contents

1: Place Value & Decimals

2: Calculations

3: Negative Numbers

4: Fractions

5: Indices

6: Introduction to Algebra

7: Working with Measures

8: Shapes, Area & Pythagoras

9: Fractions, Decimals & Percentages

Core Curriculum Book 1 Version 1.
First published 2021

Copyright Nicola Waddilove &
James Pearce 2021

Further support material, including
assessment, available at
www.mathspad.co.uk

chapter 1: place value & decimals

[Recommended Time: 11-13 hours]

Contents

reading & writing integers

learn by heart

You should know the names of the columns by heart...

millions	hundred thousands	ten thousands	thousands	hundreds	tens	units
1,000,000	100,000	10,000	1,000	100	10	1

1 million is the 7th column
1 million has 6 zeroes
1 million = 1,000,000

10 million = 10,000,000
100 million = 100,000,000
1000 million = 1 billion (UK)

example

Write the number 1439580 using commas

= 1, 439, 580

When writing numbers, starting **from the right**, we place a comma after every 3 digits. On the first comma we say 'thousand', on the second comma we say 'million'

exercise 1a

1. Write in digits:

    a) Three million and twenty two ....

    b) Five hundred and eighteen thousand ....

    c) Twenty six thousand and four ....

    d) Ninety four million, three thousand and six ....

    e) Four million, two hundred and three thousand ....

    f) Three hundred and six thousand and thirty nine ....

2. Which of these numbers is four hundred and six thousand?

    a) 46,000   b) 406,00   c) 400,6000   d) 406,000

3. Write the number 902,000 in words.

4. Which of these numbers are written incorrectly? Select four answers.

    a) 3,005   c) 9,3400   e) 24,34   g) 600,000

    b) 430,00   d) 658,000   f) 98,400   h) 903,00

5. Write each of these numbers in words. Be careful - they are all different!

A Four thousand, two hundred *4, 200*	**B** Forty thousand, two hundred	**C** Four hundred and two thousand	**D** Four hundred thousand and twenty
E Four thousand and twenty	**F** Forty thousand and twenty	**G** Four hundred thousand and two	**H** Four thousand and two
I Forty-two thousand	**J** Four hundred thousand, two hundred	**K** Forty thousand and two	**L** Four hundred and twenty thousand

6. Anna and Dan write the number "twelve thousand and nineteen" in digits.

    Anna writes: *12, 000, 19*   Dan writes: *12, 019*

    Who is right?

    What has the other person done wrong?

7. Write each of these numbers in words.

    a) 37,405   ....

    b) 9,026,030   ....

    c) 412,600   ....

8. Which of these numbers is eighteen million, forty five thousand and nine?

    a) 18,450,000   b) 18,45,000   c) 18,045,000   d) 18,000,45000

9. Which of the following numbers have the digit 8 in the ten thousands place value? Select all that apply.

    a) 809,400   b) 180,013   c) 8,432

    d) 8.0041   e) 5,080,190   f) 89,000

10. Which of the following numbers is equal to 6.2 million?

    a) 62,000,000   b) 6.2000000   c) 6.200000   d) 6,200,000

11. Which of these numbers is 1 billion?

    a) 1,000,000   b) 100,000,000   c) 1,000,000,000

Millions Multiple Choice

In each row, choose the number that matches the question.

		A	B	C	D
1	1 Million	1,000	10,000	100,000	1,000,000
2	2 Million and Fifty	2,050	2,000,50	2,000,500	2,000,050
3	15 Million and Nine Thousand	15,9000	15,009,000	15,090,000	15,000,900
4	Two Hundred Million	200,000,000	200,0000	200,000	20,200,000
5	3 Million and Six Thousand	3,6000	3,600,000	3,006,000	003,060,000
6	Seventy Two Million and Fifteen	072,000,150	72,000,15	72,000,015	72,015
7	Four Hundred and Eight Million	400,800,000	400,008,000	8,000,400	408,000,000
8	Seventeen Million and Twenty Thousand	17,020,000	17,20,000	17,200,000	170,020,000
9	Five Hundred and Two Thousand	502,000,000	500,2000	500,2,000	502,000
10	Nine Hundred and Ninety Million and Nine	900,090,009	990,000,009	990,000,090	900,900,09

extension

1. What is the name for a thousand million?
2. How many zeros are there in a million million?
3. How many zeros does a googol have?

reading & writing decimal numbers 1

learn by heart

Integer: *a whole number*	Mixed Number: *an integer + a fraction, e.g.* $3\frac{1}{10}$

Decimal: *a number including a decimal point, which separates the wholes from the parts.*	The decimal point: *is* **to the right of** *the units column*

tens	units	●	tenths	hundredths	thousandths	ten thousandths
10	1		0.1	0.01	0.001	0.0001
10	1		$\frac{1}{10}$	$\frac{1}{100}$	$\frac{1}{1000}$	$\frac{1}{10,000}$

example

Write as a decimal the number with:

a)   Two tens, three units and four hundredths   *23.04*

b)   Five units, $\frac{3}{10}$ and $\frac{7}{100}$ *5.37*

— Use a zero to show an empty column.

exercise 1b

1.   Write as a decimal the number with:

   a) 3 units and 6 tenths

   b) 4 tens and 8 tenths

   c) 3 tenths and 5 hundredths

   d) 7 hundredths and 1 thousandth

   e) 4 tenths and 7 ten thousandths

   f)   5 units and 4 thousandths

2.   State the value of the digit 6 in each of these numbers. The first is done for you.

   a) 38.1**6**5
      6 hundredths

   b) **6**.01

   c) 1.**6**924

   d) 309.85**6**

   e) 1.**6**93

   f)   0.000**6**

3.   Write these as decimals:

   a) $\frac{1}{10}$

   b) $\frac{9}{100}$

   c) $\frac{3}{10}$

   d) $\frac{7}{1000}$

   e) $1\frac{4}{10}$

   f) $5\frac{8}{100}$

   g) $2\frac{1}{1000}$

   h) $\frac{7}{10,000}$

4.   9 tens and 9 tenths make:

   a) 0.99

   b) 9.9

   c) 99

   d) 90.9

5. Write the following as decimals. The first one is done for you.

a) $5 + \frac{3}{10} + \frac{4}{100} = 5.34$ b) $1 + \frac{9}{100}$

c) $\frac{3}{10} + \frac{8}{100}$ d) $4 + \frac{2}{10} + \frac{7}{1000}$

e) $\frac{1}{10} + \frac{2}{10,000}$ f) $9 + \frac{9}{10} + \frac{9}{100}$

6. Fill in the blanks with fractions or integers, the first one is done for you:

a) $5.01 = 5 + \frac{1}{100}$ c) $31.7 = \underline{\quad} + \underline{\quad} + \underline{\quad}$

b) $0.719 = \underline{\quad} + \underline{\quad} + \underline{\quad}$ d) $54.39 = \underline{\quad} + \underline{\quad} + \underline{\quad} + \underline{\quad}$

7. Which of these is equal to 0.3 ?

a) $\frac{3}{10}$ b) $\frac{3}{100}$ c) 0.03   d) $\frac{10}{3}$

8. Write these decimals as fractions or mixed numbers:

a) 0.6   c) 1.2   e) 0.007

b) 0.09   d) 3.04   f) 5.9

9. Write down the decimal number with exactly 4 tens, 3 tenths and 2 thousandths.

10. True or false?

a) $6 + \frac{3}{10} = 6.3$ c) $20 + \frac{2}{100} = 20.2$

b) $100 + \frac{1}{100} = 200$ d) $\frac{1}{9} = 0.9$

Guess My Number ⭐ extra challenge

Use the clues to work out my number.

My number has 9 digits and a decimal point

My number is less than 1 million but more than half a million

8 is next to 9 and 8 is on the left of 9

My number has the same number of tens and tenths

My number contains the digit 4 twice, but no other repeats

My number has a 7 in the thousands column

My number does not contain the digits 2 or 6

My number has a 0 in the hundreds column and a 1 in the hundredths column

The digit 3 is next to the decimal point.

__ __ __ __ , __ __ __ . __ __

reading and writing decimal numbers 2

learn by heart

| Decimal numbers are equivalent to fractions with denominators of 10, 100, 1000, ...

0.427

$= \frac{4}{10} + \frac{2}{100} + \frac{7}{1000}$ | **Tenths**

$\frac{3}{10} = 0.3$

$3\frac{4}{10} = 3.4$

$\frac{14}{10} = 1.4$ | **Hundredths**

$\frac{3}{100} = 0.03$

$\frac{24}{100} = 0.24$

$\frac{206}{100} = 2.06$ | **Thousandths**

$\frac{3}{1000} = 0.003$

$\frac{37}{1000} = 0.037$

$\frac{409}{1000} = 0.409$ |

Mixed Number: an integer + a fraction, e.g. $3\frac{1}{10}$ means 3 wholes & 1 tenth

exercise 1c

1. Write as a decimal:

   a) $\frac{29}{100}$ b) $\frac{3}{100}$ c) $\frac{42}{1000}$ d) $2\frac{4}{100}$

   e) $\frac{9}{10}$ f) $2\frac{3}{100}$ g) $\frac{15}{1000}$ h) $12\frac{9}{100}$

   i) $14\frac{1}{100}$ j) $\frac{604}{1000}$ k) $8\frac{5}{1000}$ l) $\frac{3}{10} + \frac{4}{100} + \frac{5}{1000}$

2. Write down the value of the digit '1' in each number:

   a) 0.31   b) 2.1   c) 5.441   d) 0.6001

3. Write as a decimal the number with:

   a) 3 tens + 4 tenths   b) Twenty five hundredths

4. Write as a fraction or mixed number:

   a) 0.1   b) 0.02   c) 1.005   d) 1.3

5. Write down the decimal number that has exactly 7 hundreds, 3 tenths and 2 hundredths.

6. Write as a decimal:

   a) $\frac{27}{100}$

   c) $\frac{19}{100}$

   e) $\frac{3}{10} + \frac{1}{1000}$

   b) $\frac{172}{1000}$

   d) $2\frac{5}{10}$

   f) $4 + \frac{26}{100}$

7. The numbers 54.829 and $\frac{28}{1000}$ have the same digit in which column?

   a) units   b) tenths   c) hundredths   d) thousandths

8. Write as a fraction or mixed number, with a denominator of 10, 100 or 1000:

   a) 0.7   b) 0.92   c) 3.04   d) 0.609

9. $\frac{23}{1000}$ is the same as:

   a) 0.23   b) 0.203   c) 0.023   d) 2.3

10. True or False?

    a) $0.64 = \frac{64}{100}$

    c) $1.08 = 1\frac{8}{100}$

    e) $\frac{1}{10,000} = 0.001$

    b) $\frac{91}{1000} = 0.91$

    d) $0.7 = \frac{7}{10}$

    f) $\frac{4}{100} = 0.4$

11. Write as a decimal

    a) $\frac{4}{10} + \frac{3}{100}$

    b) $6 + \frac{1}{1000}$

    c) $300 + \frac{3}{10} + \frac{3}{1000}$

12. Write 0.0409 as a fraction.

13. The numbers 4.128 and $4\frac{1}{1000}$ have the same digit in which column?

    a) units   b) tenths   c) hundredths   d) thousandths

14. 8 tens and 8 hundredths make:

    a) 80.08   b) 80.8   c) 8.8   d) 8.08   e) 0.88

15. Fill in the blanks with fractions or integers:

    a) 0.402 = ____ + ____

    c) 20.64 = ____ + ____ + ____

    b) 3.99 = ___ + ___ + ___

    d) 305.106 = ___ + ___ + ____ + ____

16. True or false? $\frac{37}{100}$ has the same value as $\frac{3}{10} + \frac{7}{100}$.

17. True or false? $\frac{403}{1000}$ has the same value as $\frac{4}{100} + \frac{3}{1000}$.

18. How many tenths make 10?

19. How many tenths make 1000?

20. True or False? All decimal numbers are less than 1 whole.

21. True or False? The largest decimal number is 0.99.

22. How many different decimal numbers are there between 0 and 1?

Writing Decimals Match

Match these cards to their decimal equivalents at the bottom.
Record your answers in a table.

1	
2	
3	
4	
5	
6	
7	
8	
9	
10	
11	
12	
13	
14	
15	
16	
17	
18	

1 2 hundreds

2 2 hundredths

3 2 tens + 6 units

4 2 thousands + 2 units

5 6 tens + 6 tenths

6 6 tens

7 6 thousandths

8 6 thousands

9 10 tenths

10 2 tenths

11 6 tenths + 2 hundredths

12 2 tenths + 6 hundredths

13 6 tenths

14 2 tenths + 6 thousandths

15 2 tens + 6 tenths

16 6 tenths + 6 hundredths

17 6 hundreds

18 2 tens + 2 tenths

20.2	200	20.6	0.26	1	60	26	0.006	0.02
2002	6000	0.2	0.62	0.66	0.206	600	0.6	60.6

types of decimals

learn by heart

There are 3 types of decimal:

Terminating: Does not continue forever, e.g. 0.25	**Recurring:** Continues forever with a repeating pattern	**Irrational:** Continues forever with no repeating pattern, e.g. 0.123456...

We often give irrational numbers a symbol, such as π ('pi') or $\sqrt{7}$ because we can't write down all the digits. You will learn more about these symbols later on.

Recurring decimals are written using dot notation:

$0.\dot{8} = 0.888....$	$0.\dot{5}8\dot{3} = 0.58358358....$	$0.2\dot{5}\dot{3} = 0.253535....$	$5.37\dot{6}9\dot{1} = 5.37691691...$

exercise 1d

1. Which of the following equals 0.676767...?

   a) $0.6\dot{7}$ b) $\dot{0}.6\dot{7}$ c) $0.\dot{6}7$ d) $0.\dot{6}\dot{7}$

2. Which of the following equals 1.588888...?

   a) $1.5\dot{8}$ b) $\dot{1}.5\dot{8}$ c) $1.\dot{5}8$ d) $1.\dot{5}\dot{8}$

3. Which of the following equals 4.219219...?

   a) $4.21\dot{9}$ b) $4.2\dot{1}\dot{9}$ c) $4.\dot{2}1\dot{9}$ d) $4.\dot{2}1\dot{9}$

4. Write each of these recurring decimals using dot notation:

   a) 0.7222222...

   b) 4.3232323...

   c) 1.421421421...

   d) 5.5555555...

   e) 6.728282828...

   f) 3.4151515....

5. Which of these are terminating decimals? Select all that apply.

   a) 0.26   b) 1.8   c) 0.3131...   d) 0.0000004

6. The number 4.44444 is:

   a) a terminating decimal   c) a recurring decimal

   b) an irrational number   d) an integer

7. Which of the following equals $0.\dot{0}9\dot{7}$?

   a) 0.0979797...   b) 0.9797979...   c) 0.0977777...   d) 0.0970970...

8. True or false? $0.\dot{3} = 0.3\dot{3}$

9. Explain why $0.1\dot{2}5$ is an impossible number.

10. Is there a number between $0.\dot{9}$ and 1?

challenge ⭐ extra challenge

11. What is the value of $0.8\dot{5} - 0.8$?

12. What is the value of $0.\dot{3}\dot{4} - 0.\dot{3}$?

> ## example
>
> $0.9\dot{4} - 0.\dot{2}$
>
> $\quad 0.9444444....$
> $\quad \underline{0.2222222....}$ -
> $\quad \overline{0.7222222....}$
>
> $\qquad = 0.7\dot{2}$

13. Calulate:

   a) $0.6\dot{3} + 0.2\dot{4}$ d) $0.\dot{8} - 0.4\dot{2}$ g) $0.4\dot{7} - 0.\dot{4}$

   b) $0.1 + 0.8\dot{6}$ e) $1.8\dot{5} - 0.\dot{3}$ h) $0.8\dot{5} - 0.8$

   c) $0.4\dot{1} - 0.3$ f) $4.\dot{2} - 1.0\dot{2}$ i) $0.4\dot{3} + 0.2\dot{8}$

14. What's missing?

   a) $0.\dot{3} + \underline{\quad} = 0.\dot{7}$ b) $0.2 + \underline{\quad} = 0.2\dot{4}$ c) $0.1 + \underline{\quad} = 0.\dot{2}$

- -

investigate types of decimal 🖩

15. Use your calculator to write each of these as a decimal.
    State whether they are are **R**ecurring, **T**erminating or **I**rrational.

   a) $1 \div 3$ g) $1 \div 9$ m) $1 \div 100$

   b) $1 \div 4$ h) $1 \div 10$ n) $1 \div 1000$

   c) $1 \div 5$ i) $1 \div 11$ o) $3 \div 7$

   d) $1 \div 6$ j) $1 \div 12$ p) $5 \div 9$

   e) $1 \div 7$ k) $1 \div 20$ q) $4 \div 13$

   f) $1 \div 8$ l) $1 \div 25$ r) $5 \div 11$

Investigating Irrational Numbers 🔢 ⭐ extra challenge

1. An irrational number continues forever but with NO REPEATING pattern. Decide whether these numbers are recurring or irrational decimals:

   a) 0.2424242...   b) 0.123456789....   c) 0.101101101101101...

2. Is 0.45454545.... an irrational number? Explain your answer.

3. Is 0.1011121314151617.... an irrational number? Explain your answer.

4. Find the π button on your calculator. π is an irrational number. Write down the first six digits of π.

5. Is $\pi + 1$ an irrational number?

6. Is $\pi \times 2$ an irrational number?

7. Is the number 0.4242424.... an irrational number?

8. Is the number 0.12345678910111213... an irrational number?

9. Is the number 0.111222333444555666777.... an irrational number?

10. Is 0.1 + 0.01 + 0.001 + 0.0001 + 0.00001.... etc an irrational number?

11. Another way to create irrational numbers is using the $\sqrt{}$ button. Write down the first six digits of $\sqrt{3}$.

12. Use your calculator to decide whether each of the following is an integer or a recurring, terminating or irrational decimal number:

   a) $\sqrt{9}$ d) $\sqrt{10}$ g) $\sqrt{11}$

   b) $\sqrt{0.25}$ e) $\sqrt{1}$ h) $\sqrt{0}$

   c) $\sqrt{16}$ f) $\sqrt{100}$ i) $\sqrt{0.\dot{1}}$

13. Which of these give an integer answer? Select all that apply.

   a) $\pi \div \pi$ b) $\pi \times \pi$ c) $\pi + \pi$ d) $\pi - \pi$

14. Which of these will an integer answer? Select all that apply.

   a) $\sqrt{3} + \sqrt{3}$ b) $\sqrt{3} \times \sqrt{3}$ c) $\sqrt{3} \div \sqrt{3}$ d) $\sqrt{3} - \sqrt{3}$

inequality symbols

learn by heart

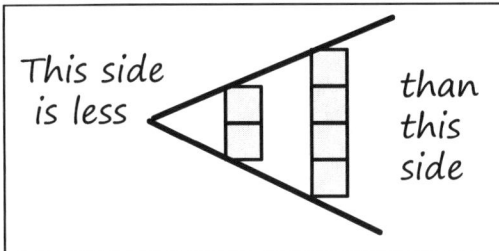

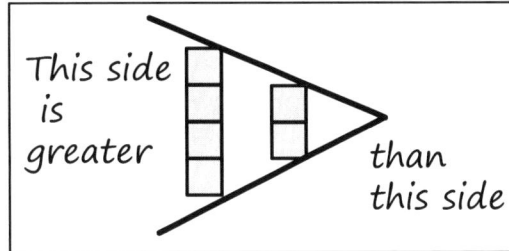

exercise 1e

1. Decide whether each of these statements are true or false.

   a) 3 > 5

   b) 6 ≥ 4

   c) 2 > 2

   d) 1 ≤ 0

   e) 3 < 7

   f) 4 < 2

   g) 7 ≠ 7

   h) 1999 > 2000

   i) 20394 ≠ 9039

2. Write 'a is greater than or equal to 17' using inequalities.

3. Complete these statements using one of these symbols: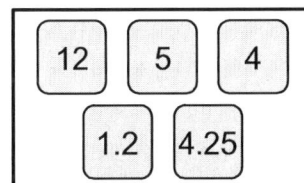

   a) 5 ◯ 0

   d) 10394 ◯ Ten thousand

   b) 9 ◯ 9

   e) 9949480 ◯ 1 million

   c) 7 ◯ 12

   f) 50193 ◯ Half a million

4. Arrange the numbers from the box to fit the chain:

   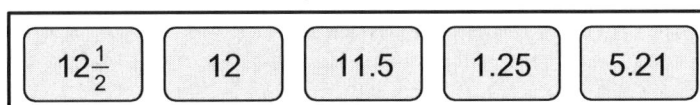

   ▢ > ▢ > ▢ > ▢ > ▢

   | 12 | 5 | 4 |
   | 1.2 | 4.25 |

5. Which of the numbers from the box could complete the statement?

   12.5 ≤ ▢

   | $12\frac{1}{2}$ | 12 | 11.5 | 1.25 | 5.21 |

comparing decimals

<u>learn by heart</u>

Decimal Places: the number of digits after the decimal point, e.g. 0.405 has 3 decimal places.

Adding zeros to the end of a decimal does not effect its size, so 0.1 = 0.10 = 0.10000000

<u>examples</u>

Which is larger 0.4 or 0.34?	True or false: 0.30 > 0.3
0.4 = 0.40, so 0.4 is larger.	False, these numbers are equal.

By adding a zero to 0.4, both numbers have two decimal places and we can easily see that '40 hundredths' is bigger than '34 hundredths'

<u>exercise 1f</u>

1. 0.6 is the same as:

    a) 0.600   b) 6.0   c) 0.06   d) 0.66

2. Which of these numbers is the **largest**?

    a) 0.92   b) 0.149   c) 0.840   d) 0.09999

3. Select the **larger** number in each pair, or write = if they are the same.

    a) 0.412 or 0.48   b) 1.38 or 1.4   c) 0.508 or 0.507

    d) 7.05 or 7.005   e) 5.125 or 5.25   f) 0.3 or 0.29

    g) 9.49 or 9.491   h)   10.46 or 1.047   i) 0.16 or 0.106

4. True or false?

    a) 0.4 = 0.400   c) 0.24 ≥ 0.240   e) 0.99 < 1.0

    b) 0.6 > 0.06   d) 0.71 < 0.707   f) 0.647 < 0.7

5. Write down a positive number that is less than 0.01

6. Which of these numbers is the **smallest**?

    a) 0.02   b) 0.4   c) 0.009   d) 0.013

7. Put these numbers in order of size, from smallest to largest:

i) A 0.401   B 0.4   C 0.42   D 0.414

ii) A 0.27   B 0.7   C 0.207   D 0.2

8. Decide whether each of these statements are true or false:

a) $0.6 \geq 0.60$

b) $0.405 > 0.41$

c) $1.2 < 1.25$

d) $0.\dot{6} < 0.67$

i) $12.001 \neq 12.0001$

e) $0.1 > 0.15$

f) $0.1 < 0.10$

g) $0.006 \geq 0.06$

h) $0.\dot{3} > 0.3$

j) $8.3405 \leq 8.341$

9. Which of the numbers from the box could complete the statement?

$1.02 \leq \boxed{}$

| 1.2 | 1.020 | 1.02 | 1.002 | 1.01 |

Guess My Number

Use the clues to work out which number in the grid is being described:

My number is less than 0.7

My number is more than 0.2

My number has an 8 in the thousandths column

My number is less than 0.42

My number contains the digit 2

The digit in the hundredths column is odd

0.144	0.8	0.248
0.288	0.25	0.825
0.418	0.141	0.118
0.88	0.44	0.114
0.458	0.258	0.552

comparing decimals and fractions (using place value)

example

Which is larger 0.84 or $\frac{9}{10}$?

$\frac{9}{10}$ = 0.9 = 0.90, so $\frac{9}{10}$ is larger

exercise 1g

1. Which of these are the same as 0.4? Circle all that apply.

   a) 0.40   b) 0.04   c) $\frac{4}{10}$ d) 0.400   e) $\frac{4}{100}$

2. In each pair, select the larger number, or write = if they are the same.

   a) 0.7 or $\frac{6}{10}$ d) 0.19 or $\frac{8}{10}$ g) $\frac{73}{1000}$ or 0.72

   b) 0.51 or $\frac{5}{100}$ e) 1.07 or $1\frac{6}{100}$ h) 0.402 or $\frac{5}{10}$

   c) 1.6 or $1\frac{6}{10}$ f) 0.26 or $\frac{3}{100}$ i) $\frac{3}{10}$ or 0.300

3. Complete these statements using one of these symbols: (<) (>) (=)

   a) 0.4 ◯ $\frac{7}{100}$ d) 0.019 ◯ $\frac{9}{100}$

   b) 0.06 ◯ $\frac{6}{100}$ e) 3.28 ◯ $3\frac{8}{100}$

   c) 0.72 ◯ $\frac{7}{10}$ f) 1.007 ◯ $1\frac{7}{10}$

4. Which of these numbers are **smaller** than 0.05? Choose all that apply.

   a) one tenth   b) one hundredth   c) one thousandth

   d) six hundredths   e) four tenths   f) nine thousandths

5. Which of these numbers are greater then $\frac{8}{10}$ and less than $\frac{9}{10}$?

   a) 0.085   b) 0.82   c) 0.10   d) 0.9   e) 0.802

6. Which of these numbers are greater then $\frac{4}{10}$ and less than 0.41?

   a) 0.408   b) 0.45   c) 0.40   d) 0.7   e) 0.39

7. By first writing these numbers as decimals, put each set in order, starting with the smallest.

i)

A	B	C	D
$\frac{1}{10}$	0.8	$\frac{2}{100}$	0.6

ii)

A	B	C	D
0.6	0.66	$\frac{6}{100}$	0.61

iii)

A	B	C	D
2.45	2.427	2.4	2.47

iv)

A	B	C	D
$\frac{83}{100}$	$\frac{83}{1000}$	$\frac{8}{10}$	$\frac{85}{100}$

v)

A	B	C	D
$\frac{70}{10}$	7.1	$7\frac{3}{100}$	$\frac{72}{100}$

8. Decide whether each of these statements is true or false.

A	B	C	D
$0.3 > 0.5$	$0.1 < 0.01$	$\frac{2}{10} > 0.1$	$0.4 \geq \frac{4}{10}$

E	F	G	H
$0.9 \neq \frac{9}{100}$	$0.12 < \frac{3}{10}$	$0.6 > 0.45$	$\frac{14}{10} < 1.5$

I	J	K	L
$2.5 \geq 2.50$	$0.3 + \frac{7}{100} = 0.37$	$0.1 + \frac{1}{100} = 0.2$	$\frac{78}{10} \geq \frac{7}{10} + \frac{8}{100}$

Arrange the Digits

| 0 | 1 | 2 | 3 | 4 | 5 | 6 | 7 | 8 | 9 |

Using each of these digits just once each, make the following statements true:

☐ · ☐☐ $<$ $6\frac{8}{10}$

☐ · ☐☐ $<$ 3.59

☐ · ☐ $\leq$ $\frac{48}{100}$

☐ · ☐ $<$ $1\frac{3}{10}$

extension: can you make up your own puzzle like this?

17

half way between

example

Write down the number half way between 0.3 and 0.31

$$0.3 = 0.300 \text{ and } 0.31 = 0.310$$
so half way between is 0.305

exercise 1h

1. Which of these numbers are between 3.4 and 3.7 ? Choose all that apply.

   a) 3.05   b) 3.65   c) 3.518   d) 3.72

2. Work out the number **halfway between** each of these pairs of numbers.

   a) 0.3 and 0.4   c) 0.235 and 0.236   e) 1.01 and 1.02

   b) 0.6 and 0.61   d) 0.07 and 0.071   f) 0.999 and 1

3. On the number line, estimate the position of 4.6

4. On the number line, estimate the position of 0.73

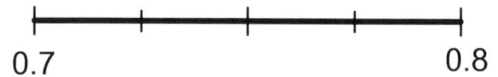

5. On the number line, estimate the position of 0.277

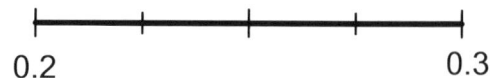

6. On the number line, estimate the position of 1.58

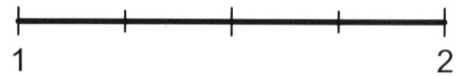

7. On the number line, estimate the position of 0.439

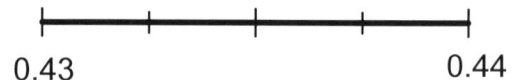

8. Which of these numbers is closest to 7.3 ?

   a) 7.305   b) 7.4   c) 7.2   d) 7.33

9. Which integer is closest to 3.39?

10. Write down a number between 0.8 and 0.8̇.

11. How many decimals are there between 2 and 3?

12. How many decimals are there between 2 and 4?

Sort It Out!

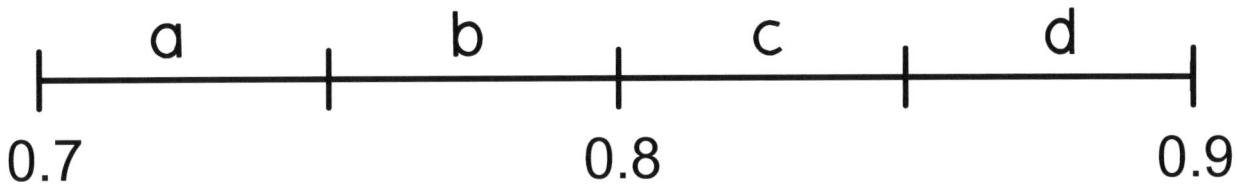

a   b   c   d

0.7   0.8   0.9

0.801   Decide which section of the number line above each of these numbers would go in   0.78   0.74

0.72   0.852   0.7501

0.799   0.887

0.76   0.709   0.7499

0.845   0.840   0.89   0.820

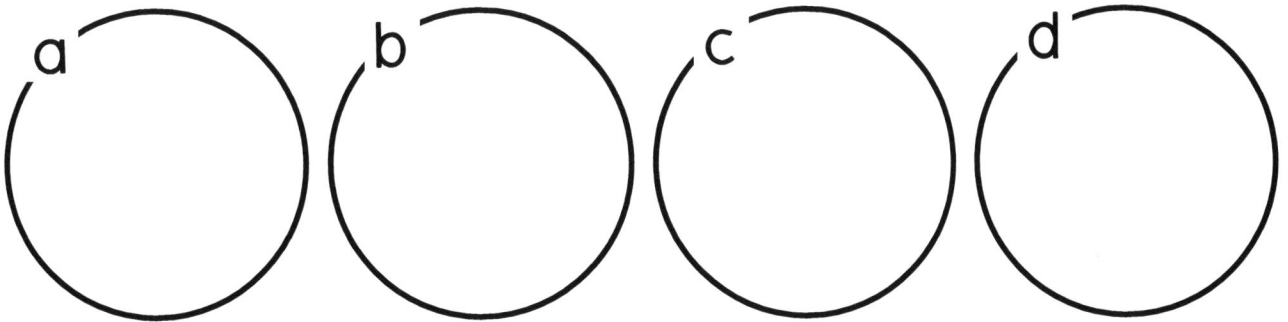

a   b   c   d

---

e   f   g   h

0.31   0.32   0.33

0.329   Decide which section of the number line above each of these numbers would go in   0.322

0.314

0.3209   0.316 $\frac{321}{1000}$

$\frac{317}{1000}$ $\frac{313}{1000}$ 0.3255

0.3199   0.311   0.328   0.31502

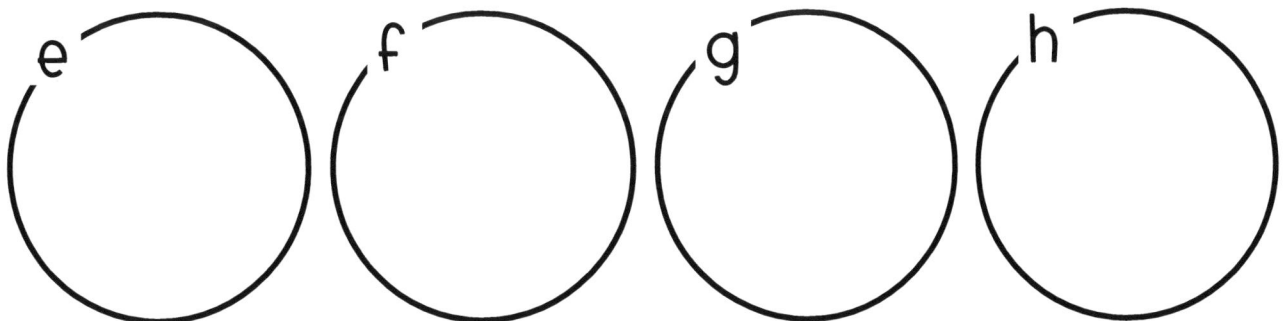

e   f   g   h

Find It On The Number Line ⭐ extra challenge

Match the numbers to the positions shown on the number lines with arrows.

1

A   C   D   F

0.6   0.7   0.8

B   E

$\frac{7}{10}$ ----	0.76 ----	$\frac{61}{100}$ ----
0.661 ----	$\frac{74}{100}$ ----	0.635 ----

2

A   C   D   F

1.3   1.4   1.5

B   E

1.392 ----	1.46 ----	$1\frac{33}{100}$ ----
$1\frac{44}{100}$ ----	1.329 ----	1.3500 ----

3

A   C D F

0.9   1.1

B   E

1.04 ----	$1\frac{1}{100}$ ----	1.05 ----
0.96 ----	0.955 ----	1.034 ----

4

A C D   F

0.4   0.5

B   E

$\frac{43}{100}$ ----	0.45 ----	0.472 ----
$\frac{439}{1000}$ ----	0.48 ----	0.441 ----

5

A   C D   F

2.1   2.2

B   E

2.16 ----	$\frac{214}{100}$ ----	$2\frac{11}{100}$ ----
2.113 ----	$2\frac{175}{1000}$ ----	2.147 ----

rounding to decimal places

learn by heart

Sometimes we do not want to write all the digits of a decimal down and we can shorten it by rounding.

A number with 1 decimal place has 1 digit after the decimal point, e.g. 3.4

If rounding, to say, 2 decimal places, the value of the digit in the 3rd decimal place tells us whether to round up or down. If the 3rd decimal place is 5 or more, we round UP, which means we increase the value of the last digit by 1.

examples

Round:

a) 4.327 to 1 decimal place	4.3|27	4.3
b) 17.0269 to 2 decimal places	17.02|69	17.03
c) 3.7997 to 3 decimal places	3.799|7	3.800
d) 1.996 to the nearest 0.1	1.9|96	2.0

→ This means 1 decimal place

exercise 1i

1. Which of these numbers have 1 decimal place? Select all that apply.

   a) 43   b) 4.5   c) 2.75   d) 62.0   e) 200.30

2. Round each number to 1 decimal place:

   a) 3.62   c) 2.45   e) 4.319   g) 105.1098

   b) 1.84   d) 13.19   f) 26.453   h) 459.821

3. Round each number to 2 decimal places:

   a) 4.085   b) 23.1279   c) 604.30567

4. Round each number to 3 decimal places:

   a) 4.0858   b) 23.127   c) 604.30567

5. Find all the numbers that round to **3.5** to 1 decimal place:

A		D		G		J		M	
	3.48		3.41		3.45		3.34		3.41
B		E		H		K		N	
	3.51		3.62		3.55		3.56		3.509
C		F		I		L		O	
	3.63		3.81		3.67		3.39		3.409

6. Complete the table by rounding each number as shown:

	Number	to 1 d.p.	to 2 d.p.	Nearest Integer
a)	3.7281			
b)	52.5917			
c)	0.1853			
d)	9.6458			
e)	4.0028			

7. Which of these numbers is 24.976 correctly rounded to one decimal place?

   a) 24.9   b) 24.10   c) 25   d) 24.98   e) 25.0

8. Which of these lengths is 32.77m given correct to the nearest 0.1m?

   a) 33m   b) 32.7m   c) 32.70m   d) 32.8m   e) 32.80m

9. Show how these cards can be arranged to make a number that rounds to 27.5 to one decimal place.

   [7] [4] [2] [8] [•]

10. Which of these numbers, when rounded to 2 decimal places, give 17.48 ? Choose all that apply.

    a) 17.485   b) 17.475   c) 17.4805   d) 17.4705

11. Round:

    a) 132.8427 to the nearest tenth

    b) 4.7396 to the nearest hundredth

challenge (rounding recurring decimals)

12. Round each of these recurring decimals as indicated:

    a) $0.\dot{6}$ (1 d.p.)

    b) $0.\dot{3}\dot{4}$ (1 d.p.)

    c) $0.\dot{5}\dot{7}$ (2 d.p.)

    d) $0.\dot{7}0\dot{5}$ (3 d.p.)

    e) $0.7\dot{0}\dot{5}$ (3 d.p.)

    f) $0.70\dot{5}$ (3 d.p.)

    g) $0.4\dot{8}$ (3 d.p.)

    h) $0.4\dot{9}$ (3 d.p.)

    i) $0.\dot{9}$ (1 d.p.)

Rounding Decimals
Code Breaker

Round each number as shown.
Find your answer in the code box and write down the letter.
The letters should spell a secret message!

code box

0.3 = K	0.69 = Q	0.8 = I	1.2 = M
0.4 = X	0.7 = G	0.81 = R	1.21 = F
0.48 = ?	0.71 = V	0.9 = S	1.22 = U
0.5 = E	0.74 = C	0.91 = D	1.23 = A
0.51 = H	0.75 = B	1 = J	1.24 = T
0.6 = O	0.78 = L	1.01 = Z	1.3 = Y
0.65 = U	0.79 = N	1.1 = P	1.31 = K

a) 0.34 to 1 d.p. = _____ = **K**

b) 0.483 o 1 d.p. = _____ =

c) 0.51 to 1 d.p. = _____ =

d) 1.05 to 1 d.p. = _____ =

e) 0.94 to 1 d.p. = _____ =

f) 1.22 to 1 d.p. = _____ =

g) 0.784 to 1 d.p. = _____ =

h) 0.784 to **2 d.p.** = _____ =

i) 0.809 to 1 d.p. = _____ =

j) 0.789 to **2 d.p.** = _____ =

k) 0.749 to 1 d.p. = _____ =

l) 1.234 to **2 d.p.** = _____ =

m) 0.781 to **2 d.p.** = _____ =

n) 0.779 to **2 d.p.** = _____ =

o) 0.911 to **2 d.p.** = _____ =

p) 1.225 to **2 d.p.** = _____ =

q) 1.27 to 1 d.p. = _____ =

r) 0.777 to **2 d.p.** = _____ =

s) 0.58 to 1 d.p. = _____ =

t) 0.792 to **2 d.p.** = _____ =

u) 0.699 to 1 d.p. = _____ =

rounding to significant figures (integers)

learn by heart

The **first significant figure** of a number is the first non-zero digit

'Trapped zeros' lie between 2 other digits. They are significant.

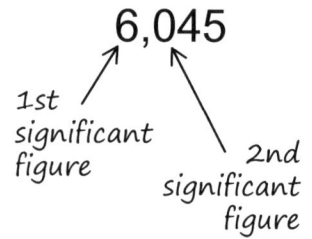

6,045
1st significant figure
2nd significant figure

examples

Round 348 to 1 significant figure (1.s.f)	Round 4,075 to 2 significant figures (2.s.f)
(1st significant figure is in the hundreds column, so round to the nearest hundred)	(2nd significant figure is in the hundreds column, so round to the nearest hundred)
= 300	= 4,100

exercise 1j

1. Round each of these numbers to 1 significant figure:

   a) 53   c) 709   e) 2,409

   b) 56   d) 358   f) 15,008

2. Round each of these numbers to 2 significant figures:

   a) 956   c) 15,809   e) 194,037

   b) 2,085   d) 12,314   f) 280,300

3. The number 6,008 has ____ significant figures.

4. The number 84,001 has ____ significant figures.

5. Round each of these numbers as indicated:

   a) 536 (2 s.f.)   d) 8,900 (1 s.f.)   g) 99 (1 s.f.)

   b) 804 (2 s.f.)   e) 84 (2 s.f.)   h) 999 (2 s.f.)

   c) 12,400 (2 s.f.)   f) 12 (1 s.f.)   i) 9,999 (3 s.f.)

6. Find all the numbers that round to 100, to 1 significant figure:

A	105	D	102	G	99	J	95	M	90	P	110
B	92	E	100	H	130	K	107	N	91	Q	96
C	98	F	90	I	170	L	89	O	55	R	140

rounding to significant figures (decimals)

learn by heart

The zeros at the start of a decimal are **not significant**

The zeros at the end of a decimal **ARE** significant

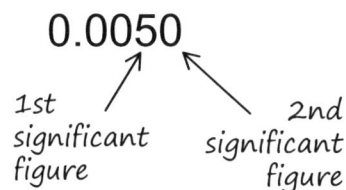

$$0.0050$$

1st significant figure

2nd significant figure

examples

Round 0.0489 to 1 significant figure (1.s.f)	Round 0.0899 to 2 significant figures (2.s.f)
(1st significant figure is in the hundredths column, so round to the nearest tenth)	(2nd significant figure is in the thousandths column, so round to the nearest thousandth)
= 0.05	= 0.090

exercise 1k

1. Which of these numbers has 3 significant figures?

    a) 2.486   b) 2.406   c) 3.490   d) 0.0300

2. Round each of these to 1 significant figure:

    a) 0.765   c) 0.038   e) 2.845

    b) 0.408   d) 0.0193   f) 0.099

3. Round each of these to 2 significant figures:

    a) 3.867   c) 0.247   e) 0.309

    b) 0.608   d) 12.859   f) 0.0049

4. The number 0.307 has ____ significant figures.

5. The number 4.8050 has ____ significant figures.

6. The number 900.009 has ____ significant figures.

7. Round each of these as indicated:

    a) 0.289 (2 s.f.)   d) 8.207 (3 s.f.)   g) 0.3007 (3 s.f.)

    b) 42.806 (3 s.f.)   e) 0.069 (2 s.f.)   h) 0.0914 (2 s.f.)

    c) 0.0987 (2 s.f.)   f) 4.98 (1 s.f.)   i) 8.999 (2 s.f.)

8. What is the value of $0.40\dot{8}$ to 4 significant figures?

rounding to significant figures (mixed practice)

exercise 1

1. What is the first significant figure in each of these numbers?

   a) 0.429　　　　　　　b) 9002　　　　　　　c) 45

   d) 0.00011　　　　　　e) 0.704　　　　　　　f) 32,415

2. How many significant figures do each of these numbers have?

   a) 506　　　　　　b) 0.03　　　　　　c) 0.4500　　　　　　d) 23.605

3. Which of these has 2 significant figures? Select all that apply.

   a) 0.08　　　　　　b) 108　　　　　　c) 0.080　　　　　　d) 1.08

4. Round each of these numbers to one significant figure:

   a) 6.928　　　　　　　b) 0.00438　　　　　　c) 82.9

   d) 417.809　　　　　　e) 0.089　　　　　　　f) 0.92

5. Which of these numbers is 72.46 rounded to one significant figure?

   a) 72　　　　　　b) 72.5　　　　　　c) 70　　　　　　d) 7

6. Which of these numbers have the digit **3** as the second significant figure? Choose all that apply.

   a) 4.312　　　b) 3.2　　　c) 403.1　　　d) 0.329　　　e) 0.0731

7. Round each of these numbers to the number of significant figures shown:

   a) 45 (1 s.f.)　　　　　　e) 0.0507 (2 s.f.)　　　　　　i) 9607 (2 s.f.)

   b) 0.956 (2 s.f.)　　　　　f) 503 (1 s.f.)　　　　　　　j) 8.099 (3 s.f.)

   c) 3005 (3 s.f.)　　　　　g) 900 (2.s.f)　　　　　　　k) 609 (2 s.f.)

   d) 551.8 (2 s.f.)　　　　　h) 0.56 (1 s.f.)　　　　　　　l) 800 (3 s.f)

8. Could the most significant figure in a number be a zero?

9. Could the second most significant figure in a number be a zero?

10. True or false: 42.389 rounded to 3 s.f. > 42.389 rounded to 3 d.p. ?

11. Which section of the diagram should each of the following numbers be in?

Some of the numbers go outside of the circles.

31.5	0.340	3001
43	2.3	0.25
396.41	403	0.9
0.90	3.52	1.01

extension: there are two empty sections, can you think of a number that would go in each of these two sections?

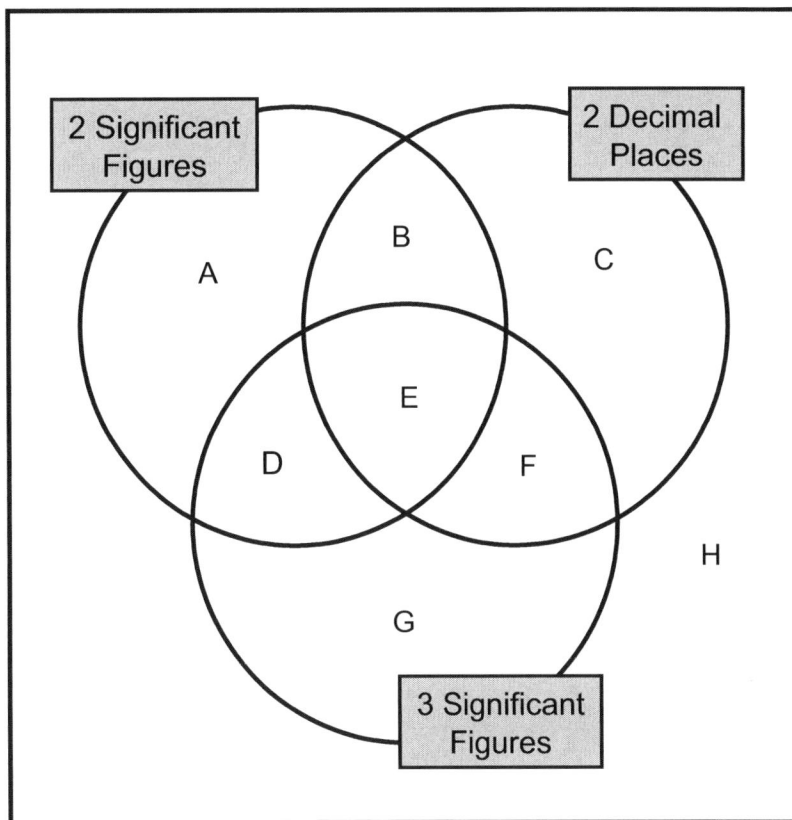

2 Significant Figures

2 Decimal Places

A

B

C

D

E

F

G

H

3 Significant Figures

Round It! ⭐ extra challenge

Place the numbers in the boxes so that all arrows indicate a correct rounding

3160	3200	3000	3164

2900	3049	2919

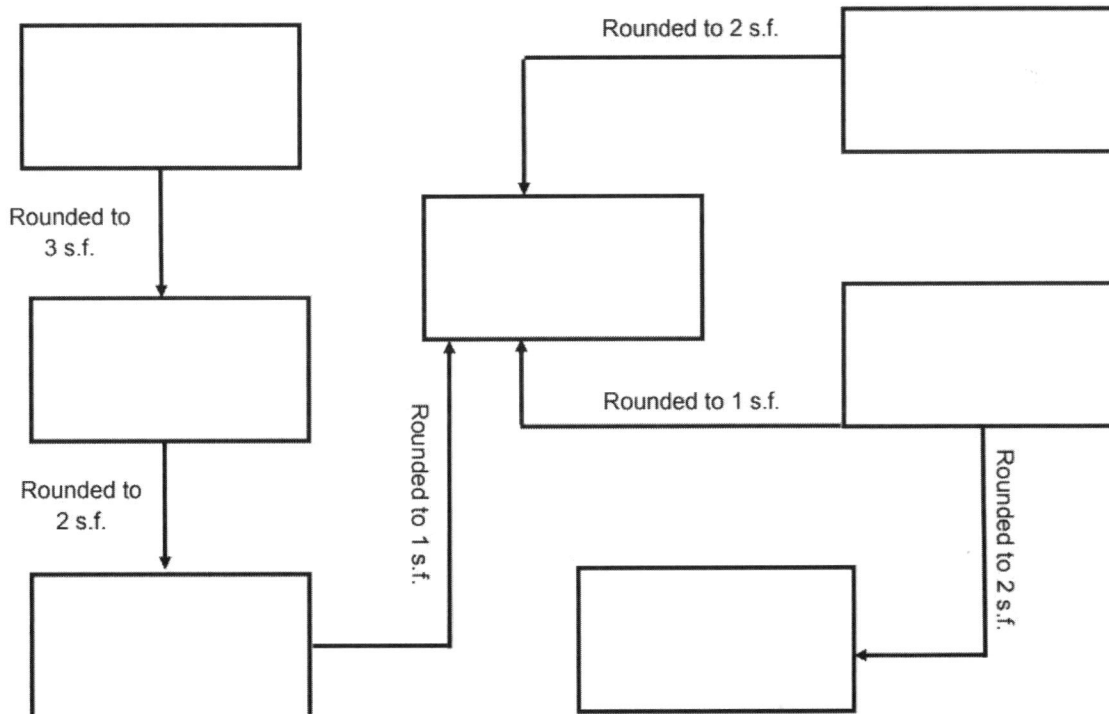

Rounded to 2 s.f.

Rounded to 3 s.f.

Rounded to 2 s.f.

Rounded to 1 s.f.

Rounded to 1 s.f.

Rounded to 2 s.f.

other number systems: base 5 ⭐ extra challenge

learn by heart

Base 10: A number system using 10 digits (0,1,2,3,4,5,6,7,8,9)

Base 5: A number system using 5 digits (0,1,2,3,4)

example

base 5 column names ↘

Write 39 in base 5

39 is 1 × 25 +
        2 × 5 +
        4 × 1
      = 124

125s	25s	5s	1s
	1	2	4

exercise 1m

1. Write these numbers in base 5:

   a) 12

   b) 6

   c) 27

   d) 3

   e) 60

   f) 37

   g) 125

   h) 255

   i) 89

   j) 11

   k) 124

   l) 624

2. Explain why 61 cannot be a number written in base 5.

3. These numbers are written in base 5. Convert them to base 10:

   a) 14

   b) 32

   c) 103

   d) 210

   e) 331

   f) 4

   g) 1000

   h) 1202

   i) 44

challenge: Convert 1,000,000 from base 5 to base 10.

3. If these numbers are written in base 5, which is biggest?

A. 44   B. 43   C. 103   D. 101

4. Working in base 5, what is the number after 44?

5. Which of these numbers is definitely not written in base 5?

A. 34   B. 35   C. 1004   D. 1234

6. Working in base 5, what is half of 31?

7. Working in base 5, which number comes before 1000?

8. Working in base 5, which of these numbers are even?

A. 21   B. 14   C. 20   D. 123

9. Working in base 5, which of these numbers are multiples of 5?

A. 40   B. 22   C. 31   D. 100

10. Write down the digits you would use if you were working in base 6.

11. In base 6, what does 10 stand for?

12. In base 6, what does 11 stand for?

true or false

Which of these statements are true?

A	B	C	D
In base 5, 11 + 1 = 12	In base 5, 14 + 1 = 15	In base 5, 12 is an even number	In base 5, 10 × 23 is 230

E	F	G	H
In base 5, 4 × 4 = 16	In base 5, all multiples of 5 end in a zero	In base 5, 12 + 12 = 24	In base 5, 100 + 10 = 110

I	J	K	L
In base 5, 23 is half of 101	In base 5, 14 has exactly two factors	In base 5, 100 ÷ 10 = 10	In base 5, $0.1 = \frac{1}{10}$

chapter review

exercise 1n

1. Write each of these as decimals:

   a) 3 tenths b) $\frac{7}{100}$ c) $\frac{9}{1000}$ d) $1\frac{7}{10}$

2. Write the number *eight hundred and ten thousand* in digits.

3. Write each of these as a fraction or mixed number:

   a) 0.07 b) 2.8 c) 0.31 d) 42.009

4. Which of these is largest?

   a) $\frac{8}{10}$ b) 0.808 c) 0.80 d) $\frac{81}{100}$

5. Copy and complete the table to show how to round these numbers:

Number	Nearest Integer	1 d.p.	1 s.f.
23.06			
482.69			
0.055			

4. Which of the following equals 0.232323....?

   a) $0.\ddot{2}\ddot{3}$ b) $0.2\dot{3}2$ c) $0.2\dot{3}$

5. Which of the following equals $0.4\ddot{1}\ddot{2}$?

   a) 0.412412... b) 0.412222... c) 0.412121...

6. Write 0.456565... using dot notation.

challenge

Decide whether each of these statements are true or false:

a) $0.\dot{3} > 0.3$ b) $0.\dot{6} > 0.67$

c) $1.2\dot{3} < 1.\ddot{2}\ddot{3}$ d) $0.\ddot{0}\ddot{9} = \frac{9}{100}$

e) $0.7\dot{7} = 0.\dot{7}$ f) $8.\dot{8} < 8.819$

g) $1.\dot{2}9\dot{5} > 1.2\dot{9}\dot{5}$ h) $0.0\ddot{4}\ddot{5} < \frac{5}{100}$

chapter review 2

exercise 1o

1. Round 486 to 1 significant figure.

2. Write $\frac{3}{10}$ as a decimal.

3. As a fraction, 0.207 is:

   a) $\frac{207}{10}$ b) $\frac{207}{100}$ c) $\frac{207}{1,000}$ d) $\frac{207}{10,000}$ e) $\frac{27}{1000}$

4. Complete the gaps using >, < or =

   a) $0.\dot{2}$ ____ $\frac{2}{10}$ c) $\frac{41}{1000}$ ____ 0.041   e) 0.1 ____ 0.001

   b) $\frac{29}{1000}$ ____ 0.290   d) 8 thousands ____ $\frac{8}{1000}$ f) 0.86 ____ 0.9

5. Round each of these to 1 significant figure:

   a) 84,026   b) 1.87   c) 0.0308

6. True or False: 0.87 and 0.870 have the same value but different accuracies.

7. Which of these is largest?

   a) $\frac{9}{10}$ b) 0.90   c) 0.809   d) $\frac{909}{1000}$

8. Which of these is an irrational number?

   a) 0.3333...   b) 0.1234   c) $2.\dot{7}$ d) 0.12345678....

9. Round 0.999 to 2 decimal places.

10. Round 0.999 to 2 significant figures.

11. Write as a decimal:

    a) $\frac{8}{10}$ c) $3\frac{1}{10}$ e) $\frac{29}{1000}$

    b) $\frac{1}{1000}$ d) $\frac{89}{100}$ f) $12\frac{3}{100}$

12. Write as a fraction or mixed number:

    a) 0.09   b) 0.023   c) 4.87

13. How many numbers are there between 4.1 and 4.2 with 2 decimal places?

Place Value Puzzles

In each of these puzzles, work out which number from the grid is being described:

Puzzle 1

My number is not an integer.

My number has a 1 in the units column

My number is greater than thirty

My number is ≠ 31.3

My number has 1 in the hundredths column

1.01	301	31.1
3.1	3.101	31.3
30.1	31.01	1.03

Puzzle 2

My number is less than eighteen thousand

My number is ≠ 180

My number is > 18

My number has 8 in both the tens and tenths columns

180	18.01	1.81
0.18	1800	188
180.8	18180	18.8

Puzzle 3

My number is ≤ 0.2

My number is ≠ 0.15

My number is greater than one tenth

My number has no hundredths

0.24	0.2	0.12
0.02	0.01	0.5
0.15	2.02	0.1

Puzzle 4

My number is < 44,000

My number is more than five thousand four hundred and fifty

My number is ≠ 5454

My number has 5 hundreds

My number is greater than fifteen thousand

14,500	15,501	45000
5401	5444	5454
14,534	4544	10,500

- -

Puzzle 5

What is the largest number that can be made by rearranging these cards?

| 1 | 2 | 4 | . | 8 |

Puzzle 6

What is the **smallest** number that can be made by rearranging these cards?

| 5 | 3 | 2 | . | 6 |

Puzzle 7

Put these numbers in order of size, from smallest to largest

0.04,   0.4,   4.4,   1.4,   0.104

Puzzle 8

Complete these statements using the symbols

= , > , <

0.40	0.400
0.35	0.300
0.2	0.25
1.5	1.05
1.8	1.80
0.01	0.1
0.99	0.999

chapter 2: calculations

[Recommended Time: 10-12 hours]

Contents

written calculations: addition/subtraction of decimals

examples

Calculate 8.2 - 1.64

$$8.20$$
$$1.64 \ -$$
$$\overline{6.56}$$

Calculate 1 - 0.043

$$1.000$$
$$0.043 \ -$$
$$\overline{0.957}$$

Which is closer to 1
  0.98 or 1.04 ?

$$1.00$$
$$0.98 \ -$$
$$\overline{0.02}$$

$$1.04$$
$$1.00 \ -$$
$$\overline{0.04}$$

so 0.98 is closer because it is only 0.02 away

exercise 2a

1. Which of the following is the correct calculation of 3847 - 554?

    a)
    $$3 \ 8 \ 4 \ 7$$
    $$5 \ 5 \ 4 \ -$$
    $$\overline{2 \ 3 \ 0 \ 7}$$

    b)
    $$3 \ 8 \ 4 \ 7$$
    $$\ 5 \ 5 \ 4 \ -$$
    $$\overline{3 \ 3 \ 1 \ 3}$$

    c)
    $$3 \ 8 \ 4 \ 7$$
    $$5 \ 5 \ 4 \ -$$
    $$\overline{-2 \ 3 \ 0 \ 7}$$

    d)
    $$3 \ 8 \ 4 \ 7$$
    $$\ 5 \ 5 \ 4 \ -$$
    $$\overline{3 \ 2 \ 9 \ 3}$$

2. Calculate:

    a) 62 - 1.84

    b) 2.05 - 1.9

    c) 1 - 0.086

    d) 30.004 - 9.26

3. Which of these is closest to 1?   a) 0.91   b) 1.08   c) 1.004

4. Which of these is closest to 4?   a) 4.02   b) $4\frac{1}{10}$ c) 3.97

5. Calculate $\frac{49}{100}$ - 0.3

6. Which is closer to 1? $\boxed{1.21}$ or $\boxed{\frac{89}{100}}$
    Explain your answer.

7. Which of these numbers is closest to 1?

    a) 0.95   b) 1.02   c) 1.0$\dot{3}$ d) 0.985

challenge

8. Calculate

    a) 4.$\dot{2}$ - 1.0$\dot{2}$ b) 1.8$\dot{5}$ - 0.$\dot{3}$?

9. Calculate:

    a) 0. 89$\dot{5}$ - 0.00$\dot{5}$ b) 0.2$\dot{3}$ - 0.$\dot{2}\dot{3}$ c) 0.35$\dot{6}$ - 0.31$\dot{2}$

Arrange the Digits ⭐ extra challenge

A. Place the digits
   [1] [3] [4] [6] [7]
   in the boxes to make
   this statement true:

   ☐[5] . ☐ + ☐ . ☐ = [3]☐

B. Place the digits
   [1] [2] [3] [5] [6]
   in the boxes to make
   this statement true:

   ☐[1] . ☐ − ☐ . [3] = ☐☐

C. Place the digits
   [1] [2] [4] [8] [9]
   in the boxes to make
   this statement true:

   ☐ . ☐ + ☐ . ☐ = ☐[7] . [6]

D. Place the digits
   [0] [1] [2] [3] [5]
   in the boxes to make
   this statement true:

   [8] . ☐☐ + ☐ . [5] = ☐☐

E. Place the digits
   [0] [1] [4] [5] [8]
   in the boxes to make
   this statement true:

   ☐☐ . [1] − ☐ . ☐ = ☐ . [3]

- -

Very Tricky Calculation Puzzles ⭐ extra challenge

Below are three subtractions and one addition. Work out the missing digits:

a)
```
  ☐ . 1 ☐ ☐
  1 . ☐ 6 8  −
  0 . 5 6 6
```

b)
```
  ☐ . ☐ 2 7
  0 . 6 ☐    −
  0 . 0 9 ☐
```

c)
```
  1 . 1 ☐ ☐
  3 . ☐ 5 8  +
  ☐ . 2 5 0
```

d)
```
  6 . ☐ ☐ ☐
  ☐ . 7 9 9  −
  5 . 7 2 7
```

written calculations: short division

learn by heart

Fraction Bar: *the line in a fraction – it means divide*

$\frac{3}{5}$ ...*this means* 3 ÷ 5

examples

Write $\frac{1}{8}$ as a decimal.

$$\begin{array}{r} 0.125 \\ 8\overline{)1.^{1}0^{2}0^{4}0} \end{array}$$

1 ÷ 8 = 0.125

Calculate half of 0.87

$$\begin{array}{r} 0.435 \\ 2\overline{)0.87^{1}0} \end{array}$$

= 0.435

Which number is half way between 35 and 82?

(35 + 82) ÷ 2
= 117 ÷ 2 = 58.5

exercise 2b

1. Work out:

   a) 448 ÷ 8   b) 211 ÷ 5   c) 941 ÷ 5

   d) 218 ÷ 5   e) 4.5 ÷ 4   f) 0.0171 ÷ 3

2. Use short division to write these fractions as decimals:

   a) $\frac{3}{8}$ b) $\frac{1}{6}$ c) $\frac{5}{8}$ d) $\frac{5}{11}$

3. Calculate half of:

   a) 0.85   b) 1.01   c) $2\frac{3}{10}$ d) $4\frac{83}{100}$

4. Find the number half way between:

   a) 17 and 35   c) 82.5 and 91   e) 2.09 and $2\frac{3}{10}$

   b) 143 and 641   d) 1.801 and 1.84   f) 5.8 and $5\frac{8}{100}$

5. Which of these is largest?

   a) $\frac{4}{9}$ b) 0.39   c) $0.4\dot{5}$ d) $\frac{1}{3}$

6. Which of these are recurring decimals?

   a) $\frac{1}{3}$ b) $\frac{2}{3}$ c) $\frac{1}{6}$ d) $\frac{4}{9}$

7. Put these numbers in order of size, starting with the smallest:

   a) $0.\dot{3}\dot{0}$ b) $\frac{3}{10}$ c) $\frac{3}{11}$ d) 0.029

challenging

1. Write $\frac{1}{16}$ as a decimal.

2. Is $\frac{3}{22}$ a recurring or terminating decimal?

3. Can you work out half of $0.\dot{8}$?

4. Can you work out half of $0.\dot{5}$?

5. Complete the statements:

   a) _____ is half way between 42 and 63

   b) 0.5 is half way between _____ and 0.72

   c) 1.5 is half way between _____ and 2.22

6. Calculate the following using short division. What do you notice?

   a) $1 \div 9$ d) $4 \div 9$ g) $7 \div 9$

   b) $2 \div 9$ e) $5 \div 9$ h) $8 \div 9$

   c) $3 \div 9$ f) $6 \div 9$ i) $9 \div 9$

7. Given the pattern above, can you work out $\frac{10}{9}$ without using short division?

8. Can you work out $\frac{13}{9}$ in a similar way?

Fractions & Decimals Match

Match each fraction to its decimal equivalent.
Record your pairs in a table, starting with the smallest number.

$\boxed{0.3}$ $\boxed{0.\dot{3}}$

$\boxed{\frac{2}{9}}$ $\boxed{0.4}$

$\boxed{0.2}$ $\boxed{0.\dot{2}}$ $\boxed{\frac{3}{5}}$ $\boxed{\frac{1}{10}}$ $\boxed{0.\dot{1}}$ $\boxed{\frac{1}{4}}$ $\boxed{\frac{2}{5}}$ $\boxed{\frac{3}{10}}$ $\boxed{0.35}$ $\boxed{\frac{1}{5}}$ $\boxed{0.\dot{6}}$ $\boxed{\frac{1}{3}}$ $\boxed{\frac{1}{8}}$

Start with the smallest decimal here ↘

$\boxed{0.25}$ $\boxed{\frac{2}{3}}$ $\boxed{\frac{4}{9}}$ $\boxed{\frac{35}{100}}$ $\boxed{0.6}$ $\boxed{\frac{1}{9}}$ $\boxed{0.\dot{4}}$ $\boxed{0.125}$ $\boxed{0.1}$

Decimal														
Fraction														

multiplying and dividing by 10, 100, 1000...

learn by heart

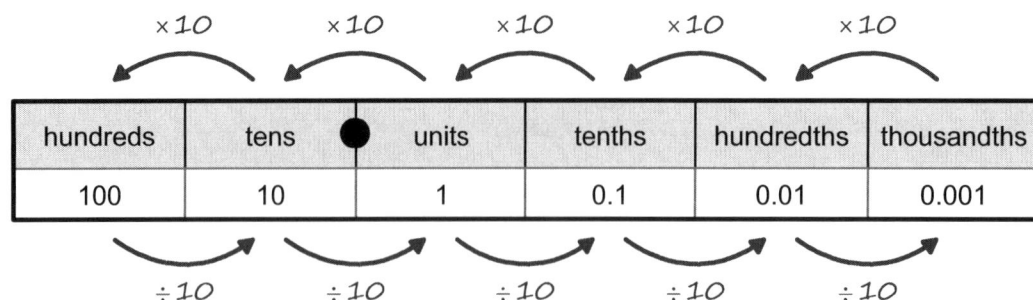

| | ×10 | ×10 | ×10 | ×10 | ×10 |

hundreds	tens	● units	tenths	hundredths	thousandths
100	10	1	0.1	0.01	0.001

| ÷10 | ÷10 | ÷10 | ÷10 | ÷10 |

examples

$34 \times 100 = 3400$	$10 \times 5.902 = 59.02$	$0.84 \times 1000 = 840$
$1700 \div 10 = 170$	$439 \div 100 = 4.39$	$0.7 \div 1000 = 0.0007$

exercise 2c

1. Work out:

   a) 84×10 b) 9.1×1000 c) 60×100

   d) $1700 \div 100$ e) $45 \div 10$ f) $300 \div 1000$

   g) $10,000 \div 100$ h) $120 \div 1000$ j) $907 \div 10$

2. Work out the missing numbers:

   a) $65 \times$ _____ $= 6500$ b) $2710 \div$ _____ $= 271$

   c) _____ $\times 10 = 95,600$ d) _____ $\div 100 = 20$

   e) $450 \div$ _____ $= 0.45$ f) $1000 \times$ _____ $= 29,000$

3. Removing the decimal point makes which number 100 times bigger?

   a) 43.1   b) 1.92   c) 0.4   d) 5.904

4. If a zero is added to the end of one of these numbers, its value will stay the same. Which number?

   a) 3   b) 42   c) 0.9   d) 10

5. Work out:

   a) 2.7×10 c) 0.5×100 e) $1.250 \div 10$

   b) $9.02 \div 10$ d) $1.1 \div 1000$ f) 0.007×100

6. Complete these statements:

   a) 450 is _____ times smaller than 450,000

   b) 80 is _____ times bigger than 0.08

   c) 0.037 is _____ times _____ than 3.7

   d) 1.004 is _____ times _____ than 1004

   e) 13.2 is 100 times smaller than _____

   f) 0.85 is 100 times bigger than _____

7. Work out the missing numbers:

   a) 0.43 × _____ = 430   b) 50.7 ÷ _____ = 5.07

   c) _____ ÷ 100 = 83.2   d) _____ × 10 = 5.2

   e) _____ ÷ 1000 = 2.3   f) 100 × _____ = 40

8. Complete: 0.48 × 100 = 480,000 ÷ _____

9. Calculate 4859.6 × 1,000 ÷ 1000

10. Calculate:

    a) $1.\overset{..}{23}$ × 10   b) $4.\overset{.}{3}$ ÷ 100   c) $96.\overset{..}{526}$ ÷ 10

11. Fill in the blank: $0.03\overset{.}{4}$ × _____ = $34.\overset{.}{4}$

- -

matching activity

Match these calculations to their answers:

A 0.45 × 10	B 20.6 ÷ 100	C 4.5 × 100
D 450 ÷ 1000	E 0.45 × 100	F 4.5 ÷ 100
G 4.5 × 1000	H 2.6 × 100	I 260 ÷ 1000
J 206 ÷ 100	K 2.06 × 100	L 0.026 × 1000

4500	0.045
450	45
4.5	0.45
26	2.06
0.206	260
0.26	206

Record your answers in a table:

A	B	C	D	E	F	G	H	I	J	K	L

multiplying by 0.1, 0.01 etc ⭐ extra challenge

learn by heart

$0.1 = 1$ tenth $= \frac{1}{10}$ and so mutiplying by 0.1 is the same as dividing by 10

Multiplying by 0.1 *is equivalent to* **dividing by 10**	**Multiplying by 0.01** *is equivalent to* **dividing by 100**	**Multiplying by 0.001** *is equivalent to* **dividing by 1000**

examples

432×0.1 $\qquad = 43.2$	86.04×0.01 $\qquad = 0.8604$	$\frac{1}{1000} \times 5060 \qquad = 5060 \div 1000$ $\qquad\qquad\qquad = 5.06$

exercise 2d

1. Work out:

   a) 7600×0.1

   b) 8301×0.01

   c) 432×0.1

   d) $97,000 \times 0.001$

   e) 420×0.01

   f) 604×0.001

2. Which of these are equal to **5.07**? Choose all that apply.

   a) 507×0.01

   b) 0.507×0.1

   c) 57×0.1

   d) 5.07×1

3. Which of these are equal to **0.68**? Choose all that apply.

   a) 68×0.1

   b) 0.068×0.1

   c) 680×0.001

   d) 680×0.01

4. Work out:

   a) 0.75×0.1

   b) 3.7×0.001

   c) 0.9×0.001

   d) 28.06×0.01

   e) 0.07×0.1

   f) 0.01×0.01

5. Work out the missing numbers:

   a) $84 \times \underline{\qquad} = 0.84$

   b) $231 \times \underline{\qquad} = 2.31$

   c) $0.3 \times \underline{\qquad} = 0.0003$

   d) $\underline{\qquad} \times 0.01 = 4.002$

   e) $\underline{\qquad} \times 0.1 = 8.9$

   f) $\underline{\qquad} \times 0.001 = 0.1$

6. Complete these statements using one of these symbols: $<$ $>$ $=$

   a) 400×0.1 ◯ 4000

   b) 0.25×0.1 ◯ 0.0205

   c) 52×0.01 ◯ $52 \div 1000$

   d) 90×0.01 ◯ 9×0.1

7. Which of these operations will turn 4.72 into an integer?

a) ÷ 100   b) × 0.1   c) × $\frac{1}{100}$ d) × 100

8. Calculate the following, giving your answer as a decimal:

a) $12 \times \frac{1}{10}$ b) $15 \times \frac{1}{100}$ c) $52.6 \times \frac{1}{10}$

d) $0.3 \times \frac{1}{10}$ e) $9\frac{4}{10} \times \frac{1}{10}$ f) $72 \times \frac{1}{10} \times \frac{1}{10}$

g) $\frac{12}{100} \times \frac{1}{10}$ h) $34\frac{1}{10} \times \frac{1}{100}$ i) $9\frac{9}{100} \times \frac{1}{10}$

- -

Multiplying by Powers of 10: Fill in the Gaps

Write an integer or decimal in each blank space to make each statement true:

A $6 \times 0.1 = 6 \div$ _____

B $9 \times \frac{1}{100} = 9 \times$ _____

C $12 \div 1000 = 12 \times$ _____

D $17 \times$ _____ $= 17 \times \frac{1}{10}$

E $80 \times 0.1 = 0.8 \times$ _____

F $900 \times \frac{1}{100} = 90 \times$ _____

G $7 \div 100 = \frac{7}{10} \times$ _____

H $\frac{26}{100} \times 100 =$ _____

I $5 \div 100 = 0.5 \times$ _____

J   _____ $\times \frac{1}{10} = 15 \div 100$

K $2\frac{2}{10} \times 0.1 =$ _____ $\times \frac{1}{10}$

L $\frac{13}{100} \times 0.1 = 13 \div$ _____

M $52\frac{1}{10} \times \frac{1}{10} =$ _____ $\div 10$

N $3 \times \frac{1}{10} \times \frac{1}{10} = 3 \div$ _____

O $18 \times 0.01 =$ _____ $\times 0.1$

P   _____ $\times \frac{1}{100} = 8.7 \div 10$

Q $9\frac{3}{10} \times 100 =$ _____ $\times \frac{1}{100}$

R $17 \times 0.1 \times \frac{1}{10} = 17 \times$ _____

multiplying decimals

example

each number is 10 times smaller...

...so the answer is 100 times smaller

Given that 28 × 14 = 392,   calculate 2.8 × 1.4   = 3.92

exercise 2e

1. Fill in the blanks:

   a) 4.5 is _____ times smaller than 45

   b) 2 is _____ times smaller than 200

   c) 1.9 is _____ times bigger than 0.19

   d) 800 is _____ times bigger than 0.8

   e) _____ is 1000 times bigger than 0.75

   f) 9.4 is 100 times smaller than _____

2. Given that **17 × 24 = 408**, work out the value of:

   a) 1.7 × 24

   b) 17 × 0.24

   c) 1.7 × 2.4

   d) 0.17 × 2.4

3. Given that **35 × 46 = 1610**, work out the value of:

   a) 0.35 × 46

   b) 4.6 × 0.035

   c) 350 × 4.6

   d) 0.35 × 4600

4. Given that **92 × 186 = 17,112**, work out the value of:

   a) 9.2 × 1.86

   b) 920 × 18.6

   c) 0.92 × 186

   d) 0.092 × 1860

5. Compared with the answer to 64 × 18, the answer to 6.4 × 1.8 would be:

   a) 10 times smaller   b) 100 times smaller   c) 1000 times smaller

6. Compared with the answer to 23 × 2.4, the answer to 2.3 × 2.4 would be:

   a) 10 times smaller   b) 100 times smaller   c) 1000 times smaller

7. If 18 × 2.3 = 41.4, which of these also equal 41.4? Circle all that apply.

   a) 1.8 × 2.3   b) 1.8 × 23   c) 0.18 × 23   d) 1.8 × 230

8. Given that 6 × 28 = 168 , fill in the blanks:

   a) _____ × 28 = 16.8

   b) 6 × _____ = 1.68

example

If the base calculation is not given, work it out first....

> Calculate 9 × 0.03
> ...Think 9 × 3 = 27, but 0.03 is 100 times smaller, so 9 × 0.03 = **0.27**

- -

exercise 2f

1. Work out:

   a) 7 × 0.2

   b) 9 × 0.03

   c) 0.4 × 6

   d) 0.04 × 3

   e) 6 × 0.3

   f) 0.07 × 4

   g) 15 × 0.03

   h) 12 × 0.4

   i) 11 × 0.3

2. Decide whether these statements are true or false:

   a) 0.6 × 100 = 6

   b) 0.2 × 0.4 = 0.8

   c) 0.3 × 4 = 0.12

   d) 0.05 × 0.3 = 0.015

   e) 0.6 × 6 = 3.6

   f) 0.5 × 0.5 = 2.5

3. Fill in the missing boxes to make these statements true:

   a) 0.6 × ☐ = 1.8

   b) 1.2 × ☐ = 6

   c) 0.3 × ☐ = 0.24

   d) 0.5 × ☐ = 0.3

   e) 0.8 × ☐ = 0.64

   f) 1.5 × ☐ = 0.015

4. Work out:

   a) $\frac{24}{100} \times 10$

   b) $6 \times \frac{5}{100}$

   c) $\frac{4}{10} \times \frac{9}{10}$

   d) $0.5 \times \frac{3}{10}$

   e) $\frac{12}{100} \times 20$

   f) $1\frac{2}{10} \times 5$

5. True or false? **8 × 0.05** is half of **8 × 0.1**

6. True or false? **0.04 × 4** is one tenth of **4 × 4**.

7. Is each of these calculations less than, or greater than 1? (<)(>)

   a) 800 × 0.4 ◯ 1

   b) 90 × 0.002 ◯ 1

   c) 0.06 × 300 ◯ 1

   d) 0.004 × 700 ◯ 1

multiplying decimals additional practice

1. Given that 0.42 × 85 = 35.7, work out:

   a) 42 × 85   b) 42 × 0.85   c) 8.5 × 0.042

2. Given that 2.9 × 0.8 = 2.32, work out:

   a) 29 × 80   b) 8 × 0.29   c) 290 × 8

4. Calculate:

   a) 8 × 0.3   e) 0.8 × 0.3   i) 0.07 × 0.7

   b) 4 × 0.05   f) 0.04 × 8   j) 4.5 × 0.2

   c) 0.4 × 7   g) 0.2 × 0.04   k) 0.25 × 0.8

   d) 5 × 0.06   h) 0.12 × 0.3   l) 2.5 × 40

5. Which of the following are equal to 2.85 × 41.6? Select all that apply.

   a) 28.5 × 416   c) 28.5 × 41.6   e) (285 ÷ 10) × 41.6

   b) 0.285 × 4.16   d) 2.85 × 4.16 × 10   f) (2.85 × 4160) ÷ 100

6. True or False: 49 × 6.5 = 49 × 65 ÷ 10

7. Which of the following is equal to : 4 × 10 × 3 ÷ 1000?

   a) 12 ÷ 10   b) 12 × 10   c) 12   d) 12 ÷ 100

8. True or False: 0.1 × 0.2 × 0.3 = 6 ÷ 1000.

9. True or False: 0.4 × 0.8 = 3.2

10. True or False: If two decimal numbers are multiplied, the answer will always be a decimal number.

11. If 4.27 and 0.63 are multiplied, how many decimal places will the answer have? Explain how you know.

12. If 8.65 and 0.4 are multiplied, how many decimal places will the answer have? Explain how you know.

13. True or False: Multiplying a number by something always makes it bigger. Explain your answer.

Decimal Multiplication Arithmagons

Copy and complete the arithmagons so that the numbers in the circles multiply together to make the numbers in the rectangles between them.

a)

0.2

6   0.4

b)

0.3

0.6   3

c)

0.1

0.5   8

d)

0.6

7   0.5

e)

0.4

1.6

0.3

f)

6

1.8

0.5

g)

0.15

0.9   3

h)

0.2

0.06

0.9

i)

0.6

0.3

0.4

j)

0.2

0.8   0.06

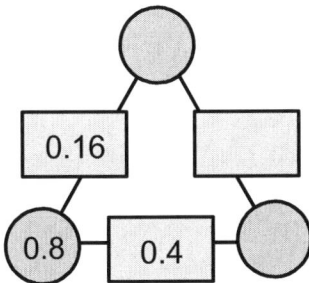

k)

0.16

0.8   0.4

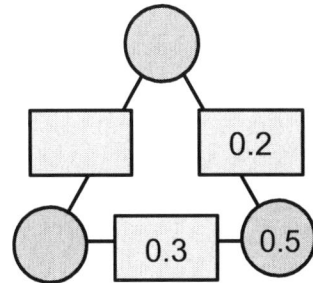

l)

0.2

0.3   0.5

Decimals Grid Puzzles

1. Put the numbers below into the empty boxes, so that all the statements are true.

1.2	0.015
0.75	0.04
6	0.03
7.5	0.3
1.5	0.4

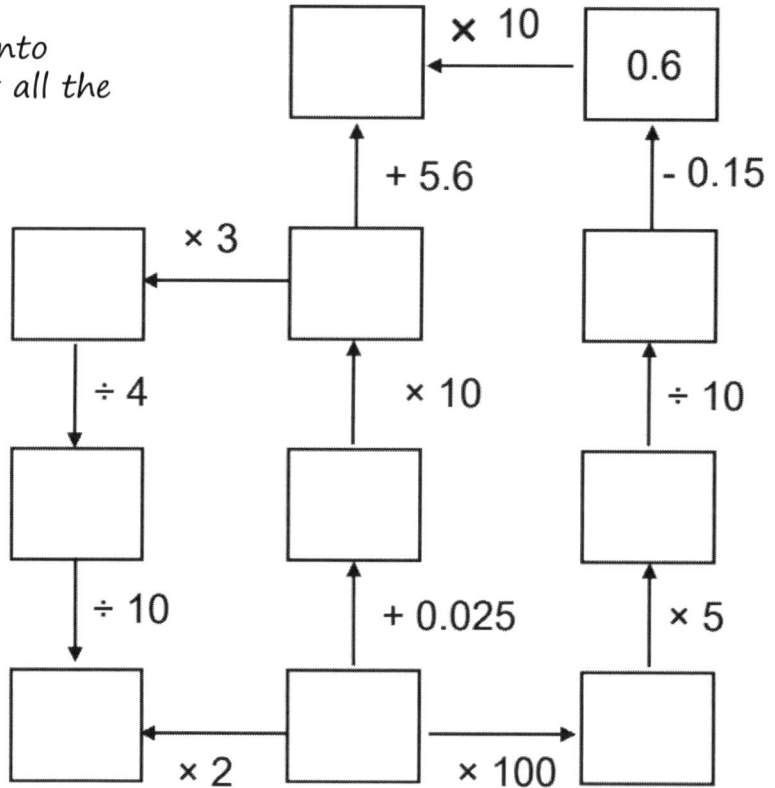

[ ] ← × 10 ← [0.6]

↑ + 5.6   ↑ - 0.15

[ ] ← × 3 ← [ ]   [ ]

↓ ÷ 4   ↑ × 10   ÷ 10

[ ]   [ ]   [ ]

↓ ÷ 10   ↑ + 0.025   ↑ × 5

[ ] ← × 2 ← [ ] → × 100 → [ ]

---

2. Complete the empty boxes, so that all the statements are true. Pay CAREFUL ATTENTION to the direction of the arrows. ⭐ extra challenge

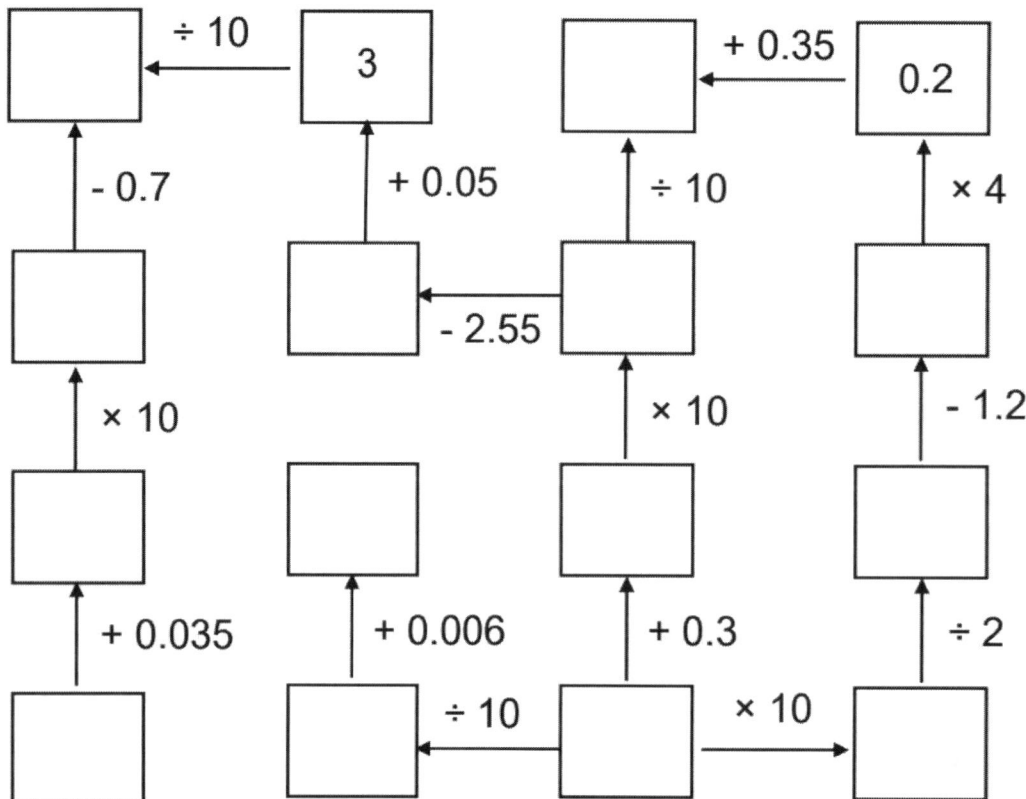

[ ] ← ÷ 10 ← [3]   [ ] ← + 0.35 ← [0.2]

↑ - 0.7   ↑ + 0.05   ↑ ÷ 10   ↑ × 4

[ ]   [ ] ← - 2.55 ← [ ]   [ ]

↑ × 10   ↑ × 10   ↑ - 1.2

[ ]   [ ]   [ ]   [ ]

↑ + 0.035   ↑ + 0.006   ↑ + 0.3   ÷ 2

[ ]   [ ] ← ÷ 10 ← [ ] → × 10 → [ ]

the effect of dividing by 0.5, 0.1, 0.01 and 0

learn by heart

Dividing by 0.5 is like doubling
Dividing by 0.1 is like multiplying by 10
Dividing by 0 is undefined

examples

Calculate
$12 \div 0.5$

$= 24$

Calculate
$12 \div 0.1$

$= 120$

Calculate
$12 \div 0.01$

$= 1200$

exercise 2g

1. Calculate, if possible:

   a) $8 \div 0.5$

   b) $12 \div 0.1$

   c) $4 \div 0.01$

   d) $0.23 \div 0.1$

   e) $\frac{9}{0.5}$

   f) $\frac{7}{0.1}$

   g) $\frac{9}{0.01}$

   h) $6.1 \div 0.5$

   i) $15 \div 0$

   j) $0 \div 15$

   k) $0.2 \div 0.5$

   l) $0.1 \div 0.1$

2. True or false?

   a) $18 \div 0.5 = 9$

   b) $6 \div 0.1 = 0.6$

   c) $4 \div 0.5 = 8$

   d) $84 \div 0.01 = 840$

3. Which of these cannot be calculated?

   a) $8 \div 0.3$ b) $8 \div 0.01$ c) $8 \div 900$ d) $8 \div 0$

4. Calculate

   a) $18 \div 0.01$

   b) $1.3 \div 0.01$

   c) $0.5 \div 0.5$

   d) $0.3 \div 0.1$

   e) $\frac{8.6}{0.01}$

   f) $\frac{0.039}{0.01}$

5. True or false? *Division always makes things smaller.*

6. Which of these give an answer of 190? Circle all that apply.

   a) $\frac{19}{100}$ b) $\frac{19}{10}$ c) $\frac{19}{1}$ d) $\frac{19}{1.0}$ e) $\frac{19}{0.1}$

7. Dividing by 0.1 is the same as multiplying by _____.

8. Dividing by 0.01 is the same as multiplying by _____.

9. Dividing by _____ is the same as doubling.

10. Complete the sentence: Dividing 32 by 0.1 has the same effect as...

    a) multiplying by 10   c) adding 10

    b) dividing by 10   d) subtracting 10.

11. Calculate:

    a) $3 \div 0.01$ c) $0.5 \div 0.5$ e) $0 \div 0.1$

    b) $12 \div 0.5$ d) $0.1 \div 0$ f) $0.2 \div 0.5$

12. Dividing 25 by ____ will give an answer bigger than 25. Choose from below:

    a) 100   b) 25   c) 1   d) 0.5   e) 0.1

13. To work out $6 \div 0.1$, we could calculate:

    a) 6×0.1 b) $6 \div 1$ c) $6 \div 10$ d) 6×10

14. Calculate:

    a) $\frac{9}{10} \div 0.1$ b) $\frac{14}{100} \div 0.1$ c) $1\frac{3}{10} \div 0.1$

    d) $\frac{4}{10} \div 0.5$ e) $\frac{8}{100} \div 0.01$ f) $2\frac{1}{10} \div 0.5$

matching activity

Match these calculations to their answers:

A $6 \div 0.5$	B 6×0.5	C $6 \div 10$		300	3
D $3 \div 0.01$	E 0.6×0.3	F $18 \div 0.1$		0.3	180
G $6 \div 0.01$	H $12 \div 0.01$	I 3×0.5		600	6
J $3 \div 0.5$	K 3×0.1	L $3 \div 0.1$		12	30
				1200	0.6
				0.18	1.5

Record your answers in a table:

A	B	C	D	E	F	G	H	I	J	K	L

the effect of division: changing the divisor

learn by heart

When dividing 2 numbers, we can call the numbers $\dfrac{dividend}{divisor}$ or $\dfrac{numerator}{denominator}$

When dividing 2 numbers, as the divisor gets smaller, the answer gets bigger

example

Given that $\dfrac{268}{4} = 67$, work out $\dfrac{268}{0.04}$

The divisor is 100 times smaller, the answer will be 100 times bigger, so 6700

Which is larger: $\dfrac{14}{7}$ or $\dfrac{14}{0.7}$?

$\dfrac{14}{0.7}$ is larger because it has a smaller divisor.

exercise 2h

1. Given that $\dfrac{12}{3} = 4$, work out:

   a) $\dfrac{12}{0.3}$

   b) $\dfrac{12}{0.03}$

   d) $\dfrac{12}{30}$

   e) $\dfrac{12}{300}$

   g) $\dfrac{12}{3.0}$

   h) $\dfrac{12}{6}$

2. Given that $\dfrac{84}{8} = 10.5$, work out:

   a) $\dfrac{84}{80}$

   b) $\dfrac{84}{0.8}$

   c) $\dfrac{84}{8.0}$

3. Given that $\dfrac{306}{17} = 18$, calculate:

   a) $\dfrac{306}{1.7}$

   b) $\dfrac{306}{170}$

   c) $\dfrac{306}{0.17}$

   d) $\dfrac{306}{17.0}$

   e) $\dfrac{306}{1700}$

   f) $\dfrac{306}{51}$

4. Which of these will be 10 times larger than $\dfrac{238}{14}$?

   a) $\dfrac{238}{1400}$

   b) $\dfrac{238}{140}$

   c) $\dfrac{238}{14.0}$

   d) $\dfrac{238}{1.4}$

5. Which of these is largest?

   a) $62 \div 0.1$ b) $62 \div 0.01$ c) $62 \div 10$ d) $62 \div 1.0$

6. Calculate:

   a) $\dfrac{12}{2}$ b) $\dfrac{12}{20}$ c) $\dfrac{12}{200}$ d) $\dfrac{12}{2000}$

7. Calculate:

   a) $15 \div 0.3$ b) $18 \div 0.06$ c) $4 \div 0.2$

8. If $8 \div 4 = 2$, then $8 \div 40 =$ _____

9. Calculate:

   a) $49 \div 0.7$ d) $15 \div 0.03$ g) $18 \div 0.9$

   b) $49 \div 0.07$ e) $15 \div 0.3$ h) $18 \div 0.09$

   c) $49 \div 70$ f) $15 \div 30$ i) $18 \div 90$

10. Which of these is 100 times smaller than $\dfrac{27}{0.4}$?

    a) $\dfrac{27}{4}$ b) $\dfrac{27}{40}$ c) $\dfrac{27}{400}$ d) $\dfrac{27}{4000}$

11. Which of these is 10 times smaller than $\dfrac{18}{50}$?

    a) $\dfrac{18}{0.5}$ b) $\dfrac{18}{5}$ c) $\dfrac{18}{500}$ d) $\dfrac{18}{5000}$

12. Calculate:

    a) $18 \div 0.9$ b) $36 \div 1.2$ c) $\dfrac{12}{0.06}$ d) $\dfrac{27}{0.03}$

13. Dividing by _____ is the same as multiplying by 10

14. Dividing by _____ is undefined

15. $\dfrac{28}{4}$ is 100 times bigger than....

    a) $\dfrac{28}{4.00}$ b) $\dfrac{28}{0.4}$ c) $\dfrac{28}{0.04}$ d) $\dfrac{28}{400}$

16. Given that $\dfrac{b}{12} = 4.1$, $\dfrac{b}{6} =$ _____

Dividing by a Decimal Code Breaker

Calculate the following and find your answer in the code box.
Write the words down as you go to reveal an inspirational message!

code box

0 = change	20 = to	50 = are	300 = world
2 = the	22 = last	70 = past	320 = door
2.5 = do	25 = river	100 = crazy	450 = game
8 = on	30 = the	120 = people	600 = believe
10 = they	40 = who	200 = fairy	640 = between
11 = every	45 = time	250 = can	700 = who
12 = enough	48 = ones	270 = snow	1000 = partner

a) $\dfrac{15}{0.5}$ = ___30___ = **The**

b) $\dfrac{12}{0.1}$ = _____ =

c) $\dfrac{8}{0.2}$ = _____ =

d) $\dfrac{15}{0.3}$ = _____ =

e) $\dfrac{10}{0.1}$ = _____ =

f) $\dfrac{6}{0.5}$ = _____ =

g) $\dfrac{12}{0.6}$ = _____ =

h) $\dfrac{6}{0.01}$ = _____ =

i) $\dfrac{9}{0.9}$ = _____ =

j) $\dfrac{25}{0.1}$ = _____ =

k) $\dfrac{0}{0.3}$ = _____ =

l) $\dfrac{9}{0.3}$ = _____ =

m) $\dfrac{36}{0.12}$ = _____ =

n) $\dfrac{20}{0.4}$ = _____ =

o) $\dfrac{16}{8.0}$ = _____ =

p) $\dfrac{24}{0.5}$ = _____ =

q) $\dfrac{7}{0.01}$ = _____ =

r) $\dfrac{0.25}{0.1}$ = _____ =

– Quote by Steve Jobs

51

the effect of division: changing the dividend

learn by heart

When dividing 2 numbers, we can call the numbers $\dfrac{dividend}{divisor}$ or $\dfrac{numerator}{denominator}$

When dividing 2 numbers, as the **dividend** gets smaller, the answer gets smaller

examples

Which is more, $\dfrac{8}{3}$ or $\dfrac{10}{3}$?

$\dfrac{10}{3}$ is larger because the dividend is larger

Given that $\dfrac{268}{4}$ = 67, work out $\dfrac{2.68}{4}$

The dividend is 100 times smaller, so the answer will be 100 times smaller, so 0.67

exercise 2i

1. Given that $\dfrac{16}{5}$ = 3.2, calculate:

   a) $\dfrac{160}{5}$ c) $\dfrac{1600}{5}$ e) $\dfrac{16.0}{5}$

   b) $\dfrac{1.6}{5}$ d) $\dfrac{0.16}{5}$ f) $\dfrac{1.60}{5}$

2. Which is larger: $42 \div 8$ or $420 \div 8$? Explain your answer.

3. Which is larger: $\dfrac{21}{0.6}$ or $\dfrac{2.1}{0.6}$? Explain your answer.

4. Which of the following is largest?

   a) $\dfrac{18}{45}$ b) $\dfrac{180}{45}$ c) $\dfrac{1.8}{45}$ d) $\dfrac{0.18}{45}$

5. Given that $243 \div 9 = 27$, work out the value of:

   a) $24.3 \div 9$ b) $2430 \div 9$ c) $0.243 \div 9$

6. Given that $414 \div 23 = 18$, work out the value of:

   a) $41.4 \div 23$ b) $41,400 \div 23$ c) $0.414 \div 23$

7. Which of these is largest?

   a) $\dfrac{120}{65}$ b) $\dfrac{0.12}{65}$ c) $\dfrac{12}{65}$ d) $\dfrac{1.2}{65}$

8. Calculate: *given that*

a) $\dfrac{360}{3}$

b) $\dfrac{3600}{3}$

c) $\dfrac{3.6}{3}$

d) $\dfrac{0.36}{3}$

e) $\dfrac{36.0}{3}$

f) 3.6 million ÷ 3

9. Calculate:

a) 1.5 ÷ 3

b) 2.4 ÷ 12

c) 440 ÷ 11

d) 0.55 ÷ 11

e) 1.8 ÷ 9

f) 2.7 ÷ 3

g) 1500 ÷ 5

h) 0.49 ÷ 7

i) 8.1 ÷ 9

10. $\dfrac{18}{6}$ is 100 times bigger than...

a) $\dfrac{180}{6}$

b) $\dfrac{1800}{6}$

c) $\dfrac{1.8}{6}$

d) $\dfrac{0.18}{6}$

11. Fill in the gaps with >, < or =

a) $\dfrac{6}{8}$ —— $\dfrac{12}{8}$

b) $\dfrac{12}{35}$ —— $\dfrac{19}{35}$

c) $\dfrac{14}{0.1}$ —— $\dfrac{1400}{0.1}$

d) $\dfrac{1.8}{15}$ —— $\dfrac{1.9}{15}$

e) $\dfrac{16}{4.6}$ —— $\dfrac{1.6}{4.6}$

f) $\dfrac{0.9}{15}$ —— $\dfrac{0.84}{15}$

12. Put these in order of size, starting with the smallest:

A	B	C	D
$\dfrac{15}{7}$	$\dfrac{1.5}{7}$	$\dfrac{150}{7}$	$\dfrac{0.15}{7}$

13. Compared with $\dfrac{19}{4.5}$, the answer to $\dfrac{0.19}{4.5}$ is :

a) 100 times smaller

b) 100 times bigger

c) 10 times smaller

d) 10 times bigger

67

the effect of changing dividend or divisor (mixed practice)

examples

Given that $\frac{42}{12}$ = 3.5, work out $\frac{42}{1.2}$

The divisor is 10 × smaller, so the answer will be 10 × bigger, i.e. 35

Given that $\frac{42}{12}$ = 3.5, work out $\frac{420}{12}$

The dividend is 10 × bigger, so the answer will be 10 × bigger, i.e. 35

exercise 2j

1. Which of these is largest?

   a) $\frac{45}{0.7}$

   b) $\frac{45}{7}$

   c) $\frac{45}{700}$

   d) $\frac{45}{7.0}$

2. Given that $63 \div 42$ = 1.5, work out the value of:

   a) $6300 \div 42$

   b) $6.3 \div 42$

   c) $63 \div 4.2$

3. Given that $\frac{84}{8}$ = 10.5, work out:

   a) $\frac{84}{80}$

   b) $\frac{84}{0.8}$

   c) $\frac{84}{8.0}$

4. Given that $\frac{62}{5}$ = 12.4, work out:

   a) $\frac{6.2}{5}$

   b) $\frac{620}{5}$

   c) $\frac{0.62}{5}$

5. Calculate:

   a) $45 \div 0.1$

   b) $7 \div 0.5$

   c) $1.9 \div 10$

6. Dividing 32 by _____ will produce the largest answer. Choose from below.

   a) 1.0

   b) 0.1

   c) 0.01

   d) 0.001

7. The answer to $\frac{23}{4.5}$ could be made bigger by...

   a) increasing the denominator

   c) halving the denominator

   b) increasing the numerator

   d) adding a zero to the end of the denominator

8. Which of these are 10 times bigger than $\frac{8}{0.4}$? Circle all that apply.

   a) $\frac{8}{4}$

   b) $\frac{80}{0.4}$

   c) $\frac{8}{0.04}$

   d) $\frac{800}{0.4}$

   e) $\frac{8}{0.40}$

dividing decimals practice

example

Work out $15 \div 0.3$

Start with a whole number 'base' calculation

$$15 \div 3 = 5$$
$$15 \div 0.3 = 50$$

Think what the effect is of changing one of the numbers to a decimal, in this case, it makes the answer 10 times bigger.

exercise 2k

1. Work out:

    a) $30 \div 5$ c) $30 \div 50$ e) $3 \div 5$

    b) $30 \div 0.5$ d) $30 \div 0.05$ f) $0.3 \div 5$

2. Work out:

    a) $36 \div 0.6$ c) $49 \div 70$ e) $27 \div 0.9$

    b) $36 \div 0.06$ d) $49 \div 700$ f) $27 \div 0.09$

4. Work out:

    a) $1.5 \div 3$ c) $2.1 \div 7$ e) $10.8 \div 9$

    b) $0.15 \div 3$ d) $0.21 \div 7$ f) $0.108 \div 9$

5. Which of these will have the **largest** answer?

    a) $0.2 \div 4$ b) $0.20 \div 4$ c) $2 \div 4$ d) $0.22 \div 4$

6. Work out:

    a) $4.2 \div 6$ d) $5.5 \div 11$ g) $250 \div 5$

    b) $420 \div 6$ e) $55 \div 0.11$ h) $2.5 \div 5$

    c) $42 \div 0.6$ f) $55 \div 1.1$ i) $25 \div 0.05$

7. True or false?

    a) $24 \div 0.3 > 24 \div 3$ b) $32 \div 80 < 32 \div 8$

8. $\frac{16}{9}$ is _____ times more than $\frac{1.6}{9}$

9. $\frac{1.2}{50}$ is _____ times smaller than $\frac{1.2}{0.5}$

10. Calculate:

a) $6 \div 0.03$　　　　　　　　　　h) $24 \div 0.3$

b) $10 \div 0.2$　　　　　　　　　　i) $28 \div 0.02$

d) $1.2 \div 4$　　　　　　　　　　k) $0.48 \div 6$

f) $25 \div 0.5$　　　　　　　　　　m) $72 \div 0.09$

g) $0.36 \div 6$　　　　　　　　　　n) $108 \div 1.2$

11. Which of these is 10 times more than $\frac{8}{1.8}$?

a) $\frac{80}{1.8}$　　　　　b) $\frac{8}{0.18}$　　　　　c) $\frac{8}{0.018}$　　　　　d) $\frac{8}{180}$

12. Calculate, if possible:

a) $24 \div 0.5$　　　b) $8 \div 0.1$　　　c) $3 \div 0$　　　d) $\frac{4}{0.5}$

13. Which number is it impossible to divide by?

matching activity

A	B	C
$7.2 \div 9$	$0.64 \div 8$	$55 \div 0.1$

D	E	F
$5.5 \div 10$	$2.4 \div 6$	$12 \div 0.01$

G	H	I
$72 \div 0.6$	$56 \div 0.7$	$4 \div 0.01$

J	K	L
$0.24 \div 2$	$11 \div 0.2$	$28 \div 0.7$

120	0.55
0.4	0.08
550	400
80	55
40	0.12
1200	0.8

A	B	C	D	E	F	G	H	I	J	K	L

Multiplying and Dividing Decimals Match

Work out each calculation and find your answer at the bottom:

A
$42 \div 100 =$ _____

B
$\dfrac{6}{0.1} =$ _____

C
$0.3 \times 0.4 =$ _____

D
$\dfrac{12}{0.3} =$ _____

E
$8 \times 0.2 =$ _____

F
$0.94 \times 1000 =$ _____

G
$1.6 \div 2 =$ _____

H
$\dfrac{2.5}{5} =$ _____

I
$\dfrac{36}{60} =$ _____

J
$\dfrac{18}{0.9} =$ _____

M
$36 \div 0.1 =$ _____

K
$0.08 \times 3 =$ _____

L
$\dfrac{9}{30} =$ _____

N
$0.6 \times 60 =$ _____

O
$\dfrac{0}{5} =$ _____

P
$\dfrac{5}{0} =$ _____

Q
$0.2 \times 900 =$ _____

R
$\dfrac{12}{0.5} =$ _____

S
$15 \div 300 =$ _____

T
$0.4 \div 10 =$ _____

U
$\dfrac{4}{200} =$ _____

V
$\dfrac{6}{0.02} =$ _____

W
$\dfrac{1.9}{0.1} =$ _____

X
$\dfrac{0.8}{8} =$ _____

Y
$0.6 \times 0.9 =$ _____

Z
$2.2 \div 11 =$ _____

- -

jumbled answers

180		

36   0.5   0.1   19   0.05

0.6

undefined   20   0.2   940   0.54

0.42

0.3   0.12   300   360   0.04   0.02   40

1.6   24   0.8   0.24   60   0

57

example

Given that $\dfrac{45}{9} = 5$, calculate $\dfrac{450}{0.9}$

Bigger numerator ($\times 10$) = Bigger Answer ($\times 10$)

Smaller denominator ($\div 10$) = Bigger Answer ($\times 10$)

So the answer is 100 times bigger = 500

exercise 21

1. Given that $\dfrac{36}{12} = 3$, calculate:

   a) $\dfrac{360}{1.2}$

   b) $\dfrac{3.6}{0.12}$

   c) $\dfrac{3.6}{120}$

   d) $\dfrac{0.36}{1.2}$

   e) $\dfrac{3600}{1.2}$

   f) $\dfrac{3.6}{120}$

2. Calculate:

   a) $180 \div 0.9$

   b) $0.18 \div 9$

   c) $1800 \div 90$

3. Which of these is 10 times bigger than $\dfrac{26}{5}$? Choose 2 answers.

   a) $\dfrac{260}{5}$

   b) $\dfrac{26}{50}$

   c) $\dfrac{2.6}{0.05}$

   d) $\dfrac{2600}{500}$

4. True or false?

   a) $1.4 \div 0.7 = 2$

   b) $250 \div 0.5 = 500$

   c) $0.36 \div 6 = 0.6$

   d) $\dfrac{1.2}{20} = 6$

   e) $\dfrac{1.2}{20} = 0.06$

   f) $\dfrac{0.3 \times 40}{0.2} = 60$

5. Given that $\dfrac{12}{0.48} = 25$, which of these also equal 25? Select all that apply.

   a) $\dfrac{120}{0.48}$

   b) $\dfrac{120}{4.8}$

   c) $\dfrac{1.2}{4.8}$

   d) $\dfrac{1.2}{0.048}$

Decimal Calculation Puzzles ⭐ extra challenge

1. Write in order of size, smallest first.

   A 0.3 + 0.2   **B** 0.3 - 0.2

   C 0.3 × 0.2   **D** 0.3 ÷ 0.1

2. Write in order of size, smallest first.

   A 2.4 + 0.6   **B** 2.4 - 0.6

   C 2.4 × 0.6   **D** 2.4 ÷ 0.6

3. Complete without calculating:

   a) 6.2 × 8 = 62 × _____

   b) 0.57 × 0.9 = 9 × _____

   c) 520 × 3.8 = 10.4 × _____

4. Jack walks at a constant rate of 0.18km per minute. How far will he travel in 1 hour?

5. (a) What is a quarter of 1.11 ?

   (b) What is an eighth of 2.03 ?

6. Work out the sum:

   0.1 + 0.2 + 0.3 + ... + 0.12

7. A bat and ball together cost £1.10.

   The bat costs £1 more than the ball. How much do they cost seperately?

8. Two numbers have a product of 0.18 and a sum of 1.1. Work out the two numbers.

9. Work out the missing values:

   a) 5 ÷ _____ = 25

   b) _____ ÷ 0.4 = 0.7

   c) _____ ^{2} = 0.0144

10. How many different digits appear in the answer to the sum:

   $0.\overset{..}{1}\overset{}{2} + 0.\overset{.}{3}4\overset{.}{5}$

clever calculation tricks 1 ⭐ extra challenge

learn by heart

| 125 × 8 = 1000 |

| 25 × 4 = 100 |

Factorise: *Break a number down into smaller factors*

examples

Factorising:
Calculate 16 × 25

$$= 4 × 4 × 25$$
$$= 4 × 100$$
$$= 400$$

Related Calculations:
Calculate 12.5 × 6

×2 ↘   ÷2 ↘

$$= 25 × 3$$
$$= 75$$

exercise 2n

1. Calculate by factorising:

   a) 12 × 25

   b) 20 × 15

   c) 125 × 16

   d) 25 × 20

   e) 64 × 125

   f) 80 × 50

   g) 24 × 25

   h) 75 × 16

   i) 200 × 15

   j) 25 × 160

   k) 125 × 80

   l) 375 × 8

2. Fill in the blanks:

   a) 15 × 6 = 5 × ____

   b) 25 × 12 = 5 × ____

   c) 27 × 20 = 10 × ____ = ____

   d) 50 × 16 = 100 × ____ = ____

   e) 35 × 8 = 4 × ____ = ____

   f) 20 × 15 = 100 × ____ = ____

   g) 12 × 40 = 10 × ____ = ____

   h) 14 × 20 = 10 × ____ = ____

   i) 8 × ____ = 4 × 50 = ____

   j) 25 × ____ = 100 × 4 = ____

---

challenges

a) 15000 ÷ 8 ÷ 125

b) (9006 × 423) - (423 × 9004)

---

clever calculation tricks 2 ⭐ extra challenge

learn by heart

To divide by 5:	To multiply by 5:
divide by 10 and double	multiply by 10 and halve

examples

Calculate $18 \div 5$
$= 18 \div 10 \times 2$
$= 1.8 \times 2$
$= 3.6$

Calculate $(4 \times 17) + (6 \times 17)$
$= 10 \times 17$
$= 170$

Calculate 99×42
$= 100 \times 42 - 42$
$= 4200 - 42$
$= 4158$

exercise 20

1. Calculate:

    a) $(17 \times 8) + (3 \times 8)$

    b) $(14 \times 6) - (4 \times 6)$

    c) $(19 \times 7) + (1 \times 7)$

    d) $(23 \times 14) - (14 \times 3)$

    e) $(4 \times 125) + (4 \times 125)$

    f) $(30 \times 25) + (25 \times 10)$

2. Calculate:

    a) $42 \div 5$

    b) 9×17

    c) $312 \div 5$

    d) 99×14

    e) $21 \div 5$

    f) 19×12

    g) 101×15

    h) 41×7

    i) $850 \div 5$

    j) $2300 \div 5$

    k) 23×201

    l) 126×8

3. Calculate

    a) $(121 \times 16) + (4 \times 16)$

    b) 41×250

    c) $(10 \times 126) - (2 \times 126)$

    d) $49 \div 3.5$

    e) 127×0.8

    f) $35 \div 14$

challenges

a) $4 \times 35 \times 15$ b) $11 \times 8 \times 25$ c) 251×16

<u>exercise 2p</u>

1. Given that 24 × 46 = 1104, what is the value of 0.24 × 460?

    a) 1104   b) 110.4   c) 11.04   d) 1.104

2. Which is larger $\frac{9}{3}$ or $\frac{9}{0.3}$? Explain your answer.

3. Which of the following is equal to 12 ÷ 0.4?

    a) 30   b) 3   c) 0.3   d) 4.8

4. Which of these cannot be calculated?

    a) 8 ÷ 0.3   b) 8 ÷ 0.01   c) 8 ÷ 900   d) 8 ÷ 0

5. Calculate 1 - 0.083

6. Calculate:

    a) 4.82 ÷ 100   c) 0.8 × 1000   e) 4.6 ÷ 10

    b) 34.7 × 100   d) 208 ÷ 100   f) 9 ÷ 100

7. Calculate:

    a) 6 × 0.1   d) 8 ÷ 0.2   g) 4.2 ÷ 7

    b) 6 ÷ 0.1   e) 0.9 × 0.3   h) 4.2 ÷ 70

    c) 8 × 0.2   f) 0.9 ÷ 0.3   i) 42 ÷ 0.7

8. Write each fraction as a decimal using short division:

    a) $\frac{1}{8}$ b) $\frac{4}{6}$ c) $\frac{4}{9}$ d) $\frac{1}{11}$

9. Dividing by 0.5 is the same as multiplying by _____

10. Dividing by _____ is the same as multiplying by 100

11. Which of these is 100 times more than $\frac{8}{1.2}$?

    a) $\frac{0.08}{1.2}$ b) $\frac{0.8}{1.2}$ c) $\frac{80}{1.2}$ d) $\frac{800}{1.2}$

12. Use short division to write $\frac{8}{5}$ as a decimal.

13. Calculate:

    a) 0.406×1000 c) $42.5 \div 1000$

    b) $0.2\dot{3} \times 100$ d) 12.5×4

14. Given that $3.8 \times 8.5 = 32.3$, what is the value of 380×85?

    a) 323   b) 3230   c) 32,300   d) 323,000

15. Calculate:

    a) $\frac{12}{0.01}$ b) $\frac{15}{0.3}$ c) $\frac{2.4}{6}$

what's missing?

16. Fill in the missing boxes to make these statements true:

    a) $6 \times \boxed{} = 2.4$ g) $0.5 \times \boxed{} = 2$

    b) $0.2 \times \boxed{} = 0.12$ h) $0.4 \times \boxed{} = 0.16$

    c) $0.8 \times \boxed{} = 0.24$ i) $0.03 \times \boxed{} = 0.15$

    d) $0.4 \times \boxed{} = 160$ j) $5 \times \boxed{} = 0.4$

    e) $6 \times \boxed{} = 0.18$ k) $0.09 \times \boxed{} = 0.036$

- -

definitely wrong?

Six of these statements are definitely wrong, which ones?

A $3 \div 0.5 = 6$	**B** $14 \div 0.1 = 14.1$	**C** $0 \div 9$ = undefined	**D** $12 \div 0.5 = 24$
E $7 \div 0.1 = 70$	**F** $\frac{9}{15} > \frac{9}{16}$	**G** $12 \div 0 = 0$	**H** $\frac{4}{14} > \frac{0.4}{14}$
I $12 \div 100 = 0.12$	**J** $8 \div 0.5 = 4$	**K** $6 \div 60 = 10$	**L** $\frac{4}{0.1} = 0.4$

cumulative review (chapters 1 & 2)

exercise 2r

1. Write three million, eighteen thousand and six in digits.

2. Write as decimals:

    a) 7 hundredths   b) $\frac{1}{10}$ c) $\frac{9}{1000}$ d) $1\frac{3}{10}$

3. In each pair, circle the larger number:

    a) 0.64 or 0.7   b) 0.203 or 0.21   c) 1.84 or 1.804

4. Which of these numbers has 2 significant figures?

    a) 204   b) 1.08   c) 0.5   d) 0.60

5. Round each of these numbers to 1 significant figure:

    a) 425   b) 0.456   c) 1900   d) 1.053

6. Put these in order of size, starting with the smallest:

    $\frac{3}{10}$ 0.209 $\frac{29}{1000}$ 0.29   _____   _____   _____   _____

7. Calculate:

    a) 22.6 ÷ 5   b) 0.8 × 0.3   c) 1 ÷ 8   d) $0.1 \times 3\frac{9}{10}$

8. Write as fractions or mixed numbers:

    a) 0.1   b) 1.1   c) 1.01   d) 0.011

9. Calculate 106 ÷ 0.5

10. Write each of these using dot notation:

    a) 0.49494...   b) 0.603603603...   c) 0.56666...   d) 2.0324324324....

11. Complete each statement with >, < or =

    a) 4.0 ____ 4   c) 0.203 ____ 0.23   e) 0.13 _____ $\frac{13}{1000}$

    b) 0.4 ____ $\frac{4}{100}$ d) 5.6 ____ $5\frac{6}{10}$ f) 0.047 ____ 0.407

exercise 2s

1. Which of the following has 2 significant figures?

   a) 4.0   b) 0.203   c) 209   d) 5.62

2. Write as a decimal:

   a) $\frac{4}{100}$ b) $3\frac{8}{1000}$ c) $\frac{29}{100}$ d) $\frac{29}{1000}$

3. Round 0.04099 to 3 significant figures.

4. Which of these numbers is half way between 0.3 and 0.31?

   a) 0.35   b) 0.035   c) 0.315   d) 0.305

5. Calculate:

   a) 1 - 0.1   b) 1 - 0.01   c) 1 - 0.001   d) 1 - 0.0001

6. Fill in the blanks with >, < or =

   a) $\frac{21}{3}$ ___ $\frac{21}{3.1}$ c) $\frac{19}{4.5}$ ___ $\frac{19}{4.1}$

   b) $\frac{8}{0.4}$ ___ $\frac{9}{0.4}$ d) $\frac{0.2}{8}$ ___ $\frac{0.3}{8}$

7. Which of the following is equal to $0.\dot{3} - \frac{3}{10}$?

   a) 0.03   b) $0.0\dot{3}$ c) $0.0\dot{3}$ d) $0.\dot{3}\dot{0}$

8. Given that 8.2 × 76 = 623.2, work out:

   a) 820 × 7.6   b) 0.82 × 0.76   c) 8.2 × 7.7

9. Given that $\frac{200}{16}$ = 12.5, work out:

   a) $\frac{200}{160}$ b) $\frac{2}{16}$ c) $\frac{2000}{1.6}$

   d) $\frac{0.2}{16}$ e) $\frac{20}{0.16}$ f) $\frac{2}{160}$

10. Estimate the positions of these numbers on the numberline below.

a) 0.42   b) 0.60   c) $\frac{9}{10}$ d) $\frac{3}{100}$

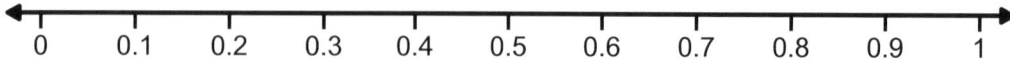

11. Estimate the positions of these numbers on the numberline below.

a) $\frac{3}{100}$ b) $\frac{2}{10}$ c) $\frac{1}{100}$ d) $\frac{16}{100}$

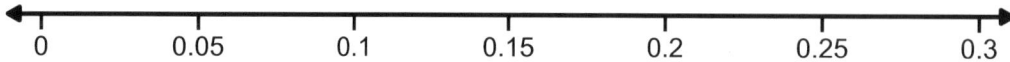

12. Estimate the positions of these numbers on the numberline below.

a) 0.17   b) 0.145   c) $\frac{2}{10}$ d) $\frac{185}{1000}$

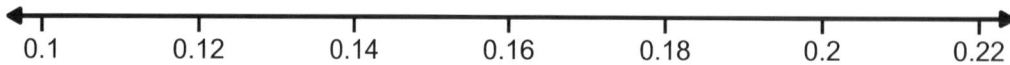

13. Estimate the positions of these numbers on the numberline below.

a) 1.2   b) 2.1   c) $3\frac{1}{10}$ d) $\frac{35}{10}$

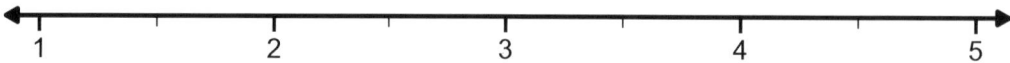

14. Estimate the positions of these numbers on the numberline below.

a) 2.6   b) 3.45   c) $3\frac{2}{10}$ d) $3\frac{95}{100}$

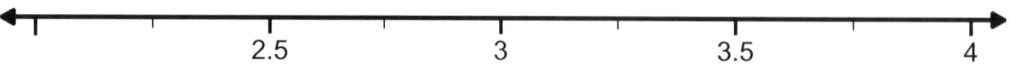

15. Estimate the positions of these numbers on the numberline below.

a) 1.01   b) 0.88   c) $\frac{11}{10}$ d) $\frac{105}{100}$

chapter 3: negative numbers

[Recommended Time: 9-13 hours]

Contents

ordering negatives

The further down the number line, the smaller the number

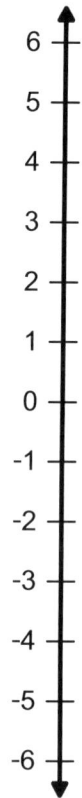

example

Put these numbers in order,
starting with the smallest: **1, -2, -7, 3**

In order: −7, −2, 1, 3

```
6
5
4
3
2
1
0
-1
-2
-3
-4
-5
-6
```

exercise 3a

1. Which is the **larger** number in each pair?

   a) -3 or 2   b) 4 or -2   c) 5 or -5

   d) 0 or -6   e) -1 or -10   f) 6 or 8

   g) -4 or -5   h) 2 or -9   i) -3 or -7

2. State the number that is:

   a) one larger than -3   b) one smaller than -5

   c) one smaller than -12   d) one larger than -1

   e) one larger than -2.5   f) one smaller than -4.5

3. List the numbers from the box that are:

   a) **larger** than -12

   b) **smaller** than -12

-15	13	-8	-11
-12.5	0	-1200	120

4. Write each set of numbers in order, from smallest to largest.

   a)   -5   3   -7   1

   b)   -3   -9   1   -4   0

   c)   -8   -4.5   -2   -4

   d)   0.5   3   -0.5   -1   -1.5

5. State the number that is directly above each of these on the number line:

   a) -1   b) -12   c) -54   d) -1,000

6. Fill in the blanks using >, < or =

   a) -3 _____ 1   c) -12 _____ -13   e) -8 _____ -8.5

   b) 6 _____ -6   d) -5 _____ 0   f) -0.1 _____ $-\frac{1}{10}$

7. State the number that each arrow is pointing to on the number line.

8. Each of these number sequences goes **down in equal steps**.
Work out the missing numbers.

a) | 3 | 2 | | | | | | |

b) | 5 | 3 | | | | | | |

c) | 20 | 15 | | | | | | |

d) | 25 | 15 | | | | | |

9. List the numbers from the box that are:

a) between -3 and 8

b) between -8 and -3

-5	6	-2	-7
0	1	-3.5	-2.5

10. List all the integers between -3 and 2

11. Simon thinks of a number. His number is an integer, it is larger than -9 and less than -6. List the possible numbers Simon could be thinking of.

12. Decide whether each of these statements is true or false.

a) -3 > -4   c) 0 < -4   e) -3 > 3

b) -1.5 < -1   d) -4.5 > -5   f) -0.5 > 0.5

13. Which number is the largest negative integer?

14. Which number is the smallest negative integer?

15. True or false: the closer a number is to zero, the smaller it is.

16. Which of these numbers is closest to 0?

a) -1   b) 0.5   c) -0.4   d) 0.505   e) 1.5

17. How many integers are there:

a) between -3 and 3   b) between -5 and 5   c) between -40 and 40

18. Write down all the possible integer values of x if: $-5 < x < 3.2$

negative number journeys (addition)

learn by heart

When **adding a positive number**, move **up** the the number line.

examples

| -8 + 3 $= -5$ | -2 + 5 $= 3$ | -12 + ___ = 5 $= 17$ |

exercise 3b

1. Work out:

   a) -6 + 4

   b) -2 + 7

   c) -7 + 6

   d) -4 + 8

   e) -3 + 1

   f) -6 + 6

   g) -30 + 20

   h) -20 + 30

   i) -15 + 35

2. Which one of these calculations is correct?

   | A -4 + 10 = 4 | B -4 + 10 = 6 | C -4 + 10 = -14 |

3. Which of the following have **negative** answers?

   | A -3 + 4 | B -3 + 1 | C -3 + 10 | D -6 + 3 | E -4 + 4 |

4. Calculate:

   a) -492 + 1

   b) -500 + 1

   c) -1000 + 1

5. Fill in the blanks:

   a) -4 + ____ = 0

   d) -10 + ____ = -3

   g) -6 + ____ = -4

   b) -4 + ____ = 2

   e) -10 + ____ = -1

   h) -6 + ____ = 5

   c) -4 + ____ = 10

   f) -10 + ____ = 1

   i) -6 + ____ = 12

6. Fill in the missing number: _____ + 34 = 0

7. True or False:

   a) 8 + 5 = 5 + 8

   c) -6 + 10 = -4

   b) -9 + 9 = 0

   d) $-a + a = 0$

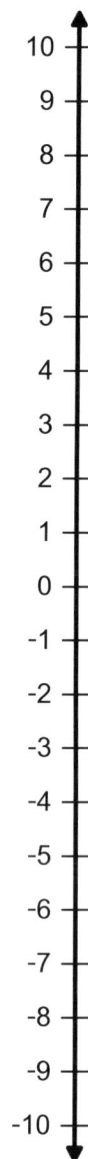

8. Decide whether the answer will be positive, negative or zero:

   a) -4 + 5

   b) -10 + 8

   c) -3 + 6

   d) -8 + 8

   e) -200 + 45

   f) -1000 + 854

9. Calculate:

   a) -10 + 6

   b) -8 + 12

   c) -15 + 10

   d) -6 + 10

   e) -20 + 30

   f) -30 + 20

   g) -5 + 18

   h) -3 + 16

   i) -29 + 27

10. True or False: -5 + 10 = 10 - 5

11. True or False: -4 + 15 = 15 - 4

12. Complete these statements with the symbols: >, < or =:

    a) -3 + 4 ___ 0

    b) -6 + 6 ___ 0

    c) -60 + 75 ___ 0

    d) -45 + 20 ___ 0

    e) -12 + 36 ___ 0

    f) -82 + 103 ___ 0

13. Complete the flow charts:

    a)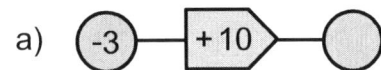

    b)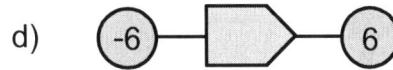

    c)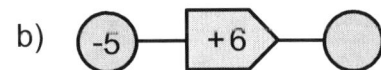

    d)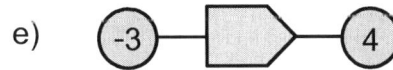

    e)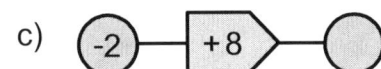

    f)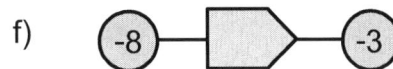

14. Calculate:

    a) -4.5 + 5

    b) -0.2 + 1.5

    c) -3.1 + $2\frac{1}{10}$

    d) -5 + $\frac{1}{10}$

    e) -2.5 + $2\frac{5}{10}$

    f) -6.0 + 0.6

15. Decide if the answer is positive, negative or zero:

    a) -0.25 + $\frac{3}{10}$

    b) -0.46 + $\frac{47}{100}$

    c) -1.89 + $1\frac{9}{100}$

16. -0.7 + _____ = $-\frac{7}{10}$?

17. $-1\frac{5}{10}$ + _____ = -1.2

negative number journeys (subtraction)

learn by heart

When **subtracting a positive number**, move **down** the number line.

examples

$8 - 10$
$= -2$

$0 - 5$
$= -5$

$8 - \underline{} = -10$
$= 18$

$12 - 15$
$= -3$

You could find the difference between the numbers (3) then decide if it will be positive or negative

exercise 3c

1. Work out:

   a) 3 - 7

   b) 3 - 2

   c) 1 - 2

   d) 5 - 6

   e) 8 - 12

   f) 8 - 8

   g) 3 - 8

   h) 8 - 3

   i) 3 - 8

2. Which of these will have a negative answer? Circle two answers.

   a) 5 - 4

   b) 5 - 5

   c) 5 - 6

   d) 5 - 7

3. Fill in the blank 777 - _____ = 0

4. Which of these is correct?

   A 82 - 83 = 1

   B 82 - 83 = -1

   C 82 - 83 = 0

5. Calculate:

   a) 81 - 84

   b) 81 - 90

   c) 810 - 900

6. Fill in the blanks:

   a) 12 - ____ = 0

   d) 6 - ____ = -3

   g) 18 - _____ = -1

   b) 12 - ____ = -1

   e) 6 - ____ = -8

   h) 18 - ____ = -3

   c) 12 - ____ = -5

   f) 6 - ____ = -12

   i) 18 - ____ = 10

7. Calculate:

   a) 7 - 7 - 7

   c) 5 - 4 - 3

   e) $2.3 - 2\frac{3}{10}$

   b) 4.5 - 5

   d) 10 - 10 - 10

   f) $1.7 - 1\frac{9}{10}$

further examples

| -8 - 10 $= -18$ | -2 - 5 $= -7$ | -8 - ____ = -10 $= 2$ |

In total you will travel 7 places down the number line

- -

exercise 3d

1. Work out:

   a) -4 - 3

   b) -2 - 6

   c) -8 - 1

   d) -1 - 99

   e) -42 - 3

   f) -12 - 12

2. Calculate -4 - 4 - 4

3. Fill in the blanks:

   a) -4 - ____ = -8

   b) -4 - ____ = -10

   c) -5 - ____ = -5

   d) -5 - ____ = -12

   e) -16 - ____ = -20

   f) -16 - ____ = -25

4. Calculate $-0.7 - \frac{3}{10}$

mixed subtractions

5. Calculate:

   a) 12 - 12

   b) 12 - 15

   c) -12 - 15

   d) -5 - 3

   e) 5 - 3

   f) 5 - 8

   g) -9 - 2

   h) 9 - 12

   i) 12 - 9

6. Which of these will have a negative answer? Circle 2 answers.

   a) -6 - 3   b) 6 - 3   c) 3 - 6   d) 6 - 6

7. Calculate 5 - 5 - 5

8. Fill in the blanks:

   a) 3 - ____ = -6

   b) -3 - ____ = -6

   c) -12 - ____ = -15

   d) 12 - ____ = -15

   e) 42 - ____ = -2

   f) -42 - ____ = -100

negative number journeys mixed problems

exercise 3e

1. Calculate:

   a) 8 - 10

   b) 5 - 9

   c) -4 + 2

   d) -7 + 14

   e) -8 - 3

   f) -11 - 22

   g) -16 + 11

   h) -12 + 20

   i) 17 - 32

   j) -14 - 18

   k) -81 + 90

   l) -4.5 + 9

2. Work out the missing numbers to make the calculations correct.

   a) $\boxed{-1}$ + $\boxed{}$ = $\boxed{3}$

   b) $\boxed{-7}$ + $\boxed{}$ = $\boxed{-2}$

   c) $\boxed{-2}$ - $\boxed{}$ = $\boxed{-10}$

   d) $\boxed{4}$ - $\boxed{}$ = $\boxed{-6}$

   e) $\boxed{-9}$ + $\boxed{}$ = $\boxed{-3}$

   f) $\boxed{-6}$ - $\boxed{}$ = $\boxed{-13}$

3. Which of the following have **negative** answers?

A	B	C	D	E
96 - 132	-67 + 59	-34 - 97	-48 + 56	-85 + 89

4. What number must be added to -8 to make zero?

5. Which **two** of these calculations have the **same answer**?

A	B	C
3 - 5	5 - 3	-3 + 5

6. Work out the missing numbers to make the calculations correct.

   a) $\boxed{}$ + $\boxed{5}$ = $\boxed{4}$

   b) $\boxed{}$ - $\boxed{6}$ = $\boxed{-1}$

   c) $\boxed{}$ - $\boxed{6}$ = $\boxed{-9}$

   d) $\boxed{}$ + $\boxed{10}$ = $\boxed{3}$

7. True or False: 7 - 5 = 5 - 7

8. Which of the following have a negative answer?

   a) -72 + 54   b) -381 + 392   c) 642 - 386   d) 209 - 391

9. Write down a calculation that has the same answer as -243 + 400

10. Calculate:

    a) -56 + 100 b) 47 - 59 c) 204 - 374 d) -401 + 323

11. Which of the following has the same answer as 421 - 500?

    a) -421 + 500 b) 500 - 421 c) -500 + 421 d) -421 - 500

12. Calculate:

    a) -3 - 3 - 3 - 3 b) -4.2 - 4 c) -10.4 - 2.3

13. Complete these statements:

    a) -42 + _____ = 0

    b) 18 - _____ = 0

    c) -0.8 - _____ = -1

    d) -4.2 + _____ = 5

    e) -13 + _____ = 22

    f) 22 - _____ = -9

    g) $-\frac{4}{10}$ + _____ = 0

    h) $-1\frac{3}{10}$ - _____ = -2

14. Work out:

    a) 4 - 5 - 6 b) -2 + 1 + 2 c) -3 - 4 - 5

    d) -2 - 2 - 2 e) -3 - 3 - 3 - 3 - 3 f) -6 + 6 + 6

15. The lowest temperature recorded in London one day was -2°C.
    The lowest temperature recorded in Edinburgh was four degrees colder.
    What was the temperature recorded in Edinburgh?

16. Harry measures the temperature in his freezer to be -20°C.
    The temperature in his fridge is 5°C.
    How many degrees warmer is Harry's fridge than his freezer?

17. The temperature at midnight was -1°C.
    At midday, the temperature is five degrees warmer than at midnight.
    John says the temperature at midday must be 6°C.
    What has John done wrong?

challenge ⭐ extra challenge

18. True, Sometimes True, or False? : $a - b = b - a$

19. Is it always true that: $-a - b = -(a + b)$?

20. Is it always true that $a - b = -(b - a)$?

Hint
Try replacing 'a' and 'b'
with two numbers and
see if the statement is
true. Can you find two
numbers that make it true?

Number Line Journeys

Work out the numbers or operations that go in the empty boxes to complete these number line journeys.

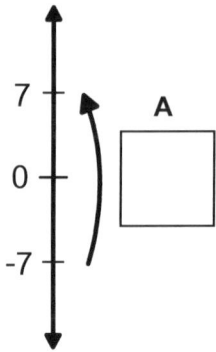

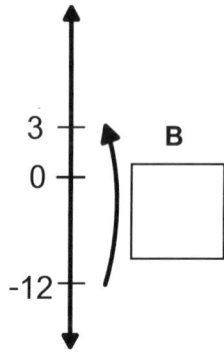

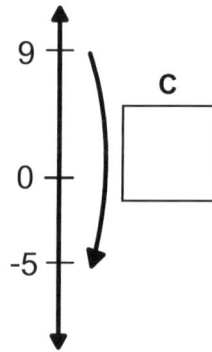

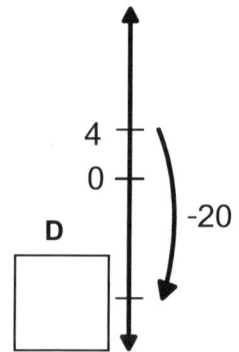

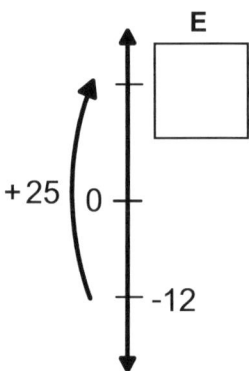

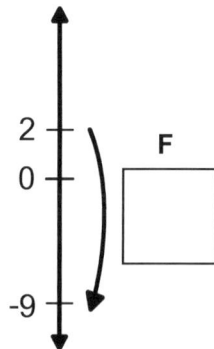

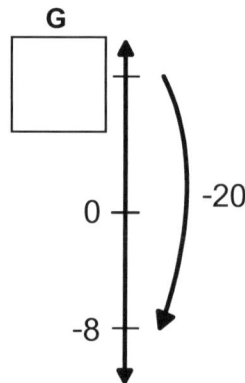

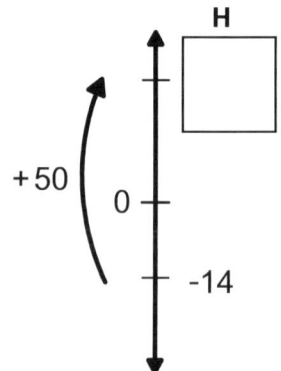

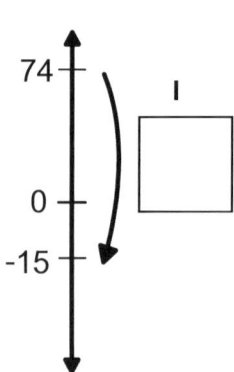

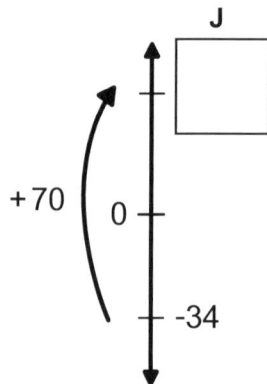

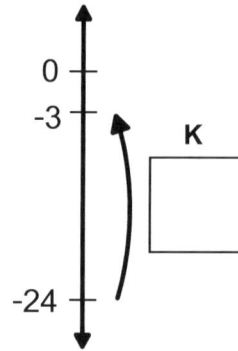

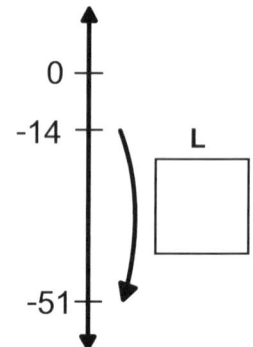

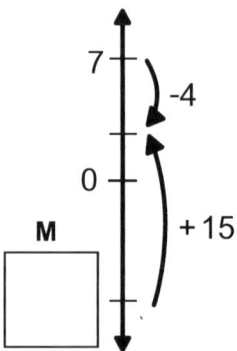

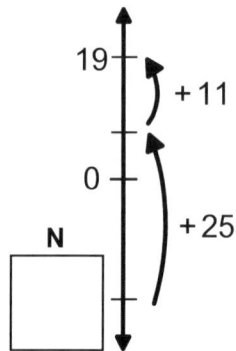

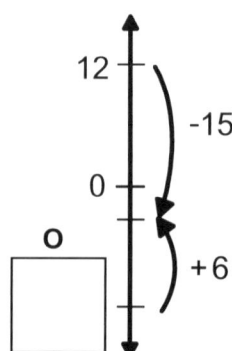

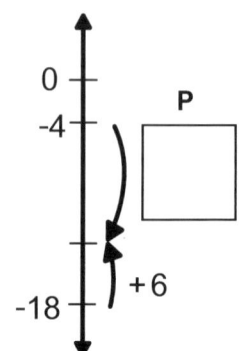

A.

B.

C.

D.

E.

F.

G.

H.

I.

J.

K.

L.

M.

N.

O.

P.

adding a negative

learn by heart

When **adding a negative number**, move **down** the number line.

examples

$$5 + -2$$
$$= 5 - 2$$
$$= 3$$

$$-5 + -2$$
$$= -5 - 2$$
$$= -7$$

exercise 3f

1. Work out:

   a) 4 + -2

   b) 1 + -6

   c) -2 + -5

   d) 3 + -10

   e) 9 + -9

   f) -8 + -8

   g) 9 + -10

   h) -1 + -1

   i) 4 + -1

2. True or false: -8 + -7 = -7 + -8

3. True or false: 9 + -10 = -9 + 10

4. True or false:
   when two negative numbers are added, the result is always a negative number.

5. Work out:

   a) 20 + -50

   b) 20 + -32

   c) -20 + -15

   d) 400 + -40

   e) 100 + -17

   f) -100 + -17

   g) -9 + -9 + -9

   h) -1 + -2 + -3

   i) 7 + -7 + -7

6. Work out the missing numbers to make the calculations correct.

   a) 4 + ☐ = 1

   b) -3 + ☐ = -1

   c) -5 + ☐ = 4

   d) -1 + ☐ = -11

   e) ☐ + -2 = -8

   f) ☐ + -9 = 7

7. Josie thought of a pair of whole numbers that added to -4. Neither of Josie's numbers were bigger than 5. Find all the possible pairs of numbers.

8. Calculate:

   a) $1.4 + -\frac{3}{10}$

   b) $-\frac{7}{10} + -0.1$

   c) $-5.5 + 6\frac{1}{10}$

Pyramid Puzzles

Copy and complete the pyramids so that each pair of numbers add up to make the box directly above them.

a)

-3	-2	4

b)

-4	-5	-1

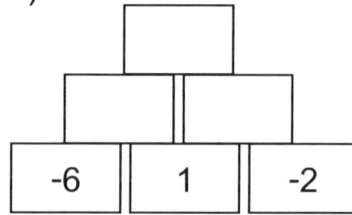

c)

-6	1	-2

d)

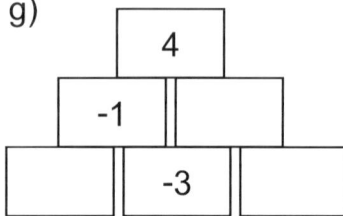

	-6	
-7	-4	

e)

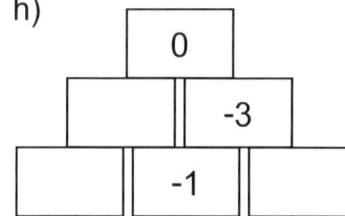

3		
	-3	2

f)

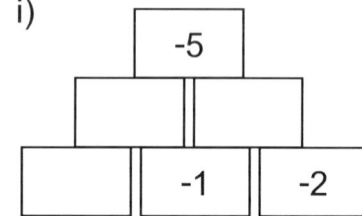

	-6	
-4		-9

g)

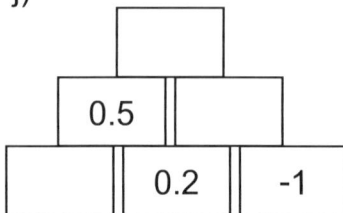

4		
-1		
	-3	

h)

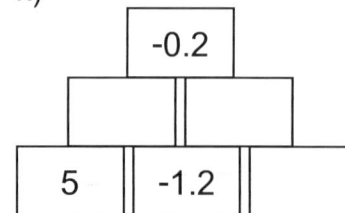

0		
	-3	
	-1	

i)

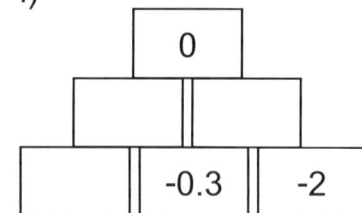

-5		
	-1	-2

more challenging

j)

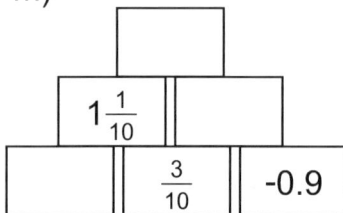

0.5		
	0.2	-1

k)

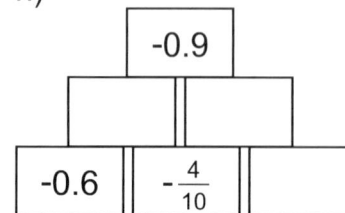

-0.2		
5	-1.2	

l)

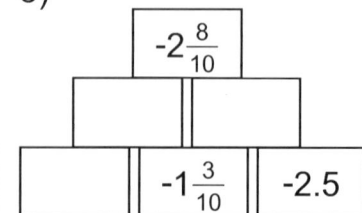

0		
	-0.3	-2

m)

$1\frac{1}{10}$		
	$\frac{3}{10}$	-0.9

n)

-0.9		
-0.6	$-\frac{4}{10}$	

o)

$-2\frac{8}{10}$		
	$-1\frac{3}{10}$	-2.5

78

subtracting a negative

learn by heart

When **subtracting a negative number**, move **up** the number line.

examples

$5 - -2$
$$= 5 + 2$$
$$= 7$$

$-5 - -2$
$$= -5 + 2$$
$$= -3$$

exercise 3g

1. Work out:

   a) 4 - -5

   b) 3 - -1

   c) -6 - -1

   d) 1 - -2

   e) -1 - -1

   f) -3 - 2

   g) -9 - -4

   h) -6 - 7

   i) 8 - -8

2. Which of the following has the same answer as 42 - -36?

   a) 42 - 36

   b) 42 + 36

   c) 36 - 42

   d) -42 - 36

3. Which of the following has the **largest** answer?

   a) 87 + -76

   b) 87 - -76

4. Which **two** of these calculations have the **same answer**?

A	B	C
-2 - -6	-2 - 6	-2 + 6

5. Work out:

   a) -5 - -10

   b) 15 - 45

   c) -40 - -30

   d) 6 - -20

   e) 6 - 20

   f) -80 - -8

   g) -10 - -6 - 7

   h) -3 - 5 - -7

   i) 100 - -10 - 1

6. Work out the missing numbers to make the calculations correct.

   a) 6 - ☐ = 7

   b) -3 - ☐ = 3

   c) -3 - ☐ = -8

   d) 0 - ☐ = 5

   e) ☐ - -7 = -1

   f) ☐ - -10 = 13

Adding & Subtracting Negatives Match

Complete these calculations and find your answer at the bottom.
Record your answers in a table.

A	-4 + 8	B	-6 - 3	C	-12 + 2	D	4 + -10
E	-6 + -2	F	8 - -3	G	-4 - -2	H	-12 + -3
I	-1 + -4	J	-8 - 8	K	6 + -9	L	14 + -14
M	23 - 30	N	-22 - 30	O	15 + -12	P	-14 + -16
Q	-55 + -25	R	-13 - -14	S	-18 - 22	T	-160 + 40
U	-4.8 + 5	V	-2 - 0.4	W	$\frac{9}{10}$ - 1.5	X	$1\frac{3}{10}$ - 2.8

- -

jumbled answers

| 0.2 | 11 | -120 |

| -40 | -2.4 | 0 | 4 | -30 |

| -8 |

| -0.6 | -5 | -52 | -6 | 1 | -80 |

| -7 |

| -2 | -1.5 | -10 | -15 | 3 |

| -3 | -16 | -9 |

A	
B	
C	
D	
E	
F	
G	
H	
I	
J	
K	
L	
M	
N	
O	
P	
Q	
R	
S	
T	
U	
V	
W	
X	

adding & subtracting negatives practice

exercise 3h

1. Work out:

   a) 4 - -6   b) -3 + -7   c) -6 - 9

   d) 1 - 6   e) -1 + -1   f) -3 - -2

   g) -4 + 9   h) -4 - -4   i) 5 + -2

2. Decide whether the answer is positive, negative or zero:

   a) -7 + 7   c) -17 - 5   e) 9 - 9

   b) -24 + 8   d) 8 + -5   f) -3 + -8

3. Calculate:

   a) 72 + -12   b) -14 + 20   c) -24 + -80

4. Work out the missing numbers to make the calculations correct.

   a) -5 + ☐ = 1   b) 2 - ☐ = 6

   c) -1 - ☐ = -7   d) 1 + ☐ = -9

   e) ☐ + -4 = -3   f) ☐ - 4 = -7

5. Use the given facts to help you work out:

   a) 763 - -189

   b) -763 + -189

   c) -763 - -189

   d) 763 + -189

763 + 189 = 952
763 - 189 = 574
-763 + 189 = -574
-763 - 189 = -952

6. What is the sum of all the integers between -4 and 2 (including these numbers)?

7. True or false? If two negative numbers are added, the result can be a positive number.

8. Arrange the numbers **-9, -2, 3** and **10** in the boxes to make these two statements true:

   ☐ + ☐ = 8

   ☐ - ☐ = -12

9. Decide whether each of these statements is true or false.

a)
> To work out
> 20 - 75,
> you could work out
> 75 - 20, then
> make your answer
> negative.

b)
> To work out
> -40 + 15,
> you could work out
> 40 + 15, then
> make your answer
> negative.

c)
> To work out
> -44 - 33,
> you could work out
> 44 + 33, then
> make your answer
> negative.

10. Work out:

a) 4 - 4 - 4

b) -7 - 7 - 7

c) -5 + 5 + 5

d) -8 - 8 - 8

e) -6 + 6 + 6

f) -10 - 10 - 10

11. The circle and square stand for two different numbers. Can you work out what they are?

$\bigcirc$ + $\square$ = 0 $\bigcirc$ - $\square$ = -8

12. Which of the following have the same answer as -71 - 18? Select 2 answers.

a) -18 - 71

b) -71 + 18

c) 71 + -18

d) -71 + -18

13. True or false: -723 - - 465 = 465 - 723

14. Which of the following has the same answer as 64 + - 21?

a) -64 + 21

b) 64 - 21

c) 21 - 64

d) -(64 + 21)

matching activity

Match the questions to their answers.

A	B	C
-9 - 1	-8 + -3	-14 - -15

D	E	F
-12 + 3	13 - 20	-8 - 8 - 8

G	H	I
-17 - -17	-31 + 8	-21 - -31

J	K	L
120 - - 14	31 + -27	2 + -14

M	N	O
-45 + -12	-2 - -4 - 5	-46 - -38

-3

-12	-7
-10	-11
1	-8
0	4
10	-9
-23	134
-24	-7

A	B	C	D	E	F	G	H	I	J	K	L	M	N	O

Addition & Subtraction Puzzles

1. Magic Squares

Complete the grid so that every row, column and the two diagonals add up to the same magic number.

a)

1	-4	-3
		2
-1		

Magic number: ......

b)

-2		-4
	-1	
2		

Magic number: ......

c)

-5		
2		-6
-3		

Magic number: ......

2. Missing signs

Write an addition (+) or subtraction (-) symbol in the boxes to complete the calculations.

a) 3 ☐ -5 = -2

b) -3 ☐ 3 = -6

c) 4 ☐ -4 = 0

d) -4 ☐ 1 = -3

e) -1 ☐ -8 = 7

f) -2 ☐ -2 = -4

g) 2 ☐ -3 = 5

h) -7 ☐ 6 = -1

i) 0 ☐ -5 = -5

3. Two-way puzzles

Write numbers in the boxes to make the calculations work both across and down.

a)

-5	+	2	=	
+		+		
-3	+	-1	=	
=		=		

b)

5	-	-3	=	
+		-		
-6	+	-2	=	
=		=		

c)

-4	+	-3	=	
-		+		
-4	-	-3	=	
=		=		

4. Arrange the numbers ⭐ extra challenge

a)

☐ + ☐ = -2

☐ - ☐ = 10

☐ + ☐ = 2

-6 -4 -4 4 6 6

b)

☐ - ☐ = 0

☐ + ☐ = -5

☐ - ☐ = -3

-4 -3 -3 -1 2 5

c)

☐ - ☐ = -3

☐ - ☐ = -2

☐ - ☐ = -1

-3 -2 -1 -1 1 2

d)

☐ + ☐ = -9

☐ - ☐ = 3

☐ + ☐ = -5

-1 -2 -3 -4 -5 -6

More Challenging Problems ⭐ extra challenge

1. True or false: *two negative numbers could add up to 0*

2. If two negative integers are added, the largest possible sum is _____

3. If three negative integers are added, the largest possible sum is _____

4. True or false: *if two negative numbers are subtracted, the answer will always be positive*

5. If a is a negative integer, then the smallest possible value of $-a$ is _____

6. Is it always true that $a + -a = 0$?

7. If a and b are different integers, is it possible for $a - b = 0$?

8. If a pair of negative numbers are subtracted, could the answer be 0?

9. If a pair of negative numbes are subtracted, could the answer be positive?

10. Calculate:

   a) -2.1 - 0.5   d) -4.3 + 0.7   g) 3.1 - 2.9

   b) 1.2 + - 5.3   e) -5.5 + 1.2   h) -5.8 + 6.4

   c) 2.1 - 5.4   f) 6.3 - 2.8   i) -3.3 - 2.9

11. Which of the following are between -0.5 and -3.1?

   a) -0.2   b) -0.7   c) 1.5   d) -3.2   e) -3.01   f) -0.45

12. Fill in the blanks:

   a) -4.2 - _____ = -6   b) 7.01 + _____ = 6   c) -3.02 + _____ 3.02

negative number pyramids

Complete each pyramid so that each block is the sum of the two beneath it.

a)
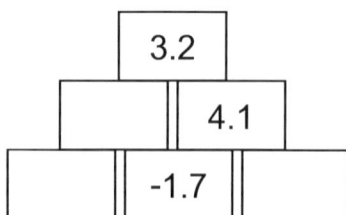

b)
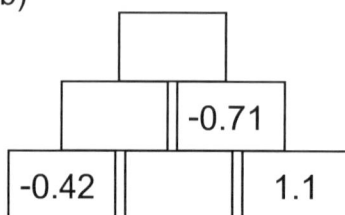

c)

84

multiplying negative numbers

learn by heart

| Negative × Negative = Positive | | Negative × Positive = Negative |

The order here doesn't matter, positive × negative = negative

| Product = the result of multiplying |

examples

| -3 × 5 = -15 | | -3 × -5 = 15 | | -2 × -3 × -4 = -24 |

exercise 3i

1. Calculate

   a) -5 × 3   d) -4 × 1   g) -2 × 7

   b) -5 × -3   e) -4 × 0   h) -2 × -7

   c) 5 × -3   f) -4 × -1   i) -2 + -7

2. The product of -2 and 5 is _____

3. Fill in the blanks:

   a) -3 × _____ = 24   e) -6 × _____ = 36

   b) 3 × _____ = -18   f) _____ × -3 = 0

   c) _____ × 4 = -16   g) -17 × _____ = 17

   d) _____ × -2 = 22   h) -1 × _____ = 200

4. The product of -6 and -4 is _____

5. The product of -2 and _____ is 0

6. Gemma says that -427 × -23 = -9821
   Without calculating, explain how you know she is definitely wrong.

7. Given that 19 × 24 = 456, work out:

   a) -19 × 24   b) -19 × -24   c) 19 × -24

8. Choose the correct word: The product of 2 negative numbers will be (more / less) than 0.

9. Calculate:

   a) -2 × 3 × 4

   b) -2 × -3 × 4

   c) -2 × -3 × -4

   d) -1 × -4 × 2

   e) -1 × -4 × -2

   f) 1 × 4 × -2

10. The product of 7, 2 and -3 is _____

11. Which of these has the largest product?

   a) -6 × -5 × -1

   b) -5 × -6 × -1

   c) -6 × -5 × 1

   d) -6 × 5 × 1

12. Gemma says that -17 × -12 × 15 = -3060
    Without calculating, explain how you know she is definitely wrong.

13. Given that 7 × 8 × 9 = 504, work out:

   a) -7 × 8 × 9

   b) -7 × -8 × -9

   c) 7 × -8 × -9

14. Choose the correct word: The product of 3 negative numbers will be (more / less) than 0.

15. If $a × b × c$ = -24, decide if these statements are true or false:

   a) a, b and c could all be negative

   c) a, b and c could all be positive

   b) a, b and c could all be integers

   d) a and b could be positive, and c is negative

mixed multiplications, additions & subtractions

16. Calculate:

   a) -4 + 6

   d) 7 × -3

   g) -8 - 2

   j) 5 × -5

   b) -4 × 6

   e) -3 × -7

   h) -8 × 2

   k) 5 + -5

   c) -4 + -6

   f) -3 + -7

   i) 8 + -2

   l) -5 × -5

17. If the product of two numbers is positive, can their sum be negative?

18. If the sum of two numbers is 0, can their product be positive?

multiplying lots of negative numbers ☆ extra challenge

learn by heart

| The product of 3 negative numbers is negative |

| The product of 4 negative numbers is positive |

If there are an odd number of negatives, the product will be negative

example

| Calculate -3 × -3 × -3 × -3 |

Work it out slowly, $-3 \times -3 = 9$
$9 \times -3 = -27$
$-27 \times -3 = 81$

exercise 3j

1. Calculate the following:

   a) -2 × -2 × -2

   b) -2 × -2 × -2 × -2

   c) -2 × -2 × -2 × -2 × -2

   d) -2 × -2 × -2 × -2 × -2 × -2

2. If you multiply 5 negative numbers together, is the product positive or negative?

3. If you multiply 20 negative numbers together, is the product positive or negative?

4. If you multiply 200 negative numbers together, is the product positive or negative?

5. If we multiply a set of negative numbers together, how do you know if the product will be positive or negative?

6. Calculate -1 × -1 × -1 × -1 × -1 × -1 × -1

7. Calculate -2 × -1 × -3 × -2

8. If the product of $a \times b \times c \times d$ is a negative number, can all four numbers be negative?

9. Work out the product of all the integers between -5 and 0 (not including 5 and 0)

10. If the product of $a \times b \times c$ is a negative number, then
    -4 × a × b × c is _____(choose positive or negative)

dividing negatives

learn by heart

Negative ÷ Negative = Positive	Negative ÷ Positive = Negative

examples

$15 ÷ -3 = -5$	$-15 ÷ -3 = 5$	$-15 ÷ 3 = -5$	$\dfrac{-12}{4} = -3$	$\dfrac{-12}{-4} = 3$

exercise 3k

1. Calculate:

   a) $-20 ÷ 5$ d) $-20 ÷ 1$ g) $-6 ÷ -6$

   b) $-20 ÷ -5$ e) $-20 ÷ -1$ h) $-40 ÷ 10$

   c) $20 ÷ -5$ f) $0 ÷ -5$ i) $200 ÷ -100$

2. Calculate:

   a) $\dfrac{-40}{8}$ c) $\dfrac{14}{-7}$ e) $\dfrac{-25}{-5}$ g) $\dfrac{14}{-1}$

   b) $\dfrac{-22}{-11}$ d) $\dfrac{-100}{2}$ f) $\dfrac{0}{-3}$ h) $\dfrac{-240}{-10}$

3. Fill in the blanks:

   a) $-30 ÷ \underline{\hspace{1cm}} = -3$ e) $-7 ÷ \underline{\hspace{1cm}} = 1$

   b) $15 ÷ \underline{\hspace{1cm}} = -5$ f) $\underline{\hspace{1cm}} ÷ -5 = 0$

   c) $\underline{\hspace{1cm}} ÷ 4 = -7$ g) $-23 ÷ \underline{\hspace{1cm}} = 23$

   d) $\underline{\hspace{1cm}} ÷ -2 = 12$ h) $-50 ÷ \underline{\hspace{1cm}} = 1$

4. Sally says that $2356 ÷ -19 = 124$. Explain why she must be wrong.

5. Given that $476 ÷ 17 = 28$, write down the answer to:

   a) $476 ÷ -17$ b) $-476 ÷ 17$ c) $-476 ÷ -17$

6. Which number is it impossible to divide by?

multiplying & dividing negatives mixed practice

exercise 3|

1. Calculate:

   a) $4 \times -7 =$ ☐

   b) $-3 \times -1 =$ ☐

   c) $-20 \div 4 =$ ☐

   d) $15 \div -5 =$ ☐

   e) $-9 \times -9 =$ ☐

   f) $42 \div -6 =$ ☐

   g) $-12 \times 4 =$ ☐

   h) $-4 \times 0 =$ ☐

   i) $-8 \div -4 =$ ☐

2. Two numbers are to be chosen from the box and multiplied together.

4	-5	2	-3

   a) Which two numbers give the largest possible product?

   b) Which two numbers give the smallest possible product?

3. Work out:

   a) $4 \times -3 \times 2$

   b) $-5 \times -3 \times -4$

   c) $-1 \times 8 \times -4$

4. Which of these is largest?

   a) $-7 \times 8 \times 9$

   b) $-7 \times -8 \times 9$

   c) $-7 \times -8 \times -9$

5. Work out: $-2 \times -3 \times -2 \times -3$

6. When three numbers are multiplied, the result is a negative number.
   Peter says that all of the numbers must be negative. Explain why Peter is wrong.

7. A negative number is multiplied by itself. Is the result positive or negative?

8. Arrange the number to make each set of calculations correct:

   a)
   ☐ × ☐ = 12
   ☐ × ☐ = -12
   ☐ × ☐ = 5
   -1   -2   -3   -4   -5   6

   b)
   ☐ ÷ ☐ = -2
   ☐ × ☐ = 18
   ☐ × ☐ = -24
   -12   -8   -6   -3   2   4

   c)
   ☐ ÷ ☐ = 4
   ☐ ÷ ☐ = -3
   ☐ ÷ ☐ = 2
   -24   -18   -12   -9   -3   8

   d)
   ☐ ÷ ☐ = -2
   ☐ × ☐ = -24
   ☐ ÷ ☐ = 2
   -6   -6   -4   -3   4   8

9. Which two of these calculations produce the same result?

   a) 18 ÷ 10   b) -18 ÷ 10   c) -18 ÷ -10

10. Work out:

    a) $\frac{15}{-3}$ b) $\frac{-21}{-7}$ c) $\frac{-84}{12}$ d) $\frac{48}{-8}$

11. Work out the missing number in each calculation:

    a) -6 × ___ = -24   b) -40 ÷ ___ = -5

    c) -3 × ___ = 18   d) -5 × ___ = 25

    e) -8 ÷ ___ = 8   f) ___ × -7 = 63

    g) ___ ÷ -4 = 12   h) ___ ÷ -6 = 12

12. Given that **26 × 17 = 442**, state the value of:

    a) 26 × -17   b) -26 × -17   c) -442 ÷ -17

13. Work out:

    a) double -4   b) half of -12   c) half of -3

14. Find pairs of numbers that have:

    a) a product of -12 and a sum of 4

    b) a product of 9 and a sum of -10

    c) a product of -18 and a sum of -3

15. True or false? If **a × b** is negative, then **a ÷ b** must also be negative.

16. Josie thinks of a number. When the number is multiplied by itself, the result is 49. Josie's number is **not** 7. What must Josie's number be?

17. True or false? If **a × b** is negative, then **a + b** must also be negative.

18. **Multiplication Arithmagons:** *The numbers in the circles multiply to make the numbers in the squares between them.*

    a) 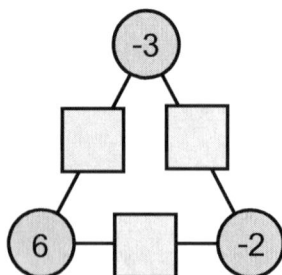   b) 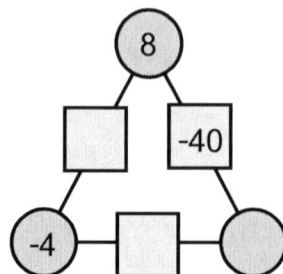   c)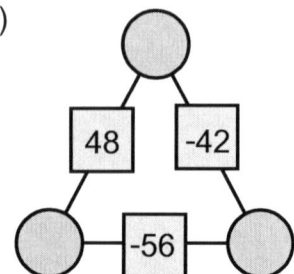

all four operations with negative numbers

1. Calculate

    a) -4 × -2

    b) -6 + -2

    c) -3 × -1

    d) 20 ÷ -5

    e) 6 ÷ -3

    f) 8 × -2

    g) 4 × -3

    h) -5 + -5 + -5

    i) -6 - 3

    j) 10 - 12

    k) -2 × -2 × -3

    l) 7 + -3

    m) 5 - - 2

    n) -2 + 5

    o) 14 ÷ -7

2. Fill in the blanks:

    a) When two negative numbers are added, the answer is _____

    b) When two negative numbers are multiplied, the answer is _____

3. Which of these calculations have a **negative** answer? Circle all that apply.

    a) -3 + 6

    b) -3 × 6

    c) -4 × -5

    d) -4 + -5

    e) -10 - 5

    f) -10 ÷ -5

    g) -2 + -6

    h) -2 × -6

4. Calculate:

    a) 7 - - 3

    b) -8 - 2

    c) -5 × -5

    d) -12 × 3

    e) -2 + -8

    f) 35 ÷ -5

    g) -4 - - 4

    h) -6 - 10

four operations puzzle

Choose 8 of the numbers below to make the sums correct:

-8	-11	-4
5	-4	-9
10	8	-8

☐ - ☐ = -1

☐ + ☐ = 18

☐ × ☐ = -55

☐ ÷ ☐ = 2

5. Complete the magic squares so that all the rows, columns and diagonals add up to the same number:

a)

0	5	-2
4		

b)

		2
5	1	
0		

c)

-7		
-3	-8	-1

6. Calculate:

a) -24 ÷ 3

b) -24 + 3

c) -24 - - 3

7. ○ + □ = 0   ○ - □ = -10

The circle and the square stand for different numbers.
Can you work out which numbers they stand for?

8. Can you work out the missing numbers on these number lines?

a)

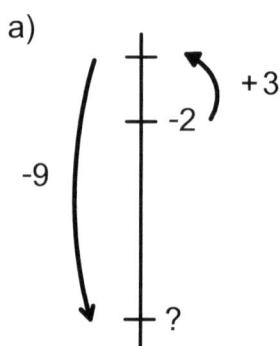

-9   -2   +3   ?

b)

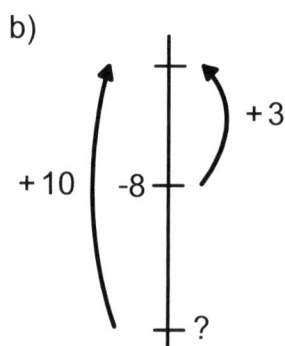

+10   -8   +3   ?

c)

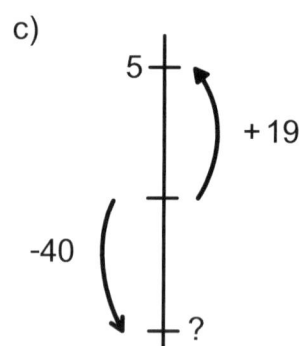

5   -40   +19   ?

9. a) Make each calculation correct by inserting + or − in each box.

i) 2 ☐ -3 ☐ -4 ☐ -5 = 0

ii) 2 ☐ -3 ☐ -4 ☐ -5 = 6

iii) 2 ☐ -3 ☐ -4 ☐ -5 = -10

iv) 2 ☐ -3 ☐ -4 ☐ -5 = 14

b) Find all the possible numbers can be made by inserting + or − in each box.

2 ☐ -3 ☐ -4 ☐ -5

c) Is it possible to make an odd number?

Negative Numbers Countdown

In each section, use the four numbers on the left to make the target number on the right. You do not need to use all the numbers and you can only use each number once. You can add, subtract, multiply or divide in any order.

A
| -5 | -1 | 2 | 3 |

target
-14

B
| -4 | -3 | -2 | -1 |

target
-10

C
| -4 | -3 | -2 | -1 |

target
9

D
| -5 | -2 | 3 | 4 |

target
-11

E
| -9 | -6 | -3 | 2 |

target
0

F
| -10 | -4 | 1 | 7 |

target
39

four operations with negative decimals ☆ extra challenge

examples

Calculate -0.3 × 4	Calculate 4.1 + -0.2	Calculate -15 ÷ -0.5
= -1.2	= 3.9	= 30

exercise 3n

1. Calculate:

   a) -0.7 × -3

   b) -4 + 0.1

   c) -8.1 - 0.4

   d) -12 ÷ 0.1

   e) 6.5 + -2.3

   f) 0.9 × -0.2

   g) -4 ÷ 0.4

   h) -6 ÷ 0.5

   i) -2.3 - 4.5

   j) -2.1 + 6

   k) 8 × -0.03

   l) -70 ÷ -0.1

2. Fill in the blanks:

   a) -4 × _____ = 2.4

   b) 0.3 × _____ = -30

   c) -2.4 ÷ _____ = -24

   d) 1.5 + _____ = 1

   e) -2 - _____ = -3.5

   f) 8 ÷ _____ = -800

3. True or false:

   a) -0.1 × -0.1 = $-\frac{1}{100}$

   b) -0.1 × -0.1 × -0.1 = $-\frac{1}{1000}$

   c) -4 ÷ 0.1 = -4 × 10

   d) -2 × -0.2 ÷ 0.1 = 4.0

4. Use 8 of the numbers below to make the sums on the right true:

-2.4	0.5	7.5
-6	5	$\frac{1}{10}$
-0.1	-4	3

   ☐ - ☐ = -2.5

   ☐ + ☐ = 0

   ☐ × ☐ = -3

   ☐ ÷ ☐ = 0.6

5. Given that 18 × 42 = 756, work out:

    a) -1.8 × 42

    c) -0.18 × 4.2

    e) 1.8 × -420

    b) -1.8 × -42

    d) -18 × 420

    f) -1.8 × -4.2

6. Calculate:

    a) 0.4 × -4

    c) 0.3 × -12

    e) -50 × -500

    b) -0.2 × -0.6

    d) -4 × -0.08

    f) -0.036 × 100

7. Without calculating the answer, can you work out which of these has the largest answer?

    a) 274 ÷ 0.1

    b) 274 ÷ -0.01

    c) -274 ÷ 0.1

8. Given that $\frac{378}{14} = 27$, work out:

    a) $\frac{378}{-14}$

    c) $\frac{-378}{-14}$

    e) $\frac{-378}{-140}$

    b) $\frac{378}{-1.4}$

    d) $\frac{-37.8}{14}$

    f) $\frac{-378}{0.14}$

9. If $a \div -1 = 0$, what is a?

    a) undefined

    b) -1

    c) 0

    d) 1

10. Which two of these calculations produce the same answer?

    a) 6 × -0.6

    b) 3.6 ÷ -6

    c) 0.3 × 0.2

    d) -36 ÷ 10

11. What's missing? Fill in the blanks.

    a) -12 × _____ = 6

    c) 8 × _____ = -0.08

    b) 24 ÷ _____ = -0.024

    d) -80 ÷ _____ = 0.08

12. Calculate:

    a) -14 ÷ 70

    c) 0.5 ÷ -5

    e) $-1.5 \times -\frac{1}{10}$

    b) $\frac{-25}{-500}$

    d) 0.3 × -0.2 × 0.1

    f) $\frac{1}{100} \times -34$

Negative Decimals Code Breaker ⭐ extra challenge

Calculate the following and find your answer in the code box.
Write the words down as you go to reveal an inspirational message!

code box

-300 = certain	-4.6 = The	-0.18 = more	1 = journey
-94 = hope	-1.9 = is	-0.1 = in	2 = to
-70 = Our	-1.8 = lies	0.06 = one	2.2 = find
-50 = reason	-1.5 = way	0.24 = most	4.5 = always
-40 = weakness	-0.5 = up.	0.3 = tax	5.7 = cat
-14 = giving	-0.2 = to	0.5 = time.	224 = kind
-8 = succeed	-0.3 = try	0.8 = greatest	350 = just

a) $7 \div -0.1 =$ _____ =   **Our**

b) $-4 \times -0.2 =$ _____ =

c) $24 \div -0.6 =$ _____ =

d) $-0.3 \times 6 =$ _____ =

e) $0.2 \div -2 =$ _____ =

f) $-7 \div 0.5 =$ _____ =

g) $0.3 - 0.8 =$ _____ =

h) $-1.2 + -3.4 =$ _____ =

i) $-0.8 \times -0.3 =$ _____ =

j) $3 \div -0.01 =$ _____ =

k) $-3 - -1.5 =$ _____ =

l) $-8 \div -4.0 =$ _____ =

m) $0.8 \div -0.1 =$ _____ =

n) $19 \times -0.1 =$ _____ =

o) $5 + -0.5 =$ _____ =

p) $-2.2 \div 11 =$ _____ =

q) $-9 \div 30 =$ _____ =

r) $-3.5 \times -100 =$ _____ =

s) $-0.6 \times -0.1 =$ _____ =

t) $180 \div -1000 =$ _____ =

u) $-45 \div -90 =$ _____ =

–Quote by Thomas Edison

Negatives & Decimals Sorting Activity ⭐ extra challenge

Look at the calculations below and decide which section of
the grid they belong in. Write the letter of the calculation in the correct place.

	Answer is Negative	Answer is Positive
Answer is an Integer		
Answer has 1 decimal place		
Answer has 1 significant figure		

A $-24 \div -10$

B $\dfrac{-250}{-10}$

C $-3 + 14$

D -26×0.5

E $\dfrac{24}{-2}$

F $12 - 24$

G -2×0.6

H $\dfrac{0.15}{-3}$

I -5×3

J $-6 \div 100$

K $-\dfrac{1}{1000} \times -10$

L $-3.5 + 4\dfrac{6}{10}$

M $-2 \div -100$

N $\dfrac{-60}{-5}$

O -0.8×8

P $\dfrac{2}{-200}$

Q $-0.3 \div -10$

R $\dfrac{-6}{-300}$

S $\dfrac{-15}{-2}$

T $4.8 \div -4$

U -0.4×-0.2

V $\dfrac{17}{-0.5}$

exercise 3o

1. Calculate:

   a) -4 - 8

   b) -4 + 8

   c) -4 × 8

   d) 12 - - 6

   e) 12 ÷ -6

   f) -12 × -6

   g) 72 - 100

   h) -100 - 72

   i) 100 × -72

2. Fill in the blanks:

   a) -3 + ____ = 10

   b) -4 × ____ = 16

   c) ____ - 12 = -12

   d) -4 - ____ = -10

   e) -12 ÷ ____ = 1

   f) 8 - ____ = 15

3. Which of these have a negative answer?

   a) 6 - - 8
   b) -6 × -8
   c) -12 + 10
   d) -9 - -10

4. **Multiplication Arithmagons:** The numbers in the circles multiply to make the numbers in the squares between them.

   a)

   -6   -4

   24

   b)

   36   -18

   -8

   c)

   -15   12

   -20

four operations puzzle

5. Use 8 of the numbers below to make the sums on the right true:

-3	3	10
4	-2	-9
7	-4	-12

   ☐ - ☐ = -3

   ☐ + ☐ = 0

   ☐ × ☐ = -27

   ☐ ÷ ☐ = 4

6. Calculate:

a) 8 - 17

b) -4 + 13

c) -24 - 9

d) 7 - -16

e) -3 + -28

f) 4 × -12

g) -9 × -6

h) -1 - -18

i) 18 + -19

j) 82 ÷ -4

k) -12 × 5

l) -9 × 0.1

m) -1.2 × -1.1

n) 0.7 + -2.7

o) -9 + -6 - -12

p) 0.42 × -100 × -0.1

q) -1.2 × 0.4

r) 0.32 ÷ -0.04

7. Use the numbers on the right to complete these calculations:

a) ☐ - 10 = ☐

b) -14 + ☐ = -20

c) ☐ + ☐ = 0

d) -2 - ☐ = ☐

e) ☐ × 5 = ☐

f) -36 ÷ ☐ = ☐

4	-6	-60
-9	-12	-3
-2	0	9
1	-1	-13

8. Cover up pairs of numbers that follow the rule.
Which number is left alone?

a) *Pairs that sum to -6.*

7	-4	-8
-10	-5	-2
-13	-1	4

b) *Pairs with a difference of 9.*

-2	-8	4
1	7	0
-9	-5	-7

c) *Pairs with a product of -24.*

-10	-1.2	3
20	12	-8
2.4	-4	6

9. Calculate:

a) $\frac{3}{10}$ × -4

b) -0.2 × $\frac{5}{10}$

c) -12 ÷ -0.1

d) -4 ÷ $\frac{1}{100}$

e) 2.5 ÷ -0.5

f) -1.2 ÷ -6

cumulative review (chapters 1, 2 & 3)

exercise 3p

1. Write "two million, eight hundred and four thousand", in digits.

2. Round 1,894 to 3 significant figures.

3. Round 0.0498 to 1 significant figure.

4. Write "four tenths" as a decimal.

5. Three tens and three tenths make:

   a) 3.3   b) 30.3   c) 30.03   d) 33

6. Fill in the blanks with >, < or =

   a) 0.406 _____ 0.46   c) 0.84 _____ $\frac{84}{100}$ e) $\frac{81}{1000}$ _____ 0.81

   b) $\frac{3}{100}$ _____ 0.002   d) 1.9 _____ $1\frac{9}{100}$ f) $\frac{1}{100}$ _____ 0.01

7. Calculate:

   a) -8 × 100   d) -12 × 4   g) -108 ÷ -12

   b) 2 × -5   e) -18 ÷ 2   h) 50 ÷ -25

   c) -5 × 20   f) -45 ÷ -10   i) -9 × -5

8. Which of these means 'x is greater than or equal to y'

   a) $x > y$ b) $x < y$ c) $x \geq y$ d) $x \leq y$ e) $x \neq y$

9. Round 40.0389 to 3 decimal places.

10. Which of these are integers? Circle all that apply.

    a) -5   b) -4.5   c) 0   d) 1   e) 3.2

11. Calculate:

    a) -4 + 8   c) 0.4 × 0.3   e) -5 - 5 - 5

    b) 0.308 × 10   d) 3 ÷ 8   f) 2.1 ÷ 0.3

12. Calculate:

a) 6 ÷ 100

b) 0.4 × 3

c) 0.1 × 24

d) 0.203 × 100

e) 3.9 ÷ 3

f) 1.2 × 4

g) 45 ÷ 100

h) 23.6 + 4.09

i) 2.5 ÷ 5

13. Which number below does not get bigger when you add a zero onto the end?

a) 2.4

b) 5

c) 60

d) 206

14. In the number 2.307, if the decimal point is moved 2 places to the right, then the number is:

a) 2 times bigger

b) 2 times smaller

c) 10 times bigger

d) 10 times smaller

e) 100 times bigger

f) 100 times smaller

15. Write these as decimals:

a) 7 tenths

b) $\frac{9}{100}$

c) $4\frac{3}{10}$

16. Fill in the blanks

a) _____ ÷ 10 = 1.5

b) _____ × 100 = 4

c) _____ × 0.1 = 9.2

d) _____ ÷ 2 = 0.6

e) _____ × 2 = 0.3

f) _____ × 0.1 = 43

17. Put these in order of size, from smallest to largest:

0.61   0.06   0.601   0.6

_____   _____   _____   _____

18. True or False:

a) Dividing by 10 is the same as multiplying by 0.1

b) 7 and 7.0 have the same value but a different number of significant figures.

c) 8 tenths is the same as 0.08

d) 0.4 < $\frac{4}{100}$

e) When two negative numbers are added, the result is always a negative number.

f) The product of two negative numbers is always a negative number.

Multiplying & Dividing Decimals Spiral

Start in the middle and work your way around the spiral, finding your answers at the bottom as you go.

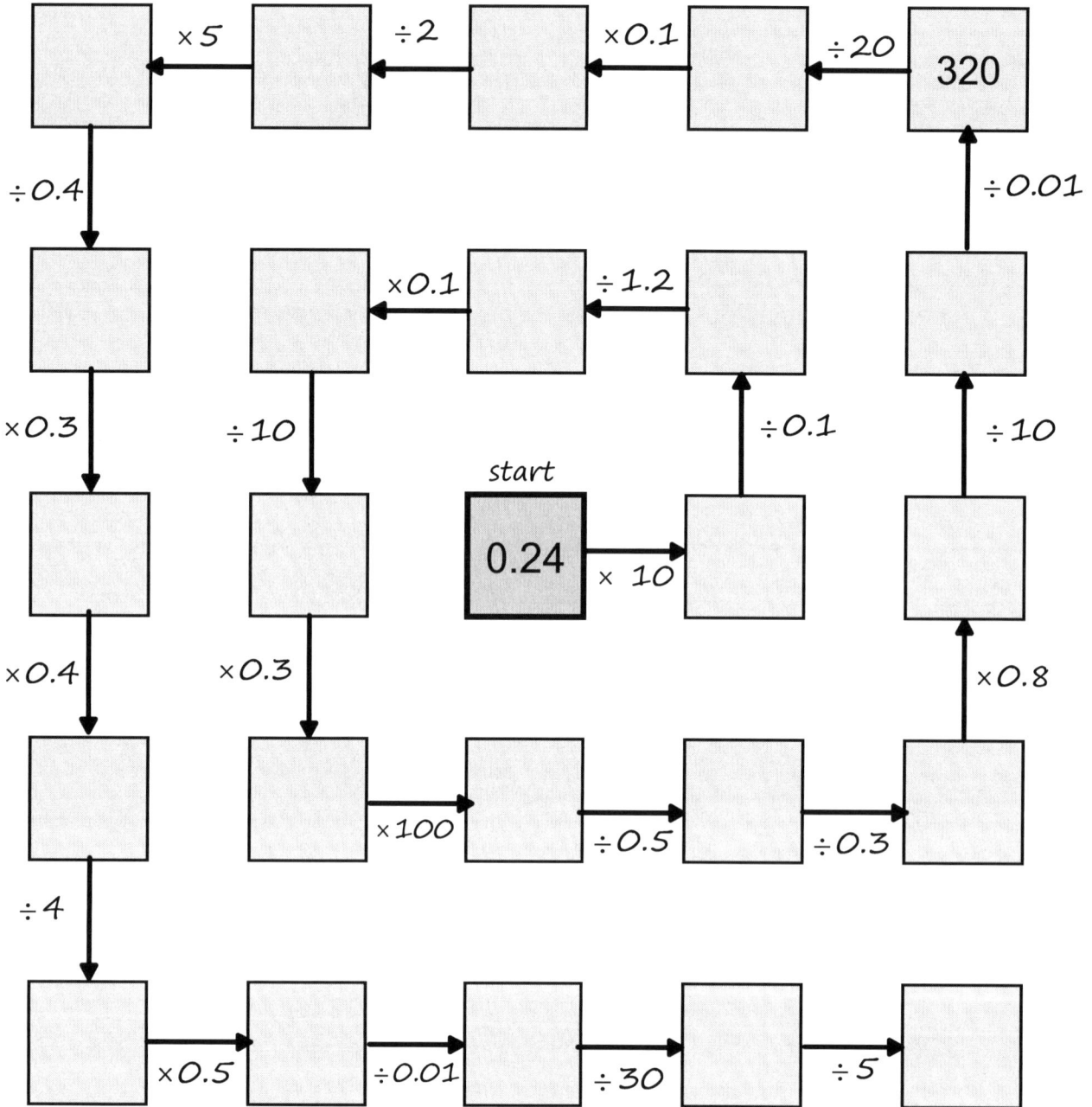

	×5		÷2		×0.1		÷20	320

÷0.4

÷0.01

×0.3   ÷10   ×0.1   ÷1.2

÷0.1   ÷10

start

0.24   ×10

×0.4   ×0.3   ×0.8

×100   ÷0.5   ÷0.3

÷4

×0.5   ÷0.01   ÷30   ÷5

- -

jumbled answers   24   0.5   12   0.06   1.2   16   10

40   0.1   3.2   0.3   32   0.2   15   6   0.15

3   2.4   2   1.6   4   0.8   20

chapter 4: fractions

[Recommended Time : 13 - 17 hours]

Contents

fractions & wholes

learn by heart

$\frac{2}{5}$

Numerator: the top number in a fraction.
This is how many parts are selected.

Denominator: the bottom number in a fraction
This is how many equal parts the whole is split into.

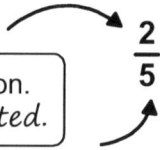

Whole:
All of the parts,
e.g. $\frac{5}{5}$ or $\frac{101}{101}$

Unit Fraction:
The numerator
is 1, e.g. $\frac{1}{5}$

exercise 4a

1. Write these in fraction notation:

   a) two fifths   b) one quarter   c) three thirds

2. In which diagram is $\frac{1}{3}$ shaded?

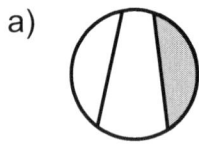

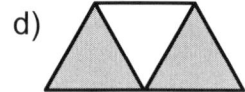

   a)   b)   c)   d)

3. In which diagram(s) is $\frac{2}{5}$ shaded? Choose all that apply.

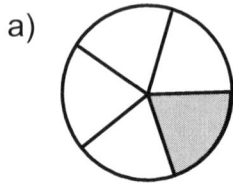

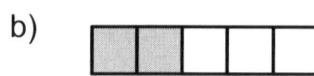

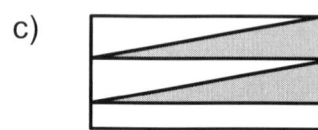

   a)   b)   c)

4. What fraction is shaded in each diagram?

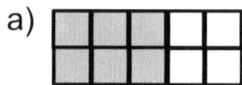

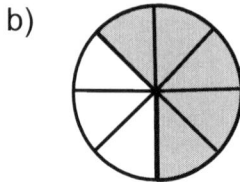

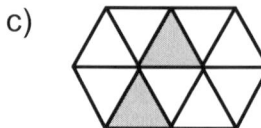

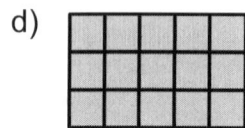

   a)   b)   c)   d)

5. If $\frac{1}{7}$ of a diagram is shaded, what fraction is **not** shaded?

6. If $\frac{3}{11}$ of a diagram is shaded, what fraction is **not** shaded?

7. 1 whole is the same as _____ fifths

8. 1 whole is the same as _____ eighths

9. Select the fractions that **equal** 1 whole:

   a) $\frac{4}{5}$ b) $\frac{6}{6}$ c) $\frac{9}{3}$ d) $\frac{2}{2}$ e) $\frac{1}{7}$

10. State the fraction that each arrow is pointing to.

a)

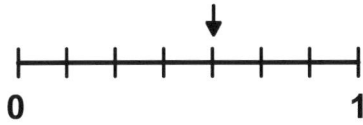

b)

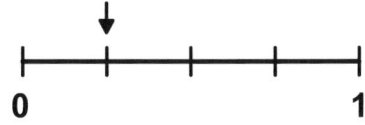

c)

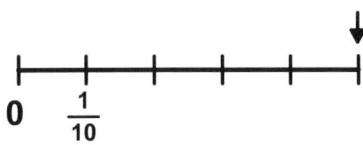

d)

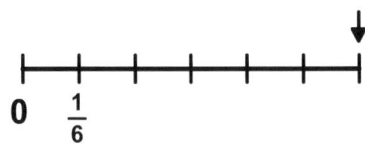

11. a) How many tenths make 1 whole?

b) How many sevenths make 1 whole?

c) How many lots of $\frac{1}{5}$ make 1 whole?

d) Explain why $\frac{3}{3}$ = 1

e) $\frac{1}{5}$ + _____ = 1

f) _____ + $\frac{4}{10}$ = 1

g) $\frac{1}{4}$ + _____ = 1

h) $\frac{1}{10}$ + $\frac{3}{10}$ + _____ = 1

i) $\frac{7}{5}$ - _____ = 1

j) $\frac{5}{3}$ - _____ = 1

k) _____ + $\frac{4}{9}$ = 1

l) 1 - _____ = $\frac{2}{3}$

m) 1 - _____ = $\frac{7}{10}$

n) $\frac{3}{3}$ + _____ = 1

o) 1 - _____ = $\frac{5}{5}$

p) _____ lots of $\frac{1}{8}$ = 1

13. Complete these statements with >, < or =

a) $\frac{5}{3}$ ◯ 1

b) $\frac{3}{3}$ ◯ 1

c) $\frac{1}{5}$ + $\frac{3}{5}$ ◯ 1

d) $\frac{2}{3}$ + $\frac{5}{3}$ ◯ 1

e) $\frac{1}{3}$ + $\frac{4}{3}$ ◯ 1

f) $\frac{5}{4}$ - $\frac{2}{4}$ ◯ 1

14. Complete the sentences:

a) 1 whole is _____ tenths

b) 1 whole is _____ fifths

c) 1 whole is _____ ninths

d) 1 whole is 6 _____

e) 2 wholes are _____ thirds

f) 2 wholes are _____ fifths

15. Select the fractions that are **more** than 3 wholes:

a) $\frac{1}{3}$ b) $\frac{5}{3}$ c) $\frac{16}{5}$ d) $\frac{5}{2}$ e) $\frac{3}{1}$ f) $\frac{301}{100}$ g) $\frac{4}{12}$

What fraction? ⭐ extra challenge

In each diagram, work out the fraction shaded.
The shapes are drawn on square dotty grids.

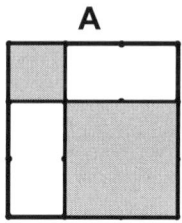

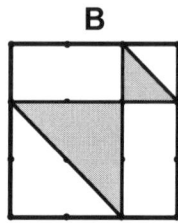

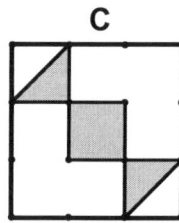

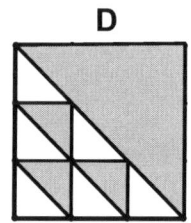

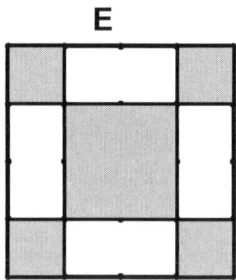

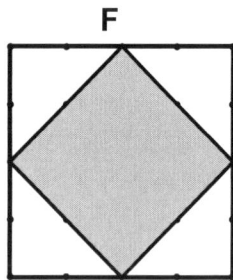

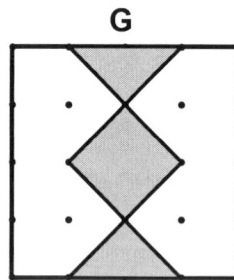

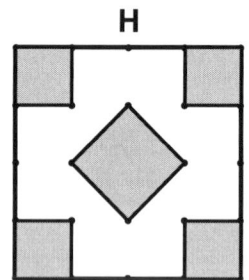

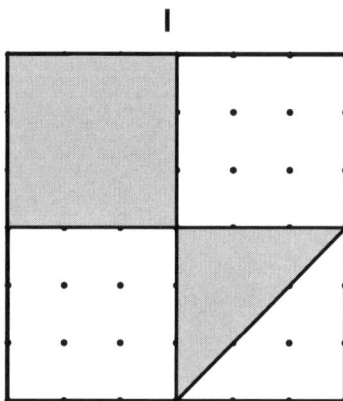

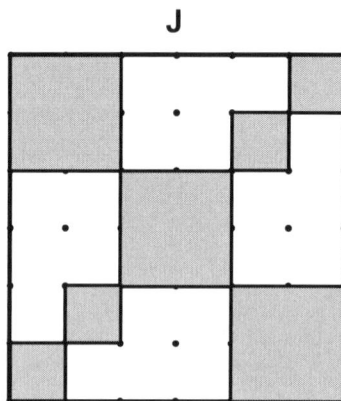

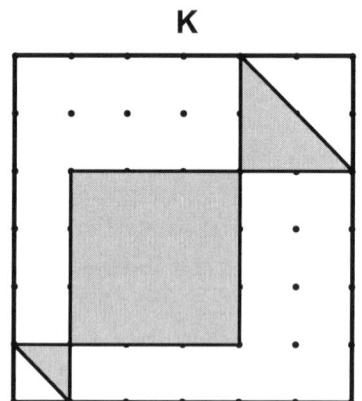

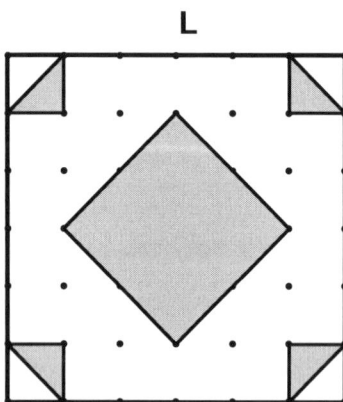

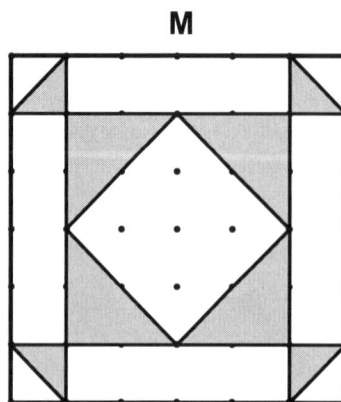

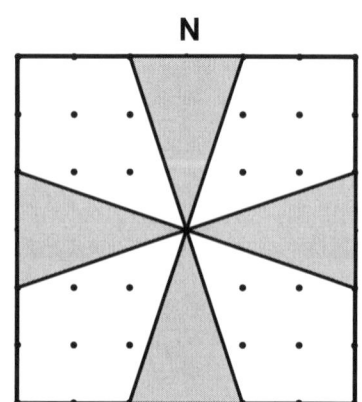

A

B

C

D

E

F

G

H

I

J

K

L

M

N

improper fractions & mixed numbers

learn by heart

Proper Fraction: e.g. $\frac{4}{10}$, denominator > numerator ← **between 0 and 1**

Improper Fraction: e.g. $\frac{10}{4}$, numerator ≥ denominator

Mixed Number: e.g. $3\frac{4}{5}$ (integer + fraction)

more than 1 whole

examples

Write $\frac{9}{4}$ as a mixed number.

$$= 2\frac{1}{4}$$

Write $3\frac{2}{5}$ as an improper number

$$= \frac{17}{5}$$

exercise 4b

1. Write as whole numbers:

   a) $\frac{15}{3}$ b) $\frac{18}{2}$ c) $\frac{14}{7}$ d) $\frac{24}{6}$

2. Write as whole or mixed numbers:

   a) $\frac{13}{9}$ b) $\frac{9}{4}$ c) $\frac{7}{6}$ d) $\frac{13}{3}$

   e) $\frac{23}{10}$ f) $\frac{9}{3}$ g) $\frac{43}{20}$ h) $\frac{12}{11}$

3. Select the **improper** fractions:

   a) $\frac{3}{7}$ b) $\frac{5}{2}$ c) $\frac{7}{1}$ d) $\frac{100}{100}$ e) $\frac{9}{10}$

4. Write as improper fractions:

   a) $2\frac{2}{5}$ b) $3\frac{1}{6}$ c) $1\frac{1}{8}$ d) $2\frac{3}{7}$

   e) $5\frac{2}{5}$ f) $6\frac{1}{4}$ g) $1\frac{7}{10}$ h) $3\frac{4}{9}$

5. Work out which number is largest in each pair:

   a) $4\frac{1}{3}$ or $\frac{11}{3}$ b) $2\frac{6}{7}$ or $\frac{18}{9}$ c) $\frac{50}{7}$ or 7

   d) $5\frac{1}{6}$ or $\frac{12}{2}$ e) $1\frac{1}{3}$ or $\frac{5}{3}$ f) $\frac{25}{3}$ or 8

6. Which of the following are proper fractions?

   a) $\frac{1}{5}$ b) $\frac{2}{3}$ c) $\frac{4}{3}$ d) $\frac{8}{8}$ e) $1\frac{1}{4}$

7. Which of these fractions are greater than 1?

   a) $\frac{9}{10}$ b) $\frac{5}{5}$ c) $\frac{3}{2}$ d) $\frac{4}{1}$ e) $\frac{3}{4}$

8. Write down three different improper fractions that are equal to 3 wholes.

9. True or False?

   a) A proper fraction can be changed into a mixed number.

   b) All mixed numbers are greater than 1.

   c) There are only 6 different proper fractions with a denominator of 7.

more challenging ⭐ extra challenge

10. If $\frac{a}{9}$ is a proper fraction, how many values of a are possible?

11. If $\frac{b}{7}$ is an **improper** fraction, what is the smallest possible value of b?

12. What must be added to $\frac{29}{4}$ to make 8?

13. What must be added to $\frac{12}{10}$ to make 2?

14. Write down all the integers between $\frac{14}{3}$ and $\frac{36}{5}$

15. Write down all the negative integers that are greater than $-\frac{25}{4}$

16. Arrange the digits 3, 4 and 5 to make a mixed number between $\frac{9}{2}$ and $\frac{47}{10}$

17. If $0 < x < 1$, which of the following could be x? Circle all that apply.

    a) $\frac{6}{7}$ b) $\frac{7}{6}$ c) $\frac{3}{8}$ d) $\frac{0}{2}$ e) $\frac{4}{1}$

18. Which of these are between 7 and 8?

    a) $\frac{15}{3}$ b) $\frac{27}{4}$ c) $\frac{22}{3}$ d) $\frac{15}{2}$

19. Which integer is closest to $\frac{11}{7}$?

fraction of an amount

learn by heart

Finding $\frac{1}{4}$ of an amount is the same as dividing by 4, so for example $\frac{1}{4}$ of 20 is 20 ÷ 4 = 5

This works for all unit fractions, so finding $\frac{1}{10}$ is the same as dividing by 10, e.g. $\frac{1}{10}$ of 18 = 1.8

For other fractions, divide by the denominator and multiply by the numerator, so for example $\frac{2}{5}$ of 15 is (15 ÷ 5) × 2 = 3 × 2 = 6

examples

$\frac{1}{3}$ of 33	$\frac{1}{4}$ of £6	$\frac{2}{5}$ of 45	$\frac{3}{10}$ of 52	$\frac{2}{5}$ of 6
= 33 ÷ 3	= £6 ÷ 4	= (45 ÷ 5) × 2	= (52 ÷ 10) × 3	= (6 ÷ 5) × 2
= 11	= £1.50	= 9 × 2	= 5.2 × 3	= 1.2 × 3
		= 18	= 15.6	= 3.6

exercise 4c

1. To work out $\frac{1}{12}$ of an amount, we should:

   a) multiply by 12   b) add 12   c) divide by 12

2. Work out $\frac{1}{5}$ of

   a) 5   b) 30   c) 0   d) £20

3. Calculate the following, giving your answer as an integer or decimal:

   a) $\frac{1}{3}$ of 60   f) $\frac{2}{3}$ of 2.4   k) $\frac{3}{4}$ of 2

   b) $\frac{2}{5}$ of 40   g) $\frac{3}{5}$ of 60   l) $\frac{2}{5}$ of 9

   c) $\frac{4}{5}$ of 30   h) $\frac{3}{5}$ of 6   m) $\frac{2}{10}$ of 14

4. Work out $\frac{1}{3}$ of

   a) 27   b) 0.3   c) -9   d) £4.50

5. Match each of the cards A-L with one of the cards M-X.
   Record your answers in a table.

A $\frac{7}{10}$ of £5	B $\frac{5}{8}$ of £4	C $\frac{1}{20}$ of £8		M £3.20	N 40p	O £7.50
D $\frac{3}{8}$ of £8	E $\frac{1}{5}$ of £6	F $\frac{1}{2}$ of £9		P 80p	Q £3.50	R £1.20
G $\frac{3}{2}$ of £5	H $\frac{4}{5}$ of £4	I $\frac{3}{20}$ of £6		S 90p	T £5	U £2.50
J $\frac{2}{5}$ of £2	K $\frac{5}{2}$ of £2	L $\frac{9}{10}$ of £6		V £3	W £4.50	X £5.40

A	B	C	D	E	F	G	H	I	J	K	L

6. Work out $\frac{1}{10}$ of the following, giving your answer as a **decimal**:

   a) 58

   b) 0.4

   c) -20

   d) $\frac{1}{4}$

   e) $\frac{2}{10}$

   f) 3 hundredths

   g) $\frac{29}{100}$

   h) $2\frac{1}{10}$

   i) 18.5

   j) 1

   k) 0

   l) $0.\dot{1}$

7. Work out $\frac{3}{5}$ of 0.8

8. Work out $\frac{2}{3}$ of 0.9

more challenging

9. At Emerton School, $\frac{1}{5}$ of the children are in year seven. Of those children in year seven, $\frac{2}{9}$ are in the basketball club. If there are 810 children in total at Emerton school, how many are in the year seven basketball club?

10. At a school, $\frac{3}{4}$ of the sixth form students study mathematics.

    $\frac{3}{5}$ of the sixth form students who study maths also study physics.

    If there are 220 students in the sixth form, how many study maths and physics?

Fractions of Amounts Puzzles

Match the cards to the statements. Use each card once only.
All fractions are proper and in the simplest form.

A

$\dfrac{\square}{6}$ of 12 = $\square$ $\dfrac{\square}{5}$ of 15 = $\square$

$\dfrac{\square}{6}$ of 30 = $\square$ $\dfrac{\square}{7}$ of 49 = $\square$

[1] [2] [3] [5] [5] [9] [10] [14]

B

$\dfrac{\square}{8}$ of 24 = $\square$ $\dfrac{5}{6}$ of $\square$ = $\square$

$\dfrac{\square}{5}$ of 55 = $\square$ $\dfrac{3}{\square}$ of 40 = $\square$

[3] [4] [7] [20] [21] [24] [30] [33]

C

$\dfrac{\square}{3}$ of 18 = $\square$ $\dfrac{\square}{5}$ of 20 = $\square$ $\dfrac{\square}{6}$ of 42 = $\square$

$\dfrac{\square}{9}$ of 99 = $\square$ $\dfrac{\square}{8}$ of 40 = $\square$ $\dfrac{\square}{4}$ of 48 = $\square$

[2] [2]
[3] [4]
[5] [5]
[12] [16]
[22] [25]
[35] [36]

D

$\dfrac{3}{4}$ of $\square$ = $\square$ $\dfrac{\square}{8}$ of 56 = $\square$ $\dfrac{3}{\square}$ of $\square$ = 27

$\dfrac{4}{9}$ of $\square$ = $\square$ $\dfrac{\square}{11}$ of 55 = $\square$ $\dfrac{4}{\square}$ of $\square$ = 32

[5] [5]
[8] [9]
[35] [40]
[44] [45]
[45] [60]
[72] [99]

111

examples

$\frac{1}{3}$ of a number is 8.
What is the number?

$\frac{2}{3}$ of a number is 8.
What is the number?

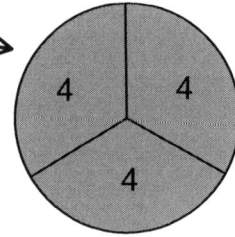

$$\frac{1}{3} \times 3 = 1 \text{ whole}$$
$$8 \times 3 = 24$$

If $\frac{2}{3}$ are 8, then $\frac{1}{3}$ is 4
So the whole is 12

exercise 4d

1. $\frac{1}{5}$ of a number is 6. What is the number?

2. $\frac{3}{4}$ of a number is 15. What is the number?

3. $\frac{2}{7}$ of a number is 8. What is the number?

4. $\frac{5}{4}$ of a number is 25. What is the number?

5. $\frac{3}{5}$ of a number is 9. What is $\frac{2}{5}$ of the number?

6. Copy and complete the table:

Original Number	$\frac{1}{3}$ of the number	$\frac{2}{3}$ of the number	$\frac{1}{5}$ of the number	$\frac{6}{5}$ of the number
30				
	15			
		40		
			0.3	
			0.12	
				1.2

equivalent fractions & simplifying

learn by heart

Equivalent fractions: *have the same value*
They are created by multiplying or dividing both numerator and denominator by the same number

The simplest form of a fraction is when :
*the numerator and denominator have **no** common factors.*

example

$$\frac{4}{6} = \frac{?}{15}$$

sometimes you need to simplify a fraction before you can work out an equivalent fraction

$$\div 2 \qquad \times 5$$

$$\frac{4}{6} = \frac{2}{3} = \frac{10}{15}$$

$$\div 2 \qquad \times 5$$

exercise 4e

1. Decide whether these statements are true or false:

   a) $\frac{2}{5} = \frac{4}{7}$

   b) $\frac{4}{25} = \frac{8}{50}$

   c) $\frac{3}{8} = \frac{6}{10}$

   d) $\frac{1}{5} = \frac{3}{10}$

   e) $\frac{1}{4} = \frac{3}{12}$

   f) $\frac{4}{3} = \frac{44}{33}$

2. Simplify each of these fractions:

   a) $\frac{6}{15}$

   b) $\frac{36}{48}$

   c) $\frac{44}{66}$

   d) $\frac{24}{28}$

3. Select four fractions below that are equivalent to $\frac{4}{6}$:

   $\frac{40}{60}$ $\frac{2}{5}$ $\frac{24}{26}$ $\frac{2}{3}$ $\frac{6}{8}$ $\frac{6}{4}$ $\frac{8}{12}$ $\frac{18}{27}$ $\frac{9}{15}$

4. Complete these fractions so that they are equivalent:

   a) $\frac{4}{7} = \frac{}{35}$

   b) $\frac{5}{6} = \frac{40}{}$

   c) $\frac{12}{15} = \frac{}{5}$

   d) $\frac{6}{36} = \frac{1}{}$

   e) $\frac{}{24} = \frac{3}{4}$

   f) $\frac{}{8} = \frac{3}{12}$

   g) $\frac{12}{42} = \frac{}{63}$

   h) $\frac{9}{} = \frac{15}{60}$

5. True or False: $\frac{5}{15}$ is equivalent to $\frac{6}{16}$ because 1 has been added to both the numerator and denominator.

6. Which of these fractions are equivalent to $\frac{6}{15}$? Circle all that apply.

   a) $\frac{4}{10}$

   b) $\frac{10}{25}$

   c) $\frac{20}{50}$

   d) $\frac{9}{18}$

   e) $\frac{5}{14}$

7. True or False: $\frac{5}{15}$ is 5 times bigger than $\frac{1}{3}$.

8. True or False: Unit fractions cannot be simplified.

9. James says that $\frac{3}{6}$ and $\frac{4}{8}$ are not equivalent because you cannot multiply 3 to make 4. Is James right?

10. Which of these fractions cannot be simplified?

   a) $\frac{3}{10}$ b) $\frac{7}{7}$ c) $\frac{1}{12}$ d) $\frac{6}{9}$ e) $\frac{10}{4}$ f) $\frac{27}{30}$

11. True or false: the simplest form of $\frac{3}{5}$ is $\frac{1.5}{2.5}$

12. Find six fractions that are in the simplest form:

A $\frac{2}{8}$	C $\frac{2}{7}$	E $\frac{9}{16}$	G $\frac{6}{15}$	I $\frac{8}{10}$	K $\frac{6}{9}$	M $\frac{5}{8}$	O $\frac{4}{6}$
B $\frac{1}{12}$	D $\frac{20}{30}$	F $\frac{15}{25}$	H $\frac{9}{15}$	J $\frac{3}{5}$	L $\frac{14}{21}$	N $\frac{1}{6}$	P $\frac{12}{21}$

13. Kim and Jenny each have an identical cake.
   Kim cuts her cake into 8 pieces and eats 3.
   Jenny cuts her cake into 16 pieces and eats 6. Who has more cake left?

14. List all the proper fractions with a denominator of 30 that cannot be simplified.

Odd One Out ⭐ extra challenge

In each box, find pairs of equivalent numbers. Cover them up and find the odd one out – the number in each box that has no pair.

A

$\frac{4}{28}$	$\frac{12}{15}$	$\frac{9}{24}$
$\frac{8}{16}$	$\frac{9}{36}$	$\frac{7}{49}$
$\frac{7}{28}$	$\frac{21}{56}$	$\frac{32}{40}$

B

$\frac{25}{10}$	$\frac{28}{4}$	6
$\frac{35}{5}$	$\frac{18}{6}$	$\frac{5}{2}$
$\frac{48}{8}$	$\frac{24}{8}$	$\frac{4}{1}$

C

$1\frac{1}{2}$	$\frac{7}{2}$	$\frac{7}{3}$
$3\frac{1}{2}$	$2\frac{1}{3}$	$4\frac{1}{2}$
$\frac{4}{2}$	$\frac{18}{4}$	$\frac{3}{2}$

D

$1\frac{3}{4}$	$\frac{15}{4}$	$2\frac{1}{4}$
$\frac{9}{4}$	$\frac{11}{4}$	$\frac{7}{4}$
$2\frac{3}{4}$	$\frac{17}{4}$	$4\frac{1}{4}$

E

$1\frac{4}{6}$	$\frac{6}{5}$	$3\frac{8}{4}$
$\frac{15}{6}$	5	$\frac{5}{3}$
$3\frac{2}{5}$	$2\frac{1}{2}$	$\frac{17}{5}$

F

$\frac{-5}{2}$	$\frac{-7}{-14}$	$\frac{5}{-4}$
$-1\frac{1}{4}$	$\frac{-1}{2}$	$\frac{10}{-4}$
$\frac{-2}{3}$	$\frac{1}{2}$	$\frac{-6}{9}$

converting fractions & decimals (using equivalent fractions)

learn by heart

If a fraction has a denominator of 10,100 etc, we can use place value to write it as a decimal, e.g. $\frac{14}{100}$ = 0.14

If the denominator of a fraction is a **factor** of 10,100 etc, first change its denominator to 10,100 etc using equivalent fractions, then write as a decimal, e.g. $\frac{2}{5}$ = $\frac{4}{10}$ = 0.4

examples

Write $\frac{4}{5}$ as a decimal

$$\frac{4}{5} = \frac{8}{10} = 0.8$$

Write $\frac{4}{50}$ as a decimal

$$\frac{4}{50} = \frac{8}{100} = 0.08$$

Write $\frac{12}{200}$ as a decimal

$$\frac{12}{200} = \frac{6}{100} = 0.06$$

exercise 4f

1. Write these fractions as decimals:

   a) $\frac{7}{10}$

   b) $\frac{9}{100}$

   c) $\frac{1}{1000}$

   d) $\frac{37}{100}$

   e) $\frac{9}{10}$

   f) $\frac{409}{1000}$

   g) $\frac{2}{10}$

   h) $\frac{28}{1000}$

   i) $\frac{8}{100}$

2. Write the following as decimals:

   a) $\frac{3}{50}$

   d) $\frac{6}{50}$

   g) $\frac{3}{20}$

   b) $\frac{1}{5}$

   e) $\frac{10}{25}$

   h) $\frac{3}{25}$

   c) $\frac{1}{20}$

   f) $\frac{12}{50}$

   i) $\frac{4}{5}$

3. Write $\frac{405}{500}$ as a decimal

4. Which of the following are equivalent to 0.24? Choose 3 answers.

   a) $\frac{24}{10}$ b) $\frac{24}{100}$ c) $\frac{24}{1000}$ d) $\frac{12}{50}$ e) $\frac{6}{25}$

5. Write 0.14 as a fraction in its simplest form.

6. Write these fractions as decimals:

   a) $\frac{35}{50}$

   b) $\frac{7}{25}$

   c) $\frac{9}{200}$

   d) $\frac{43}{50}$

   e) $\frac{8}{20}$

   f) $\frac{304}{500}$

   g) $\frac{28}{40}$

   h) $\frac{286}{2000}$

   i) $\frac{32}{400}$

7. Convert each of these decimals to fractions and then write them in the **simplest form**:

   a) 0.62

   b) 0.015

   c) 0.4

   d) 0.44

   e) 0.35

   f) 0.12

8. Which of the following are equivalent to $\frac{1}{5}$? Circle 3 answers.

   a) 1.5

   b) $\frac{2}{10}$

   c) $\frac{20}{100}$

   d) 0.2

   e) 0.05

9. Which of the following are equivalent to $\frac{8}{50}$? Circle 2 answers.

   a) 0.08

   b) 0.16

   c) 0.04

   d) $\frac{16}{100}$

   e) $\frac{8}{10}$

10. Match pairs of equivalent fractions and decimals.
    Record your answers in a table.

A $\frac{3}{100}$	B $\frac{11}{50}$	C $\frac{6}{2000}$	D $\frac{11}{250}$	M 0.6	N 0.006	O 0.044	P 0.3
E $\frac{22}{50}$	F $\frac{3}{5}$	G $\frac{1}{5}$	H $\frac{3}{50}$	Q 0.2	R 0.202	S 0.03	T 0.22
I $\frac{11}{500}$	J $\frac{3}{10}$	K $\frac{3}{500}$	L $\frac{101}{500}$	U 0.003	V 0.44	W 0.022	X 0.06

A	B	C	D	E	F	G	H	I	J	K	L

converting fractions & decimals (all types)

examples

Type 1: Denominator is 10, 100, 1000 etc..	Type 2: Denominator is a factor of 10,100,1000 etc..	Type 3: Other denominators
Write $\frac{23}{100}$ as a decimal Use place value – this is 23 hundredths = $\underline{0.23}$	Write $\frac{7}{25}$ as a decimal Use equivalent fractions $\frac{7}{25} = \frac{28}{100} = \underline{0.28}$	Write $\frac{1}{8}$ as a decimal Use short division $1 \div 8 = \underline{0.125}$

learn by heart

$0.\dot{1} = \frac{1}{9}$	$0.\dot{4} = \frac{4}{9}$	$0.2 = \frac{1}{5}$	$0.8 = \frac{4}{5}$	$0.625 = \frac{5}{8}$
$0.\dot{2} = \frac{2}{9}$	$0.\dot{5} = \frac{5}{9}$	$0.4 = \frac{2}{5}$	$0.125 = \frac{1}{8}$	$0.1\dot{6} = \frac{1}{6}$
$0.\dot{3} = \frac{1}{3}$	$0.\dot{6} = \frac{2}{3}$	$0.6 = \frac{3}{5}$	$0.375 = \frac{3}{8}$	$0.05 = \frac{1}{20}$

exercise 4g

1. Write as a decimal:

   a) $\frac{1}{4}$

   b) $\frac{9}{1000}$

   c) $\frac{12}{1000}$

   d) $\frac{9}{10}$

   e) $2\frac{1}{100}$

   f) $\frac{18}{200}$

   g) $\frac{8}{50}$

   h) $\frac{2}{6}$

   i) $\frac{9}{25}$

   j) $\frac{6}{20}$

   k) $\frac{7}{9}$

   l) $\frac{6}{5}$

2. Which of these numbers is different from the others? $0.04, \frac{4}{10}, 0.40$

3. Which of these are recurring decimals?

   a) $\frac{1}{2}$　　b) $\frac{1}{3}$　　c) $\frac{1}{4}$　　d) $\frac{1}{5}$　　e) $\frac{1}{6}$　　f) $\frac{1}{7}$

4. True or false?

   a) $\frac{1}{8} = 0.8$

   b) $\frac{1}{9} = 0.999...$

   c) $\frac{1}{5} = 0.2$

   d) $\frac{2}{5} = 0.25$

   e) $\frac{12}{12} = 1.0$

   f) $\frac{8}{100} = 0.8$

Converting Fractions & Decimals Code Breaker

Write each of the following as a decimal and find your answer in the code box. Write down the words as you go to reveal a message!

a) $\dfrac{12}{100}$ = __0.12__ = **A**

b) $\dfrac{1}{8}$ = _____ =

c) $\dfrac{3}{5}$ = _____ =

d) $1\dfrac{2}{100}$ = _____ =

e) $\dfrac{3}{20}$ = _____ =

f) $\dfrac{4}{9}$ = _____ =

g) $\dfrac{1}{3}$ = _____ =

h) $\dfrac{15}{1000}$ = _____ =

i) $\dfrac{23}{50}$ = _____ =

j) $1\dfrac{15}{100}$ = _____ =

k) $\dfrac{60}{200}$ = _____ =

l) $\dfrac{2}{5}$ = _____ =

m) $\dfrac{23}{1000}$ = _____ =

n) $\dfrac{9}{5}$ = _____ =

o) $1\dfrac{1}{4}$ = _____ =

p) $\dfrac{7}{3}$ = _____ =

– Quote by Albert Einstein

adding & subtracting fractions

examples

Type 1: Same denominators	Type 2: Related denominators	Type 3: Different denominators
$\frac{2}{5} + \frac{1}{5}$	$\frac{5}{8} - \frac{1}{4}$	$\frac{2}{3} + \frac{1}{5}$
Add numerators	Convert one fraction to the denominator of the other	Convert both fractions to the same denominator
$\frac{2}{5} + \frac{1}{5} = \frac{3}{5}$	$\frac{5}{8} - \frac{2}{8} = \frac{3}{8}$	$\frac{10}{15} + \frac{3}{15} = \frac{13}{15}$

exercise 4h

1. True or false?

a) $\frac{1}{4} + \frac{1}{3} = \frac{1}{7}$

b) $\frac{3}{5} + \frac{1}{7} = \frac{4}{35}$

c) $\frac{2}{9} + \frac{5}{9} = \frac{7}{9}$

d) $\frac{2}{3} + \frac{1}{5} = \frac{3}{8}$

e) $\frac{1}{5} + \frac{1}{2} = \frac{1}{10}$

f) $\frac{3}{10} - \frac{1}{10} = \frac{2}{10}$

2. For each question, give your answer in the simplest form.

a) $\frac{1}{4} + \frac{3}{5}$

b) $\frac{5}{8} - \frac{3}{7}$

c) $\frac{1}{3} + \frac{1}{6}$

d) $\frac{1}{5} - \frac{1}{7}$

e) $\frac{3}{15} + \frac{7}{15}$

f) $\frac{2}{7} - \frac{3}{14}$

g) $\frac{3}{4} + \frac{1}{4}$

h) $\frac{6}{10} - \frac{3}{5}$

i) $\frac{7}{5} - \frac{1}{3}$

j) $\frac{8}{3} - \frac{5}{3}$

k) $\frac{2}{5} + \frac{12}{10}$

l) $\frac{7}{9} - \frac{5}{9}$

3. What is the sum of the first 3 unit fractions?

4. Complete the following:

a) $\frac{1}{7} + \boxed{} = 1$

b) $1 - \boxed{} = \frac{3}{5}$

c) $1\frac{3}{10} - \boxed{} = \frac{9}{10}$

5. Which of the following are equal to $\frac{7}{8} + \frac{3}{8}$? Circle three answers.

a) $\frac{10}{8}$

b) $\frac{10}{16}$

c) $\frac{5}{4}$

d) $1\frac{1}{4}$

6. Copy and complete the number pyramids so that each pair of side-by-side fractions add to give the number above. Write each fraction in the simplest form.

a)

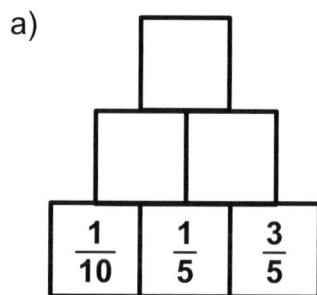

Bottom row: $\frac{1}{10}$ | $\frac{1}{5}$ | $\frac{3}{5}$

b)

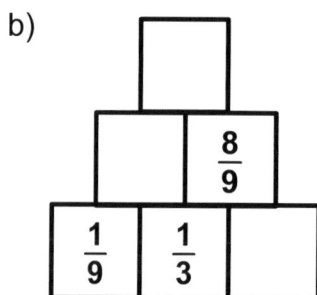

Second row: $\frac{8}{9}$
Bottom row: $\frac{1}{9}$ | $\frac{1}{3}$ |

c)

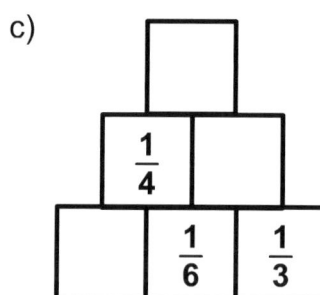

Second row: $\frac{1}{4}$
Bottom row: | $\frac{1}{6}$ | $\frac{1}{3}$

7. Match each of the cards A-L with one of the cards M-X.
   Record your answers in a table.

A $\frac{3}{10} + \frac{1}{5}$	B $\frac{5}{6} - \frac{1}{4}$	C $\frac{2}{3} + \frac{1}{4}$	M $\frac{1}{6}$	N $\frac{3}{4}$	O $\frac{2}{3}$
D $\frac{1}{2} - \frac{1}{3}$	E $\frac{9}{10} - \frac{7}{10}$	F $\frac{1}{2} + \frac{1}{6}$	P $\frac{1}{12}$	Q $\frac{5}{6}$	R $\frac{1}{2}$
G $1 - \frac{7}{12}$	H $\frac{3}{8} + \frac{3}{8}$	I $\frac{5}{6} - \frac{1}{8}$	S $\frac{11}{12}$	T $\frac{2}{5}$	U $\frac{7}{12}$
J $\frac{13}{12} - 1$	K $\frac{3}{2} - \frac{2}{3}$	L $\frac{7}{10} - \frac{3}{10}$	V $\frac{1}{5}$	W $\frac{17}{24}$	X $\frac{5}{12}$

A	B	C	D	E	F	G	H	I	J	K	L

---

investigate ⭐ extra challenge

Unit fractions are fractions such as $\frac{1}{2}, \frac{1}{3}, \frac{1}{4}, \frac{1}{5}$, where the numerator is 1.
In ancient Egypt only unit fractions were allowed and all other fractions had to be written as the sum of **different** unit fractions.

For example, $\frac{9}{20}$ would be written as $\frac{1}{4} + \frac{1}{5}$.

Can you write $\frac{5}{6}$ in the Egyptian way?

How about $\frac{2}{5}$? Can you write any other fractions in the Egyptian way?

Are there any fractions that cannot be written in the Egyptian way?

Missing Digit Puzzles ⭐ extra challenge

Using integers only, fill in the missing digits to make these sums true:

A

$$\frac{1}{\square} + \frac{1}{5} = \frac{9}{20}$$

B

$$\frac{\square}{2} + \frac{2}{\square} = \frac{9}{10}$$

C

$$\frac{1}{\square} + \frac{3}{\square} = \frac{12}{12}$$

D

$$\frac{1}{5} + \frac{\square}{\square} = \frac{13}{15}$$

E

$$\frac{\square}{7} + \frac{\square}{4} = \frac{15}{28}$$

F

$$\frac{1}{5} + \frac{\square}{\square} = \frac{17}{10}$$

G

$$\frac{1}{\square} + \frac{\square}{7} = \frac{17}{35}$$

H

$$\frac{\square}{2} + \frac{3}{\square} = \frac{7}{8}$$

I

$$\frac{\square}{6} - \frac{\square}{5} = \frac{14}{30}$$

J

$$\frac{5}{\square} - \frac{5}{\square} = \frac{10}{24}$$

extension:

a. Find three different fractions that add up to $\frac{1}{2}$

b. Which fraction, when added three times, makes $\frac{1}{2}$?

multiplying fractions

learn by heart

Multiplying Fractions: Multiply numerators and denominators

With negative fractions, the negative sign can be placed at the front, on the top or bottom: $-\dfrac{1}{5} = \dfrac{-1}{5} = \dfrac{1}{-5}$

examples

Evaluate $\dfrac{1}{2} \times \dfrac{3}{5}$

$= \dfrac{3}{10}$

Evaluate $5 \times \dfrac{3}{4}$

$= \dfrac{5}{1} \times \dfrac{3}{4} = \dfrac{15}{4}$

Evaluate $-\dfrac{3}{4} \times -\dfrac{2}{5}$

$= \dfrac{6}{20} = \dfrac{3}{10}$

Evaluate $\dfrac{15}{28} \times \dfrac{14}{3}$

$= \dfrac{15 \times 14}{28 \times 3}$

$= \dfrac{\cancel{3} \times 5 \times \cancel{14}}{2 \times \cancel{14} \times \cancel{3}}$

$= \dfrac{5}{2}$

Quick Tip:
If there are common factors you can cancel them before multiplying

exercise 4i

1. Calculate:

a) $\dfrac{2}{3} \times \dfrac{3}{4}$

b) $\dfrac{1}{8} \times 5$

c) $\dfrac{2}{5} \times \dfrac{5}{3} \times 2$

d) $\dfrac{1}{4} \times \dfrac{3}{5}$

e) $20 \times \dfrac{2}{9}$

f) $5 \times \dfrac{2}{5}$

g) $\dfrac{1}{4} \times \dfrac{1}{2} \times \dfrac{1}{3}$

h) $3 \times \dfrac{3}{8}$

i) $\dfrac{6}{5} \times 6$

2. Multiply these fractions by cancelling common factors first:

a) $\dfrac{24}{5} \times \dfrac{10}{18}$

b) $\dfrac{40}{7} \times \dfrac{14}{8}$

c) $\dfrac{8}{15} \times \dfrac{3}{4}$

d) $\dfrac{15}{42} \times \dfrac{7}{5}$

e) $\dfrac{9}{100} \times \dfrac{20}{15}$

f) $\dfrac{105}{60} \times \dfrac{18}{25}$

3. Which of the following are equal to $\dfrac{3}{8}$? Circle 2 answers.

a) $\dfrac{1}{8} \times \dfrac{2}{8}$

b) $\dfrac{1}{2} \times \dfrac{6}{16}$

c) $\dfrac{3}{4} \times \dfrac{1}{2}$

d) $\dfrac{2}{8} \times \dfrac{3}{2}$

4. What's missing? Fill in the blanks to make these statements true:

a) $\frac{1}{5} \times \boxed{} = \frac{4}{5}$

c) $\frac{1}{8} \times \boxed{} = \frac{5}{8}$

e) $\frac{3}{4} \times \boxed{} = \frac{12}{4}$

b) $\frac{3}{4} \times \boxed{} = \frac{21}{20}$

d) $\frac{1}{6} \times \boxed{} = \frac{5}{12}$

f) $\frac{2}{3} \times \boxed{} = \frac{2}{3}$

5. Multiply these fractions. Simplify your answers.

a) $\frac{4}{3} \times \text{-}3$

d) $\text{-}2 \times \frac{\text{-}4}{5}$

g) $\text{-}3 \times \text{-}\frac{3}{8}$

b) $\frac{\text{-}8}{3} \times \frac{9}{4}$

e) $\text{-}\frac{2}{5} \times \text{-}5$

h) $\text{-}\frac{5}{2} \times \text{-}\frac{22}{5}$

c) $\text{-}\frac{2}{7} \times \text{-}\frac{7}{3}$

f) $\text{-}\frac{5}{4} \times \frac{2}{5}$

i) $\text{-}\frac{1}{3} \times \text{-}\frac{3}{4} \times \text{-}\frac{5}{3}$

6. Which of the following have an answer greater than 1? Circle 2 answers.

a) $6 \times \frac{1}{7}$

b) $\frac{6}{5} \times \frac{5}{4}$

c) $\frac{2}{5} \times 3$

d) $\frac{8}{9} \times \frac{8}{9}$

7. True or False: $\frac{2}{3} \times 5 = \frac{10}{15}$

8. True or False: $\frac{1}{7} + \frac{1}{7} + \frac{1}{7} = 3 \times \frac{1}{7}$

more challenging ⭐ extra challenge

9. Chose one of the cards from below to complete each calculation.
   Each card can be used once only.

a) $\text{-}\frac{3}{4} \times \boxed{} = \frac{9}{20}$

b) $4 \times \boxed{} = \frac{4}{5}$

c) $\frac{3}{5} \times \boxed{} = \text{-}\frac{3}{10}$

d) $\frac{2}{7} \times \boxed{} = 1\frac{1}{7}$

e) $\frac{1}{2} \times \boxed{} = 2\frac{1}{2}$

f) $\frac{3}{4} \times \boxed{} = 5\frac{1}{4}$

g) $\frac{4}{9} \times \boxed{} = 0$

h) $\frac{5}{6} \times \boxed{} = 5$

i) $\frac{5}{6} \times \boxed{} = 1$

$\boxed{0} \quad \boxed{5} \quad \boxed{\tfrac{1}{5}} \quad \boxed{6} \quad \boxed{7} \quad \boxed{\text{-}\tfrac{3}{5}} \quad \boxed{4} \quad \boxed{\tfrac{6}{5}} \quad \boxed{\text{-}\tfrac{1}{2}}$

reciprocals

A number multiplied by its reciprocal equals 1.
To find the reciprocal of a fraction, swap over the numerator and denominator.

examples

The reciprocal of $\frac{3}{4}$ is $\frac{4}{3}$

The reciprocal of $\frac{1}{5}$ is $\frac{5}{1} = 5$

exercise 4j

1. Work out the reciprocal of each number:

   a) $\frac{2}{5}$ b) $\frac{1}{7}$ c) $\frac{8}{5}$ d) 9

   e) $\frac{1}{2}$ f) $\frac{2}{7}$ g) $\frac{9}{4}$ h) $\frac{4}{9}$

2. When a number is multipled by it reciprocal, the answer is always ____.

3. Work out the reciprocal of each mixed number, by first converting it into an improper fraction:

   a) $1\frac{3}{4}$ b) $5\frac{1}{2}$ c) $3\frac{1}{8}$

4. Work out the reciprocal of each number, by first converting it into a fraction:

   a) 0.7   b) 0.25   c) 0.2   d) 0.049

5. Write down the reciprocal of the following numbers:

   a) $\frac{2}{3}$ d) $\frac{1}{3}$ g) $-\frac{5}{2}$ j) 16   m) 0.2

   b) 5   e) $\frac{2}{9}$ h) $2\frac{3}{5}$ k) 1   n) 3.5

   c) $\frac{1}{4}$ f) -3   i) $\frac{1}{7}$ l) 0.5   o) $0.\dot{8}$

6. Work out a number to make each calculation correct:

   a) $\frac{2}{9} \times \boxed{} = 1$ b) $\frac{1}{12} \times \boxed{} = 1$ c) $\frac{3}{8} \times \boxed{} = 1$

   d) $6 \times \boxed{} = 1$ e) $0.8 \times \boxed{} = 1$ f) $0.9 \times \boxed{} = 1$

7. Which number has a reciprocal equal to itself?

8. Calculate cleverly: $\frac{1}{5} \times 243 \times 5$

9. Calculate cleverly: $92.6 \times \frac{1}{4} \times 40$

dividing fractions

learn by heart

Dividing Fractions: *To divide by a fraction, multiply by its reciprocal*

examples

Evaluate $\frac{4}{3} \div \frac{1}{2}$

$= \frac{4}{3} \times 2 = \frac{8}{3}$

Evaluate $\frac{4}{3} \div \frac{2}{5}$

$= \frac{4}{3} \times \frac{5}{2} = \frac{20}{6}$

Evaluate $3 \div \frac{2}{5}$

$= 3 \times \frac{5}{2} = \frac{15}{2}$

Evaluate $\frac{2}{5} \div 6$

$= \frac{2}{5} \times \frac{1}{6} = \frac{2}{30}$

exercise 4k

1. Work out the following, giving your answer in the simplest form:

   a) $\frac{5}{9} \div \frac{2}{3}$

   b) $\frac{2}{7} \div 4$

   c) $\frac{1}{8} \div \frac{2}{3}$

   d) $\frac{3}{4} \div \frac{1}{3}$

   e) $9 \div \frac{1}{4}$

   f) $10 \div \frac{3}{4}$

   g) $\frac{5}{12} \div 3$

   h) $\frac{4}{9} \div \frac{4}{9}$

3. To calculate $8 \div \frac{1}{2}$, we could work out:

   a) $\frac{1}{2} \div 8$ b) $8 \div 2$ c) 8×2 d) $2 \div 8$

4. To calculate $\frac{4}{5} \div 3$, we could work out:

   a) $\frac{4}{5} \times 3$ b) $\frac{4}{5} \times \frac{3}{1}$ c) $\frac{4}{5} \div \frac{1}{3}$ d) $\frac{4}{5} \times \frac{1}{3}$

6. Which of the following are equal to $\frac{1}{6}$? Select all that apply.

   a) $\frac{5}{6} \div 5$ b) $\frac{1}{11} \div \frac{6}{11}$ c) $\frac{1}{12} \div \frac{1}{2}$ d) $\frac{1}{3} \div 2$

7. Calculate:

   a) $\frac{2}{3} \times \frac{5}{7}$

   c) $4 \times \frac{1}{5}$

   e) $\frac{2}{3} \div 5$

   b) $\frac{2}{3} \div \frac{5}{7}$

   d) $4 \div \frac{1}{5}$

   f) $\frac{2}{3} \times 5$

Multiplying & Dividing Fractions Match

Match cards on the left with their answers on the right:
Record your answers in a table.

A $\frac{1}{5} \div \frac{1}{4}$

B $\frac{4}{5}$ of $\frac{1}{4}$

C $\frac{1}{5} \times \frac{1}{4}$

D $\frac{1}{5} \times 5$

E $\frac{1}{4} \times \frac{5}{4}$

F $\frac{1}{5} \div 5$

G $\frac{4}{5} \times 4$

H $\frac{24}{5} \div \frac{1}{4}$

I $\frac{21}{4} \times \frac{4}{4}$

J $\frac{17}{4} \div 4$

K $\frac{4}{5} \times \frac{1}{5}$

L $5 \div \frac{1}{4}$

M $5 \times \frac{1}{4}$

N $\frac{4}{5} \div \frac{1}{5}$

O $\frac{1}{5}$ of $\frac{1}{4}$

P $4 \div \frac{4}{5}$

Q $\frac{5}{4}$ of 5

R $\frac{6}{5} \times \frac{1}{4}$

S $\frac{4}{5} \div \frac{5}{4}$

T $\frac{4}{5} \div 5\frac{1}{4}$

1

$\frac{1}{20}$

$\frac{16}{105}$

$\frac{96}{5}$

$\frac{21}{4}$

$\frac{1}{5}$

$\frac{5}{4}$

$\frac{1}{25}$

$\frac{16}{25}$

4

$\frac{1}{20}$

$\frac{16}{5}$

$\frac{4}{25}$

5

$\frac{4}{5}$

$\frac{3}{10}$

$\frac{5}{16}$

$\frac{17}{16}$

20

$\frac{25}{4}$

A	B	C	D	E	F	G	H	I	J	K	L	M	N	O	P	Q	R	S	T

mixed fraction calculations practice

exercise 4

1. Calculate the following, giving your answer in the simplest form:

   a) $\frac{4}{3} \div 8$

   b) $\frac{5}{6} \times 2$

   c) $\frac{1}{8} \div \frac{2}{3}$

   d) $\frac{4}{10} - \frac{1}{5}$

   e) $9 \div \frac{1}{3}$

   f) $\frac{1}{10} + \frac{5}{20}$

   g) $\frac{1}{9} \times 4 \times \frac{2}{3}$

   h) $\frac{1}{2} + \frac{1}{5}$

   i) $1 - \frac{3}{5}$

2. True or false: $5 \div \frac{1}{4} = 5 \times 4$

3. Calculate $3 \times \frac{1}{3}$

4. True or false: $\frac{2}{3} \times 5 = \frac{10}{15}$

5. Calculate:

   a) $\frac{22}{5} \times \frac{15}{11}$

   b) $\frac{2}{5} \times 40$

   c) $\frac{3}{5} \times 4$

   d) $\frac{1}{8} - \frac{1}{10}$

   e) $8 \times \frac{1}{8}$

   f) $\frac{9}{10} - \frac{12}{10}$

6. Which of the following are equal to 10? Select all that apply.

   a) $\frac{1}{5}$ of 50

   b) $\frac{2}{3}$ of 15

   c) $\frac{3}{5}$ of 25

   d) $\frac{1}{8}$ of 40

puzzle: make a whole

Place these fractions in the boxes on the left to make 4 calculations with an answer of 1.

$$\frac{13}{5} \qquad \frac{2}{5} \qquad \frac{1}{5} \qquad \frac{7}{2}$$

$$\frac{4}{10} \qquad \frac{2}{7} \qquad \frac{4}{5} \qquad \frac{8}{5}$$

Fraction Spiral

Start in the middle and work your way around the spiral, finding your answers at the bottom as you go.

← ×2	← $-\frac{1}{2}$	← $\div\frac{2}{3}$	← simplify	$\frac{9}{12}$

simplify ↓

$\times\frac{1}{3}$ ↓ $\times\frac{1}{3}$ ↓   ← simplify   ← ×5

$+\frac{7}{12}$ ↑

$+\frac{1}{12}$ ↓ $-\frac{1}{5}$ ↓

start

$\frac{1}{5}$

$+\frac{1}{5}$ →

$\times\frac{3}{5}$ ↑ $\div 4$

$\times\frac{2}{3}$ ↑

$-\frac{1}{2}$ ↓

$\div\frac{1}{4}$ →   simplify → $+\frac{1}{5}$ →

$+\frac{1}{3}$ →   squared → $+\frac{1}{4}$ →   ×2 →

- -

jumbled answers

$\frac{6}{15}$ $\frac{3}{4}$ $\frac{1}{3}$ $\frac{1}{9}$ $\frac{6}{12}$ $\frac{2}{12}$ 1 $\frac{13}{36}$ $\frac{2}{3}$ $\frac{12}{15}$

$\frac{26}{36}$ $\frac{30}{25}$ $\frac{4}{5}$ $\frac{6}{5}$ $\frac{9}{8}$ $\frac{5}{8}$ $\frac{2}{5}$ $\frac{5}{12}$ 0 $\frac{5}{4}$ $\frac{3}{15}$ $\frac{10}{8}$ $\frac{6}{25}$

four operations with mixed numbers ☆ extra challenge

Calculate...

$1\frac{1}{4} + 2\frac{1}{5}$

$= \frac{5}{4} + \frac{11}{5}$

$= \frac{25}{20} + \frac{44}{20} = \frac{69}{20}$

$1\frac{1}{4} \times 3$

$= \frac{5}{4} \times 3$

$= \frac{15}{4}$

$1\frac{1}{4} \times 2\frac{1}{5}$

$= \frac{5}{4} \times \frac{11}{5}$

$= \frac{11}{4}$

$1\frac{1}{4} \div 3$

$= \frac{5}{4} \times \frac{1}{3}$

$= \frac{5}{12}$

exercise 4m

1. Calculate the following, giving your answer as a mixed number in its simplest form:

   a) $1\frac{1}{4} + \frac{2}{5}$

   b) $2\frac{1}{3} - 1\frac{1}{10}$

   c) $2\frac{1}{5} - \frac{3}{7}$

2. Calculate the following, leaving your answer as an improper fraction:

   a) $3 \times 4\frac{1}{5}$

   b) $2\frac{1}{3} \times 1\frac{2}{5}$

   c) $2 \times 3 \times 1\frac{1}{4}$

3. Calculate the following, leaving your answer as a proper/improper fraction:

   a) $2 \div 1\frac{3}{4}$

   c) $6\frac{1}{5} \div \frac{1}{2}$

   b) $\frac{1}{5} \div 3\frac{2}{3}$

   d) $2\frac{1}{3} \div 5$

4. Calculate $1\frac{1}{2} + 1\frac{1}{3} + 1\frac{1}{4}$

5. Calculate $1\frac{1}{2} \times 1\frac{1}{3} \div 1\frac{1}{4}$

- -

Countdown Target : $1\frac{2}{5}$

Using each number only once, how close can you get to $1\frac{2}{5}$?

You can add, subtract, multiply or divide the numbers.

| $\frac{1}{10}$ | $\frac{1}{5}$ | $\frac{1}{4}$ | 1 | $1\frac{1}{2}$ | 1.8 | 2 |

Mixed Up Multiplications

Complete these calculations and find your answer at the bottom.
Record your answers in a table.

A		B		C		D	
$\frac{1}{5} \times \frac{2}{3}$		-3×-7		0.2×0.3		$4 \times \frac{2}{7}$	

E	F	G	H
-5×3	0.6×10	$\frac{3}{5} \times 4$	1.2×3

I	J	K	L
0.07×100	8×-2	0.8×3	$\frac{3}{4} \times \frac{4}{3}$

M	N	O	P
0.24×1000	$6 \times \frac{2}{3}$	-2×-12	6×0.3

Q	R	S	T
90×0.3	$\frac{4}{5}$ of 25	-16×0	80×0.1

U	V	W	X
$-\frac{1}{3} \times 4$	$0.7 \times \frac{3}{4}$	$0.8 \times \frac{1}{10}$	-3×0.9

- -

jumbled answers

| 3.6 | 20 | -2.7 |

| 2.4 | $\frac{2}{15}$ | 4 | 24 | -15 |

| 0 | | | | | 8 |

| 30 | 0.06 | $-\frac{4}{3}$ | 0.08 | -16 | 7 |

| | | | | | 1.8 |

| $\frac{12}{5}$ | $\frac{21}{40}$ | 21 | 240 | $\frac{8}{7}$ | 6 | 1 |

A	
B	
C	
D	
E	
F	
G	
H	
I	
J	
K	
L	
M	
N	
O	
P	
Q	
R	
S	
T	
U	
V	
W	
X	

fractions, decimals and negatives 1

examples

Calculate $\frac{1}{5} \div 0.3$	Calculate $-\frac{4}{3} \times 0.2$	Calculate $\frac{3}{25} \div 0.5$
$= \frac{1}{5} \div \frac{3}{10}$		
$= \frac{1}{5} \times \frac{10}{3}$	$= -\frac{4}{3} \times \frac{2}{10}$	$= \frac{3}{25} \times 2$
$= \frac{10}{15}$	$= -\frac{8}{30}$	$= \frac{6}{25}$
$= \frac{2}{3}$	$= -\frac{4}{15}$	$= \frac{24}{100} = 0.24$

remember from chapter 2 that dividing by 0.5 is like doubling

exercise 4n

1. Calculate the following, giving your answer as a **decimal**:

   a) $\frac{1}{5} \times 0.1$

   b) $\frac{3}{10} \div 0.5$

   c) $\frac{2}{10} \times 0.7$

   d) $0.9 \div \frac{1}{2}$

   e) $\frac{1}{2} \times 0.3$

   f) $\frac{14}{20} \times 0.1$

   g) $0.4 \div \frac{1}{4}$

   h) $\frac{4}{50} \div 0.1$

   i) $\frac{1}{3} \times 0.3$

   j) $0.6 \div \frac{6}{10}$

   k) $1.5 \div \frac{1}{10}$

   l) $\frac{14}{50} \times 100$

2. Calculate the following, giving your answer as a **fraction in its simplest form**:

   a) $-\frac{1}{4} \times \frac{2}{3}$

   b) $-\frac{1}{3} \times 4$

   c) $-2 \times \frac{3}{4}$

   d) $-\frac{1}{6} \times -\frac{1}{6}$

   e) $\frac{2}{7} \times -10$

   f) $-3 \times -\frac{2}{5}$

3. Calculate the following, giving your answer as **an integer or fraction in its simplest form**:

   a) $\frac{3}{4} \div -\frac{2}{5}$

   b) $-\frac{1}{5} \div 7$

   c) $-\frac{1}{5} \div -\frac{2}{3}$

   d) $-\frac{1}{7} \div 7$

   e) $-3 \div -\frac{2}{5}$

   f) $12 \div -\frac{2}{10}$

4. Calculate the following and find your answers on the right:

a) $-0.3 \times \frac{3}{5}$

b) $0.7 \times -\frac{1}{5}$

c) $-12 \div \frac{1}{5}$

d) -4×-0.9

e) $\frac{1}{4} \div -5$

f) $-\frac{2}{3} \times -3$

g) $-1.2 \div -3$

h) $\frac{2}{5} \div -0.5$

i) $0.9 \div -3$

j) $-\frac{1}{2} \times -\frac{1}{5}$

k) $-0.2 \times -\frac{1}{4}$

l) $\frac{1}{5} \div -0.5$

-0.8	0.05
0.1	0.4
-0.05	-0.14
-0.4	3.6
-60	-0.3
-0.18	2

5. Fill in the blanks with integers or **decimals**:

a) $\frac{2}{5} \times \frac{5}{2} =$ _____

b) $\frac{5}{3} \times$ _____ $= 1$

c) $\frac{20}{6} \times$ _____ $= 1$

d) $0.1 \times$ _____ $= 1$

e) $\frac{2}{10} \div$ _____ $= 1$

f) $\frac{1}{3} \times$ _____ $= 1$

- -

Countdown Target : -3.8

extra challenge

Using each number only once, how close can you get to -3.8?
You can add, subtract, multiply or divide the numbers.

-5	-4	$-\frac{1}{2}$	$-\frac{1}{10}$	$-\frac{1}{100}$	1	3

fractions, decimals & negatives 2

examples

Calculate $\frac{3}{8}$ - 0.1 $\frac{3}{8}$ = 0.375 (by short division) 0.375 - 0.1 = 0.275	Calculate 0.6 - - $\frac{4}{10}$ = 0.6 + 0.4 = 1

exercise 40

1. Calculate the following, giving your answer as an integer or decimal:

    a) $\frac{1}{10}$ × 0.4

    b) $\frac{1}{8}$ + 0.1

    c) 0.05 - $\frac{1}{100}$

    d) $\frac{4}{5}$ ÷ 0.5

    e) 0.2 ÷ $\frac{1}{10}$

    f) 1.2 ÷ $1\frac{2}{10}$

    g) $\frac{5}{4}$ × $\frac{4}{5}$

    h) $\frac{1}{10}$ - 0.7

    i) 0.3 × $\frac{4}{10}$

2. Which of these will equal 100? Choose all that apply.

    a) 50 ÷ 0.5

    b) 50 ÷ $\frac{1}{2}$

    c) 50 × $\frac{1}{2}$

    d) 50 × -2

3. Calculate:

    a) -0.1 × 4

    b) -$\frac{1}{5}$ × $\frac{2}{3}$

    c) 0.4 - - 0.2

    d) $\frac{1}{10}$ + -$\frac{1}{10}$

    e) -5 × $\frac{1}{5}$

    f) 0.3 - - $\frac{1}{10}$

    g) -5 - $\frac{1}{10}$

    h) -12 ÷ $\frac{1}{2}$

    i) 45 × $\frac{1}{10}$

4. Which of these equal zero? Choose all that apply.

    a) 0.4 - $\frac{4}{10}$

    b) 0.4 - $\frac{4}{100}$

    c) 0.4 - 0.40

    d) $\frac{4}{10}$ - $\frac{40}{100}$

5. True or false: *Dividing by $\frac{1}{3}$ has the same effect as multiplying by 3*

6. In each case, decide if the answer will be positive, negative or zero:

a) $0.4 - 0.5$

b) $0.4 - \frac{5}{10}$

c) $\frac{1}{100} - 0.01$

d) $\frac{1}{4} - 0.5$

e) $\frac{9}{10} - 0.8$

f) $\frac{1}{10} - 0.01$

g) $\frac{1}{3} - 0.3$

h) $\frac{1}{3} - 0.\dot{3}$

i) $\frac{3}{10} - \frac{1}{3}$

7. Calculate $-\frac{1}{2} \times -\frac{1}{2} \times -\frac{1}{2} \times -\frac{1}{2}$

8. Fill in the blanks with **decimals**:

a) $\frac{4}{10} +$ _____ $= 0.6$

b) $\frac{1}{100} +$ _____ $= 0.02$

c) $1\frac{1}{10} -$ _____ $= 0$

d) $\frac{1}{10} +$ _____ $= 0.25$

e) $\frac{3}{10} -$ _____ $= \frac{4}{10}$

f) $\frac{7}{10} -$ _____ $= 0.55$

g) $\frac{3}{10} -$ _____ $= \frac{1}{5}$

h) $\frac{1}{10} -$ _____ $= 0.01$

i) $\frac{1}{3} -$ _____ $= 0$

- -

matching activity

9. Match each of the cards A-L with one of the cards M-X.
   Record your answers in a table.

A	B	C
$\frac{2}{10} \times 0.1$	$0.4 + \frac{6}{10}$	$-5 \div \frac{1}{4}$

D	E	F
-7×-0.1	$-\frac{1}{5} \times -\frac{1}{2}$	$1 - \frac{3}{5}$

G	H	I
$12 \div -0.5$	$\frac{2}{3} \times 0.3$	$0.2 + \frac{1}{100}$

J	K	L
$\frac{1}{4} - 0.1$	$\frac{2}{5} + 0.2$	$-4 \times \frac{1}{5}$

M	N	O
0.21	0.4	0.02

P	Q	R
-20	0.6	0.7

S	T	U
-0.8	1	0.2

V	W	X
0.1	0.15	-24

A	B	C	D	E	F	G	H	I	J	K	L

Same, or Different?

Without calculating any answers, decide whether each card shows two calculations with the same answer, or with different answers.

A

| $\frac{1}{5}$ of 82 | $82 \div 5$ |

B

| $\frac{2}{3} \times 4$ | $4 \times \frac{2}{3}$ |

C

| $-3 \times -\frac{1}{5}$ | $3 \times \frac{1}{5}$ |

D

| $6 \div 0.2$ | $6 \div \frac{2}{10}$ |

E

| $\frac{4}{5} \div 3$ | $\frac{4}{5} \times \frac{3}{1}$ |

F

| $\frac{2}{5}$ of 0.7 | $\frac{2}{5} \times \frac{7}{10}$ |

G

| $\frac{2}{5} \times \frac{4}{4}$ | $\frac{2}{5} \times 1$ |

H

| $4 \div 0.5$ | $4 \times \frac{1}{2}$ |

I

| $-12 \div 3$ | $12 \div -3$ |

J

| 14×0.1 | $14 \div 0.1$ |

K

| $16 \div \frac{1}{5}$ | 16×5 |

L

| $0.2 - -0.3$ | $0.2 + 0.3$ |

M

| $\frac{1}{10}$ of -8 | -8×0.1 |

N

| $1\frac{1}{5} \times 3$ | $\frac{6}{5} \times 3$ |

O

| $7 \div \frac{3}{10}$ | $\frac{3}{10}$ of 7 |

P

| $\frac{3}{5} \times \frac{5}{3}$ | $\frac{3}{5} \div \frac{3}{5}$ |

The cards with DIFFERENT calculations are : ____   ____   ____   ____

exercise 4p

1. Calculate the following, simplifying your answers as much as possible:

   a) $\frac{1}{4} \times 3$

   b) $\frac{1}{5} + \frac{1}{4}$

   c) $\frac{2}{3} \div 5$

   d) $1 - \frac{1}{3}$

   e) $\frac{4}{5} \times \frac{2}{3}$

   f) $\frac{1}{3} \div 2$

   g) $\frac{4}{10} \div \frac{2}{3}$

   h) $\frac{24}{50} \times \frac{25}{6}$

   i) $\frac{8}{50} + \frac{3}{100}$

   j) $\frac{2}{5} - \frac{1}{3}$

   k) $2 \div \frac{7}{10}$

   l) $-\frac{1}{5} \times -5$

2. Write each of these as a decimal:

   a) $\frac{2}{5}$

   b) $\frac{3}{25}$

   c) $\frac{18}{100}$

   d) $\frac{6}{1000}$

   e) $2\frac{1}{10}$

   f) $\frac{204}{1000}$

   g) $\frac{1}{9}$

   h) $\frac{8}{40}$

- -

Fractions Spider

Copy the diagram and work out the answers.
Simplify your answers.

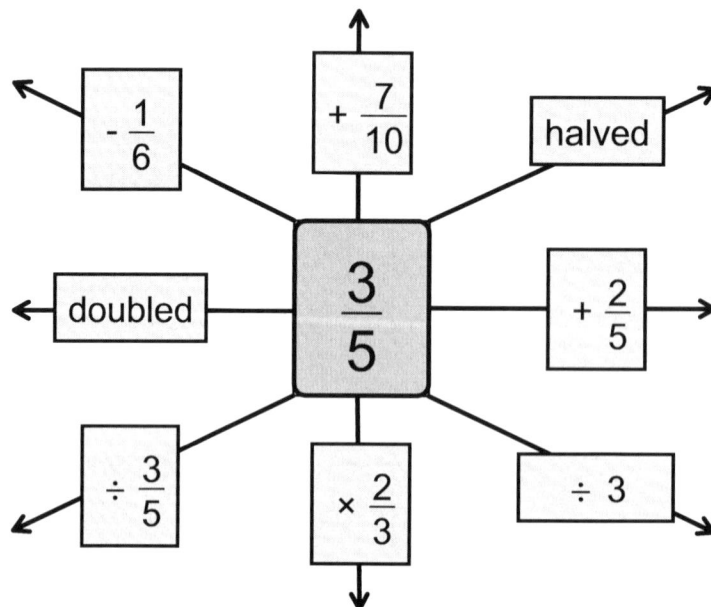

3. Work out:

   a) $\frac{1}{10}$ of £18   b) $\frac{1}{5}$ of £4   c) $\frac{2}{3}$ of £1.50

4. Which of the following will have the same answer as $\frac{2}{3} \div 3$?

   a) $\frac{2}{3} \times \frac{1}{3}$ b) $\frac{3}{2} \times \frac{1}{3}$ c) $\frac{2}{3} \times 3$ d) $\frac{3}{2} \times 3$

5. Write as whole or mixed numbers:

   a) $\frac{6}{3}$ b) $\frac{7}{3}$ c) $\frac{8}{3}$ d) $\frac{9}{3}$

6. Simplify $\frac{24}{30}$ fully. Circle your answer below.

   a) $\frac{12}{15}$ b) $\frac{1}{2}$ c) $\frac{6}{7.5}$ d) $\frac{4}{5}$

matching activity

Which of these calculations will produce the same answers?
Match each card on the left with an equivalent card on the right.
Simplify your answers as you go to help match the cards.

A. $\frac{2}{3} \div 5$	B. $\frac{2}{3} \div \frac{2}{3}$		K. $\frac{2}{3} \times \frac{3}{2}$	L. $\frac{25}{12} \div \frac{5}{18}$
C. $\frac{2}{3} - \frac{1}{5}$	D. $\frac{2}{3} \times 4$		M. $\frac{8}{27} \div \frac{4}{9}$	N. $\frac{1}{10} \times \frac{1}{2}$
E. $\frac{4}{5} - \frac{3}{4}$	F. $\frac{1}{3} + \frac{1}{5}$		O. $\frac{1}{5} \div \frac{3}{7}$	P. $\frac{2}{3} \times \frac{1}{5}$
G. $3 \div \frac{2}{5}$	H. $\frac{3}{2} \div 6$		Q. $1 - \frac{1}{6}$	R. $1 - \frac{7}{15}$
I. $\frac{4}{6} + \frac{1}{6}$	J. $\frac{4}{9} \div \frac{2}{3}$		S. $-\frac{1}{32} \times -8$	T. $\frac{4}{3} + \frac{4}{3}$

A	B	C	D	E	F	G	H	I	J

exercise 4q

1. Calculate 4.2 × 1000

2. Write **three million and forty** in digits

3. Round 0.049 to 1 significant figure

4. Calculate the following:

   a) -7 - 5   c) -5 - 4   e) -40 ÷ 8   g) -12 + 8

   b) -8 + -3   d) 12 × -3   f) 17 + -20   h) -3 × 9

5. Calculate 1 - 0.6

6. Complete the sum: 0.39 × _____ = 3,900

7. Given that 92 × 18 = 1656, calculate:

   a) 9.2 × 1,800   b) 0.92 × 1.8   c) 92 × 9

8. Work out:

   a) $\frac{6}{0.1}$ b) $\frac{12}{0.5}$ c) $\frac{3}{0.01}$ d) $\frac{14}{0.2}$

9. Calculate the following:

   a) $\frac{1}{4} + \frac{3}{5}$ c) $\frac{3}{5} - \frac{1}{7}$ e) $\frac{4}{5} \times \frac{2}{7}$

   b) $\frac{1}{12} + \frac{8}{24}$ d) $1 - \frac{1}{7}$ f) $4 \div \frac{2}{5}$

10. Which of these is 5 hundreds + 5 hundredths?

   a) 50.5   b) 0.55   c) 500.5   d) 500.05

11. Calculate 14 ÷ 9

12. Calculate 1.2 × 0.6

13. Calculate -3 × -3 × -3

14. Put these in order of size, starting with the smallest: | 0.32 | | $\frac{3}{10}$ | | 0.301 | | $\frac{31}{100}$ |

15. Fill in the blanks with decimals:

a) $0.2 + \frac{4}{10} +$ _____ $= 1$ c) $0.7 + \frac{5}{100} +$ _____ $= 1$

b) $\frac{12}{100} + 0.5 +$ _____ $= 1$ d) $0.45 + \frac{6}{100} +$ _____ $= 1$

16. Calculate:

a) $7 - 10$ c) $0.4 + \frac{1}{4}$ e) -4×-3

b) $\frac{1}{3} \times 3$ d) $1 - 0.3$ f) $12 \div -6$

17. Calculate $\frac{1}{3} \times \frac{1}{5} \times 3$

18. Calculate:

a) $\frac{15}{0.1}$ b) $\frac{1}{3}$ of 18   c) $\frac{1.4}{7}$ d) $\frac{4}{5}$ of 25

19. Work out the reciprocal of $3\frac{1}{4}$

20. The product of any number and its reciprocal is _____

21. Calculate -402×-0.1

22. Calculate $\frac{402}{1000} \times \frac{1}{10}$ and give your answer as a decimal.

- -

exercise 4r: negative numbers practice

1. Calculate:

a) $8 - 10$ d) $8 - - 2$ g) $-9 + 2$

b) -2×-3 e) $-9 - 1$ h) $-4 + -5$

c) $4 + -10$ f) $-10 + 15$ i) $20 \div -10$

2. Fill in the blanks with positive or negative:

a) When two negative numbers are added, the result is _____

b) When two negative numbers are multiplied, the result is _____

c) When a negative number is subtracted from 0, the result is _____

3. Which of these has the same answer as $463 + -305$?

a) $463 - 305$ b) $463 + 305$ c) $463 \div 305$ d) $-463 - 305$

4. Look at this number line:

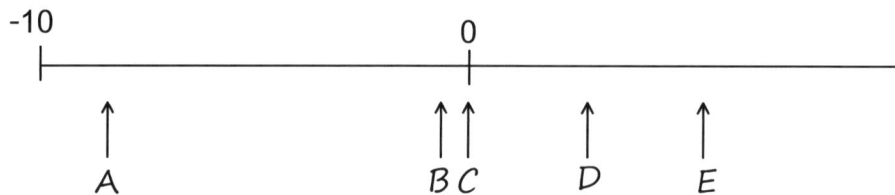

```
   -10                              0
    |————————————————————————————|——————————————————————
         ↑                      ↑↑        ↑          ↑
         A                      B C       D          E
```

Which arrow points to:

i) The largest negative number

ii) The number which is -(-3.5)

iii) The number which is neither positive nor negative

iv) The number whose reciprocal is 0.2

v) The number which adds with 8 to make 0.

5. Fill in the blanks:

a) 6 + _____ = -3   c) 4 - _____ = 8   e) -9 - _____ = -12

b) -5 + _____ = 3   d) -4 - _____ = 0   f) -5 + _____ = -20

6. If a and b are different numbers and $a + b = 0$, then $a \times b$ is:

a) positive   b) negative   c) zero   d) cannot be certain

- -

Negative Numbers Mystery Activity

Copy the grid and use the clues to complete it.

the number in the top left is 3 less than -4

the number in the top right is 3 - 8

the number below -5 is 10 - 16

the number below -7 is 2 less than 0

the top row adds up to 0

the number in the bottom left is -4 + 8

the number next to 4 is -3 - 6

the numbers in the right hand column add up to -15

	0	

140

chapter 5: indices

[Recommended Time: 13 - 17 hours]

Contents

repeated multiplication (warm up)

learn by heart

2 × 2 × 2 is not the same as 2 × 3
2 × 2 × 2 = 8 (work it out one bit at a time)

recall

A negative × a negative = a positive

Product = the result of multiplying,
e.g. the product of -6 and 2 is -12

examples

Calculate....

$3 \times 3 \times 3 \times 3$

$= 81$

$\frac{1}{3} \times \frac{1}{3} \times \frac{1}{3}$

$= \frac{1}{27}$

$0.1 \times 0.1 \times 0.1$

$= 0.001$

$-2 \times -2 \times -2 \times -2$

$= 16$

If an **even** number of negatives are multiplied, the product is positive

exercise 5a

1. Work out:

    a) $3 \times 3 \times 3$

    b) -3×-3

    c) $4 \times 4 \times 4$

    d) $2 \times 2 \times 2 \times 2$

    e) -2×-2

    f) $5 \times 5 \times 5$

2. True or False: 2 × 2 × 2 = 6

3. The product of two negative numbers is (positive / negative)

4. True or False: -3 × -3 = -9

5. Work out:

    a) $\frac{1}{5} \times \frac{1}{5}$

    b) $\frac{2}{3} \times \frac{2}{3}$

    c) $\frac{1}{3} \times \frac{1}{3} \times \frac{1}{3}$

    d) $\frac{2}{5} \times \frac{2}{5}$

    e) $\frac{1}{2} \times \frac{1}{2} \times \frac{1}{2} \times \frac{1}{2}$

    f) $\frac{1}{4} \times \frac{1}{4}$

6. Work out:

    a) $-3 \times -3 \times -3$

    b) $-1 \times -1 \times -1$

    c) $-2 \times -2 \times -2 \times -2$

7. Work out 1 × 1 × 1 × 1 × 1 × 1 × 1 × 1 × 1 × 1 × 1 × 1 × 1 × 1

8. Work out 2 × 2 × 2 × 2 × 2 × 2 × 2

9. Work out $\frac{1}{2} \times \frac{1}{2} \times \frac{1}{2} \times \frac{1}{2} \times \frac{1}{2} \times \frac{1}{2} \times \frac{1}{2}$

10. Given that 5 × 5 = 25, work out 0.5 × 0.5

11. Given that 2 × 2 = 4, work out 0.2 × 0.2

12. Given that 6 × 6 × 6 = 216, work out 0.6 × 0.6 × 0.6

13. Work out 0.1 × 0.1

14. True or False: when **50** negative numbers are multiplied, the answer is a positive number.

15. Work out -1 × -1 × -1 × -1 × -1 × -1

16. **99** negative numbers are multiplied. Is the answer positive or negative?

17. Write the **same** number in each box to make the sum true:

$$\boxed{} \times \boxed{} \times \boxed{} \times \boxed{} = 81$$

18. Calculate:

a) $\frac{1}{3} \times \frac{1}{3} \times \frac{1}{3}$

b) -2 × -2 × -2 × -2

c) 0.1 × 0.1 × 0.1

d) 6 × 6 × 6

e) $\frac{1}{6} \times \frac{1}{6} \times \frac{1}{6}$

f) -1 × -1 × -1 × -1 × -1

g) $\frac{2}{5} \times \frac{2}{5}$

h) $-\frac{1}{2} \times -\frac{1}{2} \times -\frac{1}{2}$

i) 0.2 × 0.2 × 0.2

19. Fill in the blanks with >, < or =

a) -2 × -2 _____ -5 × -5 × -5

b) $\frac{1}{2} \times \frac{1}{2}$ _____ 0.5 × 0.5

c) 1 × 1 × 1 × 1 _____ -1 × -1

d) $\frac{1}{10} \times \frac{1}{10} \times \frac{1}{10}$ _____ 0.1 × 0.1 × 0.1

e) 3 × 3 × 3 _____ 2 × 2 × 2 × 2

f) 5 × 5 × 5 _____ 6 × 6 × 6

g) $\frac{1}{5} \times \frac{1}{5} \times \frac{1}{5}$ _____ 0

h) -5 × -5 × -5 × -5 × -5 _____ 0

20. Given that 6 × 6 × 6 × 6 = 1296, work out

a) -6 × -6 × -6 × -6

b) 0.6 × 0.6 × 0.6 × 0.6

index notation: positive integer bases

learn by heart

To show repeated multiplication we use a base and an index.

The base is the number being multiplied, the index shows how many times to multiply.

An index of 1 is not written, so $4 = 4^1$

People use many different names for 'index', including 'exponent' and 'power'

An index of 2 is pronounced 'squared', so 3^2 is read 'three squared'. The result is called a square number.

An index of 3 is pronounced 'cubed', so 5^3 is read 'five cubed'. The result is called a cube number.

Higher indices are read as 'to the power of', so 3^5 is read '3 to the power of 5'

3^5

index

base

examples

Evaluate 2^3

$$2 \times 2 \times 2 = 8$$

Write $7 \times 7 \times 7 \times 7$ using indices

$$= 7^4$$

exercise 5b

1. Write using indices:

   a) Five to the power nine

   b) Three to the power four

   c) Seventeen squared

   d) Forty one cubed

2. Write the following using indices:

   a) $4 \times 4 \times 4$

   b) $3 \times 3 \times 3 \times 3$

   d) $10 \times 10 \times 10 \times 10 \times 10$

   e) 9

3. Calculate:

   a) 3^2

   b) 2^3

   c) 10^2

   d) 2^4

   e) 0^4

   f) 3^3

   g) 4^2

   h) 10^3

   i) 2^1

   j) 10^4

   k) 1^8

   l) 5^3

   m) 6^3

   n) 1^{400}

   o) 400^1

   p) 2^6

4. Which of the following is the same as 2^5?

a) 2×5 b) $2 + 2 + 2 + 2 + 2$ c) $2 \times 2 \times 2 \times 2 \times 2$

5. Six squared = _____ and two cubed = _____

6. Write down the first 12 square numbers.

7. Write down the first 6 cube numbers.

8. True or False: a) 7^5 is the same as 7×5 b) 5^1 is the same as 5

9. Which of these is a cube number?

a) 1   b) 3   c) 6   d) 9

10. Which is bigger, 3^2 or 2^3?

11. Evaluate $5^2 - 2^3$

12. What's missing? Work out the missing indices:

a) $2^a = 8$ d) $3^d = 27$ g) $4^g = 64$

b) $2^b = 16$ e) $4^e = 4$ h) $3^k \times 3 = 27$

c) $2^c = 32$ f) $10^f = 10{,}000$ i) $2^l \times 2^l = 64$

- -

Square and Cube Numbers Puzzle ⭐ extra challenge

Using all the square and cube numbers that are less than or equal to 100, fill in the circles to make these sums true. You must use a different number in each circle.

◯ + ◯ = ◯

◯ + ◯ = ◯ + ◯

◯ + ◯ + ◯ + ◯ = ◯

index notation: fractional and decimal bases

learn by heart

Fractional bases require brackets, so $\frac{2}{3} \times \frac{2}{3}$ is written $\left(\frac{2}{3}\right)^2$

examples

Evaluate $\left(\frac{1}{2}\right)^4$

$\frac{1}{2} \times \frac{1}{2} \times \frac{1}{2} \times \frac{1}{2} = \frac{1}{16}$

Evaluate 0.2^2

$0.2 \times 0.2 = 0.04$

Think $2 \times 2 = 4$, each number is 10 times smaller, so the answer is 100 times smaller

exercise 5c

1. Work out the following, giving your answer as a fraction:

    a) $\frac{1}{3} \times \frac{1}{3}$

    b) $\frac{1}{2} \times \frac{1}{2} \times \frac{1}{2}$

    c) $\left(\frac{1}{4}\right)^2$

    d) $\left(\frac{1}{5}\right)^3$

    e) $\left(\frac{2}{3}\right)^3$

    f) $\left(\frac{5}{4}\right)^2$

2. Work out the following, giving your answer as a decimal:

    a) 0.1^2

    b) 0.2^2

    c) 0.3^2

    d) 0.4^2

    e) 0.5^2

    f) 0.2^3

    g) 0.3^3

    h) 0.2^4

3. True or false?

    a) $4^2 = 8$

    b) $5 = 5^1$

    c) $\left(\frac{1}{3}\right)^2 = \frac{2}{9}$

    d) $\left(\frac{2}{3}\right)^3 = \frac{6}{9}$

    e) $0.3^2 = 0.9$

    f) $\left(\frac{1}{10}\right)^2 = 0.01$

4. Which of the following is 0.001?

    a) $\frac{1}{10}$

    b) $\left(\frac{1}{10}\right)^2$

    c) $\left(\frac{1}{10}\right)^3$

    d) $\left(\frac{1}{10}\right)^4$

5. Work out

    a) $\left(\frac{1}{2}\right)^2 \times \frac{1}{3}$

    b) $\left(\frac{1}{2}\right)^2 \times \left(\frac{1}{2}\right)^3$

    c) $\left(\frac{4}{5}\right)^2 \times \left(\frac{1}{2}\right)^2$

6. True or false: $\left(\frac{1}{5}\right)^2 = 0.1$

7. Evaluate:

a) 9^1

e) $\left(\frac{7}{10}\right)^2$

i) 1^{20}

m) 2^4

b) $\left(\frac{1}{3}\right)^3$

f) 0.3^2

j) 3^3

n) 1.0^2

c) 4^2

g) 5^1

k) $\left(\frac{2}{5}\right)^3$

o) $\left(\frac{3}{10}\right)^3$

d) 0.1^3

h) 0^4

l) 1.2^2

p) 0.2^3

8. Which of these is the odd one out?

a) $\left(\frac{3}{10}\right)^2$

b) 0.9

c) 0.3^2

d) 0.09

9. Write each of the following as a decimal:

a) $\frac{1}{10}$

d) $\left(\frac{2}{10}\right)^3$

g) $\left(\frac{12}{10}\right)^2$

b) $\left(\frac{1}{10}\right)^2$

e) $\left(\frac{5}{10}\right)^2$

h) $\left(\frac{1}{2}\right)^3$

c) $\left(\frac{3}{10}\right)^2$

f) $\left(\frac{1}{5}\right)^2$

i) $\left(\frac{1}{100}\right)^2$

10. Evaluate $\left(1\frac{3}{4}\right)^2$

11. Evaluate $\left(2\frac{1}{5}\right)^2$

Investigate: The Last Digit ⭐ extra challenge

First, work out the following and look for patterns:

a) 5^1 b) 5^2 c) 5^3 d) 5^4 e) 5^5

Can you now work out the last digit of 5^{100} ?

Can you work out the last digit of $5^{1,000,000}$?

Try using a similar method to work out the last digit of 10^{100} and 2^{40}

index notation: negative bases

learn by heart

If the base number is negative, it requires a bracket, so -3 × -3 = $(-3)^2$

If the base is negative, and the index is **even**, the answer will be a **positive** number.

examples

Evaluate $(-3)^2$

$$-3 \times -3$$
$$= 9$$

Evaluate $(-1)^5$

$$-1 \times -1 \times -1 \times -1 \times -1$$
$$= -1$$

If the base is negative, and the index is **odd**, the answer will be a **negative** number.

exercise 5d

1. Evaluate:

    a) $(-7)^2$ c) $(-3)^3$ e) $(-2)^3$ g) $(-4)^2$

    b) $(-5)^2$ d) $(-1)^3$ f) $(-10)^2$ h) $(-2)^4$

2. True or False: $(-3)^2 = -9$

3. Copy and complete the table to show what happens for the powers of -1:

$(-1)^1$	$(-1)^2$	$(-1)^3$	$(-1)^4$	$(-1)^5$	$(-1)^6$	$(-1)^7$	$(-1)^8$	$(-1)^9$	$(-1)^{10}$	$(-1)^{11}$

4. Which of these equal -1?

    a) $(-1)^{18}$ b) $(-1)^{19}$ c) $(-1)^{20}$ d) $(-1)^{21}$

5. If we multiply **31** negative numbers, the answer will be _____ (choose positive or negative)

6. Which of the following will have a positive answer? Choose all that apply:

    a) 1^4 b) $(-2)^2$ c) 3^1 d) $(-3)^3$ e) $(-2)^3$

7. Evaluate:

    a) 3^3 b) $(-3)^3$ c) $(-4)^2$ d) 1^3

8. Given that $6^4 = 1296$, work out $(-6)^4$

9. Given that $6^5 = 7776$, work out $(-6)^5$

exercise 5e : mixed positive & negative bases

1. Evaluate:

   a) 2^3

   b) 1^4

   c) 5^2

   d) 3^1

   e) 3^3

   f) 2^4

   g) 1^{10}

   h) 7^1

   i) 6^2

   j) $(-4)^2$

   k) 4^3

   l) $(-2)^2$

   m) $(-1)^3$

   n) 8^2

   o) $(-3)^3$

   p) $(-5)^1$

2. Work out the missing indices:

   a) $6^? = 36$

   b) $4^? = 4$

   c) $5^? = 125$

   d) $2^? = 8$

   e) $(-3)^? = 9$

   f) $2^? = 32$

3. There are 6 false statements in this grid. Can you find them?

A $5^2 = 10$	F $2 \times 3 = 2^3$	K $2^3 = 8$	P $3 \times 3 \times 3 = 9$
B $2^5 = 32$	G $9^2 = 3$	L $2^2 \times 2 = 2^3$	Q $4^2 = 2^4$
C $(-1)^5 = -1$	H $7^6 > 7^5$	M $10^3 = 1{,}000$	R $1^1 = 1$
D $1^5 = 5$	I $3^3 = 27$	N $10^4 = 10{,}000$	S $(-3)^2 = 3^2$
E $8^2 = 64$	J $10^6 = 1$ million	O $3^4 = 12$	T $9^2 = 81$

4. Fill in the blanks with >, < or =

   a) 2^3 _____ 0

   b) $(-2)^3$ _____ 0

   c) $(-1)^6$ _____ 1

   d) $(-1)^{90}$ _____ 1

   e) 1^6 _____ 1^7

   f) $(-1)^7$ _____ 1^7

   g) 2^6 _____ 2^7

   h) (-2^4) _____ 0

   i) $(0.2)^3$ _____ $(-0.2)^3$

5. Annie says that $(-2)^{13} = 8192$. Explain why she must be wrong.

6. Evaluate $(-1)^{1{,}000{,}000}$

7. If $(-2)^b$ equals a positive number, then b is a:

   a) positive number   b) negative number   c) odd number   d) even number

Two Lies & a Truth

In each row, two statements are false and one is true.

Can you find the **true** statement?

	A	B	C
1	$2 \times 2 \times 2 = 6$	$2 \times 2 \times 2 = 8$	$2 \times 2 \times 2 = 10$
2	3^2 means 3×3	3^2 means $3 + 3$	3^2 means $3 - 3$
3	$(-3)^2 = 6$	$(-3)^2 = -9$	$(-3)^2 = 9$
4	$2^3 = 6$	$2^3 = 8$	$2^3 = -8$
5	$(-10)^2 = -20$	$(-10)^2 = 20$	$(-10)^2 = 100$
6	$1^5 = 1$	$1^5 = 5$	$1^5 = -1$
7	$3^3 = 9$	$3^3 = 27$	$3^3 = 6$
8	$6^1 = 36$	$6^1 = \frac{1}{6}$	$6^1 = 6$
9	$(-2)^3 = -8$	$(-2)^3 = 6$	$(-2)^3 = -6$
10	$(-3)^3 = -9$	$(-3)^3 = 9$	$(-3)^3 = -27$
11	$1^{400} = 1,400$	$1^{400} = 1$	$1^{400} = 400$
12	$5^2 = 10$	$5^2 = 7$	$5^2 = 25$
13	$(-3)^4 = -12$	$(-3)^4 = -81$	$(-3)^4 = 81$

index notation: mixed bases practice

examples

Evaluate $(4)^2$

$= 4 \times 4$
$= 16$

Evaluate $\left(\frac{2}{3}\right)^3$

$= \frac{2}{3} \times \frac{2}{3} \times \frac{2}{3}$
$= \frac{8}{27}$

Evaluate $(0.6)^2$

$= 0.6 \times 0.6$
$= 0.36$

Evaluate $\left(-\frac{1}{5}\right)^3$

$= -\frac{1}{5} \times -\frac{1}{5} \times -\frac{1}{5}$
$= -\frac{1}{125}$

exercise 5f

1. Evaluate:

   a) $\left(\frac{2}{5}\right)^2$

   b) 3^3

   c) $(-1)^5$

   d) 0.2^2

   e) $\left(\frac{1}{3}\right)^3$

   f) 1^{10}

   g) 46^1

   h) 9^2

   i) $(-2)^4$

2. Evaluate:

   a) $\left(-\frac{2}{3}\right)^2$

   b) $\left(-\frac{1}{2}\right)^3$

   c) $\left(-\frac{1}{3}\right)^3$

   d) $\left(-\frac{4}{7}\right)^2$

   e) $\left(-\frac{3}{2}\right)^3$

   f) $\left(-\frac{1}{5}\right)^3$

3. True or false?

   a) $(-3)^3 = 27$

   b) $\left(\frac{1}{3}\right)^2 = \frac{1}{6}$

   c) $3^1 = 1$

   d) $0^{10} = 0$

4. Which of the following will have a negative answer? Circle all that apply.

   a) $(-2)^2$

   b) $(-3)^3$

   c) $\left(\frac{1}{2}\right)^2$

   d) 0^3

   e) $(-1)^{50}$

5. Decide if the answer will be positive or negative:

   a) 1^{30}

   b) $(-1)^{30}$

   c) $(-1)^{31}$

   d) $(-2)^{15}$

   e) 2^{199}

   f) $(-3)^{55}$

6. Evaluate:

a) $(-2)^1$

b) $(-2)^2$

c) $(-2)^3$

d) $(-3)^2$

e) $(-1)^5$

f) $(-4)^2$

g) $\left(-\frac{1}{2}\right)^2$

h) $\left(-\frac{1}{2}\right)^3$

i) $\left(-\frac{1}{4}\right)^2$

j) $\left(-\frac{1}{3}\right)^3$

k) $\left(-\frac{3}{2}\right)^3$

l) $(-0.5)^2$

m) $(-0.2)^3$

n) $(-4)^1$

o) $(-3)^2 \times -3$

p) $\left(-\frac{1}{10}\right)^3$

7. Which of the following are true?

a) $5^3 > 5^2$

b) $(-2)^3 = 2^3$

c) $82^4 > 82^5$

d) $1^{84} = 1$

e) $(-1)^{10} = -1$

8. Given that $12^3 = 1728$, evaluate $(-12)^3$

9. Which of these is 1 million?

a) 10^2

b) 10^3

c) 10^4

d) 10^5

e) 10^6

10. Calculate

a) $(-4)^2 \times 3$

b) $\left(\frac{1}{3}\right)^2 \times \left(\frac{1}{2}\right)^2$

c) $3^2 \times \left(\frac{1}{3}\right)^2$

d) $0.2^2 \times 100$

e) 0.1×10^2

f) $(-5)^2 \times (-2)^2$

g) $1^4 \times 4^1$

h) $\left(\frac{1}{3}\right)^2 + \frac{4}{9}$

i) $\left(\frac{2}{5}\right)^2 - 0.16$

11. Given that $7^3 = 343$, work out:

a) $(-7)^3$

b) $\left(-\frac{1}{7}\right)^3$

c) $(-0.7)^3$

12. Given that $9^4 = 6561$, work out:

a) $(-9)^4$

b) $\left(-\frac{1}{9}\right)^4$

c) $\left(-\frac{2}{9}\right)^4$

further mixed bases problems (extension) ⭐ extra challenge

1. Work out the missing powers:

   a) $(-4)^a = 16$

   b) $(-2)^b = -8$

   c) $(-3)^c = 9$

   d) $(-5)^d = -125$

   e) $(-8)^e = -8$

   f) $(-1)^f = -1$

2. If a is an integer, and $(-3)^a > 0$, which of the following could be a?

   a) 1   b) 2   c) 3   d) 8   e) 50   f) 101

3. If is true that $2 \times a$ is the same as a^2, which of these could be a?

   a) 0   b) 1   c) -1   d) 2   e) -2

4. If $6 < (-2)^a < 100$, which of the following could be a?

   a) 1   b) 2   c) 3   d) 6   e) 7

5. Given that $14^3 = 2744$, work out:

   a) 1.4^3

   b) $(-14)^3$

   c) $\left(\frac{1}{14}\right)^3$

   d) $\left(1\frac{4}{10}\right)^3$

   e) 0.14^3

   f) $(-1.4)^3$

   g) 140^3

   h) $14^3 \div -100$

   i) $\left(-\frac{14}{100}\right)^3$

- -

investigate zero & negative indices

1. Copy and complete these power tables by looking for a pattern in each table:

a)

2^4	
2^3	
2^2	
2^1	
2^0	
2^{-1}	

b)

3^3	
3^2	
3^1	
3^0	
3^{-1}	
3^{-2}	

c)

5^3	
5^2	
5^1	
5^0	
5^{-1}	
5^{-2}	

d)

10^3	
10^2	
10^1	
10^0	
10^{-1}	
10^{-2}	

2. Look at what happens when the power is 0. Can you work out 92^0? 123^0?
   Explain what happens when we raise something to the power 0.

index notation: zero & negative indices

learn by heart

(except 0^0)

Any number to the power zero = 1

A negative power tells us to take the reciprocal of the base first & then apply the index (or the other way round)

examples

Evaluate 2^0

$= 1$

Evaluate $(5)^{-2}$

$= \left(\frac{1}{5}\right)^2 = \frac{1}{25}$

Evaluate $(3)^{-3}$

$3^3 = 27$, so $3^{-3} = \frac{1}{27}$

exercise 5g

1. Evaluate:

a) 6^0

b) $(-2)^0$

c) 10^{-2}

d) 1^0

e) 4^{-2}

f) 2^{-3}

g) 3^{-2}

h) 3^{-3}

i) $\left(\frac{1}{3}\right)^0$

j) 7^{-1}

2. True or False: $8^0 = 0$

3. Evaluate:

a) 8^2

b) 15^0

c) 6^1

d) 6^{-1}

e) 6^{-2}

f) 3^0

g) 2^{-3}

h) 9^{-2}

4. Can you work out the missing powers?

a) $6^? = 1$

b) $2^? = 8$

c) $4^? = \frac{1}{4}$

d) $0.2^? = 1$

e) $7^? = 49$

f) $5^? = \frac{1}{25}$

g) $2^? = \frac{1}{8}$

h) $2^? = 2$

i) $2^? = 1$

5. Which of these are less than 1? Choose all that apply.

a) 6^0

b) 5^{-1}

c) 2^1

d) 4^{-2}

6. Which of these is largest?

a) 2^3

b) 25^0

c) 1000^0

d) 1^{100}

e) 100^{-1}

7. Copy and complete these power tables:

a)

2^3	
2^2	
2^1	
2^0	
2^{-1}	
2^{-2}	
2^{-3}	

b)

10^3	
10^2	
10^1	
10^0	
10^{-1}	
10^{-2}	
10^{-3}	

c)

3^3	
3^2	
3^1	
3^0	
3^{-1}	
3^{-2}	
3^{-3}	

8. Write 10^{-2} as a decimal.

9. Work out:

a) $5^2 \times 5^0$

b) $2^3 \div 2$

c) $3^{-1} \times 3^{-1}$

d) $(3 \times 2)^0$

e) $\left(\frac{1}{3}\right)^2 \times 3$

f) $5^{-1} \times 5$

10. Explain why 0^{-3} is undefined.

- -

Arrange the Digits

$\boxed{-2}\ \boxed{-1}\ \boxed{0}\ \boxed{1}\ \boxed{2}\ \boxed{3}\ \boxed{4}\ \boxed{5}\ \boxed{6}$

Using each of these digits just once each, make the following statements true:

$$\square^{\square} = 0$$

$$\left(\frac{\square}{\square}\right)^{\square} = \frac{1}{32}$$

$$\left(\square\right)^{\square} = 1$$

$$\square^{\square} = \frac{1}{36}$$

mixed index notation practice

exercise 5h

1. Evaluate:

   a) 3^0

   b) $(-4)^2$

   c) 4^{-2}

   d) $\left(\frac{1}{2}\right)^2$

   e) 2^3

   f) $(-9)^2$

   g) $\left(\frac{3}{4}\right)^2$

   h) 5^1

   i) $(-3)^3$

   j) $\left(-\frac{1}{3}\right)^3$

   k) 2^{-3}

   l) 1^{20}

   m) $(-2)^3$

   n) $\left(\frac{1}{5}\right)^1$

   o) $(-1)^6$

2. Given that $4^5 = 1024$, work out the value of:

   a) $(-4)^5$

   b) 4^{-5}

   c) $\left(\frac{1}{4}\right)^5$

3. There are 10 **false** statements in this grid. Can you work out which ones?

A $5^{-1} = -5$	B $\left(\frac{2}{3}\right)^1 = \frac{2}{3}$	C $2^{-2} = \frac{1}{4}$	D $2^{-3} = -8$
E $3 \times 3 \times 3 = 9$	F $4^{-3} = \frac{1}{64}$	G $2^5 = 32$	H $1^0 = 1$
I $5^{-2} = \frac{1}{25}$	J $100^0 = 0$	K $\frac{1}{49} = 7^2$	L $2^{-1} = \frac{1}{2}$
M $3^3 = 27$	N $4^{-2} = \frac{1}{8}$	O $7^6 < 7^5$	P $4^3 = 12$
Q $2^{-3} = \frac{1}{6}$	R $1^5 = 5$	S $8 \times 2^{-1} = 4$	T $2^{-1} = \frac{1}{2}$

Odd One Out

In each box, cover up pairs that are equal.
Find the number that is left over.

A

2^3	16	8
1^3	6^2	4^2
36	12	1

B

3^3	1^8	5^2
25	8	27
2^4	1	16

C

49	81	11^2
12^1	121	5^3
7^2	125	3^4

D

2^4	10^3	8
4^3	32	64
1000	2^3	2^5

E

$\left(\frac{1}{2}\right)^3$	$\frac{1}{25}$	$\frac{1}{64}$
$\left(\frac{1}{4}\right)^3$	$\left(\frac{1}{4}\right)^2$	$\frac{1}{8}$
$\frac{1}{16}$	$\frac{1}{6}$	$\left(\frac{1}{5}\right)^2$

F

$\frac{4}{25}$	$\left(\frac{2}{3}\right)^3$	$\left(\frac{3}{5}\right)^2$
$\left(\frac{2}{3}\right)^2$	$\frac{8}{27}$	$\left(\frac{2}{5}\right)^2$
$\left(\frac{4}{5}\right)^3$	$\frac{9}{25}$	$\frac{4}{9}$

G

$(-1)^3$	8	4
$(-2)^2$	$(-1)^{10}$	-8
1	$(-2)^3$	-1

H

0^4	1	4
$(-1)^{19}$	19	0
5^0	19^1	-1

I

$\frac{1}{4}$	4^{-2}	5^2
5^{-1}	$\frac{1}{25}$	$\frac{1}{16}$
4^{-1}	$\frac{1}{5}$	25

J

$\frac{1}{64}$	6^{-2}	$\frac{1}{16}$
2^{-4}	8^{-2}	-16
$\frac{1}{36}$	16	4^2

K

2^{-1}	8^{-2}	4^0
1^0	3^{-4}	$\frac{1}{2}$
4^{-3}	2^2	9^{-2}

L

3^{-1}	4^{-1}	2^{-1}
0.5	5^{-1}	$0.\dot{3}$
0.3	0.2	0.25

Arrange the Digits ⭐ extra challenge

Using each of the digits just once, make all of statements true.

A

| 1 | 2 | 2 | 3 | 3 |
| 3 | 4 | 5 | 7 | 8 |

$$\square^{\square} = 2\,\square$$

$$\square^{\square} = 3\,\square$$

$$\square^{\square} = \square\,\square$$

B

| 1 | 2 | 2 | 4 | 4 |
| 5 | 6 | 6 | 8 | |

$$2^{\square} = \square$$

$$2^{\square} = \square\,\square$$

$$2^{\square} = \square\,\square\,\square$$

C

| 2 | 2 | 2 | 3 | 4 | 6 | 8 |

$$(0 \cdot \square)^{\square} > 0 \cdot 5$$

$$(\square)^{\square} = \square\,6$$

$$\left(\frac{\square}{\square}\right)^{2} = \frac{1}{4}$$

D

| -1 | 0 | 2 | 3 | 4 | 5 |

$$(\square)^{\square} < 0$$

$$(\square)^{\square} = 0$$

$$\left(\frac{1}{\square}\right)^{\square} = \frac{1}{8}$$

E

| -9 | -8 | -3 | -2 | -1 | 1 | 2 | 3 | 4 | 9 |

$$(\square)^{\square} = \frac{1}{4}$$

$$(\square)^{\square} = \square$$

$$(\square)^{\square} = \square$$

$$(\square)^{0} = \square$$

F

| -3 | -2 | 1 | 2 | 3 | 4 | 4 | 5 | 5 | 6 | 7 | 8 |

$$(\square)^{\square} = 1\,\square$$

$$\left(\frac{\square}{\square}\right)^{2} = 0 \cdot 0\,\square$$

$$\left(\frac{\square}{\square}\right)^{2} = 2\frac{\square}{9}$$

$$(\square)^{\square} = \frac{1}{\square}$$

multiplying with indices

learn by heart

$$3^{10} \times 3^2 = 3^{12}$$

Multiplication Law: *when multiplying with the same base, add the indices*

examples

Write $7^{-2} \times 7^{-4}$ as a power of 7

$= 7^{-2 + -4} = 7^{-6}$

Write $5^6 \times 5$ as a power of 5

$= 5^{6 + 1} = 5^7$

exercise 5i

1. Write as a power of 3:

   a) $3^2 \times 3^4$

   b) 3×3^2

   c) $3^{10} \times 3^{-2}$

   d) $3^7 \times 3^0$

   e) $3^3 \times 3^{-1}$

   f) $3 \times 3 \times 3$

   g) $3^4 \times 3^2 \times 3$

   h) $3^7 \times 3 \times 3^1$

   i) $3^8 \times 3 \times 3 \times 3$

2. Simplify the following, where possible.
   Two statements cannot be simplified using the multiplication law. Which two?

   a) $3^2 \times 3^5$

   b) $4^2 \times 4^3$

   c) $4^5 - 4^2$

   d) $3^0 \times 3^0$

   e) $3^4 + 3^2$

   f) $(-3)^2 \times (-3)^5$

   g) $6^{-2} \times 6^2$

   h) $5^{-4} \times 5^4$

   i) $8^{-2} \times 8^5$

3. True or false?

   a) $6^7 + 6^7 = 6^{14}$

   b) $6^7 \times 6^7 = 6^{49}$

   c) $6^7 \times 6^7 = 6^{14}$

   d) $6^7 \times 6^7 = 36^{14}$

4. Simplify, if possible:

   a) $0.5^3 \times 0.5^4$

   b) $\left(\frac{1}{5}\right)^2 \times \left(\frac{1}{5}\right)^4$

   c) $(-5)^3 \times (-5)^4$

   d) $5^{1.5} \times 5^{2.5}$

   e) $1^{27} \times 1^{400}$

   f) $4^{\frac{1}{5}} \times 4^{\frac{1}{5}}$

5. Evaluate the following: (be clever about it!)

   a) $7^{22} \times 7^{-20}$

   b) $12 \times 12 \times 12^{-1}$

   c) $(1.72 \times 147)^0$

Indices Match

Simplify each card as much as possible and then find a matching card at the bottom. Some of the answers are in index form, others have been evaluated.

A $3^{10} \times 3^{-9}$	**B** $12^3 \times 12^{-1}$	**C** $(-3)^2$	**D** $\left(\frac{1}{3}\right)^2$
E $12^2 \times 12^{-3}$	**F** $3^2 \times 3$	**G** $\left(\frac{1}{3}\right)^3$	**H** 1.4×3^0
I $\left(\frac{1}{12}\right)^2$	**J** $\left(-\frac{1}{9}\right)^1$	**K** $12^4 \times 12^6$	**L** 9×9^{-3}
M $3^3 - 3^2$	**N** $(-3)^2 \times (-3)^2$	**O** $3^4 \times 3^{-4}$	**P** 12^1
Q $(-3)^5 \times (-3)^{-2}$	**R** $(-3)^3 \div 9$	**S** $3^6 \times 3^4$	**T** $12^0 - 12^1$
U $9^7 \times 9^{-2}$	**V** $12^2 \times 10^{-1}$	**W** $\left(\frac{1}{3}\right)^{-3} \times \left(\frac{1}{3}\right)^4$	**X** $(-3)^{-1}$

- -

answers

-3	-11	81	$\frac{1}{81}$	12	144	9^5	$\frac{1}{3}$	9	14.4	27	3^{10}

$-\frac{1}{9}$	1	12^{10}	$\frac{1}{144}$	-27	$\frac{1}{27}$	$\frac{1}{9}$	$\frac{1}{12}$	$-\frac{1}{3}$	1.4	18	3

$$3^{10} \div 3^2 = 3^8$$

Division Law: *when dividing with the same base, subtract the indices*

examples

Write $5^8 \div 5^2$ as a power of 5

$$= 5^{8-2} = 5^3$$

Write $\dfrac{2^4}{2^{-3}}$ as a single power

$$= 2^{4--3} = 2^7$$

exercise 5j

1. Write as a single power:

   a) $3^5 \div 3^1$

   b) $4^{10} \div 4^3$

   c) $3^8 \div 3^2$

   d) $3^8 \div 3^8$

   e) $(-4)^3 \div (-4)^2$

   f) $8^5 \div 8^2$

   g) $6^4 \div 6^8$

   h) $5^4 \div 5^6$

   i) $8^{-2} \div 8^3$

2. True or False:

   a) $5^{10} \div 5^5 = 5^2$

   b) $10^7 \div 10^5 = 1^2$

   c) $\dfrac{5}{5^2} = 5 \div 5^2$

   d) $15^7 \div 5^3 = 3^4$

   e) $8^6 - 8^4 = 8^2$

   f) $10^5 \div 2^3 = 5^2$

3. Write as a single power of 2, if possible:

   a) $2^5 \div 2^2$

   b) $2^1 \div 2^4$

   c) $2^3 \div 2^5$

   d) $2^0 \div 2^3$

   e) $2^{-6} \div 2^5$

   f) $2^{-2} \div 2^5$

   g) $2^{-3} \div 2^3$

   h) $2^{-1} \div 2^5$

   i) $2^{-3} \div 2^{-5}$

   j) $2^7 \div 2^3$

   k) $\dfrac{2^6}{2^2}$

   l) $\dfrac{2^5}{2^3}$

   m) $\dfrac{2^5}{2^4}$

   n) $\dfrac{2^5}{2^0}$

   o) $\dfrac{2^{-2}}{2^5}$

   p) $\dfrac{2^3}{2^{-2}}$

   q) $\dfrac{2}{2^{-4}}$

   r) $\dfrac{2^{-3}}{2^{-2}}$

4. If we simplify $\dfrac{408^{409}}{408}$, the answer is:

    a) 408^{409} b) 409^{408} c) 408^{408} d) 407^{409}

5. Simplify, if possible:

    a) $3^7 \div 3^2$ e) $3^8 \times 3^2$ i) $5^{-2} \div 5^2$

    b) $(-2)^5 \times (-2)^3$ f) $10^2 \div 10^5$ j) $8^3 \div 8^{10}$

    c) $4^4 \div 4^0$ g) $6^4 \times 6$ k) $(-5)^8 \div 5^4$

    d) $5^6 \times 6^5$ h) $3^0 \times 3^{-4}$ l) $2^3 + 2^8$

6. Work out the missing powers:

    a) $4^{\square} \div 4^3 = 4^5$ e) $5^4 \div 5^{\square} = 5^{-3}$

    b) $3^{10} \div 3^{\square} = 3^5$ f) $10^{\square} \div 10 = 10^5$

    c) $2^{\square} \times 2^5 = 2^4$ g) $7^{-5} \times 7^{\square} = 1$

    d) $3^{\square} \times 3 = 3^{12}$ h) $5^8 \div 5^{\square} = 1$

7. Work out the value of $\dfrac{2400^{8500}}{2400^{8499}}$

true or false?

8. There are 5 false statements, can you find them?

A $4^3 = 12$	B $3^2 \times 3^4 = 3^8$	C $2^8 \div 2^4 = 2^4$	D $6^2 = 36$
E $2^3 \times 2 = 2^4$	F $9^2 \div 9^3 = 9^1$	G $4^3 \times 4^5 = 4^8$	H $8^0 = 1$
I $3^5 \div 3^5 = 1$	J $6^2 \div 6^4 = 6^2$	K $8^5 \times 8^3 = 8^8$	L $2^{15} \div 2^3 = 2^5$
M $6^2 - 6 = 30$	N $8^3 \div 8 = 8^2$	O $4^1 \times 5 = 20$	P $4^2 \div 4^3 = 4^{-1}$

9. Write as a power of 2:   a) $\dfrac{2^7 \times 2^{-3}}{2^5}$ b) $\dfrac{2 \times 2 \times 2^3}{2^{-3}}$

index laws (power law)

learn by heart

$$(2^3)^5 = 2^{15}$$

Power Law: When a base is raised to more than one index, multiply the indices

exercise 5k

1. Write as a single power:

   a) $(2^2)^4$

   b) $(4^3)^2$

   c) $(5^4)^5$

   d) $(2^2)^2$

   e) $(5^8)^0$

   f) $(6^{-2})^3$

2. Which of the following equal 2^8?

   a) $(2^6)^2$

   b) $(2^4)^4$

   c) $(2^2)^4$

   d) 2^4

3. Which of the following equal 4^6?

   a) $(4^{-2})^{-3}$

   b) $2^3 \times 2^3$

   c) $(2^3)^2$

   d) $(4^{-1})^6$

4. Write as a single power of 5:

   a) $(5^{0.1})^2$

   b) $(5^3)^{0.2}$

   c) $(5^{-3})^0$

   d) $(5^{100})^1$

matching activity

A $5^3 \times 5^2$	**B** $(5^5)^2$	**C** $\dfrac{5^6}{5^2}$
D $(5^{-2})^2$	**E** $5^{-4} \times 5^2$	**F** $5^7 \div 5^{-2}$
G 5^{-1}	**H** $\dfrac{5^8}{5^2}$	**I** $5^6 \times 5$
J $\dfrac{5^6}{5^3}$	**K** $\dfrac{5^7}{5^7}$	**L** $(5^{-1})^{-1}$

5^3 5^{-4}

1 5^7

5^6 5

5^9 $\dfrac{1}{5}$

5^4 5^5

5^{-2} 5^{10}

A	B	C	D	E	F	G	H	I	J	K	L

Mixed Laws of Indices
Code Breaker

Write each of the following as a single power using the laws of indices. Find your answer in the code box. Write the words down as you go to reveal a hidden joke!

code box

5^{-11} = don't	5^{-3} = will	5^4 = hair	5^{11} = an
5^{-10} = forever	5^{-2} = and	5^5 = on	5^{12} = you
5^{-9} = over	5^{-1} = never	5^6 = talk	5^{13} = can
5^{-8} = to	5^0 = go	5^7 = drink	5^{14} = cake
5^{-7} = number?	5 = ever!	5^8 = wish	5^{15} = Because
5^{-6} = paper	5^2 = Why	5^9 = should	5^{16} = cable
5^{-4} = they	5^3 = book	5^{10} = irrational	5^{17} = What

a) $5^7 \div 5^5 = \underline{5^2} = $ **Why**

b) $(5^3)^3 = \underline{\hspace{1cm}} = $

c) $5^{10} \times 5^2 = \underline{\hspace{1cm}} = $

d) $5^3 \times 5^{-4} = \underline{\hspace{1cm}} = $

e) $\dfrac{5^8}{5^2} = \underline{\hspace{1cm}} = $

f) $(5^4)^{-2} = \underline{\hspace{1cm}} = $

g) $5^{10} \times 5 = \underline{\hspace{1cm}} = $

h) $\dfrac{5^{11}}{5} = \underline{\hspace{1cm}} = $

i) $5^{-2} \div 5^5 = \underline{\hspace{1cm}} = $

j) $(5^{-3})^{-5} = \underline{\hspace{1cm}} = $

k) $5 \div 5^5 = \underline{\hspace{1cm}} = $

l) $(5^3)^{-1} = \underline{\hspace{1cm}} = $

m) $5^7 \times 5^{-7} = \underline{\hspace{1cm}} = $

n) $\dfrac{5^4}{5^{-1}} = \underline{\hspace{1cm}} = $

o) $5^{-3} \times 5^{-7} = \underline{\hspace{1cm}} = $

p) $\dfrac{5^{-10}}{5^{-8}} = \underline{\hspace{1cm}} = $

q) $\dfrac{5^{-7}}{5^{-8}} = \underline{\hspace{1cm}} = $

indices & index laws mixed practice

exercise 5

1. Evaluate:

   a) 4^2
   b) $(-3)^2$
   c) $(-2)^3$
   d) 1^4

   e) 5^1
   f) 0^3
   g) $(-1)^6$
   h) 10^4

2. True or false? $2^4 = 4^2$

3. True or false? $2^3 = 3^2$

4. Evaluate:

   a) $\left(\frac{1}{3}\right)^2$
   b) $\left(\frac{2}{5}\right)^2$
   c) $\left(\frac{1}{10}\right)^3$
   d) $\left(-\frac{3}{4}\right)^2$

5. Evaluate:

   a) $(-2)^1$
   b) $(-2)^2$
   c) $(-2)^3$
   d) $(-2)^4$

6. Work out:

   a) 8^{-1}
   b) 9^{-2}
   c) 7^0
   d) 3^{-3}

7. Write as a single power of 3:

   a) $3^5 \times 3^2$
   b) $3^6 \div 3^2$
   c) $3^8 \times 3$

   d) $\dfrac{3^5}{3^3}$
   e) $\dfrac{3^2}{3^5}$
   f) $3^4 \times 3^4$

   g) $(3^5)^2$
   h) $(3^2)^{-3}$
   i) $(3^{-4})^{-2}$

8. The table on the right shows some powers of 7.
   Use the table to work out the value of each of these:

   a) $7^2 \times 7^3$

   b) $7^8 \div 7^4$

   c) $(7^3)^2$

   d) $7 \times 7^2 \times 7^3$

   e) $\dfrac{7^9}{7^3}$

   f) $(7^2)^4$

$7^1 = 7$
$7^2 = 49$
$7^3 = 343$
$7^4 = 2401$
$7^5 = 16{,}807$
$7^6 = 117{,}649$
$7^7 = 823{,}543$
$7^8 = 5{,}764{,}801$

9. Which of these equal 1?

   a) 10^0
   b) 1^{50}
   c) $4^{-5} \times 4^5$
   d) $9^{10} \div 9^{10}$

combining index laws ⭐ extra challenge

examples

Simplify $\dfrac{4^8 \times 4}{4^{-5}}$

$$= \dfrac{4^9}{4^{-5}} = 4^{9--5} = 4^{14}$$

Write $\dfrac{(2^4)^2 \times 2^3}{2 \times 2^2}$ as a single power of 2:

$$= \dfrac{2^8 \times 2^3}{2^3} = 2^{8+3-3} = 2^8$$

exercise 5m

1. Write as a single power of 2, if possible:

   a) $(2^2)^4 \times 2^5$

   b) $(2^3)^2 \div 2^4$

   c) $(2^4)^5 \times (2^3)^{-2}$

   d) $(2^{-2})^4 \div 2$

   e) $(2^3 \times 2^5)^2$

   f) $(2^1 \times 2^5)^3$

   g) $(2^{-3} \times 2^{-2})^5$

   h) $(2^5 \times 2^5)^0$

   i) $\left(\dfrac{2^0}{2^2}\right)^2$

   j) $\left(\dfrac{2^4}{2^2}\right)^2$

   k) $\left(\dfrac{2^3}{2}\right)^3$

   l) $\left(\dfrac{2^2}{2^{-2}}\right)^3$

2. Write as a power of 4:

   a) $\dfrac{4^3 \times 4^2}{4}$

   b) $\left(\dfrac{4^3}{4}\right)^{-2}$

   c) $4^{-2} \times \left(\dfrac{4^3}{4}\right)^2$

   d) $\dfrac{4^5 \times 4^{-3}}{4^{10}}$

   e) $(4^2 \times 4^{-3})^3$

   f) $\dfrac{4^7}{4^2} \times \dfrac{4^3}{4}$

   g) $\dfrac{4 \times (4^2)^3}{4^5}$

   h) $\dfrac{4^5}{4} \div \dfrac{4^2}{4^3}$

   i) $(4^{-2} \div 4^5)^{-3}$

- -

Arrange the Digits

Arrange the digits 1,2,3,4 and 5 to make this statement true:

$$\dfrac{2^\square \times 2^\square}{2^\square} = (2^\square)^\square$$

roots (integers)

learn by heart

Square Numbers: $1, 4, 9, 16, 25, 36, 49, 64, 81, 100, 121, 144$

Cube Numbers: $1, 8, 27, 64, 125, 216, 343$

$\sqrt{}$ is read 'square root' | $\sqrt[3]{}$ is read 'cube root' | $\sqrt[4]{}$ is read 'fourth root'

Although 6^2 and $(-6)^2$ both make 36, the $\sqrt{}$ symbol refers to the positive root only, so $\sqrt{36} = 6$

examples

Evaluate $\sqrt{49}$
$= 7$

Evaluate $\sqrt[4]{16}$
$= 2$

This means, which number, to the power 4, equals 16?

exercise 5n

1. Evaluate:

   a) $\sqrt{25}$

   b) $\sqrt{49}$

   c) $\sqrt[3]{8}$

   d) $\sqrt{4}$

   e) $\sqrt[3]{27}$

   f) $\sqrt[4]{16}$

   g) $\sqrt{100}$

   h) $\sqrt[5]{32}$

   i) $\sqrt[3]{64}$

   j) $\sqrt{144}$

   k) $\sqrt{0}$

   l) $\sqrt{1}$

   m) $\sqrt[3]{1}$

   n) $\sqrt[4]{1}$

   o) $\sqrt[5]{1}$

2. Work out:

   a) the square root of 9

   b) the square of 9

   c) the cube root of 8

   d) the square root of 100

   e) the cube of 3

   f) the fourth root of 1

   g) the square of 4

   h) the cube root of 64

   i) the square root of 4

   j) the square of 8

3. Work out: a) $\sqrt[100]{1}$

   b) $\sqrt[200]{1}$

4. Which of these are square numbers? Select three answers.

   a) 1   b) 2   c) 5   d) 8   e) 9   f) 100

5. Evaluate:

   a) 4^2

   b) $\sqrt[3]{1000}$

   c) $(-3)^2$

   d) $\sqrt{64}$

   e) 3^3

   f) $\sqrt[3]{125}$

   g) $\sqrt[4]{16}$

   h) 2^3

   i) 1^5

   j) 0^3

   k) $\sqrt{25}$

   l) $\sqrt[3]{8}$

   m) 6^3

   n) $(-3)^3$

   o) 5^1

   p) $\sqrt{144}$

6. Put these in order of size, starting with the smallest:

A	B	C	D
$\sqrt{36}$	3^3	2^4	$\sqrt[3]{64}$

   ___ ___ ___ ___

7. If $6^8 = 1{,}679{,}616$, what is $\sqrt[8]{1{,}679{,}616}$?

8. Calculate:

   a) $\sqrt{4} \times 3^2$

   b) $\sqrt{36} \times 2^3$

   c) $4^1 \times \sqrt{25}$

   d) $\sqrt[3]{27} \div 3$

   e) $18 \div \sqrt{81}$

   f) $1^5 + 1^3$

   g) $9 \div \sqrt{9}$

   h) $2^3 \div \sqrt[3]{8}$

   i) $2^4 \div \sqrt{16}$

9. Fill in the blanks with >, < or =

   a) 2^3 _____ 3^2

   b) 2^4 _____ 4^2

   c) $\sqrt{9}$ _____ 4^2

   d) $\sqrt[3]{64}$ _____ $\sqrt{64}$

   e) $\sqrt[5]{1}$ _____ $\sqrt[6]{1}$

   f) 1^9 _____ 8^1

10. If $\sqrt{a} = \sqrt[3]{a}$, what could a be?

roots (decimals) 🖩

learn by heart

The square root of a square number is an integer

The cube root of a cube number is an integer

Surd: the root of an integer that is not a square number or cube number etc, e.g. $\sqrt{7}$ or $\sqrt[3]{5}$. The result is an irrational number.

recall this is a decimal that continues forever with no repeating pattern...

exercise 50

1. Which of these have decimal answers?

    a) $\sqrt{9}$ b) $\sqrt{10}$ c) $\sqrt{12}$ d) $\sqrt{16}$ e) $\sqrt{100}$

2. Which of the following have integer answers?

    a) $\sqrt{5}$ b) $\sqrt{16}$ c) $\sqrt[3]{27}$ d) $\sqrt[3]{2}$ e) $\sqrt{1}$

3. Which of the following have irrational answers?

    a) $\sqrt{5}$ b) $\sqrt{16}$ c) $\sqrt[3]{27}$ d) $\sqrt[3]{2}$ e) $\sqrt{1}$

4. Use your calculator to evaluate the following.
    If the answer is a decimal, round it to 2 decimal places.

    a) $\sqrt{10}$ c) $\sqrt[3]{20}$ e) $\sqrt[3]{100}$

    b) $\sqrt{9}$ d) $\sqrt{50}$ f) $\sqrt[3]{1000}$

5. Sort these numbers into the correct box:

    $\sqrt{16}$ $\sqrt{49}$ $\sqrt{10}$

    $\sqrt[3]{27}$ $\sqrt{0}$ $\sqrt[4]{1}$

    $\sqrt[3]{9}$ $\sqrt[3]{64}$ $\sqrt[4]{16}$

    $\sqrt{7}$ $\sqrt[3]{2}$ $\sqrt{3}$

Answer is an integer	Answer is a decimal

6. Which of these are surds? Select three answers:

   a) $\sqrt{9}$ b) $\sqrt{10}$ c) $\sqrt{11}$ d) $\sqrt{16}$ e) $\sqrt{18}$ f) $\sqrt{25}$

7. Which of these are more than 6? You can use your calculator to help you.

   a) $\sqrt{34}$ b) $\sqrt{35}$ c) $\sqrt{36}$ d) $\sqrt{37}$ e) $\sqrt{38}$

8. Which of these are more than 7? You can use your calculator to help you.

   a) $\sqrt{48}$ b) $\sqrt{49}$ c) $\sqrt{50}$ d) $\sqrt{51}$ e) $\sqrt{52}$

9. Which of these are more than 8? You can use your calculator to help you.

   a) $\sqrt{61}$ b) $\sqrt{62}$ c) $\sqrt{63}$ d) $\sqrt{64}$ e) $\sqrt{65}$

10. Can you predict which of these will be more than 9, without using your calculator?

   a) $\sqrt{80}$ b) $\sqrt{81}$ c) $\sqrt{82}$ d) $\sqrt{83}$ e) $\sqrt{84}$

11. Which part of the diagram should each of these numbers be in?

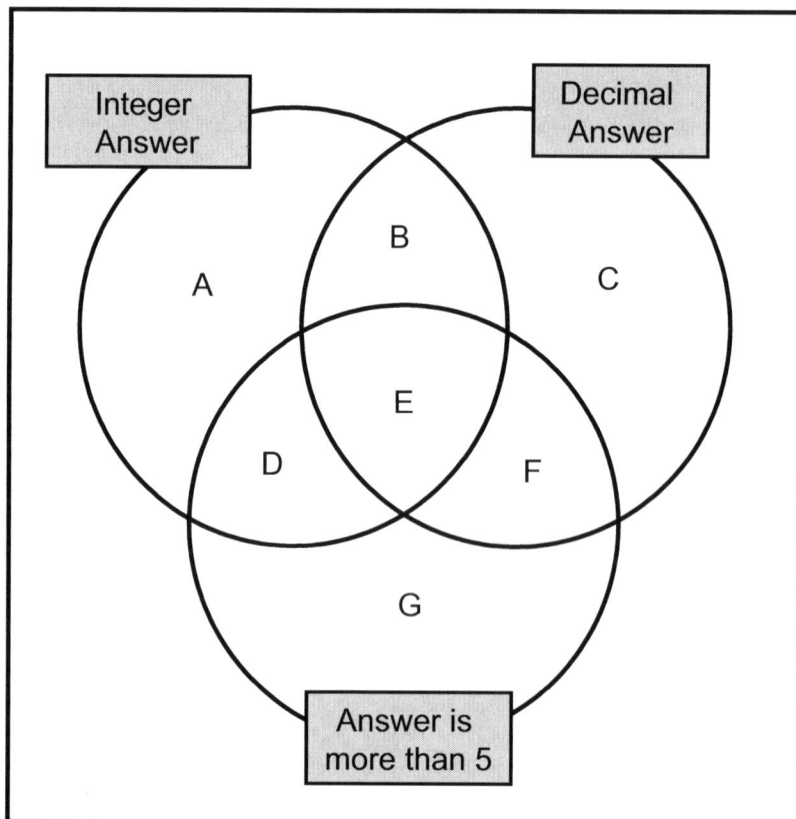

$\sqrt{16}$ $\sqrt{5}$ $\sqrt[3]{100}$

$\sqrt[3]{1}$ $\sqrt{144}$ $\sqrt{32}$

$\sqrt[3]{90}$ $\sqrt[4]{16}$ $\sqrt{99}$

$\sqrt{0}$ $\sqrt[3]{216}$ $\sqrt[3]{130}$

Integer Answer

Decimal Answer

A   B   C

D   E   F

G

Answer is more than 5

estimating roots

example

Estimate $\sqrt{15}$ $\sqrt{9} = 3$ and $\sqrt{16} = 4$, so ≈ 3.9	$\sqrt{50}$ is between __7__ and __8__ $\sqrt{49} = 7$ and $\sqrt{64} = 8$

exercise 5p

1. For each root, say which two integers it is between:

   a) $\sqrt{20}$ b) $\sqrt{30}$ c) $\sqrt{70}$

   d) $\sqrt{42}$ e) $\sqrt{29}$ f) $\sqrt{12}$

   g) $\sqrt{95}$ h) $\sqrt{130}$ i) $\sqrt{51}$

2. Estimate the following roots:

   a) $\sqrt{60}$ b) $\sqrt{98}$ c) $\sqrt{140}$ d) $\sqrt{5}$

3. Which of these are more than 10?

   a) $\sqrt{22}$ b) $\sqrt{50}$ c) $\sqrt{105}$ d) $\sqrt{1000}$

mixed powers and roots practice

1. Evaluate:

   a) 3^2 f) $(-9)^2$ k) $\sqrt[3]{8}$ p) $\sqrt{100}$

   b) 8^2 g) $(-3)^3$ l) $\sqrt{1}$ q) $\sqrt{144}$

   c) 5^3 h) $(-1)^2$ m) $\sqrt[3]{1}$ r) $\sqrt[3]{64}$

   d) 4^3 i) $(-1)^3$ n) $\sqrt[4]{1}$ s) $\sqrt{49}$

   e) $(-2)^2$ j) $(-2)^3$ o) $\sqrt[5]{1}$ t) $\sqrt[5]{32}$

2. Which of the following have negative answers?

   a) $(-2)^2$ b) $(-2)^3$ c) $(-2)^4$ d) $(-2)^5$ e) $(-2)^6$

3. Which of these numbers are surds?

   a) $\sqrt{6}$ b) $\sqrt{7}$ c) $\sqrt{8}$ d) $\sqrt{9}$ e) $\sqrt{10}$ f) $\sqrt{11}$

learn by heart

A negative number cannot be square rooted, since no number multiplied by itself equals a negative number.

examples

Evaluate $\sqrt{-16}$

$= undefined$

Evaluate $\sqrt[3]{-8}$

$= -2$

Evaluate $\sqrt{\frac{9}{4}}$

$= \frac{3}{2}$

exercise 5q

1. Evaluate the following, if possible:

   a) $\sqrt[3]{-1}$

   b) $\sqrt[3]{-27}$

   c) $\sqrt[3]{-8}$

   d) $\sqrt{-4}$

   e) $\sqrt[3]{-1000}$

   f) $\sqrt{16}$

   g) $\sqrt{81}$

   h) $\sqrt[3]{8}$

   i) $\sqrt{25}$

   j) $\sqrt{36}$

   k) $-\sqrt{25}$

   l) $\sqrt{-64}$

   m) $\sqrt{-1}$

   n) $\sqrt{-25}$

   o) $\sqrt{-16}$

   p) $\sqrt[5]{-32}$

2. Evaluate, if possible:

   a) $\sqrt{\frac{16}{25}}$

   b) $\sqrt{\frac{9}{100}}$

   c) $\left(\frac{1}{3}\right)^3$

   d) $\left(\frac{1}{4}\right)^2$

   e) $\sqrt{\frac{1}{49}}$

   f) $\left(\frac{2}{3}\right)^3$

   g) $\left(\frac{3}{4}\right)^3$

   h) $\sqrt[3]{\frac{8}{27}}$

3. Which of the following is undefined?

   a) $\sqrt[3]{-64}$

   b) $\sqrt[4]{-64}$

   c) $\sqrt[5]{-64}$

   d) $\sqrt[6]{-64}$

   e) $\sqrt[7]{-64}$

4. Decide if each of these roots will be an integer, a decimal or undefined:

   a) $\sqrt{49}$

   c) $\sqrt{-16}$

   e) $\sqrt[3]{-16}$

   g) $\sqrt{0}$

   b) $\sqrt{50}$

   d) $\sqrt{36}$

   f) $\sqrt{\frac{1}{2}}$

   h) $\sqrt[4]{16}$

Sorting Roots ⭐ extra challenge

Sort these roots into the correct box below:

$\sqrt{25}$ $\sqrt{1}$ $\sqrt[3]{-8}$ $\sqrt[4]{1}$ $\sqrt[3]{0.5}$ $\sqrt[3]{-9}$

$\sqrt{30}$ $\sqrt{0}$ $\sqrt{-8}$ $\sqrt[3]{10}$ $\sqrt[4]{10}$ $\sqrt[3]{100}$

$\sqrt[3]{27}$ $\sqrt{100}$ $\sqrt[3]{64}$ $\sqrt{-1}$ $\sqrt{64}$ $\sqrt{1000}$

A	a positive integer (7 answers)	B	a negative integer (1 answer)

C	a positive decimal (6 answers)	D	a negative decimal (1 answer)

E	none of the above (3 answers)

Mixed Powers and Roots Challenge ⊞ ⭐ extra challenge

1. Evaluate, if possible:

   a) 3^3

   b) 2^4

   c) $(-3)^3$

   d) $(2^2)^3$

   e) $\sqrt{64}$

   f) $3^2 \times 3$

   g) $2^3 \div 2^5$

   h) $\left(\frac{1}{3}\right)^2$

   i) $\sqrt{-4}$

   j) $\sqrt[3]{64}$

   k) $-\sqrt{49}$

   l) 6^{-2}

   m) $\sqrt[3]{-8}$

   n) $3^5 \times 3^{-3}$

   o) 5^0

   p) $\left(\frac{5}{2}\right)^1$

   q) $\left(\frac{1}{4}\right)^2$

   r) $3^1 \times 3^3 \div 3^5$

   s) $\sqrt{9}$

   t) $\frac{2^2}{2^{-2}}$

2. Which of these numbers are irrational?

   a) $\sqrt{16}$ b) $\sqrt{6}$ c) $\sqrt{-1}$ d) $\frac{1}{2}$ e) $\sqrt[3]{27}$ f) $\frac{1}{7}$ g) $-3.\dot{2}$ h) $\sqrt{4}$

3. Give an example of an irrational number between 4 and 5.

4. Does zero have a square root?

5. Work out $\sqrt[3]{4 \times 4 \times 4 \times 4 \times 4 \times 4}$

6. Work out $\sqrt[4]{5 \times 5 \times 5 \times 5 \times 5 \times 5 \times 5 \times 5}$

7. Work out $\sqrt[6]{3^{12}}$

8. Explain why $\sqrt{-25}$ cannot be calculated.

9. If $a \times a = 36$ what are the two possible values for a?

10. True or False: $\sqrt{2.5} = 0.5$

11. Which integer is closest to $\sqrt{8}$?

12. Calculate $\sqrt{0.09}$

really tricky index questions

13. Evaluate the following: (give your answer as an integer or fraction)

   a) $\left(\dfrac{-4}{2^2 \times (-2)^3}\right)^2$

   b) $\left(\dfrac{-2 \times 2^3}{(-2)^3}\right)^{-2}$

   c) $\sqrt{\dfrac{2^2 \times 2^5}{2^3}}$

order of operations 1

learn by heart

Addition and subtraction have equal & lowest priority. When a calculation only involves adding and subtracting, just read from left to right.

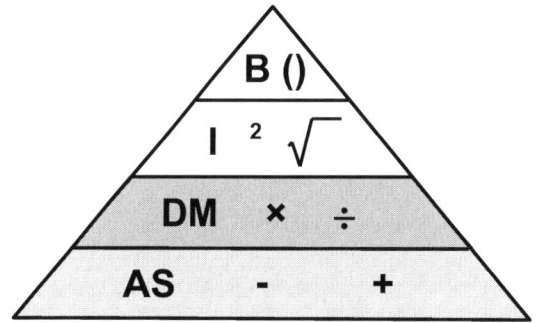

Divisions and multiplications have more impact on the size of the answer, so they have higher priority. Calculate these **before** additions and subtractions.

Divisions can be written with a fraction bar, e.g. $\frac{5 \times 3}{6 - 1}$
In this case, calculate numerator and denominator seperately and then divide

examples

Calculate 30 - 3 × 5

$$= 30 - 15 = 15$$

Calculate 4 - 2 + 1

$$= 3$$

Calculate $\frac{4 + 8}{2}$

$$= 12 \div 2 = 6$$

Work out the multiplication first, so replace 3 × 5 with 15, then read from left to right

Just read from left to right – addition and subtraction have equal priority.

exercise 5r

1. Work out:

   a) 10 - 8 + 2

   b) 4 + 3 × 2

   c) 20 ÷ 4 - 2

   d) 10 - 6 ÷ 2

   e) 3 × 5 + 4

   f) 10 - 8 ÷ 2

2. Work out:

   a) 10 + 5 ÷ 5

   b) $\frac{10 + 5}{5}$

   c) $\frac{10}{5}$ + 5

   d) 8 - 4 + 2

   e) $\frac{20}{4 - 3}$

   f) 3 × 2 + 5

   g) 5 + 24 ÷ 4 + 2

   h) 24 ÷ 2 + 4 × 3

   i) 3 × 4 - 7

   f) $\frac{9 - 3}{3}$

   i) 2 × 4 × 5

   l) 18 ÷ 2 - 3

3. True or false: 9 - 3 + 2 = 4

4. Calculate:

a) $\dfrac{5 \times 6}{3} - 4$

b) $\dfrac{18 - 2}{10 - 6}$

c) $12 - \dfrac{9}{3}$

d) $\dfrac{20 - 2}{9} - 10$

e) $\dfrac{18}{5 - 2} - 7$

f) $\dfrac{15}{3} + 4 \times \dfrac{10}{2}$

g) $5 - \dfrac{8 + 2}{3 - 1}$

h) $\dfrac{16}{2} \times \dfrac{25 - 3}{10 + 1}$

i) $9 - \dfrac{30}{2 \times 3} - 2$

j) $4 - \dfrac{8}{5 - 4} + 3 \times \dfrac{5}{5}$

k) $6 \times \dfrac{6}{2} - 6 \div \dfrac{9}{3}$

l) $20 - \dfrac{16 + 4}{3 - 4}$

- -

Order of Operations Puzzle

Can you use the numbers in the grid below to make the sums true? Use each number once only.

18	4	10	2
3	5	6	8
2	8	6	5

A $\boxed{2}$ + $\boxed{3}$ × $\boxed{}$ = $\boxed{17}$

B $\boxed{3}$ + $\boxed{}$ × $\boxed{4}$ = $\boxed{11}$

C $\boxed{5}$ + $\boxed{}$ ÷ $\boxed{5}$ = $\boxed{7}$

D $\boxed{}$ + $\boxed{5}$ ÷ $\boxed{5}$ = $\boxed{}$

E $\boxed{}$ - $\boxed{2}$ × $\boxed{5}$ = $\boxed{8}$

F $\boxed{}$ - $\boxed{8}$ ÷ $\boxed{}$ = $\boxed{2}$

G $\boxed{}$ - $\boxed{5}$ + $\boxed{}$ = $\boxed{6}$

H $\boxed{8}$ × $\boxed{}$ ÷ $\boxed{}$ = $\boxed{8}$

order of operations 2

learn by heart

Indices, including roots, have a bigger impact than the four operations (+ - ÷ ×) so they have higher priority and should be calculated first.

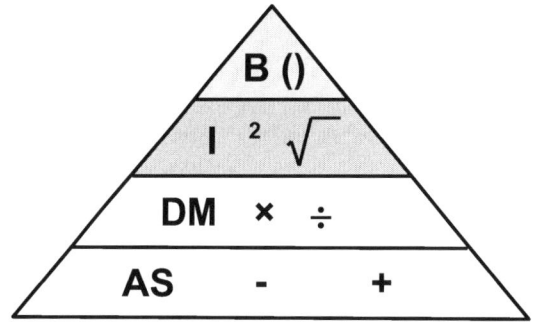

B ()

I ^{2} $\sqrt{\ }$

DM × ÷

AS - +

Brackets create a group of calculations that should be given highest priority.

examples

Calculate $(9 - (3 - 4)) \times 2$
$= (9 - -1) \times 2$
$= 10 \times 2 = 20$

Start with the innermost bracket first $(3 - 4)$

Calculate $3 + 2^2$
$= 3 + 4 = 7$

Calculate -3^2
$= -9$

Work out the index first – notice this is not $(-3)^2$

exercise 5s

1. Work out:

    a) $4 + 3^2$

    b) 2×3^2

    c) $16 - 3^2$

    d) $5 - 3^2$

    e) $10 - 2^3$

    f) $20 - 3^3$

    g) $20 \div 2^2$

    h) $2^3 + 3^2$

    i) $3^2 - 2^2$

    j) $(10 - 3)^2$

    k) $(1 + 2 \times 3)^2$

    l) $(9 - 4) \times 3^2$

2. Calculate:

    a) $6 \times (3 + 5)$

    b) $20 \div (4 + 1)$

    c) $\sqrt{9} + 7$

    d) $(3 + 2) \times (5 - 2)^2$

    e) $10 \div (1 - 2)^2$

    f) $6 - (5 - 10)$

    g) $(-6 + 3) \times (-2 - 1)$

    h) $5 - (3 + (2 \times 5))$

    i) $(\sqrt{4} + 5)^2$

    j) $10 \times (3 + (-2)^2)$

    k) $(-3 - 5) \times (8 - 10)$

    l) $4 + (3 - (8 + 1))$

3. Put brackets into each of these calculations to make them true, if required:

a) $3 \times 5 + 4 = 27$

b) $4 + 3 \times 5 + 1 = 20$

c) $8 - 2 \times 6 = 36$

d) $10 - 4^2 = 36$

e) $18 - 9 \div 3 = 15$

f) $7 \times 3 \times 3 = 63$

g) $20 - 6 + 3 = 11$

h) $15 - 6 \div 3 = 3$

i) $8 - 3^2 = 25$

j) $5 + 3 \times 2^2 = 41$

k) $5 + 2 \times 3 + 1 = 28$

l) $3 + 4^2 = 49$

4. Use the numbers on the right to make this calculation true:

$$\boxed{} \times \boxed{} - \left(\boxed{} \times \boxed{} + \boxed{} \right) = 7$$

$\boxed{1}$ $\boxed{2}$ $\boxed{4}$

$\boxed{6}$ $\boxed{8}$

- -

mixed calculation problems ⭐ extra challenge

1. Work out:

a) $-3 \times 4 + 2$

b) $-1 + 2 \times -3$

c) $9 - -1 \times 6$

d) $12 \div -3 + -1$

e) $(-6)^2 + -6$

f) $5 + -5 \times -7$

g) $(-5 + -3) \times 4$

h) $8 - (-2 + -2)$

i) $(-2 + 5)^2$

2. Work these out, giving your answers in the simplest form:

a) $\frac{2}{5} + \frac{1}{5} \times 2$

b) $\frac{3}{4} - \frac{1}{2} \times \frac{1}{2}$

c) $\frac{1}{6} \times 2 + \frac{1}{2}$

d) $\left(\frac{2}{3}\right)^2 - \frac{1}{3}$

e) $1 - \frac{2}{5} \times \frac{1}{2}$

f) $\frac{1}{5} + \frac{4}{5} \div 2$

g) $\left(\frac{1}{2} + \frac{1}{4}\right)^2$

h) $\sqrt{\frac{4}{9}} + \frac{2}{9}$

i) $\sqrt{\frac{3}{16}} - \frac{1}{8}$

Power Puzzles

Work out the missing numbers.

1 positive integers

A
$(3 + \underline{\quad})^2 = 25$

B
$4^3 + \underline{\quad}^2 = 73$

C
$100 - \underline{\quad}^2 = 36$

D
$\underline{\quad}^3 + \underline{\quad}^2 = 10$

E
$(7 - \underline{\quad})^3 = 27$

F
$\underline{\quad}^2 - 3 \times 4 = 13$

G
$2^{\square} + 3^2 = 25$

H
$\underline{\quad}^2 \div 5^2 = 4$

I
$4 \times \underline{\quad}^2 = 64$

J
$(12 - \underline{\quad})^2 = 81$

K
$(\underline{\quad} \times 2)^3 = 1000$

L
$(3 + \underline{\quad})^3 = 64$

2 positive and negative integers

A
$\underline{\quad}^3 + 2 = -6$

B
$(-2)^2 + \underline{\quad} = 12$

C
$(4 - \underline{\quad})^3 = -1$

D
$\underline{\quad}^3 + (-2)^3 = -16$

E
$(4 - 2 \times 3)^2 = \underline{\quad}$

F
$5 \times \underline{\quad}^3 = -40$

G
$(-1 \times \underline{\quad})^3 = 27$

H
$(-5)^2 + \underline{\quad}^3 = 26$

I
$(-8)^2 \div \underline{\quad} = 32$

J
$(\underline{\quad} + 1)^5 = -32$

K
$(-10)^{\square} = -1000$

L
$(-3)^2 \times \underline{\quad}^3 = -72$

M
$\underline{\quad}^3 - 4 = 4$

N
$\underline{\quad} - 10^2 = -100$

O
$10^3 - (-10)^2 = \underline{\quad}$

using a calculator 🖩

exercise 54

1. Use your calculator to answer these questions. Give your answer as a decimal. For long decimals, round your answers to 4 decimal places.

a) 27^2

b) 22^3

c) 9^4

d) $\sqrt{106276}$

e) $\sqrt[3]{6859}$

f) $\sqrt[4]{456976}$

g) $\sqrt[5]{2476099}$

h) $\sqrt{\dfrac{3}{5}}$

i) $-31.03 - 532.9$

j) $-4.71 - -50.6$

k) -19.8×-20.09

l) $(-32)^2$

m) -32^2

n) $\dfrac{21}{15} + \dfrac{18}{61}$

o) $1\dfrac{19}{20} - \dfrac{21}{72}$

p) $\dfrac{12}{17} \times \dfrac{18}{31}$

q) $\dfrac{10}{19} \div \dfrac{2}{17}$

r) $\left(-\dfrac{2}{21}\right)^2$

s) $\left(2\dfrac{3}{16}\right)^3$

t) $\dfrac{6 \times -2.8}{14.3^2}$

u) $\sqrt{6^2 + 8.3^2}$

2. Find the given digit in each case.

a) 4th digit of 1.5^5

b) 3rd digit of $\dfrac{21}{15} \times 0.375$

c) 8th digit of π

d) 3rd digit of $100^{\frac{1}{4}}$

e) 5th digit of $3 \times \left(\dfrac{2}{7}\right)^2$

f) 2nd digit of $(5 \div 1.3)^{-0.5}$

g) 5th digit of 4.23×10^{-2}

h) 8th digit of $\dfrac{1}{7}$

i) 12th digit of $\dfrac{23}{9}$

j) 10th digit of $\dfrac{4}{7}$

exercise 5U

1. Evaluate the following. Give your answer as an integer, fraction or decimal:

   a) 1^6

   b) 6^0

   c) $\sqrt[3]{27}$

   d) $\sqrt{100}$

   e) 10^{-2}

   f) $\sqrt{9}$

   g) $(-3)^2$

   h) 2^4

   i) 4^{-2}

   j) $\left(\frac{1}{2}\right)^2$

   k) 3^{-2}

   l) $(-2)^3$

   m) $(-2)^4$

   n) $\sqrt[5]{1}$

   o) $\left(\frac{2}{5}\right)^2$

   p) $(-4)^2$

   q) $\sqrt{25}$

   r) 4^3

   s) $\sqrt[3]{8}$

   t) $\sqrt{64}$

   u) 2^0

2. Which of the following is the same as $\sqrt{16}$?

   A 8   **B** 4   **C** $\frac{1}{16}$ **D** 16^2

3. Which of these is the same as 4^{-1} ?

   A -4   **B** $\sqrt{4}$ **C** 2   **D** $\frac{1}{4}$

4. Which of these are **not** equal to 1?

   A 3^0 **B** 1^{-1} **C** $\sqrt{1}$ **D** $\sqrt[3]{-1}$

5. Which of these are the same as 2^{-1} ?

   A $2^3 \div 2^4$ **B** $2^0 \div 2$ **C** $2^3 \div 2^{-4}$ **D** $2 \div 2^2$

6. Which of these have a positive answer?

   A $\sqrt{1}$ **B** $\sqrt{0}$ **C** $(-1)^{100}$ **D** $(-1)^{101}$

7. Insert brackets to make this calculation true: $4 \times 3 + 6 = 36$

8. Simplify the following using the index laws, where possible.
   Write NP if they cannot be simplifed using index laws.

   a) $5^2 \times 5^8$

   b) $5^{0.7} \div 5^{0.3}$

   c) $5^{-3} \times 5^{-4}$

   d) $5^{-4} \div 5^3$

   e) $5^4 \div 5^4$

   f) $(5^{-3})^2$

   g) $(5^{-3})^5$

   h) $5^8 \div 5$

   i) $5^6 - 5^4$

   j) $5^{-2} \div 5^6$

   k) $(5^{\frac{3}{4}})^{\frac{1}{2}}$

   l) $5^3 \div 4^3$

9. Estimate $\sqrt{14}$

10. Fill in the missing indices:

    a) $3^{\square} = 27$

    b) $(-5)^{\square} = 25$

    c) $7^{\square} = 7$

    d) $2^2 \times 2^{\square} = 16$

    e) $(-2)^{\square} = -8$

    f) $9^{\square} = 1$

11. Write the following as fractions:

    a) 2^{-1}

    b) 3^{-1}

    c) 2^{-3}

    d) 9^{-1}

    e) 5^{-2}

    f) 10^{-1}

    g) 10^{-2}

    h) 10^{-3}

12. Calculate $\sqrt{16} \times 4^{-1}$

13. Work out:

    a) $\dfrac{4 + 14}{2}$

    b) $4 + \dfrac{14}{2}$

    c) $\dfrac{9 \times 3}{3^2}$

    d) $25 - \dfrac{12 + 6}{1 + 2}$

    e) $\dfrac{4 + 2 \times 3}{2}$

    f) $\dfrac{(7 - 1)^2}{3 \times 4}$

    g) $\dfrac{5 \times (5 + 1)}{7 - 2 \times 3}$

    h) $\left(\dfrac{4 + 4 \times 4}{2^2}\right)^2$

    i) $\dfrac{\sqrt[3]{27} + 5}{2}$

14. By placing brackets into this calculation, work out as many different possible answers as you can.

    $1 \times 2 + 3 \times 4$

exercise 5v

1. Calculate:

    a) -4 × 6

    b) $\frac{1}{2}$ of 18

    c) $\frac{2}{3}$ + $\frac{3}{5}$

    d) -2 + -6

    e) 0.3 × 100

    f) $\frac{15}{0.3}$

    g) -20 ÷ 10

    h) $\frac{1}{4}$ × 5

    i) -45 ÷ -9

    j) $\frac{1}{3}$ ÷ 5

    k) -12 - - 5

    l) 6 ÷ 0.1

2. Calculate 3 - 4 × 2 + 1

3. Write as a single power of 3:

    a) 3×3^4

    b) $3^4 \div 3^5$

    c) $(3^2)^5$

    d) $\frac{3^4}{3^{-2}}$

4. Calculate -4 + -4 + -4

5. Write down the value of:

    a) $\sqrt{64}$

    b) $\sqrt[3]{27}$

    c) $\sqrt[5]{32}$

    d) $\sqrt[10]{1}$

    e) $\sqrt{16}$

    f) $\sqrt[3]{8}$

    g) $\sqrt[4]{16}$

    h) $\sqrt{25}$

6. Write 0.89 as a fraction

7. Calculate -4 × -2 × -3 × -1

8. Calculate the following and give your answers in simplest form::

    a) $\frac{27}{4} \times \frac{16}{18}$

    b) $8 \times \frac{3}{4}$

    c) $\frac{18}{40} + \frac{3}{10}$

    d) $\frac{1}{7} - \frac{1}{10}$

    e) $18 \div \frac{2}{3}$

    f) $\frac{4}{5} \div 8$

9. True or false: the product of 3 negative numbers will always be negative.

10. Calculate $\frac{4}{9} \times 3$

11. Calculate 14 ÷ 0.5

12. Which number below is smallest?

    a) 4.02   b) 0.24   c) 0.402   d) 0.204

13. Write each fraction as a decimal:

    a) $\frac{7}{100}$ d) $\frac{1}{1000}$ g) $\frac{1}{3}$

    b) $\frac{3}{5}$ e) $\frac{4}{10}$ h) $\frac{1}{2}$

    c) $\frac{1}{4}$ f) $\frac{3}{50}$ i) $\frac{1}{9}$

14. Calculate -2 × -2 × -2

15. Fill in the blanks with >, < or =

    a) 2.3 _____ 2.04   b) 0.808 _____ 0.81   c) 0.7 ___ 0.7000

16. Calculate:

    a) -5 × 2   f) -6 × 10   k) $1 - \frac{1}{9}$

    b) -3 × -4   g) $\frac{1}{3}$ of 18   l) -8 × -3

    c) $\frac{1}{9} + \frac{4}{9}$ h) 40 ÷ -5   m) 0.04 × 100

    d) 20 ÷ -2   i) $\frac{1}{4} + \frac{3}{8}$ n) -25 ÷ -5

    e) 1 - 0.2   j) -2 × 10   o) -6 ÷ -1

17. Match these cards into pairs that are equivalent.
    Record your pairs in a table.

A	-3 + 2		B	-2 - 4		C	10 -15		J	0		K	-6		L	-5
D	-1 - - 1		E	6 - 8		F	6 - - 3		M	-1		N	3		O	4
G	-2 + -2		H	4 + -1		I	-2 + 6		P	9		Q	-2		R	-4

A	
B	
C	
D	
E	
F	
G	
H	
I	

18. Calculate:

a) -3 - 3

b) -4 + 4

c) 4 ÷ 0.1

d) 0.4 × 3

e) $\frac{1}{4} + \frac{3}{4}$

f) 4^2

g) 12 × 5

h) 9 ÷ 0.3

i) -20 ÷ 5

19. Given that 37 × 43 = 1591, calculate:

a) 3.7 × 43

b) 3.7 × 4.3

c) 0.37 × 430

20. Which of these calculations will have the largest answer?

a) 206 ÷ 10

b) 206 ÷ 1

c) 206 ÷ 0.1

d) 206 ÷ 0.01

21. 8 tens + 7 hundredths equals:

a) 8.7

b) 70.8

c) 80.7

d) 80.07

e) 700.8

challenging

22. Given that 6 × 7 = 42, fill in the blanks:

a) 0.6 × 0.7 = _____

b) 600 × _____ = 42

c) 0.6 × _____ = 4.2

d) _____ × 700 = 4200

e) 60 × 0.07 = _____

f) 4.2 ÷ _____ = 70

23. Complete the missing numbers:

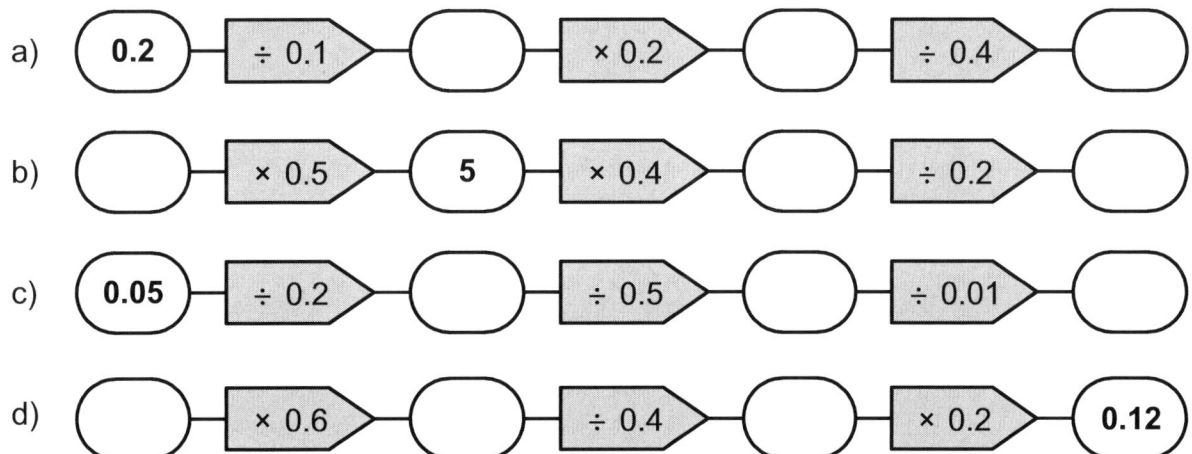

a) (0.2) → [÷ 0.1] → ( ) → [× 0.2] → ( ) → [÷ 0.4] → ( )

b) ( ) → [× 0.5] → (5) → [× 0.4] → ( ) → [÷ 0.2] → ( )

c) (0.05) → [÷ 0.2] → ( ) → [÷ 0.5] → ( ) → [÷ 0.01] → ( )

d) ( ) → [× 0.6] → ( ) → [÷ 0.4] → ( ) → [× 0.2] → (0.12)

chapter 6: introduction to algebra

[Recommended Time : 12 - 15 hours]

Contents

variables & like terms

learn by heart

Variable: a letter that stands for a number, which can vary

$1a$ is written simply as a and the letter x is written so that it looks different to a × symbol

The times sign is not used, so '2 lots of a' is written $2a$

Like terms: are multiples of the same variable, such as $3b$ and $5b$

Simplify: collect together like terms (only like terms can be collected)

examples

Simplify $a + 4a - 2a$

$$= 3a$$

Simplify $6b - 10b$

$$= -4b$$

exercise 6a

1. Simplify:

   a) $b + b + b$

   b) $4b + 2b$

   c) $8y + y$

   d) $y + 3y + y$

   e) $10y - 4y$

   f) $4y - 10y$

   g) $9y - y$

   h) $4y + 5y - 3y$

   i) $b + 4b - 2b$

   j) $8b - 3b - 5b$

   k) $2b - b - b$

   l) $b - 2b$

2. Which of these is the same as $1x$?

   a) $1y$ b) 24 c) x d) $x + 1$

3. Circle the pairs which are like terms:

   a) $4a$ & $5a$ c) y & $4y$ e) $9d$ & 9

   b) $3x$ & $3y$ d) $-2p$ & $6p$ f) $-t$ & $4t$

4. True or False?

   a) $8a + 8 = 16a$

   b) $4a - a = 4$

   c) $8a + 8b = 16ab$

   d) $10y + 10y = 20y$

   e) $100y - y = 99y$

   f) $6a - 7a = a$

5. Simplify, **if possible**:

   a) $w + w + w =$ _____

   b) $y + y + 2y =$ _____

   c) $8a - 2a - a =$ _____

   d) $2y + 4y - 6y =$ _____

   e) $3p - 6p =$ _____

   f) $4b + b - b =$ _____

   g) $6t - t =$ _____

   h) $4p + 6 =$ _____

6. Explain why this expression cannot be simplified: $3a + 4b + 5c + 6d$

7. Simplify: $6a - a + 5a - a + 4a - a + 3a - a + 2a - a$

8. Which of these **cannot** be simplified?

   a) $6b + 4b$

   b) $6b + 4a$

   c) $4b - 6b$

   d) $4b + 4$

   e) $3b - b$

   f) $b + 6$

9. Fill in the blanks:

   a) $4t +$ _____ $= 5t$

   b) $2t +$ _____ $= 0$

   c) $t -$ _____ $= 2t$

   d) $8t -$ _____ $= 10t$

   e) $12t +$ _____ $= 10t$

   f) $6t -$ _____ $= -2t$

   g) $-3t +$ _____ $= 0$

   h) $4t -$ _____ $= -10t$

10. Simplify, **if possible:**

   a) $8a - 10a$

   b) $8a - a$

   c) $8a - 8$

   d) $8a + -8a$

   e) $-8a + 8$

   f) $-8a - 8a$

11. Simplify $b - b - b$

12. Which of these equals $0.5b$?

   a) $1 - 0.5b$ b) $b - 0.5b$ c) $0.2 + 0.3$ d) $b + 0.4b$

13. Simplify:

   a) $-3y + 2y$

   b) $-4d + 6d$

   c) $-9d - d$

   d) $4b + b - 5b$

   e) $-10d + d$

   f) $12d + -5d$

collecting like terms

examples

If like terms get separated, we can still add or subtract them....

$$4a + 5 + 2a$$

$$= 6a + 5$$

the 5 cannot be added to the 4 and 2 because it's not a like term

Subtraction signs stay attached to the term they are in front of:

$$4a - 5 = -5 + 4a$$

If there is no sign at the front, it is +

Simplify: $6a - 3 - 2a$

Circle each term, including its sign:

$6a$ -3 $-2a$

Add or subtract like terms, to get
$4a - 3$ OR $-3 + 4a$

exercise 6b

1. Simplify:

    a) $b + 5 + b$

    b) $7b + 4 + 2b$

    c) $3b + a + 2b$

    d) $5y - 2 + 3y$

    e) $8y - 4 - 2y$

    f) $6y - 5 - y$

    g) $8a + 5b - 3b$

    h) $2y - 4y - 6$

    i) $9a + a - 2a$

2. True or false: $3t - 6 = -6 + 3t$

3. Which of these is the same as $-4y - 8$?

    a) $-8 - 4y$ b) $-8 + 4y$ c) $4y + 8$ d) $8 - 4y$

4. Simplify:

    a) $4a + 2 + 3a$

    b) $2a - 6 - 3a$

    c) $4y - 3 + 2y - 2$

    d) $6y + 1 - 5y + 2$

    e) $2x + 5 - 3x$

    f) $8b - 3 - 2b + 1$

    g) $9 - 7f + f - 3$

    h) $3 + b - 2 + 2b - 1 - 3b$

5. True or false?

   a) $2b + 3 = 5b$

   b) $2b + 5 + b = 3b + 5$

   c) $4y - 5 + 2y = 2y - 5$

   d) $8a + 8b = 16ab$

6. Simplify:

   a) $10y + 4 - 12y$

   b) $3y + 2 - 3y$

   c) $5y - b - 5y$

   d) $9a - 3a - 5$

   e) $y + 4 - 3y$

   f) $6t - 2 - t - 3$

7. Choose from the list below to fill in the blanks:

$3 + b$	$-6b$	$3b$	$-3a$	b^3	y^5	$5x$	$-3y$

   a) $3 \times b$ is written as _____

   b) $5y$ and _____ are like terms

   c) $2a -$ _____ $= 5a$

   d) $6b +$ _____ $= 0$

8. Which of these **cannot** be simplified?

   a) $a + b + c$ b) $2a + b + a$ c) $3y - y - 1$ d) $4c - 5c$

9. True or false: $7a - a = 7$

Make the Total

Arrange the cards into three groups, so that each group has the total indicated. You must use all the cards.

$-4x$	-6	5	$3x$	$3x$	4	1	-4	x	$-2x$	$-x$

Total: $x - 5$	Total: $2x + 1$	Total: $4 - 3x$

10. Simplify, if possible:

a) $9b - 2 - 5b + 2$

b) $6x - 4y + 4y + 2x$

c) $a - 2b + 3a - b$

d) $-4g + 2g$

e) $4 - 8y + 2 + 3y$

f) $2y - 5y + 8$

g) $9 - 3y - 12 + y$

h) $-5a - 2y + 6a - 3y$

matching activity

11. Match the cards on the left with their counter part on the right.
Record your answers in a table.

A	$6a + 3a - 5$
B	$-3a + 4a$
C	$2a - 5 + 3a$
D	$6 + 3a - a - 4$
E	$8a - 10a$
F	$6 - 3a + 5 - 2a$

G	$7a + 1 - 5a - 1$
H	$3 - 2a - 3 - 5a$
I	$-5a + 5 + 12a - 2$
J	$-4a - 4a - 4a$
K	$2a - 3 - a + 6$
L	$7 - 8a + 3 - 2a$

M	$2 + 2a$
N	$2a$
O	$-7a$
P	$9a - 5$
Q	$-12a$
R	$-2a$

S	$11 - 5a$
T	$a + 3$
U	$5a - 5$
V	$10 - 10a$
W	a
X	$7a + 3$

A	B	C	D	E	F	G	H	I	J	K	L

challenging

12. Simplify:

a) $8b - - 2b$

b) $2 + -5x - 3$

13. Fill in the blanks:

a) $9c + \underline{\quad} = 2c$

b) $4y - \underline{\quad} = 5y$

c) $6 - \underline{\quad} + \underline{\quad} + 2y = 10 - y$

d) $8a + \underline{\quad} - 4 - \underline{\quad} = -1$

e) $7 - \underline{\quad} + 2y + \underline{\quad} = y + 3$

multiplying variables

learn by heart

We don't use the × sign with algebra, variables are placed next to each other in alphabetical order.

$y \times b \times a = aby$

A single number is placed at the front (unless it is 1, which we don't write)

$y \times 3 = 3y$

If more than 1 number is being multiplied, we write their product at the front

$2 \times y \times 4 = 8y$

examples

$a \times 2$	$a \times b$	$3 \times b \times 4 \times a$	$e \times f \times -5$	$4y \times 3x$
$= 2a$	$= ab$	$= 12ab$	$= -5ef$	$= 12xy$

exercise 6c

1. Write more simply:

    a) $8 \times p$

    b) $a \times b \times c$

    c) $f \times a$

    d) $2 \times y \times 5$

    e) $10 \times a \times 4$

    f) $3 \times 4 \times p$

    g) $a \times 4 \times y$

    h) $3 \times x \times 4 \times y$

    i) $2 \times y \times 4 \times p$

2. True or false?

    a) $2p \times 4 = 8p$

    b) $4 \times 3a = 43a$

    c) $y + a = ay$

    d) $y \times 2 \times 3 = 23y$

    e) $5p \times 3 = 8p$

    f) $p \times 4 \times y = 4py$

3. Simplify:

    a) $2y \times 5$

    b) $3a \times 2$

    c) $p \times 4y$

    d) $a \times 1 \times y$

    e) $2y \times 5 \times p$

    f) $3y \times 4 \times a$

4. Which of these is the same as $3 \times p \times 4$?

    a) $34 \times p$ b) $3p \times 4$ c) $3 + p + 4$ d) $43p$

5. Which of these is the correct way to simplify $4y \times 2a$?

   a) $4y2a$ b) ay^8 c) $8ya$ d) $8ay$

6. Fill in the blanks:

   a) _____ $\times 2p = 14p$ d) $3 \times$ _____ $= 6ab$

   b) _____ $\times 3y = 21ay$ e) _____ $\times 8ab = 16abc$

   c) _____ $\times 10 = 40x$ f) $10y \times$ _____ $= 100xy$

7. Write simply:

   a) $m \times -3$ e) $b \times 3 \times a$ i) $2 \times a \times 4 \times b$

   b) $-2h \times g$ f) $a \times -3b$ j) $3b \times 5a$

   c) $-k \times -3$ g) $w \times x \times d$ k) $-4a \times -2b$

   d) $5 \times p \times q$ h) $t \times 2 \times 5 \times a$ l) $-6p \times 3$

8. Which of these is the correct simplification of $-4 \times a \times b \times -3$?

   a) $12ab$ b) $-12ab$ c) $ab12$ d) $-43ab$

9. Simplify $4a \times 3b \times 2c$

10. True or false?

    a) $2 \times a = a2$ b) $4y \times 5a = 45ay$ c) $-3y \times 4x = 12yx$

11. Fill in the blanks:

    a) $0.2y \times$ _____ $= 0.12y$ b) $1.1a \times$ _____ $= 3.3ab$

12. Which of these **cannot** be written more simply?

    a) $a \times 4$ b) $3y \times 2$ c) $8ab$ d) $p \times -3$

13. Simplify $-3x \times -3y \times -3z$

14. Simplify $2^2 \times b \times -3 \times a \times 3^2$

multiplying variables - index notation

learn by heart

If a variable is multiplied repeatedly, an index is used to show how often, e.g. $a \times a \times a = a^3$

An index of 1 is not written, so $a^1 = a$

If terms have coefficients, their product is written at the front, e.g. $3a \times 5a = 15a^2$

$$3a^2$$

coefficient, index, base

examples

Write in index form:

$y \times y = y^2$ $a \times b \times b \times a = a^2b^2$ $bbbaa = a^2b^3$ $2 \times y \times 5 \times y = 10y^2$

exercise 6d

1.   Write in index form:

a) $a \times a \times a \times a$ d) $2 \times y \times 3 \times y$ g) $xyx \times 2x$

b) $b \times c \times b \times c$ e) $4a \times 5a$ h) $4ab \times 4ab$

c) $aaabbb$ f) $3 \times a \times 3a$ i) $3y \times 3y \times 3y \times 3y$

2.   Which of the following is the best simplification of $2 \times a \times b \times a \times 5$?

a) $10aba$ b) $10aab$ c) $10a^2b$ d) $7a^2b$ e) $7a^2 + b$

3.   Which of the following statements is true?

a) $a + a + a = a^3$ c) $y + y = y2$

b) $x + y = xy$ d) $s \times 4 \times s = 4s^2$

4.   Simplify:

a) $3 \times 4a \times a$ d) $p^2 \times a^2$ g) $-4p \times -2p$

b) $1 \times p$ e) $2x \times 0$ h) $ee \times ff \times gg$

c) $a^1 \times a$ f) $9a \times 3b^2$ i) $0.2b \times 0.3b$

5.   Simplify $b \times b \times b \times b \times d \times d \times d \times d \times d$

Expressions Code Breaker

Simplify the following and find your answer in the code box.
Write the words down as you go to reveal an inspirational message!

a) $2a \times a$ = __$2a^2$__ = | **Never**

b) $2a + a$ = _____ =

c) $2a - a$ = _____ =

d) $a \times a \times a$ = _____ =

e) $3a \times -3a$ = _____ =

f) $3 \times a \times 2 \times a$ = _____ =

g) $-3 \times a \times -2$ = _____ =

h) $4a - 10a$ = _____ =

i) $3a \times a$ = _____ =

j) $-2a \times -5a$ = _____ =

k) $-2a - 5a$ = _____ =

l) $-a \times a \times 2$ = _____ =

m) $-4a + 3a$ = _____ =

n) $a - a$ = _____ =

o) $a - 5a$ = _____ =

p) $a \times 7 \times a$ = _____ =

q) $a \times 2 \times 5$ = _____ =

r) $aa \times 1$ = _____ =

s) $a - 6a + 2a$ = _____ =

t) $a - 6 + 2a$ = _____ =

u) $2a \times a \times a$ = _____ =

v) $2a \times -2a$ = _____ =

w) $4a \times a \times a$ = _____ =

– Quote by Margaret Mead

multiplying variables - using index laws

recall

Multiplication Law (add the indices): $a^3 \times a^4 = a^7$

Power Law (multiply the indices): $(a^5)^3 = a^{15}$

examples

Simplify $a^6 \times a^4 \times a$

Add the indices $= a^{11}$

Simplify $(a^6)^{-3}$

Multiply the indices $= a^{-18}$

Simplify $y^x \times y^{3x}$

Add the indices $= y^{4x}$

exercise 6e

1. Write as a single power, if possible:

    a) $a \times a^4$

    b) $y^{-10} \times y^4$

    c) $y^0 \times y^{-3}$

    d) $p^{-5} \times p^{-3}$

    e) $y^3 \times y^6$

    f) $p^5 \times p \times p^3$

    g) $y \times y \times y^{-1}$

    h) $a^8 \times b^4$

    i) $a^{0.5} \times a^{1.5}$

    j) $b^{-3} \times b^{-4}$

    k) $n^{0.8} \times n^{0.2}$

    l) $x^4 \times x^{-4}$

2. Fill in the blanks:

    a) $a^4 \times$ _____ $= a^{10}$

    b) $b^{-3} \times$ _____ $= b^2$

    c) $y \times$ _____ $= y^{-3}$

    d) $p \times p \times$ _____ $= p^2$

3. Write as a single power:

    a) $(a^4)^2$

    b) $(d^8)^{-2}$

    c) $(b^{-3})^2$

    d) $(p^{-4})^{-3}$

    e) $(y^0)^{-3}$

    f) $(x^4)^{0.1}$

4. Write as a single power:

    a) $y^a \times y^a$

    b) $a^{3b} \times a^{2b}$

    c) $(p^4)^y$

    d) $(d^a)^5$

    e) $b^y \times b^y \times b^y$

    f) $(a^b)^c$

    g) $y^{2b} \times y^{-b}$

    h) $(p^3)^{2x}$

    i) $(y^x)^x$

5. Write as a single power:

a) $(y^4)^2 \times y^3$

b) $y \times y^4 \times (y^2)^3$

c) $p^{10} \times (p^{-3})^2$

d) $a^3 \times (a^4)^{-2} \times a^2$

e) $a^{10}a^3$

f) $(p^5)^2 \times (p^{-2})^5$

g) $y^p \times (y^p)^2$

h) $(b^6)^x \times (b^x)^{-2}$

6. Simplify

a) $y^{\frac{1}{5}} \times y^{\frac{1}{5}}$

b) $(y^{\frac{1}{5}})^3$

True or False?

In the grid there are **6** true statements. Can you find them?

A	B	C	D
$5b + 1 = 6b$	$b \times b = 2b$	$b - 1 = 1$	$b - 1 = 0$
E $4b - b = 4$	**F** $b \times b \times b = b^3$	**G** $b = 1b$	**H** $b \times 4 = b^4$
I $2b \times 3b = 6b$	**J** $b^4 \times b = b^5$	**K** $(b^4)^3 = b^7$	**L** $b^5 \times b = 2b^6$
M $b + b = b^2$	**N** $6b + b = 7b^2$	**O** $2b + b = 3b$	**P** $b^4 \times b^4 = b^{16}$
Q $(b^{-2})^{-3} = b^6$	**R** $2b \times b = 3b$	**S** $(b^5)^2 = b^{25}$	**T** $3b - 4b = -b$

The true statements are: _____ _____ _____ _____ _____ _____

exercise 6f: mixed multiplications and additions

1. Simplify

   a) $2a - 3 + a - 2$

   b) $a^2 \times a^2 \times a^2$

   c) $a^3 \times a^3$

   d) $3a + 3a$

   e) $a - a - a$

   f) $-5a + b - a - 2b$

   g) $y^4 \times y^5$

   h) $(y^4)^2$

   i) $2y - 3y$

   j) $2y \times 3y$

   k) $10a - 3 - 2a + 5$

   l) $y \times y \times y \times y$

   m) $y + y + y + y$

   n) $4a - a$

   o) $4a \times a$

2. Fill in the blanks:

   a) $a \underline{\quad} b = ab$

   b) $6y \times \underline{\quad} = 42y^2$

   c) $t \times \underline{\quad} = t^3$

   d) $b \times \underline{\quad} = -3b$

   e) $4a \times \underline{\quad} = 12ab$

   f) $x \times \underline{\quad} = 3x^3$

3. Simplify:

   a) $y^2 \times y^2$

   b) $2y + 2y$

   c) $2 \times y^2$

4. Simplify $y - y - y$

5. Simplify $-y \times -y \times -y$

- -

Mixed Operations Puzzle

Use 8 of the expressions below to make these statements true:

$3x$	x^6	$-x$	$4x$
x^2	$2x$	4	x^4
x^3	5	$9x$	$5x$

$$\boxed{} - \boxed{} = -2x$$

$$\boxed{} + \boxed{} = 8x$$

$$\boxed{} \times \boxed{} = 8x^2$$

$$\boxed{} \times \boxed{} = x^9$$

Mixed Up Expressions

Simplify each expression and find your answer at the bottom.
Record your answers in a table.

A	B	C	D
$3a - 2 + a$	$a \times a \times a$	$2a \times 3a$	$(a^4)^2$

E	F	G	H
$8a + 1 - 3a$	$a^{10} \times a^{-3}$	$4a - 10a$	$(a^{-2})^{-3}$

I	J	K	L
$a + a + a$	$4 - 3a + a$	$a \times a^3 \times a$	$-5a \times -5a$

M	N	O	P
$(a^3)^{-1}$	$-a + 5a$	$a^{-4} \times a^6$	$4a \times a \times -3$

Q	R	S	T
$4a - 2 + a$	$-2 \times 4a$	$(a^5)^0$	$a \times a^9$

U	V	W	X
$6a - 10a + a$	$(a^3)^5 \times a^{-3}$	$a^7 \times (a^3)^{-2}$	$(a^4)^{-3} \times (a^2)^{-3}$

- -

jumbled answers

$-3a$ $-12a^2$ $-8a$

a^{10} $5a -2$ $6a^2$ $4a -2$ $25a^2$

a^2 a^6

a^{-18} a^5 a^3 a^{-3} a^0 a

a^8 $3a$

$-6a$ $4 - 2a$ $4a$ a^{12} $5a + 1$ a^7

A	
B	
C	
D	
E	
F	
G	
H	
I	
J	
K	
L	
M	
N	
O	
P	
Q	
R	
S	
T	
U	
V	
W	
X	

199

multiplying fractions ☆ extra challenge

examples

| Simplify: $\frac{2}{5} \times \frac{d}{7}$ $= \frac{2d}{35}$ | Simplify: $\frac{2}{3} \times d$ remember this is like $\frac{d}{1}$ $= \frac{2d}{3}$ | Simplify: $\left(\frac{y}{5}\right)^2$ $= \frac{y}{5} \times \frac{y}{5} = \frac{y^2}{25}$ |

exercise 6g

1. Simplify:

   a) $\frac{4}{5} \times b$

   b) $\frac{4}{5} \times \frac{b}{3}$

   c) $\frac{1}{4} \times y$

   d) $\frac{2}{3} \times 4y$

   e) $3 \times \frac{y}{4}$

   f) $\frac{2b}{5} \times \frac{1}{3}$

   g) $\frac{y}{3} \times \frac{y}{5}$

   h) $\frac{4y}{5} \times 2y$

   i) $\left(\frac{y}{2}\right)^3$

2. Which of the following is the same as $\frac{5}{x^2} \times 2y$?

   a) $\frac{10y}{2x^2 y}$

   b) $\frac{10}{2x^2}$

   c) $\frac{10y}{x^2}$

   d) $\frac{5}{x^2}$

3. Simplify:

   a) $6 \times \frac{3}{x}$

   b) $\frac{7p}{3} \times \frac{2p}{q}$

   c) $\frac{5m^2}{7} \times 3m$

   d) $\frac{5x^2}{3y} \times 4x$

   e) $\frac{5b^2}{3c} \times \frac{1}{6c^2}$

   f) $\left(\frac{x^3}{5}\right)^2$

   g) $\frac{k}{2} \times \frac{5}{p^2}$

   h) $\left(\frac{3x^2}{y}\right)^2$

   i) $\frac{2x}{3} \times \frac{x^4}{5} \times 4x$

4. Fill in the missing blank: $\frac{5}{a} \times \underline{\hspace{1cm}} = \frac{25}{a}$

5. Fill in the missing blank: $\left(\underline{\hspace{1cm}}\right)^2 = \frac{9a^4}{b^2}$

recall

Instead of dividing by a number, we can instead multiply by its reciprocal

examples

Simplify $5 \div \frac{2a}{b}$

$= 5 \times \frac{b}{2a} = \frac{5b}{2a}$

Simplify $\frac{1}{a} \div 3$

$= \frac{1}{a} \times \frac{1}{3} = \frac{1}{3a}$

exercise 6h

1. What is the reciprocal of   (i) $\frac{5}{x^2}$ (ii) x (iii) $\frac{1}{x}$?

2. Simplify

a) $8 \div \frac{c}{d}$

b) $3 \div \frac{6}{7x}$

c) $x \div \frac{1}{x}$

d) $y \div \frac{2}{y}$

e) $9 \div \frac{2a}{3}$

f) $\frac{1}{2} \div \frac{1}{x}$

g) $\frac{3}{4} \div \frac{a^2}{b}$

h) $\frac{p}{q^2} \div \frac{9}{2a}$

i) $\frac{7t^2}{3} \div \frac{1}{6u}$

3. Which of the following is the same as $3 \div \frac{1}{x}$?

a) $3 \times \frac{1}{x}$ b) $3 \div x$ c) $3 \times x$ d) $\frac{1}{3} \div x$

4. Which of the following is the same as $\frac{1}{a} \div 5$?

a) $a \times 5$ b) $a \div \frac{1}{5}$ c) $\frac{1}{a} \div \frac{1}{5}$ d) $\frac{1}{a} \times \frac{1}{5}$

5. Simplify $\frac{2a^3}{b} \div b^2$

more challenging

6. Simplify $\left(\frac{1}{a^2} \times \frac{b}{a} \right) \div \frac{a^3}{b}$

7. Simplify $\left(ab \times \frac{1}{3} \right) \div 5$

8. Simplify $\frac{a^2}{b} \div \left(\frac{b}{a} \times \frac{2b}{a^2} \right)$

Multiplying & Dividing Fractions Match ⭐ extra challenge

Match cards on the left with their answers on the right.
Record your answers in a table.

A $\dfrac{a}{b} \times \dfrac{a}{b}$

B $\dfrac{a^2}{b} \times a$

C $\dfrac{b}{a} \div \dfrac{a^2}{4}$

D $4 \div \dfrac{1}{b}$

E $\dfrac{4}{b} \div a$

F $\dfrac{b^3}{a^2} \times 2b$

G $\dfrac{1}{2} \times \dfrac{a}{2} \times b$

H $ab \div \dfrac{4}{b}$

I $\dfrac{1}{b} \div 4$

J $\dfrac{a^2b}{2} \div \dfrac{1}{b}$

K $2b \div \dfrac{a}{b}$

L $2 \times \dfrac{b}{a} \times 2$

M $\left(\dfrac{a^3}{2}\right)^2$

N $\dfrac{1}{2}$ of a

O $\left(\dfrac{1}{a} \times \dfrac{2}{b}\right) \div b$

P $\left(\dfrac{2}{b^2} \div a\right) \times \dfrac{1}{b}$

Q $\left(\dfrac{a}{b}\right)^2 \times \dfrac{a}{4b}$

R $\dfrac{1}{a} \div \left(\dfrac{a}{b}\right)^2$

very challenging

S $\dfrac{\dfrac{1}{a} \times \dfrac{1}{b}}{ab}$

T $\dfrac{4 \times ab}{\dfrac{1}{b} \div a}$

answers

$\dfrac{a^3}{4b^3}$ $\dfrac{b^2}{a^3}$ $\dfrac{1}{4b}$

$\dfrac{1}{a^2b^2}$ $4a^2b^2$

$\dfrac{ab}{4}$

$\dfrac{a^2b^2}{2}$ $\dfrac{a^3}{b}$

$\dfrac{4b}{a^3}$ $\dfrac{2}{ab^2}$ $\dfrac{ab^2}{4}$

$\dfrac{2}{ab^3}$ $\dfrac{a^2}{b^2}$ $\dfrac{a}{2}$

$\dfrac{4b}{a}$ $4b$ $\dfrac{2b^4}{a^2}$

$\dfrac{2b^2}{a}$ $\dfrac{4}{ab}$ $\dfrac{a^6}{4}$

A	B	C	D	E	F	G	H	I	J

K	L	M	N	O	P	Q	R	S	T

learn by heart

Dividing Variables: *the ÷ sign is not used, a ÷ 3 is written* $\frac{a}{3}$

examples

$a \div 2$	$(a \times 2) \div b$	$(x \times y) \div (2 + b)$	$(a + 1) \times 4$
$= \frac{a}{2}$	$= \frac{2a}{b}$	$= \frac{xy}{2 + b}$	$= 4(a + 1)$

we also avoid the × symbol

exercise 6i

1. Write in simple algebraic notation:

    a) $b \div 4$

    b) $(p \times p) \div 4$

    c) $(x \times 3) \div (y + 4)$

    d) $4 \div b$

    e) $b \times (2 + c)$

    f) $(d \times h) \div (p \times p \times 2)$

    g) $(y + x) \times 3$

    h) $6 \div (q + 4)$

2. Write more simply:

    a) $7 \times (3 + x)$

    b) $b + b$

    c) $d \times d$

    d) $b \div 3$

    e) $y \times y \times y \times y$

    f) $6 \div p$

    g) $p \div 6$

    h) $(y - 2) \div 3$

    i) $3 \times y \times 2$

    j) $(2 + y) \div 5$

    k) $a \times b \times a$

    l) $a + b + a$

3. Which of these means y multiplied by 4?

    a) $y + 4$ b) y^4 c) $4y$ d) $\frac{y}{4}$

4. Which of these is the correct way to write $a \times a \times a$?

    a) $3a$ b) $a3$ c) $3(a)$ d) a^2 e) a^3

5. True or false?

    a) $x + y = xy$ b) $b^4 = b + b + b + b$

6. Match each expression on the left with one on the right:

A	G	M	T
n add 4	4 divided by n	$-4n$	$4n^2$

B	H	N	U
n times 4	n squared times 4	n^3	$\dfrac{n}{4}$

C	I	O	V
n minus 4	n squared times n	$\dfrac{4 + n}{n}$	$n + 4$

D	J	P	W
4 minus n	n squared + 4	$\dfrac{4}{n}$	$n - 4$

E	K	R	X
n times -4	n - 4 divided by n	$n^2 + 4$	$\dfrac{n - 4}{n}$

F	L	S	Y
n divided by 4	4 + n divided by n	4 - n	$4n$

A	B	C	D	E	F	G	H	I	J	K	L

7. Write each of these as an algebraic expression:

a) I think of a number, n, and multiply it by 5

b) I think of a number, y, add on 3 and then divide by 4

c) I think of a number, b, times by 2 and then divide by 6

d) I think of a number, a, square it and then subtract 10

e) I think of a number, x, divide by 4 and then subtract 8

f) I think of a number, p, square it and then add 5

g) I think of a number, m, divide by 2 and then add 5

h) I think of a number, d, square it, then multiply by 4

i) I think of a number, c, subtract 15, then divide by the product of g and 7

Flow Chart Expressions

1. Write an expression for each sequence of operations on the variable n:

a) n — $\times 4$ — $+ 1$ _____

b) n — $\times n$ — $- 6$ _____

c) n — $\times a$ — $\times 3$ _____

d) n — $+6$ — $\div y$ _____

e) n — $\div y$ — $+6$ _____

f) n — $\times 3$ — $- 4$ _____

g) n — $- 2$ — $\div 5$ _____

h) n — $\div 5$ — $- 2$ _____

i) n — $\times 4$ — $\times n$ _____

2. Now complete the empty flow charts to show how each expression is made:

a) n — ☐ — ☐ $3n - 8$

b) n — ☐ — ☐ $6n + 5$

c) n — ☐ — ☐ $n^2 + 1$

d) n — ☐ — ☐ $\dfrac{n}{3} + 5$

e) n — ☐ — ☐ $\dfrac{n + 5}{3}$

f) n — ☐ — ☐ $an - 6$

g) n — ☐ — ☐ $\dfrac{5n}{9}$

h) n — ☐ — ☐ — ☐ $\dfrac{2n - 5}{9}$

substitution (positive numbers)

examples

Given $y = 3$, evaluate:

$2y + 5$ $= 2 \times 3 + 5$ $= 6 + 5$ $= 11$	$2y^3$ $= 2 \times 3^3$ $= 2 \times 27$ $= 54$	$\dfrac{4(y + 1)}{10}$ $= \dfrac{4 \times (3 + 1)}{10}$ $= \dfrac{16}{10} = 1.6$

exercise 6j

1. Given that $a = 3$, evaluate:

    a) $10a$

    b) a^2

    c) $\dfrac{4a}{6}$

    d) $5a - 1$

    e) $4a + 2$

    f) $9(a - 1)$

    g) $2a^2$

    h) $(2a)^2$

    i) $5(a - 1)$

    j) a^3

    k) $(2a)^3$

    l) $(a + 2)^2$

2. Given that $b = 5$, evaluate:

    a) b^0 b) b^1 c) b^2 d) b^3

3. If $x = 3$, which of these is smallest?

    a) $4x$ b) $x + 4$ c) $\dfrac{x}{4}$ d) x^4

4. If $x = 2$ and $y = 3$, evaluate:

    a) xy

    b) $x - y$

    c) $3x^2$

    d) $y - 2x$

    e) $3y - 10$

    f) $(xy)^2$

    g) $3xy - 2(x + y)$

    h) x^y

    i) $\dfrac{x}{y}$

5. If $a = $ _____ , then $\dfrac{6}{a}$ cannot be evaluated.

substitution (negative numbers)

examples

Given $a = 5$ and $b = -4$, evaluate:

$b - 2a$	$2b^2$	$\dfrac{4b + 1}{5}$
$\begin{aligned} &= -4 - 2 \times 5 \\ &= -4 - 10 \\ &= -14 \end{aligned}$	$\begin{aligned} &= 2 \times (-4)^2 \\ &= 2 \times 16 \\ &= 32 \end{aligned}$	$\begin{aligned} &= \dfrac{4 \times (-4) + 1}{5} \\ &= \dfrac{-16 + 1}{5} = -3 \end{aligned}$

exercise 6k

1. Given $x = -4$, evaluate:

   a) x^2

   b) $x + 4$

   c) $(2x)^2$

   d) $2x^2$

   e) $5x$

   f) $x + 8$

   g) $-3x$

   h) $\dfrac{x}{2}$

   i) $2x + 1$

   j) $x - 3$

   k) $3(x + 1)$

   l) $(x - 1)^2$

2. Given $b = -1$, evaluate:

   a) b^2

   b) b^3

   c) b^4

   d) b^5

3. If $a = -2$, which of these is smallest?

   a) a^1

   b) a^2

   c) a^3

   d) a^4

4. Given $x = -5$ and $y = -2$, evaluate:

   a) $(5y)^2$

   b) $5y^2$

   c) xy^2

   d) x^2y

   e) $3(y + 3)$

   f) $\dfrac{y + 5}{10}$

   g) $x(y + 2)$

   h) $x - y$

   i) $6 - y$

   j) y^3

   k) $y - x$

   l) $xy + yx$

Substitution Mystery Grid

Copy the grid at the bottom and use the clues to complete it:

$$a = -5 \qquad b = -6 \qquad c = 8 \qquad d = 3$$

The numbers in the bottom row add up to $10 - b$

The number below -3 is $c^2 - b^2$

The number next to 5 is $4(c + b)$

The numbers in the two diagonals have the same sum

The number above 4 is $\dfrac{ab}{10} + 2$

The number to the left of -3 is d^d

The number in the bottom left corner is $b - a$

The number below 4 is $(a + d)(b + c)$

The number next to 0 is $\dfrac{2c - a}{3}$

The numbers in the top row sum to $2 - ac$

The number in the bottom right is the product of all the other numbers and 0

The number to the right of 2 is $\sqrt{2c}$

The number to the left of 2 is $\dfrac{b}{2}$

One of the numbers in the left column is $20 - d$

The number above -3 is $2d^2$

		2	

More Challenging Substitutions ⭐ ^{extra}challenge

1. If $x = \frac{1}{4}$ and $y = 4$, what is the value of xy?

2. If $x = \frac{2}{3}$ and $y = 6$, what is the value of $x \div y$?

3. Given $x = -6$ and $y = -1$, evaluate:

    a) $x \times \frac{1}{x}$ b) $x \div \frac{1}{x}$ c) $\frac{1}{y} \div \frac{1}{x}$

4. Given $p = \frac{1}{2}$, $q = \frac{5}{6}$ and $r = -\frac{3}{4}$, evaluate:

    a) pq d) $q - r$ g) $p \div q$

    b) $2pr$ e) $1 - p^2$ h) $\frac{1}{p}$

5. Find a value of p so that $p^2 > p^3$

6. If $u = 10$, evaluate $\frac{1}{u} + \frac{1}{2u}$. Give your answer as a decimal.

7. If $n = -3$, evaluate n^n

8. Given $a = 2$, $b = 1$ and $c = -15$, evaluate $\dfrac{-b + \sqrt{b^2 - 4ac}}{2a}$

9. If $w = 1$, what is the value of : $\dfrac{w^2 - 2}{w - 1}$?

10. For what value of p is $\dfrac{8}{p + 2}$ undefined?

11. Can you find a value of a that would make the expression $2a^2$ negative?

12. Can you find a value of b that would make the expression $\dfrac{5}{b}$ greater than 5?

13. Can you find a value of c that would make $\dfrac{2}{c}$ equal 0?

solving one step equations (addition & subtraction)

learn by heart

Equation: *two expressions that are* **equal** *(=)*

Solution: *a value that makes the equation true*

examples

Solve $x + 5 = 2$
$\quad$ -5 $\quad$ -5

$x = -3$

Solve $2 = y - 5$
$\quad$ + 5 $\quad$ + 5

$y = 7$

addition is the **inverse**
of subtraction

exercise 61

1. Solve:

a) $x + 4 = 10$

b) $x - 4 = 10$

c) $x + 3 = 0$

d) $x - 0.3 = 8.2$

e) $x + 7 = -2$

f) $x - 9 = -4$

g) $6.5 = x - 2.4$

h) $-3.2 = x + 4.1$

i) $x - 5 = -5$

j) $10 = x + 6$

k) $5 = x - 3$

l) $0.2 + x = 5$

m) $13 + x = -2$

n) $9 = x - 2$

o) $\frac{6}{10} = x + \frac{1}{10}$

p) $6 + x = 4.5$

q) $x - 3 = -2$

r) $x + 5 = 0$

s) $x - 8 = 1$

t) $12 + x = -3$

u) $5 = 6.8 + x$

v) $7 + x = -4.3$

w) $6 = x - 2.2$

x) $18 = 19.2 + x$

2. For which of the following is $x = 8$ a solution? Select all that apply.

a) $2x = 16$

b) $x + 2 = 10$

c) $8 - x = 0$

d) $x^2 = 16$

e) $2(x + 1) = 20$

f) $3 - x = -5$

solving one step equations (multiplication)

examples

Solve $3x = 1.2$
$\div 3 \quad \div 3$
$x = 1.2 \div 3$
$x = 0.4$

Solve $-4x = 16$
$\div -4 \quad \div -4$
$x = 16 \div -4$
$x = -4$

Solve $0.1x = 9$
$\div 0.1 \quad \div 0.1$
$x = 9 \div 0.1$
$x = 90$

exercise 6m

1. Solve:

a) $4x = 44$

b) $35 = 5y$

c) $2x = -18$

d) $3x = 1.5$

e) $-5y = 55$

f) $0.1a = 14$

g) $0.5b = 8$

h) $-3b = -27$

i) $4y = 10$

j) $100x = 45$

k) $3x = 0.9$

l) $-5x = -2.5$

m) $6y = -36$

n) $0.8 = 2x$

o) $0.1y = 4.5$

p) $0.5x = 9$

q) $-4x = -0.4$

r) $-0.1y = 8$

2. To solve the equation $0.1x = 5$, which working is correct?

a) $x = 5 \times 0.1$
$x = 0.5$

b) $x = 5 \div 0.1$
$x = 0.5$

c) $x = 5 \div 0.1$
$x = 50$

3. To solve the equation $-3x = -4$, which working is correct?

a) $x = -4 \times -3$
$x = 12$

b) $x = -4 \div -3$
$x = \frac{4}{3}$

c) $x = -4 \div -3$
$x = -\frac{4}{3}$

solving one step equations (division)

example

Solve $\frac{x}{5} = 1.2$

$x = 1.2 \times 5$
$x = 6$

Solve $\frac{x}{-3} = -7$

$x = -3 \times -7$
$x = 21$

exercise 6n

1. Solve the following:

   a) $\frac{x}{2} = 6$

   b) $\frac{x}{2} = 0.5$

   c) $-3 = \frac{x}{3}$

   d) $\frac{x}{0.1} = 4$

   e) $0 = \frac{x}{5}$

   f) $-1 = \frac{x}{2}$

   g) $\frac{x}{-6} = -7$

   h) $\frac{x}{-3} = 2$

   i) $\frac{x}{0.4} = 5$

   j) $0.5 = \frac{x}{5}$

   k) $\frac{x}{3} = 1.2$

   l) $\frac{x}{3} = -12$

   m) $\frac{x}{-3.5} = 2$

   n) $\frac{x}{2} = 0.7$

   o) $4.1 = \frac{x}{1}$

- -

Arrange the Digits

Arrange the digits to make
five correct equations.
The value of x is the same in all five equations.

| -2 | 0 | 1 | 2 | 3 | 5 | 6 | 7 |

⭐ extra challenge

$$\frac{x}{\Box} = \Box$$

$$x = \Box$$

$$x + \Box = \Box$$

$$x - \boxed{8} = \Box$$

$$\Box x = \boxed{3}\,\Box$$

mixed one step equations

1. Solve:

   a) $-7x = -14$

   b) $x - 2 = 8$

   c) $x - 4 = -3$

   d) $10x = 100$

   e) $\frac{x}{4} = -3$

   f) $-5 = x + 3$

   g) $-8 = -4x$

   h) $144 = 12x$

   i) $3 = 2 + x$

   j) $\frac{x}{2} = 6$

   k) $6 = -2x$

   l) $x - 3 = -4$

   m) $x + 0.3 = 1.5$

   n) $2x = 1.8$

   o) $x - 2.3 = 3.1$

   p) $\frac{x}{2} = 1.6$

   q) $x - 0.03 = 5$

   r) $4x = 3.2$

   s) $10x = 40.5$

   t) $\frac{x}{10} = 1.4$

   u) $0.1x = 4$

   v) $x - 1 = -0.5$

   w) $10x = 1.4$

   x) $x + 1.5 = 4$

2. Match each equation on the left with a solution from the right. Use each card once only.

A $x + 3 = 7$	B $4x = 12$	C $5 = x - 1$		$x = -7$	$x = 8$	$x = 5$
D $3x = -6$	E $x - 3 = -2$	F $\frac{x}{2} = 4$		$x = 0$	$x = -1$	$x = 4$
G $x - 2 = -2$	H $x - 3 = -1$	I $2 + x = 9$		$x = -8$	$x = 6$	$x = 9$
J $\frac{x}{5} = 2$	K $15 = 6 + x$	L $5x = -35$		$x = 3$	$x = 10$	$x = 1$
M $x - 3 = -4$	N $-3x = -15$	O $\frac{x}{2} = -4$		$x = 2$	$x = 7$	$x = -2$

A	B	C	D	E	F	G	H	I	J	K	L	M	N	O

examples

Solve $x^2 = 16$

$$x = 4 \text{ or } -4$$
$$x = \pm 4$$

Solve $\sqrt[3]{x} = 1.8$

$$x = 1.8^3$$
$$x = 5.832$$

Solve $x^3 = -27$

$$x = \sqrt[3]{-27}$$
$$x = -3$$

exercise 6p

1. Solve:

    a) $x^2 = 100$

    b) $x^3 = 1000$

    c) $\sqrt{x} = 5$

    d) $\sqrt[3]{x} = 3$

    e) $x^3 = -8$

    f) $x^2 = 1$

2. If $x^2 = 64$, then $x =$ _____ or _____

3. If $x^3 = 64$, then $x =$ _____

4. Explain why $x^2 = -16$ cannot be solved.

5. Solve:

    a) $x^4 = 16$

    b) $x^5 = 1$

    c) $\sqrt[3]{x} = -2$

6. Solve the following using a calculator and rounding answers to 2 d.p. Some of the equations cannot be solved. For these, write 'impossible'. 🖩

    a) $x^2 = 25$

    b) $x^2 = 15$

    c) $20 = x^2$

    d) $\sqrt{x} = 8$

    e) $\sqrt[3]{x} = 2$

    f) $x^3 = 27$

    g) $6 = \sqrt{x}$

    h) $x^3 = 64$

    i) $x^4 = 10$

    j) $-1 = x^3$

    k) $x^3 = -15$

    l) $\sqrt[3]{x} = 7.2$

    m) $5.5 = \sqrt[4]{x}$

    n) $\sqrt{x} = -4$

    o) $x^2 = -9$

7. Without a calculator, solve:

    a) $x^2 = 0.01$

    b) $x^3 = 0.001$

    c) $\sqrt{x} = 0.1$

solving equations (2 steps)

learn by heart

Isolate: Get the term containing the variable alone

examples

Solve $5x + 8 = 38$
$5x = 30$ $\quad\big)$ -8
$x = 6$ $\quad\big)$ $\div 5$

Solve $2x - 7 = 25$
$2x = 32$ $\quad\big)$ $+7$
$x = 16$ $\quad\big)$ $\div 2$

exercise 6q

1. Solve:

a) $2x + 5 = 17$

b) $4x - 1 = 11$

c) $3x + 1 = 22$

d) $8 + 3x = 11$

e) $16 = 4x - 4$

f) $10x - 8 = 82$

g) $8x + 12 = 76$

h) $65 = 15x + 5$

i) $29 = 4x - 15$

j) $5x + 1 = -9$

k) $9x + 10 = 1$

l) $15 = 10x - 3$

m) $12 = 3x + 15$

n) $9 + 3x = 15$

o) $6x + 3 = -9$

p) $4x - 4 = -20$

q) $8 = 4x - 2$

r) $8 = 2x + 8$

- -

Arrange the Digits

| -6 | -4 | -2 | -1 | 2 | 3 | 5 | 7 | 8 |

☆ extra challenge

Arrange the digits to make five correct equations.
The value of x is the same in all five equations.

$$\frac{x}{\boxed{}} = \boxed{3} \cdot \boxed{}$$

$$2x + \boxed{} = \boxed{}$$

$$x = \boxed{}$$

$$x - \boxed{} = \boxed{9}$$

$$\boxed{}x + \boxed{} = \boxed{}$$

I'm Thinking of a Number

Match each statement at the top, to an equation in the next section and a solution at the bottom.

statements

A I'm thinking of a number, n, I divide it by 3 and the answer is 9

B I'm thinking of a number, n, I subtract 9 and the answer is 3

C I'm thinking of a number, n, I multiply it by 3, subtract 9 and the answer is 6

D I'm thinking of a number, n, I multiply by 6, subtract 12 and the answer is 12

E I'm thinking of a number, n, I multiply it by 6, add 3 and the answer is 9

F I'm thinking of a number, I subtract 3 and the answer is -9

G I'm thinking of a number, n, I multiply it by 9, subtract 9 and the answer is 9

H I'm thinking of a number, n, I multiply it by -6, add 6 and the answer is -12

I I'm thinking of a number, n, I divide it by -12 and the answer is 3

J I'm thinking of a number, n, I multiply by -6, add 9 and the answer is 6

K I'm thinking of a number, n, I add 6 and the answer is 3

L I'm thinking of a number, n, I multiply by 3, subtract 9 and the answer is -12

equations

M $3n - 9 = 6$

N $\dfrac{n}{-12} = 3$

O $\dfrac{n}{3} = 9$

P $n - 3 = -9$

Q $9n - 9 = 9$

R $6n + 3 = 9$

S $n + 6 = 3$

T $3n - 9 = -12$

U $6n - 12 = 12$

V $n - 9 = 3$

W $-6n + 6 = -12$

X $-6n + 9 = 6$

solutions

$n = 1$ $n = 4$ $n = -6$ $n = 12$ $n = -36$ $n = -1$

$n = -3$ $n = 2$ $n = 5$ $n = 0.5$ $n = 3$ $n = 27$

A		
B		
C		
D		
E		
F		
G		
H		
I		
J		
K		
L		

examples

Solve $\dfrac{x}{2} - 4 = 6$

$\quad\quad \dfrac{x}{2} \quad = 10 \quad \rbrace +4$

$\quad\quad x \quad\quad = 20 \quad \rbrace \times 2$

Solve $\dfrac{x + 3}{4} = 5$

$\quad\quad x + 3 = 20 \quad \rbrace \times 4$

$\quad\quad x \quad\quad = 17 \quad \rbrace -3$

exercise 6r

1. Solve:

    a) $\dfrac{x}{3} + 5 = 8$

    b) $\dfrac{x + 3}{5} = 2$

    c) $\dfrac{x - 4}{9} = 2$

    d) $\dfrac{x + 1}{8} = 3$

    e) $1 + \dfrac{x}{2} = 11$

    f) $\dfrac{7 + x}{4} = 1$

    g) $\dfrac{x}{3} - 5 = -2$

    h) $\dfrac{x - 2}{10} = -5$

    i) $5 = \dfrac{x}{4} + 3$

    j) $\dfrac{x + 1}{2} = 1.5$

    k) $2 = \dfrac{x + 4}{2}$

    l) $\dfrac{x}{2} + 3 = 3.5$

2. Solve:

    a) $45 = \dfrac{x}{4} - 5$

    b) $15 = \dfrac{x}{2} - 6$

    c) $\dfrac{\sqrt{x}}{6} + 2 = 3$

    d) $\dfrac{1}{5}x + 20 = 35$

    e) $6 = \dfrac{1}{3}x - 10$

    f) $\dfrac{1}{4}x + 8 = 14$

3. Which of these equations cannot be solved? Explain your answer.

    a) $\dfrac{3}{x} = 0$

    b) $\dfrac{x}{3} = 0$

    c) $\dfrac{0}{x} = 3$

4. Match pairs of equations that have the same solution: ⭐ extra challenge

A	B
$2x + 5 = 9$	$\frac{x}{2} - 2 = 0$

C	D
$3x + 6 = 0$	$0.2x = 1.6$

E	F
$3x = \frac{1}{2}$	$-2x = 8$

G	H
$6x + 1 = 4$	$\sqrt{x} = 4$

I	J
$\frac{x}{4} = 2$	$\frac{x}{2} = 1$

K	L
$x - 3 = -5$	$-3x = -\frac{3}{6}$

M	N
$\frac{x}{4} = \frac{1}{8}$	$10 + x = 6$

O	P
$\frac{x}{2} = 8$	$-2x = -8$

A	B	C	D	E	F	G	H

Number Tricks ⭐ extra challenge

Think of any whole number.
Double it.
Subtract 3.
Subtract your original number.
Add 5.
Subtract your original number.
What do you get?
Try again with a different starting number.

You should always end up with the same number. We can use algebra to show why this trick works. Let your original number be x. Write an expression to show what happens to x. Simplify your expression. See?

Now try the same with these tricks:

Think of any whole number.
Multiply it by 3.
Add 4.
Subtract your original number.
Subtract 5.
Subtract your original number.
Add 1.
What do you get?
Try again with a different starting number.

Think of any whole number.
Double it.
Subtract 4.
Subtract your original number.
Add 5.
Subtract your original number.
Add 1.
What do you get?
Try again with a different starting number.

exercise 6S

1. Simplify

   a) $3x - 5x$

   b) $3x + 5 - 5x - 2$

   c) $3x \times 5x$

   d) $n \times 3$

   e) $n \times n \times n$

   f) $4 \times y \times y$

   g) $x + x + x$

   h) $7y - y$

   i) $(a^4)^2$

   j) $y \times y \times y \times y$

   k) $2y + 3y$

   l) $a - a$

   m) $3y - 2 - 4y + 8$

   n) $a^4 \times a^{-1}$

   o) $3a \times 3a$

   p) $4a - 3a$

   q) $4a \times 3a$

   r) $6 + 3p + p$

2. If $a = 4$, evaluate:

   a) a^2

   b) $2a$

   c) $a - 5$

   d) $3a + 1$

   e) $2a^2$

   f) $(2a)^2$

   g) $2a - 5$

   h) $\dfrac{3a}{6}$

   i) $2(a - 1)$

   j) $(a + 1)^2$

   k) $5(3a - 2)$

   l) $\dfrac{4(a + 3)}{a}$

3. Which of these cannot be simplified?

   a) $3a + 2b$

   b) $3a \times 2b$

   c) $3a \times a$

   d) $3a + a$

true or false?   Find 4 true statements:

A $2 \times x$ is the same as x^2	B $x \times 2$ is written as: $x2$	C $x - y$ is the same as $y - x$	D $y \times y \times y$ is written y^3
E $x \times y \times x$ is written as: x^2y	F $2 \times y \times y$ is written as $2y$	G $y \times y$ is the same as $2y$	H $y - (-2)$ is the same as $y + 2$
I $5y - 4$ simplifies to y	J $3 \times y \times 4$ is written as $34y$	K $\dfrac{x}{2}$ is the same as $x \div 2$	L $y + y$ is the same as y^2

4. Solve:

a) $3x = 15$ e) $\frac{x}{3} = -4$ i) $x + 4 = -8$

b) $x + 5 = 3$ f) $x - 0.3 = 1.5$ j) $3x = -27$

c) $16 = 2x$ g) $4 + x = 1$ k) $6 = \frac{x}{-2}$

d) $-5x = 25$ h) $-3 = x - 5$ l) $2x - 5 = 9$

5. Spot the error. These equations have been solved incorrectly - circle the mistakes and state what should have been done.

a) $3x - 6 = 18$

$3x - 6 = 18$ (-6)
$3x = 12$ $(\div 3)$
$x = 4$

b) $8 = 6x + 5$

$8 = 6x + 5$ (-5)
$3 = 6x$ $(\div 3)$
$x = 2$

c) $2 + 5x = 22$

$2 + 5x = 22$ (-5)
$2x = 17$ $(\div 2)$
$x = 8.5$

6. Which of these is not an equation? Explain your answer.

a) $4x = 2$ b) $\frac{x}{3} - 4$ c) $\frac{x}{5} = -4$ d) $9 - x = 0$

matching activity

Match each equation on the left with a solution from the right.
Use each card once only.

A	B	C
$3x - 2 = 1$	$\frac{x}{4} = 2$	$-3x = -9$

$x = -1$ $x = 5$ $x = -2$

D	E	F
$-6 = 3x + 3$	$x + 2 = 0$	$6x + 5 = 17$

$x = -4$ $x = 6$ $x = -3$

G	H	I
$x - 12 = -5$	$3x + 6 = 6$	$-2x = 10$

$x = 7$ $x = 1$ $x = 9$

J	K	L
$-2x + 1 = -9$	$\frac{x}{2} = -2$	$x - 14 = -5$

$x = 4$ $x = 2$ $x = 3$

M	N	O
$14 = 4x - 10$	$-2x - 2 = 0$	$-2x - 1 = -9$

$x = 0$ $x = 8$ $x = -5$

A	B	C	D	E	F	G	H	I	J	K	L	M	N	O

Algebra in Words

Match expressions on the left with their descriptions on the right.

1 $\dfrac{b}{a}$

2 $3a + 2b$

3 a^5

4 $\dfrac{ab}{5}$

5 a^2b^2

6 ab

7 $3 - b$

8 $3b$

9 $\dfrac{5}{a - 1}$

10 $6a$

11 $(a + b)^2$

12 $5a$

13 $\dfrac{a}{b}$

14 a^4

15 $8a^2$

16 $b - 3$

17 b^0

18 $4x = -12$

19 b^3

20 $5b - b$

A The same as $b \times b \times b$

B a is divided by b

C This expression simplifies to $4b$

D a is multiplied by b

E An equation with a solution of -3

F Subtract b from 3

G An expression that cannot be simplified

H Subtract 3 from b

I The sum of $4a$ and $2a$

J The same as $b + b + b$

K The product of two squares

L Unless $b = 0$, this equals 1

M b is divided by a

N The product of $4a$ and $2a$

O a is multiplied by itself 5 times

P a is multiplied by 5

Q b is multiplied by a and the result is divided by 5

R No matter the value of a, this expression will never be negative

S a and b are added together and the result is squared

T In this expression, a cannot be 1

A	B	C	D	E	F	G	H	I	J	K	L	M	N	O	P	Q	R	S	T

exercise 64

1. Calculate 0.4×0.4

2. Simplify $3a + 2b - 5a + 1$

3. Calculate:

   a) $-4 + -5$ b) -4×-5 c) $4 + -5$

4. Write 3^{-3} as a fraction.

5. Calculate $\frac{2}{5} - \frac{1}{4}$

6. Which of the following is the same as dividing by 10? Circle all that apply.

   a) Dividing by 0.1   c) Dividing by $\frac{1}{10}$

   b) Multiplying by 0.1   d) Multiplying by $\frac{1}{10}$

7. Work out $\frac{1}{8} + \frac{1}{3}$

8. Calculate $82 \div 6$

9. Write down the first six cube numbers.

10. Write the following as decimals:

    a) $\frac{1}{9}$ b) $\frac{2}{9}$ c) $\frac{3}{9}$ d) $\frac{4}{9}$ e) $\frac{10}{9}$

11. Work out:

    a) $20 - 2^3$ b) $\left(\frac{2}{3}\right)^2$ c) 5^{-2} d) 8^0

12. Calculate:

    a) $-5 - 5 - 5$ c) $8 \div 0.5$ e) 0.306×100

    b) $-2 \times -3 \times -1$ d) $1.2 \div 0.1$ f) $4.09 \div 10$

13. Round to 1 significant figure:

    a) 0.0038   b) 4,820   c) 103

14. Calculate $\frac{24}{50} \times \frac{25}{12}$

15. Simplify $a^3 \times a^5$

16. If $b = -2$, evaluate:

    a) $3b$

    b) $b + 2$

    c) $b - 1$

    d) b^2

    e) b^3

    f) b^0

    g) $-5b$

    h) $3b + 1$

    i) $2b - 1$

17. Calculate $-7 \times 3 + 1$

18. Calculate:

    a) $\frac{1}{8} \times 5$

    b) $-3 - 3 - 3$

    c) $4 \div \frac{1}{10}$

    d) $\frac{6}{0.5}$

    e) $\frac{1}{4} \div 6$

    f) 5^{-1}

    g) $\sqrt[3]{8}$

    h) 0.4^2

    i) $0.15 \div 3$

19. Given that $42 \times 108 = 4536$, calculate 4.2×1.08

20. Calculate:

    a) $4 \div 0.5$

    b) $3 \div 0.1$

    c) 4×0.8

    d) 0.3^2

    e) $\sqrt{49}$

    f) $\sqrt[3]{27}$

    g) $(-2)^3$

    h) $-5 \times -5 \times -5$

21. Round each number to the given degree of accuracy:

    a) 4.56 (1 decimal place)

    b) 0.4666 (2 decimal places)

    c) 4702 (nearest hundred)

    d) 4.99 (1 decimal place)

22. Complete the calculation: $0.49 \times$ _____ $= 4,900$

23. Which of the following will make a number 100 times smaller?

    a) $\times 10^2$

    b) $\times 10^{-2}$

    c) $\times 0.1$

    d) $\times 0.01$

    e) $\times 0.001$

24. Calculate $428 \div 9$

25. Calculate $\frac{2}{9} + 5 \times \frac{2}{3}$

<u>exercise 6U</u>

1. Calculate:

   a) $\frac{2}{5} + \frac{3}{5}$

   b) $1 - \frac{1}{7}$

   c) $\frac{4}{5} \times 3$

   d) $\frac{3}{7} \times \frac{1}{4}$

   e) $\frac{5}{10} - \frac{1}{5}$

   f) $\frac{1}{3} + \frac{1}{8}$

   g) $\frac{4}{5} \div \frac{1}{3}$

   h) $8 \div \frac{1}{5}$

   i) $\frac{1}{5} \div 6$

2. The reciprocal of 74 is _____

3. Which number is equal to its reciprocal?

4. Which of these fractions are equivalent to $\frac{3}{30}$? Circle all that apply.

   a) $\frac{2}{29}$ b) $\frac{1}{2}$ c) $\frac{1}{10}$ d) $\frac{9}{90}$ e) $\frac{6}{15}$

5. Which of these fractions cannot be simplifed? Circle all that apply.

   a) $\frac{4}{18}$ b) $\frac{9}{10}$ c) $\frac{3}{27}$ d) $\frac{2}{5}$ e) $\frac{9}{18}$

Missing Numbers Puzzle

Use the numbers below to make the calculations on the right correct.

11	1
-1	-2
-3	-4
-5	-6
-7	-8

A ☐ + -3 = -6

B -5 + -2 = ☐

C 6 + ☐ = 5

D ☐ - ☐ = -5

E 6 - ☐ = ☐

F ☐ - ☐ = ☐

chapter 7: working with measures

[Recommended Time : 11 - 15 hours]

Contents

The diagrams in this chapter are not drawn to scale

estimating calculations

learn by heart

To estimate: *try rounding numbers to 1 significant figure before calculating*

Dividing by 0.5: *is the same as multiplying by 2*

remember dividing by a number is the same as multiplying by its reciprocal

≈ means 'is approximately'

examples

Estimate $\dfrac{4.2 \times 9.8}{0.488}$

$\approx \dfrac{4 \times 10}{0.5} \approx \dfrac{40}{0.5} \approx 40 \times 2 \approx 80$

Estimate $\sqrt{42}$

$\sqrt{36} = 6, \sqrt{49} = 7,$ so ≈ 6.5

exercise 7a

1. Round each number to 1 significant figure:

   a) 488

   b) 23.98

   d) 4.5

   e) 3,085

   g) 26,030

   h) 0.406

2. Estimate the following:

   a) 8.2×19.5

   b) 0.477×12.6

   c) 8.2^2

   d) $\sqrt{103}$

   e) $\dfrac{423}{9.8}$

   f) $\dfrac{8.9 \times 4.12}{1.8}$

   g) $\sqrt[3]{220}$

   h) 11.1×401.5

   i) $\dfrac{5.01 \times 4.7}{0.542}$

   j) $\dfrac{1.08 + 18.57}{2.01}$

   k) 0.046×9.99

   l) $(-0.99)^3$

3. Which of the following is the correct answer to **721 × 0.082** ?
   Use estimation to help you decide.

   a) 5.672   b) 5882   c) 59.122   d) 0.0572

4. Estimate the answer to $420 + 18.9 \times 5.9$

5. Which of the following is largest? Use estimations to decide.

   a) $\dfrac{9210}{29}$

   b) $\dfrac{820{,}623}{2061}$

   c) 431×0.513

6. Estimate the value of:

   a) $\dfrac{9.02}{0.11}$

   b) $\sqrt{1002} \div 9.05$

   c) $6.809 \times 10^4 \times 5.2$

   d) $\sqrt{8.9 \times 4.03}$

   e) $\sqrt{70}$

   f) $\dfrac{5.82}{0.488}$

7. Which of the following is the correct answer to **5712 ÷ 28** ?
   Use estimation to help you decide.

   a) 12.6
   b) 1036
   c) 1.28
   d) 204

8. Which of the following is largest? Use estimations to decide.

   a) 0.51×3.7
   b) 6.8×3.4
   c) 92.1×0.0039

9. Anya spends £50,106 on 4 advertisements.
   Estimate the cost of each advert.

10. Which of the following is largest? Use estimations to decide:

    a) $\dfrac{8.3}{0.4}$
    b) $\dfrac{9.2}{0.1}$
    c) $\dfrac{4.01}{0.52}$
    d) $\dfrac{7.9}{0.21}$

11. Estimate $\dfrac{372 + 109.6}{0.52}$

a good estimate?

12. Which of these estimates are clearly wrong?

   A $492 \times 8 \approx 500$

   E $\dfrac{42.6}{0.489} \approx 20$

   I $(0.62)^2 \approx 3.6$

   B $9.79 \times 0.44 \approx 5$

   F $2.02^3 \approx 8$

   J $\dfrac{4.8 \times 9.6}{2.51} \approx 20$

   C $\sqrt{8.2 \times 8.1} \approx 8$

   G $\sqrt{396} \approx 20$

   K $1208.6 - 49.66 \approx 700$

   D $\dfrac{2799.2}{10.04} \approx 280$

   H $20.19 \times 4.99^2 \approx 1000$

   L $\sqrt[3]{64.8} \approx 20$

Find the Correct Answer

In each row, work out which is the correct answer
to the calculation by estimating.

	calculation	answer 1	answer 2	answer 3
A	147 × 2.9	4.263	42.63	426.3
B	11 × 19	209	2,090	20,900
C	399 × 3.4	13.566	135.66	1356.6
D	2.8 × 4.9	1.372	13.72	137.2
E	198 × 3.1	613.8	61.38	6.138
F	34.7 × 20.15	699.205	6,992.05	69,920.5
G	1,420 + 2,999	44.19	441.9	4,419
H	7.2^2	5.184	51.84	518.4
I	92 + 54 × 3.5	28.1	281	2,810
J	340 + 2.1 × 3	346.3	34.63	3.463
K	9.9^2	9.801	98.01	980.1
L	7.1 × 140 + 52	1046	10,460	104,600
M	2.1 + 3.8 × 4.2 + 1.9	0.996	1.996	19.96
N	-14.7 × -2.8	-41.16	-4.16	41.16

error intervals

learn by heart

Error Interval: the range of values a measured quantity could have taken before it was rounded. The end points of this range are called the **upper and lower bounds.**

example

A length is measured to be 49.5cm to 1 d.p. Write an inequality to show the error interval for this length.

$$49.45cm \leq length < 49.55cm$$

Add and subtract half of the value to which the number has been rounded to find the upper and lower bounds.

Lower Bound

Upper Bound

exercise 7b

1. Find all the numbers in this grid which round to 600, to 1 significant figure:

A 64	D 521	G 653	J 580	M 700	P 550	S 599.99
B 679	E 620	H 500	K 60	N 593	Q 650	T 549.5
C 6000	F 595	I 555	L 521	O 650.8	R 742	U 608.8

2. A temperature is measured as 40°, to the nearest ten degrees.
   Complete the error interval for this measurement:

   _____ ≤ temperature < _____

3. Each of these numbers has been rounded to the degree of accuracy shown. Write down the error interval for each measurement.

   a) 40.8 (1 d.p.)   b) 560 (nearest 10)

   c) 201 (nearest integer)   d) 400 (nearest 100)

   e) 90.9 (nearest tenth)   f) 540 (nearest 20)

   g) 6000 (nearest 1000)   h) 500 (nearest 10)

4. Shade all the numbers in this grid which round to 0.5 to 1 significant figure.

A	D	G	J	M	P	S
0.8	0.56	0.407	0.55	0.491	0.4500	0.9
B 0.42	E 0.7	H 0.48	K 0.45	N 0.445	Q 0.53	T 0.05
C 0.50	F 0.40	I 5	L 0.3689	O 0.500	R 0.545	U 0.491

5. The area of a shape is measured to be 300cm^2, to 1 significant figure. Complete the error interval for this measurement:

_____ $\leq$ area < _____

6. The weight of an object is measured to be 25kg, to 2 significant figures. Complete the errror interval for this measurement:

_____ $\leq$ weight < _____

7. Each of these numbers has been rounded to the degree of accuracy shown. Write down the error interval for each measurement.

a) 55 (2 significant figures)

b) 0.8 (1 significant figure)

c) 4000 (1 significant figure)

d) 8.23 (2 d.p.)

e) 82.6 (3 significant figures)

f) 0.90 (2 significant figures)

g) 2000 (3 significant figures)

h) 2000 (4 significant figures)

8. Which of these numbers has the largest upper bound?

a) 500 (1 s.f.)   b) 510 (2 s.f.)   c) 516 (3 s.f.)   d) 500 (2 s.f.)

9. Which of these numbers has the smallest lower bound?

a) 30 (1 s.f.)   b) 24 (2 s.f.)   c) 22.5 (3 s.f.)   d) 20 (2 s.f.)

10. Which of these numbers is the same when rounded to either 1 significant figure or 2 significant figures?

a) 452   b) 0.314   c) 485   d) 196

Standard form (large numbers)

learn by heart

| When we measure very large quantities, it is helpful to write numbers in standard form, which is: $a \times 10^b$, where a is between 1 and 10. | Ordinary Form: a decimal or integer |

examples

| Write 8,742.6 in standard form. $= 8.7426 \times 10^3$ | Write 4.6×10^3 in ordinary form. $= 4600$ |

exercise 7c

1. Which of these numbers are correctly written in standard form? Select all that apply.

   a) 23×10^2

   b) 1.85×7^5

   c) 0.09×10^3

   d) 4.6×10^5

   e) 10×10^6

   f) 2.0×100

2. Write these numbers in standard form:

   a) 634

   b) 48.9

   c) 1094

   d) 3095

   e) 4.9

   f) 0.5 million

   g) 3 million

   h) 30 million

   i) 1 billion

3. Explain why 25.6×10^3 is not written in standard form.

4. Which of these is the correct ordinary form of 4.7×10^2?

   a) 4.7

   b) 47

   c) 470

   d) 4700

5. Write these numbers in ordinary form:

   a) 4.2×10^3

   b) 4.08×10^2

   c) 1.89×10^1

   d) 3.1×10^0

   e) 6.81×10^1

   f) 1.26×10^2

6. Which of these is largest?

   a) 2.6×10^1

   b) 2.6×10^2

   c) 2.6×10^3

   d) 2.6×10^4

7. Which of these is the same as 4.08?

   a) 4.08×10^0

   b) 4.08×10^1

   c) 4.08×10^2

   d) 4.08×10^3

8. The moon is 4.53 billion years old. Write this number in standard form.

Standard form (small numbers)

recall

$$10^0 = 1$$
$$10^{-1} = \frac{1}{10} = 0.1$$
$$10^{-2} = \frac{1}{100} = 0.01$$

examples

Write 0.052 in standard form

$$= 5.2 \times 10^{-2}$$

Write 4.2×10^{-3} in ordinary form

$$= 0.0042$$

Quick Tip
Count the total zeros at the front of the number, that's the index.

exercise 7d

1. Which of these numbers are correctly written in standard form? Circle all that apply.

   a) 0.5×10^3

   b) 0.201×100

   c) 1.45×10^{-3}

   d) 12×10^5

   e) 9.9×10^{-6}

   f) 5.2×7^{-10}

2. Write these numbers in standard form:

   a) 0.23

   b) 0.04

   c) 0.094

   d) 1.34

   e) 0.0006

   f) 0.0905

3. Which of these is the correct ordinary form of 6.5×10^{-2}?

   a) 650   b) 65   c) 0.65   d) 0.065

4. Write these numbers in ordinary form:

   a) 1.7×10^{-1}

   b) 4.9×10^{-3}

   c) 6×10^{-4}

   d) 2.80×10^{-2}

   e) 8.9×10^{-3}

   f) 1×10^{-5}

5. Work out the missing indices:

   a) $7 \times 10^{\square} = 0.07$

   b) $2.44 \times 10^{\square} = 0.00244$

6. Write $\frac{1}{1000}$ in standard form.

7. Write $\frac{1}{8}$ in standard form.

Standard form (mixed practice)

<u>exercise 7e</u>

1. Write each of these numbers in standard form:

   a) 75

   b) 428

   c) 93.5

   d) 0.06

   e) 0.42

   f) 186

   g) 2,400

   h) 0.003

   i) 157,000

   j) 0.0204

   k) 9.2

   l) 1 million

2. Write the following in ordinary form:

   a) 7×10^3

   b) 4.1×10^{-1}

   c) 9.9×10^5

   d) 3.4×10^{-4}

   e) 6×10^1

   f) 7.2×10^0

3. Work out the missing indices to make these statements true:

   a) $5.2 \times 10^{\square} = 5,200$

   b) $3.7 \times 10^{\square} = 0.37$

   c) $9 \times 10^{\square} = 9$ million

   d) $7.4 \times 10^{\square} = 0.074$

   e) $5.01 \times 10^{\square} = 50,100$

   f) $4.203 \times 10^{\square} = 4,203,000$

4. Which of these numbers is largest?

   a) 5.2×10^6

   b) 4.5×10^7

   c) 9.1×10^{-8}

5. Explain why 7.2×8^4 is not written in standard form.

6. Calculate

   a) $4 \times 10^2 + 3 \times 10^{-1}$

   b) $5.2 \times 10^3 - 2 \times 10^2$

   c) $(1.2 \times 10^1)^2$

   d) $\sqrt[3]{(2.16 \times 10^2)}$

1 Million Puzzles ⭐ extra challenge

1 Work out the missing numbers to make 1 million

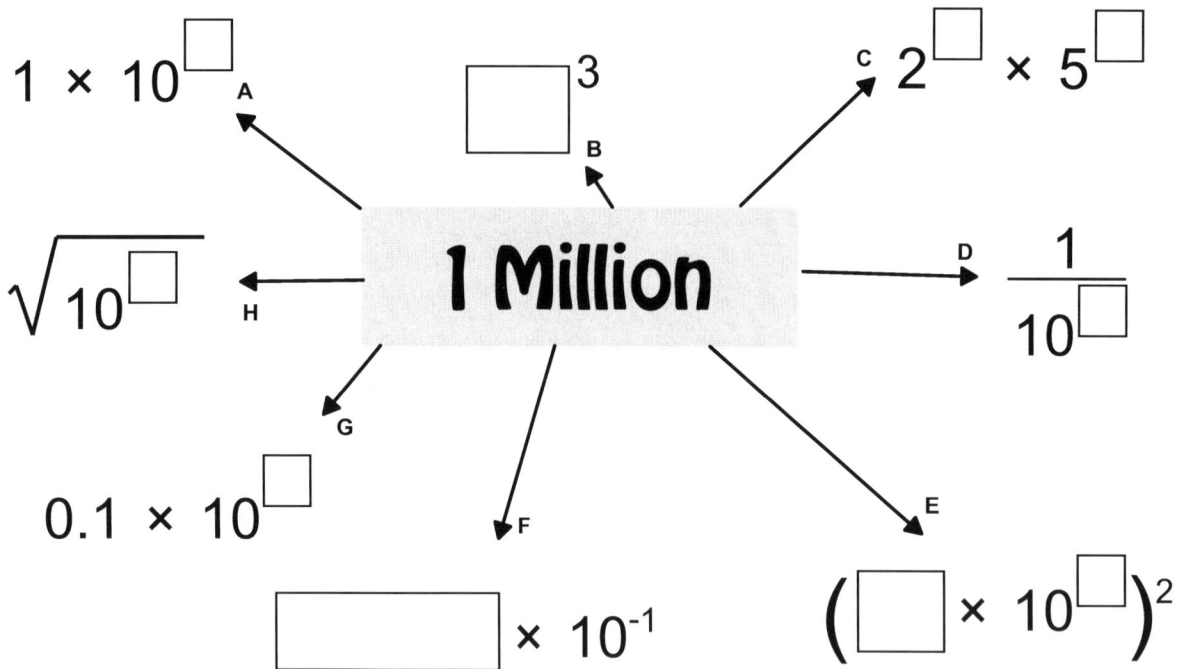

$1 \times 10^{\square}$ A

$\square 3$ B

C $2^{\square} \times 5^{\square}$

1 Million

$\sqrt{10^{\square}}$ H

D $\dfrac{1}{10^{\square}}$

G

$0.1 \times 10^{\square}$

F $\boxed{} \times 10^{-1}$

E $(\boxed{} \times 10^{\square})^2$

---

2 Using the digits 0 - 9 just once only, how close can you get to 1 million?

$\boxed{\cdot} \times 10^{\square} + \boxed{\cdot} \times 10^{\square} + \boxed{\cdot} \times 10^{\square} + \boxed{\cdot} \times 10^{\square} + \boxed{\cdot} \times 10^{\square}$

---

3 Put a different digit in each box, can you make 1 million exactly?

$\boxed{\cdot} \times 10^{\square} \times \boxed{\cdot} \times 10^{\square} + \boxed{\cdot} \times 10^{\square}$

4 Put a different digit in each box, how close to 1 million can you get?

$$\dfrac{\boxed{\cdot} \times 10^{\square}}{\boxed{\cdot} \times 10^{\square}}$$

estimating metric lengths

learn by heart

The metric measurements for length are mm, cm, m and km

| **millimetres** (mm) are small. 10mm make 1 cm. | **centimetres** (cm) 100 of them make 1 metre. | **metres** (m) A normal door is 2m. | **kilometres** (km) are big. 1 km = 1000 metres. |

exercise 7f

1. Which of these are very unlikley measurements?

A A door that is 4km tall	B A real train that is 3cm wide	C A man that is 2m tall
D A pen that is 15cm long	E A book that is 4mm wide	F A classroom that is 3m high
G The distance from Sheffield to London is 30m	H The Shard skyscraper is 306m tall	I A TV that is 1m wide

2. Which of these are metric units for length? Select 2 answers.

   a) mm   b) m^2 c) miles   d) km   e) litres   f) yards

3. Fill in the blanks with mm, cm, m or km:

   a) The length of a ruler is 30 _____.   b) The height of a door is 2 _____.

   c) The distance from the Earth to the Moon is 384,000 _____.

   d) A paperclip is 20 _____ tall.   e) A chair is 0.5 _____ tall.

   f) A house is 7_____ tall.   g) An ant is 8 _____ long.

   h) A laptop is 45 _____ wide.   i) A train is 1.2 _____ long

4. There are _____ metres in 1 kilometre.

5. Estimate the length of these objects using a sensible metric unit.

a) A hammer is _____ long.

b) A car is _____ tall.

c) The wing on a jumbo jet is _____ long.

d) A cat is _____ tall.

e) The average man is _____ tall.

6. True or False:

a) A metre is the same as 100cm.

b) mm, cm, m and km are all metric measurements.

c) A metre is longer than a kilometre.

d) 10mm are the same as 1cm.

e) A kilometre equals 100 metres.

f) The distance from York to Sheffield would be best measured in millimetres.

7. Fill in the blanks:

a) 30cm + _____ = 1 metre

b) 500m + _____ = 1 kilometre

c) 3mm + _____ = 1 centimetre

d) 2m + _____ = 1 kilometre

e) Half a centimetre is _____ mm.

f) Half a metre is _____ cm.

g) Half a kilometre is _____ m.

----

matching activity

Match each object to its length:

| A A ruler | B The length of the UK | C The length of a snake |

| D The height of a Lorry | E The height of a man |

| F A paperclip | G The length of a swimming pool | H The width of America |

| 50m | 4,300km | 3cm | 175cm |

| 1,400km | 2.5m | 30cm | 450cm |

Object	Length
A	
B	
C	
D	
E	
F	
G	
H	

converting metric lengths

learn by heart

When converting to a larger unit, divide

When converting to a smaller unit, multiply

examples

Convert 70cm into metres.	Convert 7m into kilometres.	Convert 84cm into mm.
$70 \div 100$	$7 \div 1000$	84×10
$= 0.7m$	$= 0.007km$	$= 840mm$

exercise 7g

1. Complete these statements:

   a) 3000cm = _____ m

   b) _____ mm = 36cm

   c) _____ cm = 0.72m

   d) 108m = _____ km

   e) 1.25cm = _____ mm

   f) 0.7km = _____ m

   g) 80mm = _____ cm

   h) 2km = _____ m

   i) _____ cm = 0.91m

   j) _____ km = 680m

2. Copy and complete the table to show equivalent lengths:

	mm	cm	m	km
A		600		
B			80	
C			1000	
D	2000			

3. Which of the following is equal to 200cm?

   a) 2000mm   b) 0.2km   c) 20m   d) 0.02km

4. Which of the following is the largest?

   a) 500cm   b) 7m   c) 0.08km   d) 9000mm

matching activity

5. Find 12 pairs of matching lengths. Record your results in a table.

A 4m	B 3.5m	C 250m	M 35cm	N 0.5km	O 0.015km
D 500m	E 1.5m	F 2500m	P 1.05km	Q 400cm	R 0.25km
G 0.4m	H 0.35m	I 15m	S 350cm	T 40cm	U 105cm
J 1.05m	K 1050m	L 350m	V 0.35km	W 2.5km	X 150cm

A	B	C	D	E	F	G	H	I	J	K	L

6. True or false?

a) 30m = 300cm   b) 5.4m = 54cm   c) 2.8cm = 280mm

7. Fill in the blank spaces.

a) 2cm + 3mm = _____ cm   d) 6.1cm + 9mm = _____ cm

b) 5cm + 1mm = _____ cm   e) 8cm + 10mm = _____ cm

c) 12cm + 8mm = _____ cm   f) 1.1cm + 9mm = _____ mm

8. Complete these conversions:

a) 0.24km = _____ cm   d) 52,000cm = _____ km

b) 3,400mm = _____ m   e) 0.01m = _____ mm

c) 1.9m = _____ mm   f) 290mm = _____ m

9. Which of the following is equal to 4.05m?

a) 450cm   b) 4050mm   c) 0.0405km   d) 40.5cm

10. Which of the following is the smallest?

a) 0.002m   b) 0.7cm   c) 0.000003km   d) 4mm

metric lengths in standard form ⭐ extra challenge

example

2.77 × 10^3 metres = _____ kilometres?
Give your answer in standard form

2.77 × 10^3 metres = 2,770 metres
2770 ÷ 1000 = 2.7
so 2.7 × 10^0 kilometres.

exercise 7h

1. 5 kilometres is the same as:

   a) 5 × 10^1 metres   b) 5 × 10^2 metres   c) 5 × 10^3 metres   d) 5 × 10^4 metres

2. 8.2 × 10^2 kilometres = _____ metres?
   Give your answer in standard form.

3. 1,480cm = _____ millimetres?
   Give your answer in standard form.

4. Which of these is longer, 4.8 × 10^2m or 5.2 × 10^3cm?

5. The width of a dust particle is 0.000 000 000 753 km.
   How many centimetres is this? Write your answer in standard form.

6. Which of the following are the same as 34,000 cm? Circle 2 correct answers.

   a) 3.4 × 10^4 cm   b) 3.4 km   c) 34 × 10^1 km

   d) 34 km   e) 340 km   f) 3.4 × 10^2 m

7. The distance between the Earth and Sun is 149,600,000 km.
   How many metres is this? Give your answer in standard form.

8. Which is longer, $(1.25 × 10^3)$ metres, or $(8 × 10^{-1})$ kilometres?

9. The distance between Edinburgh and Manchester is 270 km. This is the same as:

   a) 2.7 × 10^2 m b) 2.7 × 10^3 m c) 2.7 × 10^4 m d) 2.7 × 10^5 m

10. A light year is the distance that light travels in a year.
    A light year is approximately 9.5 trillion kilometres.
    1 light year = _____ metres? Give your answer in standard form.

11. The distance across our milky way galaxy is approximately 105,000 light years. 🖩
    How many kilometres is this?
    Give your answer in standard form.

Estimating Large & Small Lengths ⭐ extra challenge

Match the lengths given in standard form to the sizes described.
Two cards are blank – estimate their values.

A Length of the UK	F Length of a pencil	K Size of a galaxy
B Distance across the earth	G Thickness of a credit card	L Height of Mount Everest
C Height of the Eifell Tower	H Distance from the earth to the sun	M Length of an egg
D Width of a red blood cell	I Height of a lamp post	N Length of a grain of rice
E Height of Big Ben	J Width of an atom	O Length of a marathon

1 2×10^{-1} m	4 9.6×10^{1} m	7 1×10^{-10} m	10 1.5×10^{11} m	13 4.5×10^{0}
2 3.2×10^{2} m	5 4.2×10^{4} m	8 1×10^{18} m	11 8.8×10^{3} m	14
3 1.4×10^{6} m	6 7×10^{-4} m	9 7×10^{-4} m	12 1.3×10^{7} m	15

A	B	C	D	E	F	G	H	I	J	K	L	M	N	O

perimeter

learn by heart

| Perimeter: The distance around the edge of a shape | Equal Length Lines: are marked with one or two dashes |

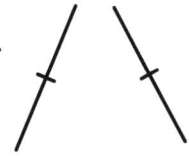

exercise 7i

1. Work out the perimeter of these shapes. Pay attention to the units!

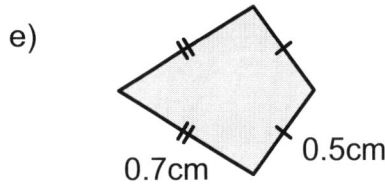

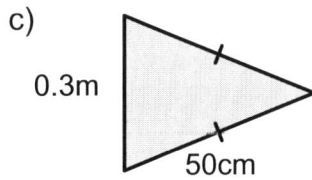

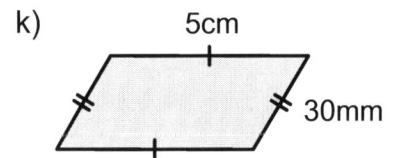

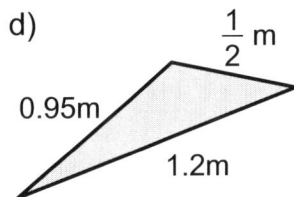

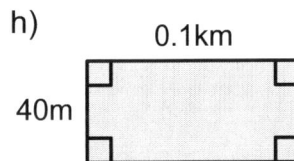

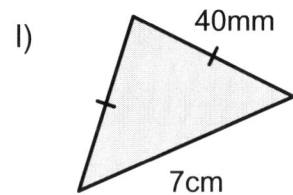

    a)
    5m

    e)
    0.7cm   0.5cm

    i)
    8m
    6m
    10m

    b)
    50cm
    1.5m

    f)
    60mm   9cm
    11cm

    j)
    5km   3000m
    4km

    c)
    0.3m
    50cm

    g)
    2m
    40cm

    k)
    5cm
    30mm

    d)
    $\frac{1}{2}$ m
    0.95m
    1.2m

    h)
    0.1km
    40m

    l)
    40mm
    7cm

2. Given the perimeter shown, work out the length of each side marked ?

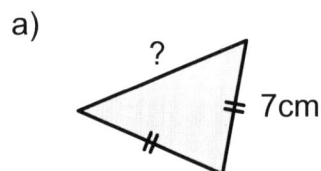

    a)
    ?
    7cm

    Perimeter = 20cm

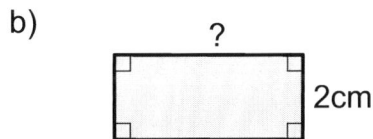

    b)
    ?
    2cm

    Perimeter = 16cm

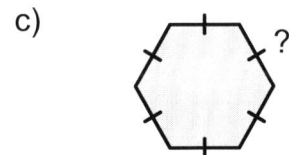

    c)
    ?

    Perimeter = 24cm

3. The side lengths of these shapes are measured in cm.
   Work out their perimeters, giving your answers **as decimals**:

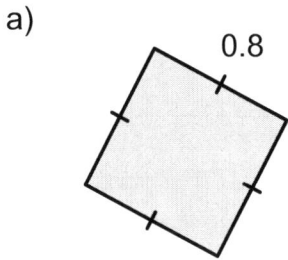

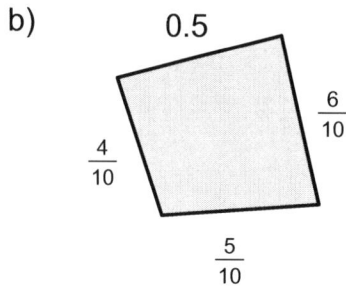

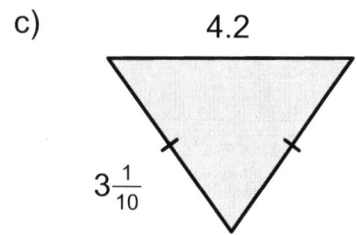

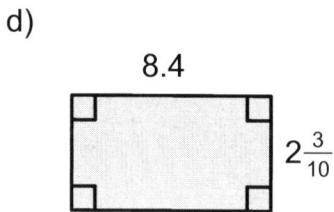

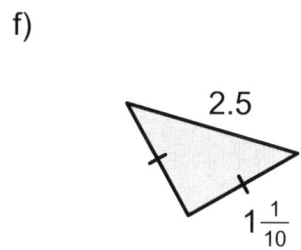

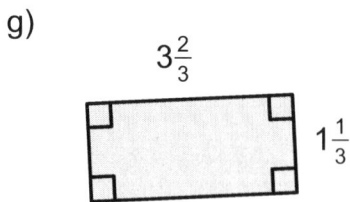

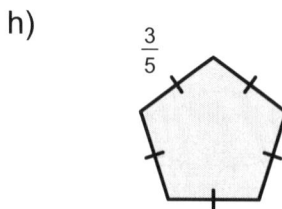

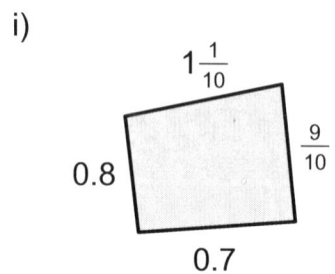

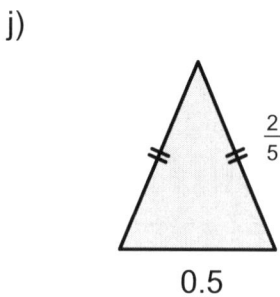

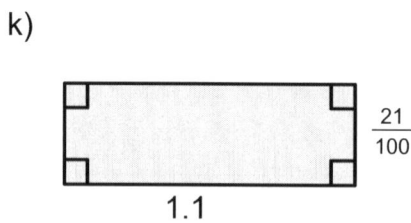

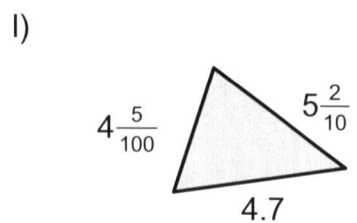

a)
0.8

b)
0.5
$\frac{4}{10}$
$\frac{6}{10}$
$\frac{5}{10}$

c)
4.2
$3\frac{1}{10}$

d)
8.4
$2\frac{3}{10}$

e)
$2\frac{3}{10}$

f)
2.5
$1\frac{1}{10}$

g)
$3\frac{2}{3}$
$1\frac{1}{3}$

h)
$\frac{3}{5}$

i)
$1\frac{1}{10}$
0.8
$\frac{9}{10}$
0.7

j)
$\frac{2}{5}$
0.5

k)
$\frac{21}{100}$
1.1

l)
$4\frac{5}{100}$
$5\frac{2}{10}$
4.7

challenge

4. The perimeter of this rectangle is 14cm.

   Five of these rectangles are put together to make this larger shape.
   Work out the perimeter of this larger shape.

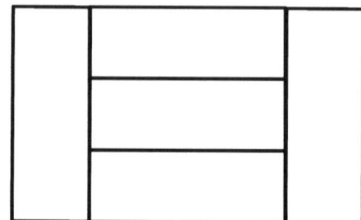

Investigation: Tiling ⭐ extra challenge

Sanya has hundreds of tiles that are 5cm by 11cm:

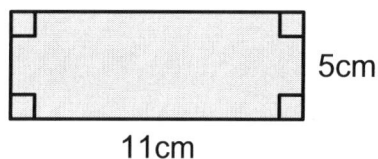

5cm

11cm

She places two together, like this:

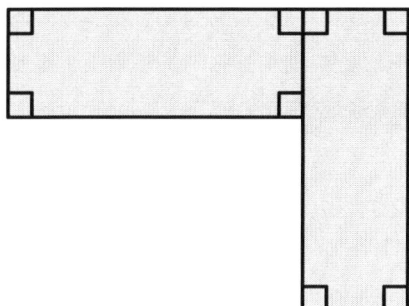

1. What is the perimeter of this new shape?

2. Using exactly 3 tiles, what is the **smallest** perimeter that can be made?

3. Using exactly 3 tiles, what is the **largest** perimeter that can be made?

6. Sanya arranges 4 of her tiles as shown. What is the perimeter?

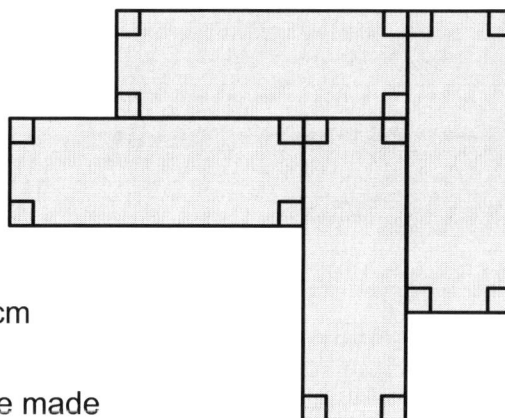

7. Show that it is possible to arrange 4 of these tiles to make a perimeter of 66cm

8. What is the largest perimeter that can be made with 4 tiles?

9. Sanya wants to use her tiles to make a **square**. What is the perimeter of the smallest square she can make?

10. Can you design a rectangular tile so that 3 tiles can be used to make a perimeter of 18cm?

11. Can you design a rectangular tile so that 10 tiles can be used to make a square?

12. Design a rectangular tile so that it has a perimeter of 24cm, its sides are integers and when two are placed together the total perimeter is just 28cm.

13. Is it possible to arrange 3 of Sanya's tiles to make a shape with a perimeter of 53cm?

14. In general, is it possible to use 3 tiles and make a perimeter that is an odd number?

15. Investigate different tiles and different arrangements, when is the perimeter even and when is it an odd number?

rectilinear shapes

exercise 7j

1.   The following shapes are all rectilinear (their sides meet at right angles).
     Find the missing side lengths marked x and y.

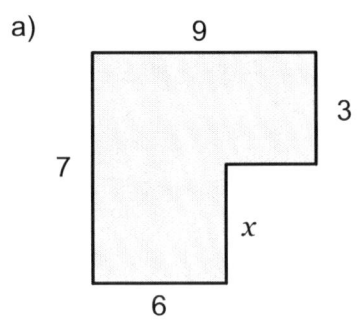

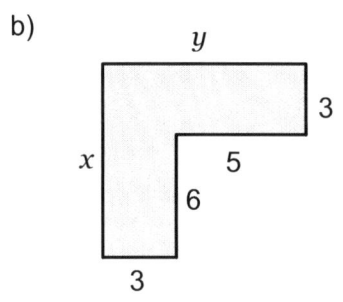

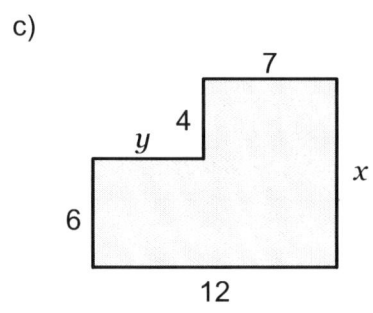

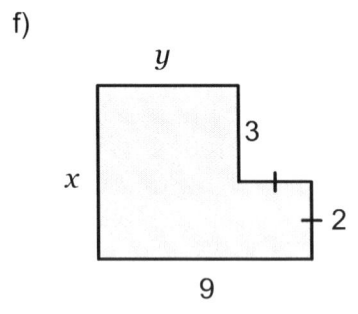

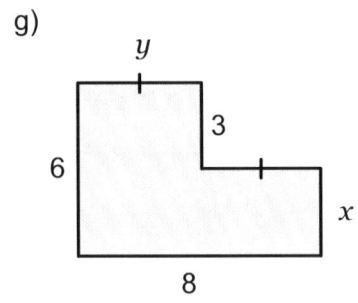

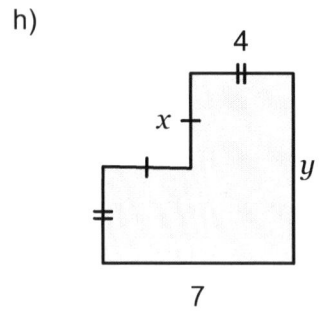

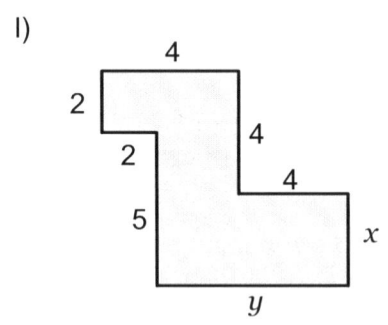

a)
9
3
7
x
6

b)
y
3
x
5
6
3

c)
7
4
y
6
x
12

d)
4
5
1
12
x

e)
1.8
6.2
8.5
2.2
x

f)
y
3
x
2
9

g)
y
3
6
x
8

h)
4
x
y
7

i)
x
4

j)
10
4
3
6
x

k)
8
y
5
x
6
3

l)
4
2
2
4
5
4
x
y

m)
x
3.3
y
4.5

n)
x
8
3

o)
20
x
12
10
5
9

244

2. Work out the perimeter of these shapes. All lengths are given in centimetres.

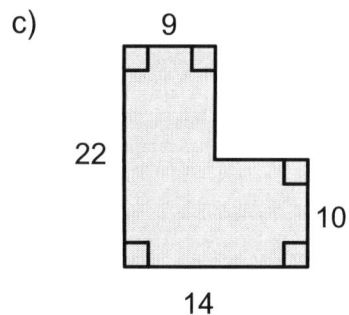

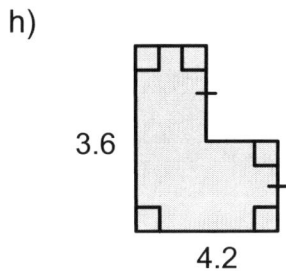

a)

3
4
4
4
6

b)

4
10
15
8

c)

9
22
10
14

d)

4
12
10

e)

8
8

f)

4
4
9
10

g)

9
10

h)

3.6
4.2

i)

18.4
7.4

4. Work out the missing lengths, given the perimeters shown.
In parts (c), (d), (e) and (f) the shapes are rectilinear.

a)

? cm
15mm

Perimeter = 5.7cm

b)

1.7m
? cm

Perimeter = 462cm

c)

3cm
? cm
5cm

Perimeter = 34cm

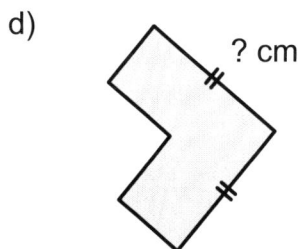

d)

? cm

Perimeter = 32cm

e)

? cm

Perimeter = 84cm

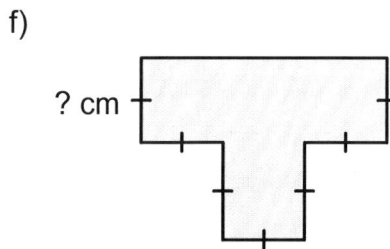

f)

? cm

Perimeter = 36cm

circles & their circumference 🔢

learn by heart

Circumference:	Arc:	Diameter:	Radius :	Chord:
The perimeter of a circle	A part of the circumference	A straight line through the centre	Half of a diameter	A straight line through a circle

Circumference of a Circle: π × diameter or 2 × π × radius

example

Calculate the length of the circumference of this circle to 2 d.p:

6cm

$C = π × 6$
$= 18.85 \ cm$

Recall that π is an irrational number.

You can find it on your calculator. It begins 3.141... and will continue forever with no repeating pattern

Because it is irrational we will need to round our answers for the circumference of a circle

exercise 7k

1. Which diagrams show a diameter?

   a)   b)   c)   d)   e)

2. Which diagrams show a radius?

   a)   b)   c)   d)   e)

3. If the radius of a circle is 8cm, then its diameter is _____.

4. If the diameter of a circle is 15cm, then its radius is _____.

5. The diagram shows two identical circles inside a larger circle. If the larger circle has a diameter of 20cm, what is the radius of each smaller circle?

6. If the radius of a circle is x, then the diameter is:

   a) $\dfrac{x}{2}$
   b) $x + 2$
   c) x^2
   d) $2x$

7. A chord that passes through the centre of a circle is called a _____.

8. Calculate the length of the circumference of these circles.
   Round your answers to 3 significant figures.

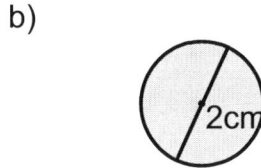

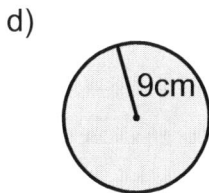

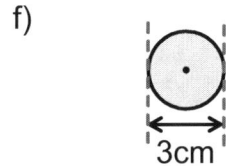

   a)

   5cm

   b)

   2cm

   c)

   5cm

   d)

   9cm

   e)

   11cm

   f)

   3cm

9. Which of these shapes has the largest perimeter? Watch out for the units!

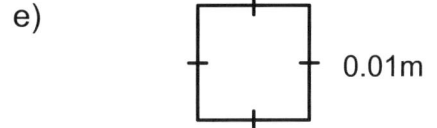

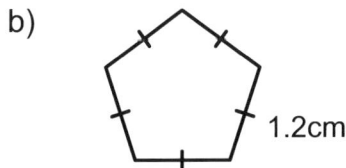

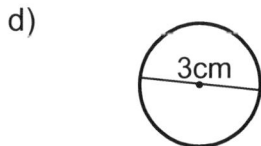

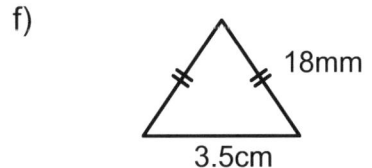

   a)

   2cm

   c)

   14mm

   e)

   0.01m

   b)

   1.2cm

   d)

   3cm

   f)

   18mm
   3.5cm

10. Jared **does not have a calculator**. Which calculation could Jared use to estimate the circumference of the circle on the right?

    | **A** 3×6 | **B** $6 \times 2 \times 3$ | **C** $3 \times (6 \div 2)$ | **D** 3×3 |

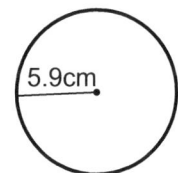

    5.9cm

11. a) The distance from the earth to the sun is approximately
       (1.5×10^8) km. Assuming the earth's orbit is a circle,
       work out the distance travelled by the earth in one year.
       Give your answer in standard form.

    b) The distance from the earth to the moon is approximately
       (3.8×10^5) km. Work out the distance travelled by the
       moon each time it orbits the earth. Give your answer in standard form.

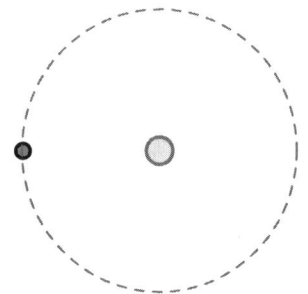

expressions for perimeter

example

Write an expression for the perimeter of this shape, simplifying your answer.

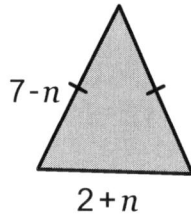

= 7-n + 7-n + 2 + n

= 16 - 2n + n

= 16 - n

exercise 7l

1. Write a simplified expression for the perimeter of each of these shapes.

a)

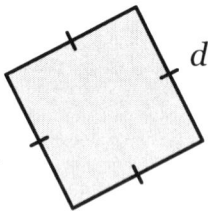

b)

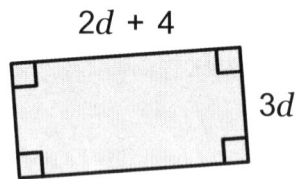

c)

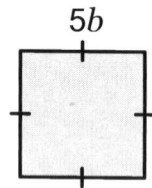

d)

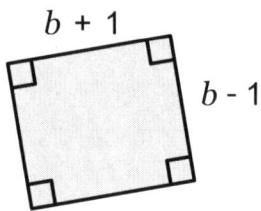

e)

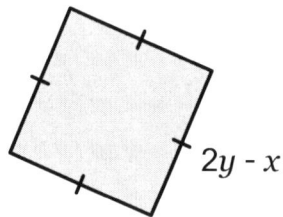

f)

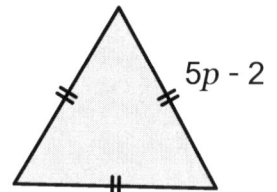

g)

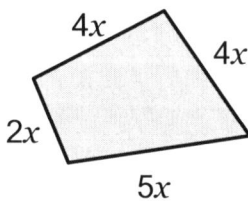

h)

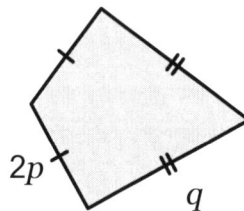

i)

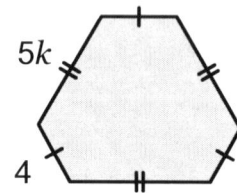

j)

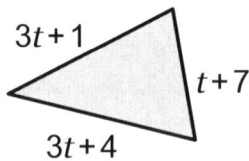

k)

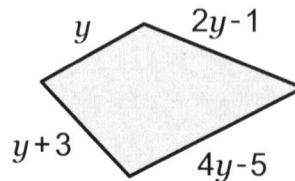

l)

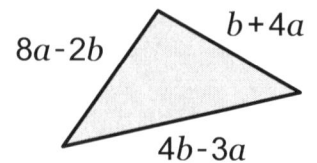

2. The perimeter of each of these shapes is **4a + 8b.**
   Work out the missing lengths.

a)

$2a + 2b$

?

$a + 3b$

b)

$a + b$

?

c)

?

3. Write a simplifed expression for the perimeter of each shape:

a)

$4x + 7$

$2x$

$6x + 2$

$4x$

b)

$3x$

$5x + 2$

$7x + 4$

$4x$

c)

$3x + 1$

$6x - 2$

x

$4x + 8$

d)

$2x + 12$

$3x$

$2x$

4. The perimeter of this triangle is $9x$ - 15.

   Write an expression for the length of one side.

?

5. The perimeter of this square is $12x$ + 16.

   Write an expression for the length of one side.

?

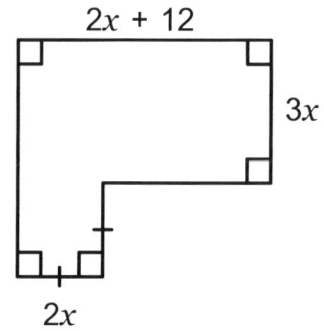

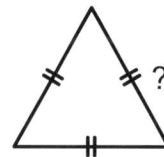

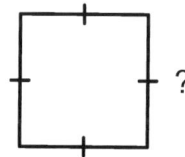

6. The total perimeter of a rectangle is $2y$ metres.
   Write an expression for the length of its perimeter in centimetres.

7. In this question, the shapes shown are made from this tile:

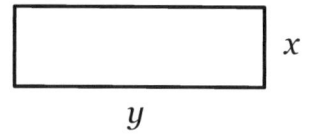

Write an expression for the total perimeter of each shape:

a)

b)

c)

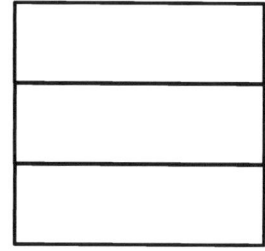

d)

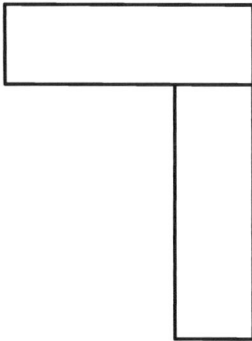

e)

f)

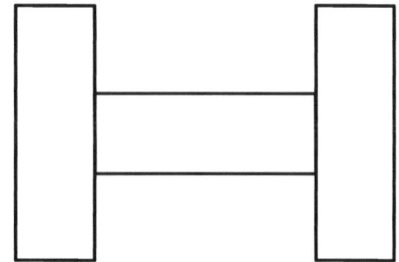

8. On this dotty grid, the distance between each pair of dots is either a or b, as shown below:

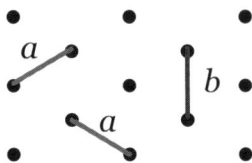

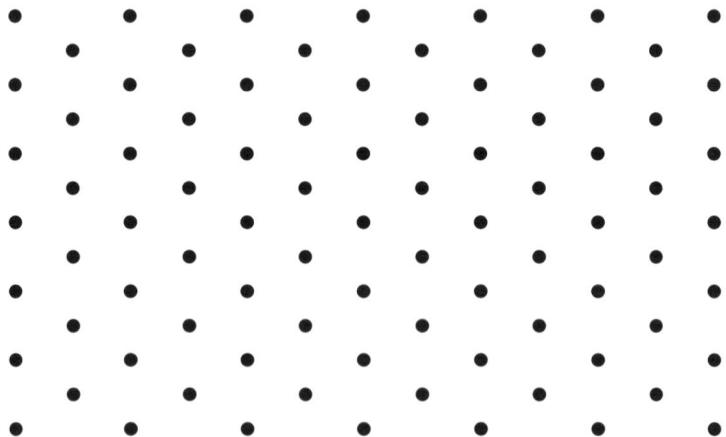

Draw a shape with a perimeter of :

a) $4a + 3b$ b) $8b + 2a$

9. A square has the same perimeter as this triangle. Find an expression for one side of the square.

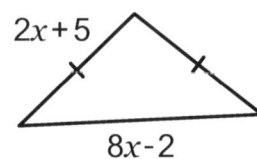

example

The perimeter of this triangle is 42cm.
Work out the value of n.

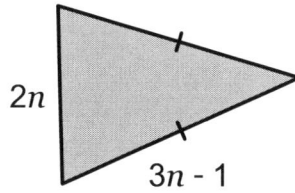

$2n$

$3n - 1$

Perimeter $= 8n - 2$
$8n - 2 = 42$
$8n = 44$
$n = 5.5$

exercise 7m

1. The perimeter P of each shape is given. Form an equation and work out the value of x.

a)
$3x$
$4x$
15

$P = 36$

b)
$2x+3$

$P = 52$

c)
$5x-2$
$2x$

$P = 68$

d)
$4x$

$P = 30$

e)
12
$3x$
$2x + 8$

$P = 68$

f)
x
$6x - 2$

$P = 38$

g)
$2x+5$
x
$5 - x$

$P = 28$

h)
$2 + 4x$
$4 - x$
$10 - x$

$P = 25$

i)
$3x+6$
$9-2x$

$P = 38$

2. The perimeter of each of these triangles is 24.
Work out the length of the side marked with a question mark.

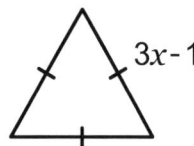

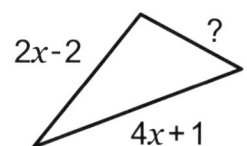

$3x-1$

$2x-2$?

$4x+1$

measuring time

Convert 150 minutes to hours
1 hour = 60 minutes,
150 ÷ 60 = 2.5

How many minutes is $\frac{1}{10}$ of an hour?

1 hour = 60 minutes,
60 ÷ 10 = 6 minutes

Convert 3.2 hours to minutes

1 hour = 60 minutes,
3.2 × 60 = 192 minutes

exercise 7n

1. Convert each of these to minutes:

   a) 5 hours

   b) $\frac{1}{2}$ an hour

   c) $\frac{1}{10}$ of an hour

   d) 2.5 hours

   e) 4 hours & 15 minutes

   f) $1\frac{1}{4}$ hours

   g) $\frac{3}{4}$ of an hour

   h) 3.25 hours

   i) $3\frac{1}{5}$ hours

   j) 0.3 hours

   k) $1\frac{3}{5}$ hours

   l) 2.9 hours

2. Convert each of the following times to hours and minutes.

   a) 110 mins

   b) 70 mins

   c) 345 mins

   d) 420 mins

3. Match each time interval below with a time in minutes from the boxes on the right.

A	B	C
2 hours 15 mins	2 hours 35 mins	$1\frac{3}{4}$ hours

D	E	F
1 hour 40 mins	3 hours 5 mins	$3\frac{1}{2}$ hours

G	H	I
1 hour 20 mins	$3\frac{1}{4}$ hours	3 hours

J	K	L
$1\frac{1}{2}$ hours	1 hour 55 mins	$2\frac{1}{2}$ hours

185 mins	90 mins
155 mins	180 mins
195 mins	100 mins
210 mins	135 mins
150 mins	80 mins
105 mins	115 mins

A	B	C	D	E	F	G	H	I	J	K	L

4. Put these times in order, starting with the shortest:

   a) 1.2 hours

   b) 65 minutes

   c) $1\frac{1}{3}$ hours

   d) 1.3 hours

Time Conversions - Odd One Out

In each box, cover up pairs of time intervals that are **equal** to each other.
Find the time interval that is left over.
Times shown are in hours (h) and minutes (m).

A

$\frac{1}{2}$h	6m	$\frac{1}{4}$h
45m	30m	$\frac{3}{4}$h
15m	$\frac{1}{10}$h	50m

B

10m	15m	$\frac{1}{5}$h
60m	$\frac{1}{6}$h	12m
$\frac{1}{3}$h	20m	1h

C

$\frac{1}{20}$h	8m	9m
4m	5m	$\frac{1}{15}$h
$\frac{1}{12}$h	$\frac{3}{20}$h	3m

D

$\frac{3}{5}$h	42m	35m
$\frac{5}{6}$h	36m	$\frac{2}{3}$h
40m	$\frac{7}{12}$h	50m

E

0.25h	6m	30m
24m	40m	0.1h
0.5h	0.4h	15m

F

0.3h	20m	0.4h
42m	24m	18m
0.6h	36m	0.7h

G

$1\frac{1}{2}$h	$1\frac{1}{3}$h	$\frac{9}{10}$h
150m	$1\frac{1}{5}$h	90m
80m	54m	72m

H

$1\frac{2}{3}$h	63m	$1\frac{1}{15}$h
$1\frac{1}{10}$h	105m	100m
64m	$1\frac{1}{20}$	$1\frac{3}{4}$h

I

$1\frac{9}{10}$h	$2\frac{1}{4}$h	108m
$1\frac{4}{5}$h	135m	$1\frac{7}{10}$h
130m	$2\frac{1}{6}$h	102m

J

$0.\dot{3}$h	18m	$0.\dot{6}$h
40m	36m	33m
0.6h	0.3h	20m

K

1.4h	114m	1.8h
108m	84m	75m
1.9h	1.6h	1.25h

L

$1.\dot{3}$h	1.1h	2.5h
100m	80m	$1.\dot{6}$h
150m	120m	66m

measuring time 2

examples

The time is 17:45.	Work out the number of minutes
What time will it be in 20 minutes?	between 13.48 and 14.25
15 minutes will make 18:00,	*60 - 48 = 12*
so it will be 18:05	*12 + 25 = 37 minutes*

exercise 70

1. Each of the following times are given in 24-hour clock format.
   Convert each to 12-hour clock format. The first one is done for you.

   a) 14 28   *2:28 pm*   b) 13 15   c) 07 45

   d) 18 30   e) 11 28   f) 21 40

   g) 04 10   h) 00 50   i) 12 33

2. Each of the following times are given in 12-hour clock format.
   Convert each to 24-hour clock format. The first one is done for you.

   a) 3:27 pm   *15 27*   b) 8:23 am   c) 8:56 pm

   d) 10:20 pm   e) 3:00 am   f) 6:30 pm

   g) 12:08 am   h) 12:38 pm   i) 11:17 pm

3. Which of these times are in the afternoon? Circle all that apply.

   a) 9:04 am   b) 15.01   c) 13.30   d) 4pm

4. Work out how many minutes there are between:

   a) 14.05 & 15.00   b) 11.10 & 12.00   c) 10.02 & 11.05

   d) 18.12 & 19.00   e) 10.06 & 10.45   f) 12.35 & 13.12

5. The time is 13.05. What time will it be in 55 minutes?

6. The time is 14.25. How many minutes is it until 3pm?

7. The time is quarter past three in the afternoon. What time will it be in 20 minutes?

8. The time is 15.15. How many minutes is it until 5pm?

9. Each flow diagram shows a starting time, an interval and an end time.
Work out the missing parts:

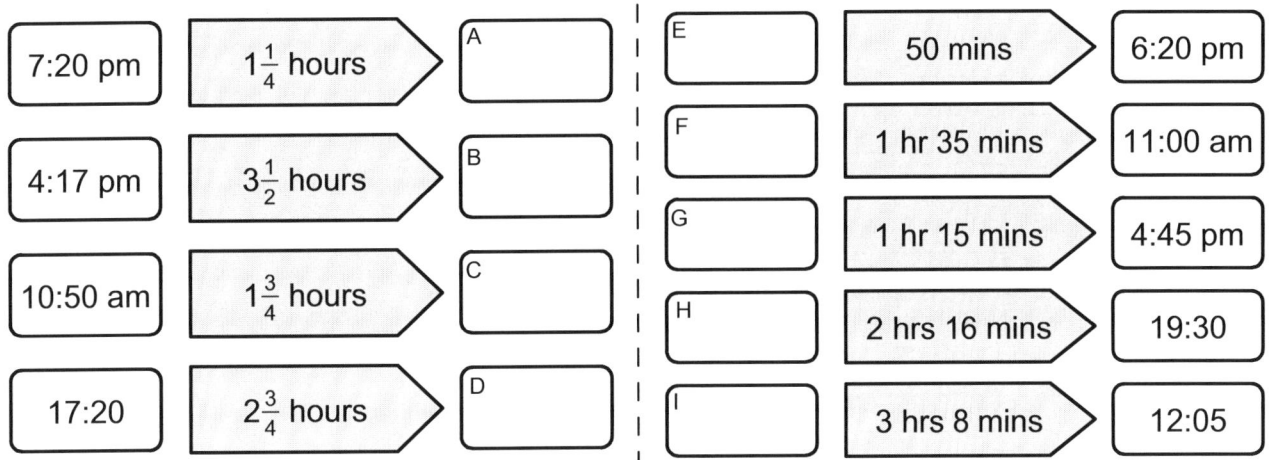

7:20 pm	1¼ hours ⟩	A
4:17 pm	3½ hours ⟩	B
10:50 am	1¾ hours ⟩	C
17:20	2¾ hours ⟩	D

E	50 mins ⟩	6:20 pm
F	1 hr 35 mins ⟩	11:00 am
G	1 hr 15 mins ⟩	4:45 pm
H	2 hrs 16 mins ⟩	19:30
I	3 hrs 8 mins ⟩	12:05

10. A film starts at 7:30pm and lasts 110 minutes. At what time does the film finish?

11. It takes Sam $1\frac{1}{4}$ hours to travel to work. Sam set off for work at 8:50am.
At what time did Sam arrive at work?

12. At an activity day, there are three sessions, each lasting 45 minutes.

   a) Work out the total duration of the three sessions.

   b) The first session starts at 10:30 am and there are no gaps between the sessions.
      Work out the time at which the last session ends.

13. A theatre show consists of two acts with a 20 minute interval.
The first act is 1 hour 10 minutes long and the second act is 55 minutes long.
The show starts at 7:30pm.
Work out the finishing time of the show.

14. It takes 40 minutes for Claudia to travel from home to work.
Claudia is due to start work at 10:30 am. Work out the lastest time that she could leave home in order to arrive at work on time.

15. Rebecca arrived at the gym at 3:50pm.
She stayed at the gym for 1 hour and 20 minutes, then walked home.

It took Rebecca $\frac{3}{4}$ hour to walk home. At what time did Rebecca get home?

16. Rob started gardening at 11:45 am and finished at 2:00 pm.
During this time, Rob took a 20 minute break.
How long was Rob gardening for?

17. Patients can book an appointment to see a doctor for ten minutes.
In the morning, the doctor sees patients between 8:50 am and 11:30 am.
The doctor also takes a 20 minute break during this time.
Work out how many patients the doctor can see in the morning.

learn by heart

$Speed = \dfrac{distance}{time}$	Examples of units of speed are m/s or km/h, where the / is read 'per'. We also use mph, standing for miles per hour.

example

Sabrina drives at an average speed of 42 miles per hour.
How long does it take for Sabrina to travel 168 miles?

$168 \div 42 = 4 \ hours$

exercise 7p

1. Each row of the table shows some information about a different journey.
   Complete the table.

	Distance	Time	Speed
a)	124 miles	2 hours	
b)	180 metres	30 seconds	
c)	240 kilometres		40 km/h
d)	75 miles		15 mph
e)		4 seconds	20 m/s
f)		3 hours	70 km/h

2. Alan drives a distance of 144 kilometres in 3 hours. Work out Alan's average speed.

3. Yasmin runs for 20 seconds at a speed of 8 m/s. How far does Yasmin run?

4. Katie drives 90 miles in 2 hours and 15 minutes.
   Work out Katie's average speed in miles per hour.

5. Nasneen jogs for 20 minutes at a speed of 9 kilometres per hour.
   Work out how far Nasneen jogs in kilometres.

6. Jason cycles at an an average speed of 12 miles per hour.
   Work out how long it takes for Jason to cover 30 miles.
   Give your answer in hours and minutes.

7. If Sarah travels 9.2km every hour for 32 hours, **estimate** how far she will travel.

7. In 130 minutes, a train travels a distance of 143 miles.
    Work out the average speed of the train in miles per hour.

8. Chris runs a race of 540 metres at an average speed of 7.5 metres per second.
    Work out how long Chris takes to complete the race, in minutes and seconds,

9. A plane travels at a speed of 275 kilometres per hour.
    Work out how long it will take for the plane to travel 880 kilometres.
    Give your answer in hours and minutes.

10. Natalie drives from home to a festival. She sets off at 8:30 am, and travels for 65 miles
    at an average speed of 52 miles per hour.
    At what time does Natalie reach the festival?

11. Jake cycled from home to work. He set off at 10:45 am and arrived at 11:15 am.
    Jake's average speed was 12 miles per hour. Work out the distance Jake cycled to work.

- -

chapter review

exercise 7g

1. A car is 4.95_____ long (choose mm/cm/m/km)

2. A kilometre is _____ cm.

3. Complete these conversions:

    a) 45cm = _____mm   d) 4,500mm = _____cm

    b) 28m = _____km   e) 0.03km = _____m

    c) 2.5m = _____cm   f) 4.2m = _____mm

4. What is 1.25 hours in minutes?

    a) 125 minutes   b) 85 minutes   c) 75 minutes   d) 15 minutes

5. Fill in the blank: 855 minutes = _____hours

6. Which of these numbers is in standard form? Choose 2 correct answers.

    a) 4.50×10^{-3} b) 4.5×7^{-2} c) 45×10^{3} d) 4×10^{0}

7. The lengths of the sides in these shapes are given in cm. Work out their perimeters.

a)

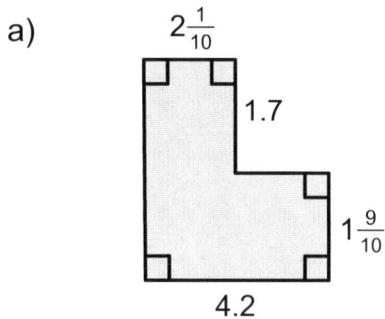

$2\frac{1}{10}$
1.7
$1\frac{9}{10}$
4.2

b)

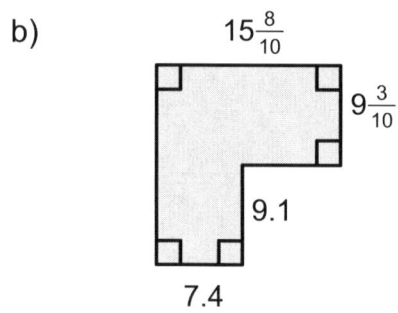

$15\frac{8}{10}$
$9\frac{3}{10}$
9.1
7.4

8. The diameter of five circular British coins are shown in the tables.
Work out the circumference of the circular face of each coin.
Round your answers to 3 significant figures.

Coin value	Diameter (mm)	Circumference (mm)
Two pounds	28.4	
Ten Pence	24.5	
Five Pence	18.0	

Coin value	Diameter (mm)	Circumference (mm)
Two Pence	25.9	
One Penny	20.3	

9. Complete the error intervals for each of these measured quantities:

a) 25cm measured to nearest cm

_____ $\leq$ 25cm < _____

b) 4.5g measured to 1 d.p.

_____ $\leq$ 4.5g < _____

10. Write 48,600 in standard form.

11. Write 0.00387 in standard form.

12. Write 2.8×10^{-2} in ordinary form.

13. Write 3.18×10^{6} in ordinary form.

14. Write a simplified expression for the perimeter of this shape:

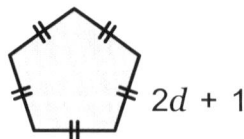

$2d + 1$

15. The perimeter of this shape is 24. Work out the value of x:

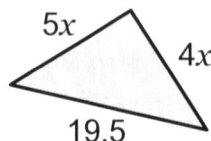

$5x$
$4x$
19.5

16. A cell is measured to be 4.5×10^{-1} mm wide.
Write down the error interval for this measurement in ordinary form.

cumulative review (chapters 1-7)

exercise 7r

1. Calculate:

   a) -5 + -7

   b) 3 × -7

   c) 4^{-2}

   d) $\frac{1}{3} \times \frac{1}{5}$

   e) $\left(\frac{4}{3}\right)^2$

   f) 3 + 5 × 7

   g) $\sqrt[3]{27}$

   h) $(-1)^5$

   i) $\frac{2}{3} + \frac{1}{7}$

2. Which of the following numbers are written in standard form?

   A. 36×10^3

   B. 5×4^3

   C. 2.8×10^{-1}

   D. 48,000

   E. 0.5×10^4

   F. 51×10^{-2}

3. Write down the first 6 cube numbers.

4. If you had to measure the following, which units would you most likely record your answers in? Choose **mm, cm, m or km**:

   a) The distance from Edinburgh to London

   b) The height of a book

   c) The length of a fly

   d) The height of a skyscraper

   e) The height of a man

   f) The distance around the Earth

5. Given that 2.4 × 83 = 199.2, work out:

   a) 24 × 83

   b) 0.24 × 83

   c) 240 × 8.3

   d) 24 × 0.083

6. Calculate 0.4 + 3 × 0.2

7. Calculate $\frac{1}{2} \times \frac{1}{2} \times \frac{1}{2}$

8. Work out:

   a) 5.4 + 3.6   b) 0.3^2 c) 4.12 ÷ 0.1

9. Calculate:

   a) $(-3)^3$ d) -6 + -4   g) 0.4 × 6   j) 6 ÷ 0.1

   b) $\frac{1}{3}$ of 18   e) $\sqrt[3]{27}$ h) 4 - -10   k) $2^7 \times 2^{-5}$

   c) 0.4 × 100   f) 1^{100} i) 2^4 l) -12 ÷ 3

10. Fill in the missing numbers:

    a) **0.43** — × 10 — [ ]   b) **0.304** — × 100 — [ ]

    c) **2** — × 0.01 — [ ]   d) **1.3** — ÷ 100 — [ ]

    e) **1.04** — × 1000 — [ ]   f) **18.4** — × 0.1 — [ ]

11. What is the reciprocal of 8?

12. It is impossible to divide by _____

13. Use the cards to complete the statements. Use each card once only.

    a) _____ × 0.2 = _____

    b) _____ × _____ = 0.018

    c) _____ × _____ = 1.6

    d) _____ × _____ × _____ = 0.001

    | 10 | 8 | 0.024 |
    | 0.6 | 0.12 | 0.1 |
    | 0.2 | 0.001 | 0.03 |

14. Work out the circumference of each circle, correct to 2 d.p.

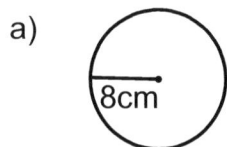

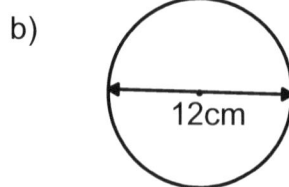

    a) 8cm   b) 12cm   c) 3.5cm

15. Given that **45 × 182 = 8190**, which of the following is equal to **45 × 1.82**?

    a) 8.19   b) 81.9   c) 0.819   d) 819

indices & roots practice

exercise 7S

1. Calculate:

   a) 4^2 d) $(-1)^3$ g) $(-2)^3$

   b) 2^3 e) $\left(\frac{2}{3}\right)^2$ h) $(-2)^4$

   c) 1^{10} f) 0.1^2 i) $(-2)^5$

2. Which of these equal 1? Circle all that apply.

   a) 1^4 b) 3^1 c) 5^0 d) 0^1 e) $(-1)^2$

3. Anything to the power zero equals _____.

4. Which of these is the same as 3^{-1} ?

   a) -3 b) $\frac{1}{3}$ c) -31 d) $\frac{3}{1}$

5. Write as a fraction or whole number:

   a) 4^{-1} b) 5^{-2} c) 10^{-3} d) 3^{-3}

6. Evaluate:

   a) $\sqrt{25}$ c) $\sqrt{1}$ e) $\sqrt[3]{27}$ g) $\sqrt[3]{-125}$

   b) $\sqrt{100}$ d) $\sqrt[3]{8}$ f) $\sqrt[3]{64}$ h) $\sqrt[3]{-1}$

7. Which of these has an integer answer? Circle all that apply.

   a) $\sqrt{20}$ b) $\sqrt[3]{27}$ c) $\sqrt{1000}$ d) $\sqrt{1}$ e) $\sqrt[3]{8}$

8. Estimate the value of $\sqrt{40}$

9. Given that $4^5 = 1024$, evaluate:

   a) $(-4)^5$ b) 4^{-5} c) 0.4^5

exercise 7+ (laws of indices)

1. Work out the missing number in each statement.

   a) $8^3 \times 8^5 = 8^{\square}$

   b) $8^7 \div 8^3 = 8^{\square}$

   c) $7^{\square} \times 7^3 = 7^9$

   d) $5^7 \div 5^{\square} = 5$

   e) $6^4 \times 6^4 \times 6^4 = 6^{\square}$

   f) $4^{12} \div 4^{\square} = 4^5$

2. Match each calculation to a card with equivalent value.

   a) $6^3 \times 6^2$

   b) $(6^3)^3$

   c) $\dfrac{6^7}{6^6}$

   d) $6^2 \times 6^3 \times 6$

   e) $(6^4)^2$

   f) $6^8 \div 6^8$

   g) $6^2 \times 6$

   h) $\dfrac{6^6}{6^2}$

P	Q	R	S	T	U	V	W
6^6	6^4	6^9	1	6^8	6^5	216	6

3. Write in the form 4^n:

   a) $(4^5)^2$

   b) $(4^7)^3$

   c) $(4^4)^{-3}$

   d) $(4^{-5})^{-1}$

4. Work out the missing number in each statement.

   a) $3^2 \times 3^{-5} = 3^{\square}$

   b) $2^{-2} \div 2^5 = 2^{\square}$

   c) $4^{-4} \times 4^{-1} = 4^{\square}$

   d) $2^3 \div 2^{-6} = 2^{\square}$

   e) $9 \times 9^{-5} = 9^{\square}$

   f) $5^{-1} \div 5^{-4} = 5^{\square}$

5. Match each calculation to a card with equivalent value.

   a) $3^2 \div 3^5$

   b) 3×3^6

   c) $\dfrac{3}{3^9}$

   d) $3^{-5} \times 3^5$

   e) $3^{-4} \times 3^{-3}$

   f) $3^{-3} \div 3$

   g) $3^2 \times \dfrac{1}{3}$

   h) $3^{-1} \div 3^{-3}$

P	Q	R	S	T	U	V	W
3^{-4}	1	$\dfrac{1}{3^3}$	3^{-7}	3^7	9	$\dfrac{1}{3^8}$	3

chapter 8: shapes, area & pythagoras

[Recommended Time: 14-18 hours]

Contents

The diagrams in this chapter are not drawn to scale

P For resources marked P, students will need a photocopy or print out of this activity to work on

parallel & perpendicular lines

learn by heart

Parallel Lines: *straight lines that will never meet. Marked with arrows (one or two)*	Perpendicular: *lines that cross at right angles*	Equal Length Lines : *marked with a dash (or two)*

For lines to be parallel, they must have the same 'up' and 'across' patterns.
E.g. both of these lines go 3 across 1 up, the longer line does it twice

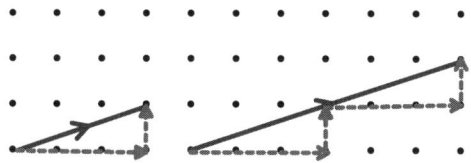

exercise 8a

1. Which of these lines are parallel? Circle all that apply:

a) 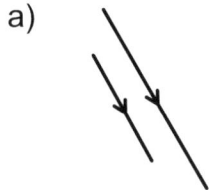   b) 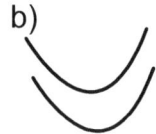   c) 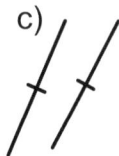   d)

2. For each pair of lines, decide whether they are:

Parallel	Perpendicular	Equal Length	None

a)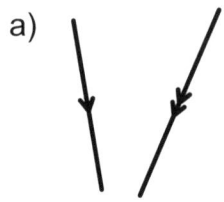

b)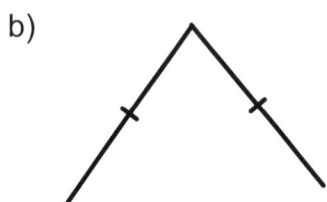

c)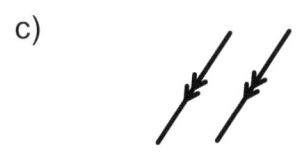

- - - - - - - - - - - - - -   - - - - - - - - - - - -   - - - - - - - - - - - -

d)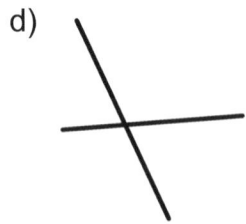

e)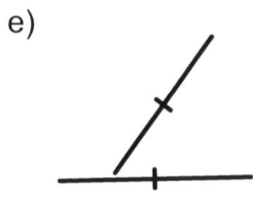

f)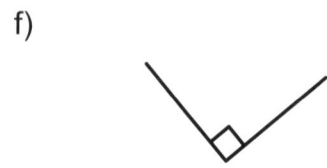

- - - - - - - - - - - - - -   - - - - - - - - - - - -   - - - - - - - - - - - -

3. True or False?

a) Parallel lines will never cross.

b) Parallel lines can curve, so long as they never meet.

c) All straight lines are parallel.

d) If lines are the same length, they must be parallel.

e) Perpendicular lines meet or cross each other at right angles.

f) A triangle can never contain parallel lines.

4. Copy each line and draw another line that is parallel and **twice** as long:

a) 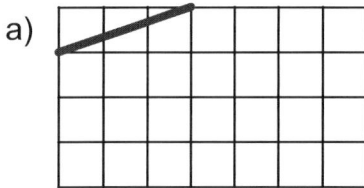   b) 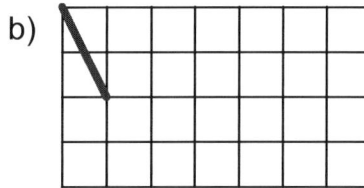   c)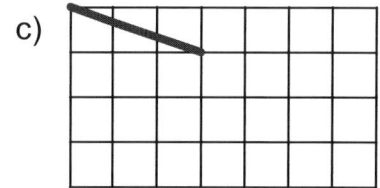

5. Copy each line and draw another line that is parallel and **three times** as long:

a) 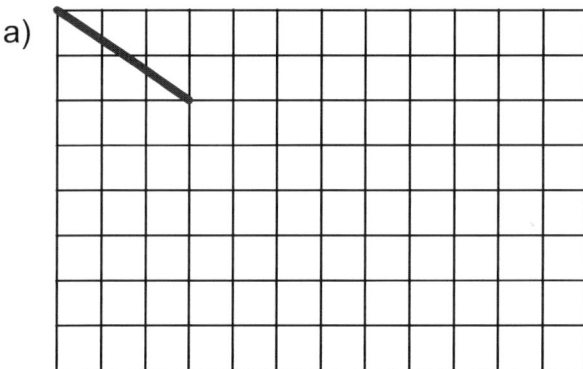   b)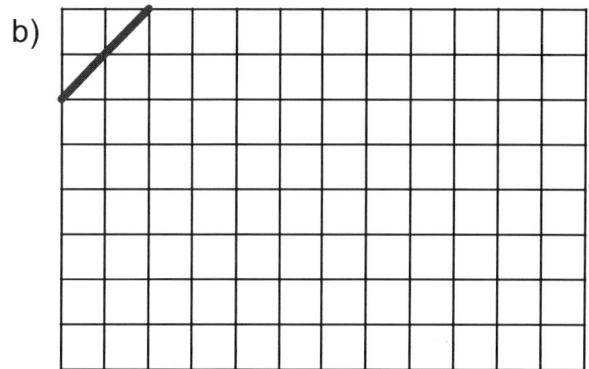

6. Fill in the blanks:

Parallel lines are marked with single or double _____.

Equal length lines are marked with single or double _____.

Perpendicular lines are marked with a _____.

7. a) In the diagram, lines _____

and _____ are equal length.

b) In the diagram, lines _____

and _____ are parallel.

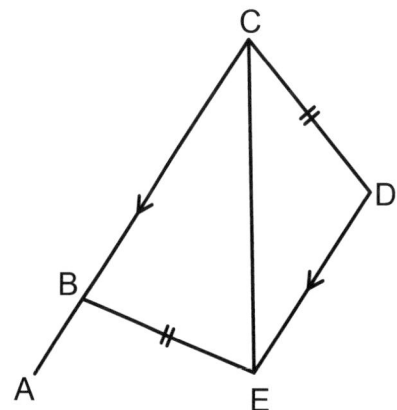

8.   One of the boxes below contains perpendicular lines. Which one?

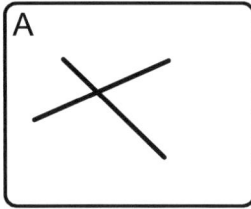

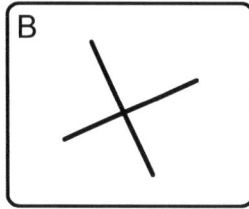

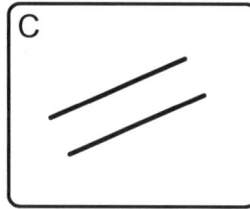

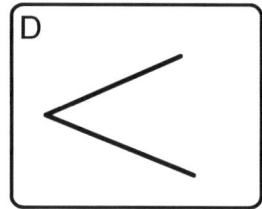

A

B

C

D

9.   On the diagram, mark lines
     that are parallel with arrows:

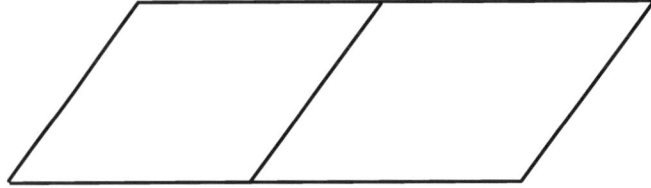

10. Complete the statements about
     the lines in the diagram.

     AI is perpendicular to _____

     BH is perpendicular to _____

     CG is perpendicular to _____

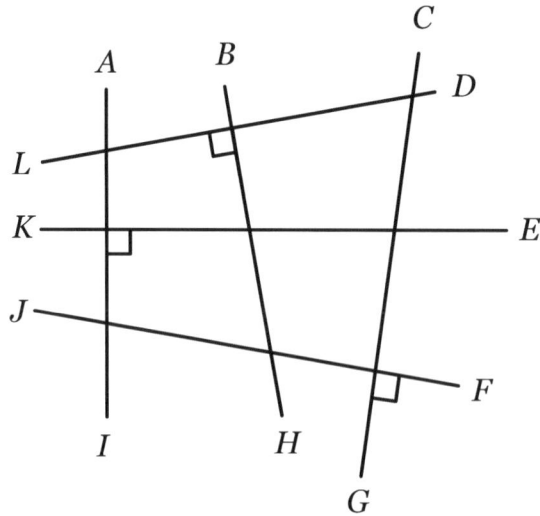

11. Add arrows, dashes and squares to the diagrams below to show that:

     a) AB is equal in length to AD

     b) EF is perpendicular to FG

     c) EH is parallel to FG

     d) BC is equal length to CD

     e) EF is parallel to GH

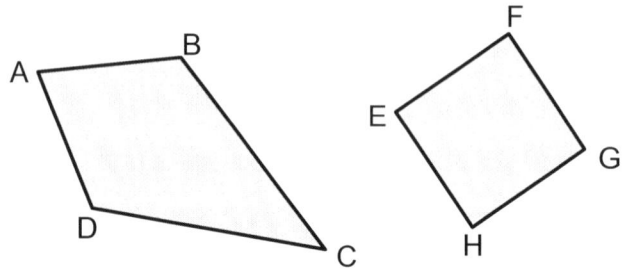

12. Copy each line and draw a line that is perpendicular to it.

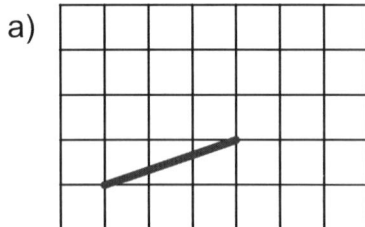

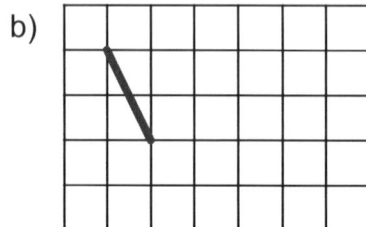

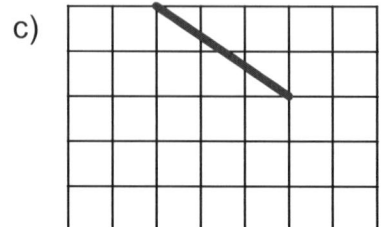

     a)

     b)

     c)

Drawing Squares P

A square has all sides the same length and all angles 90°
Complete each box to form a square.

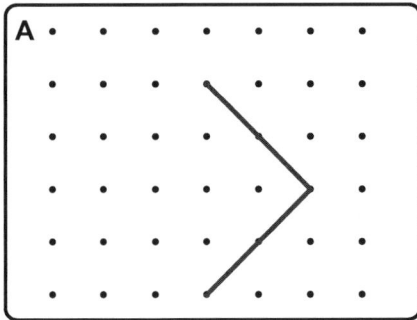

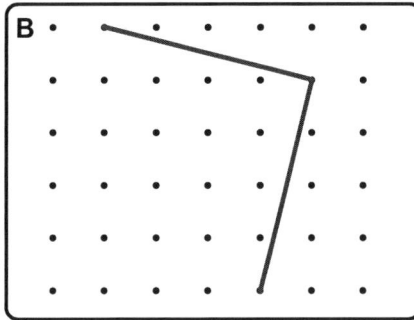

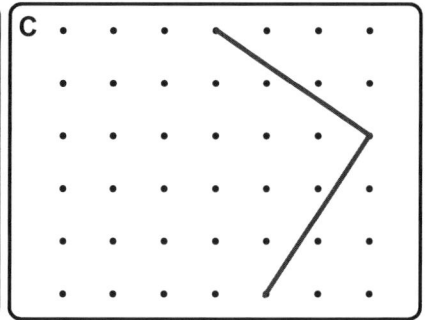

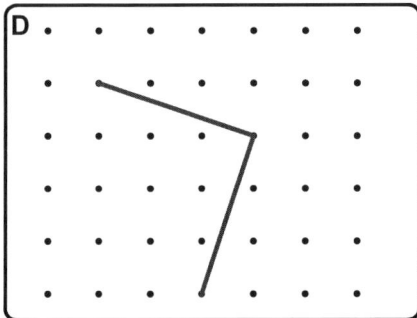

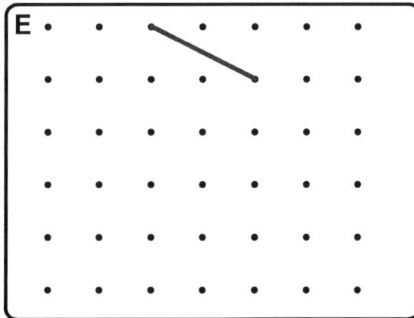

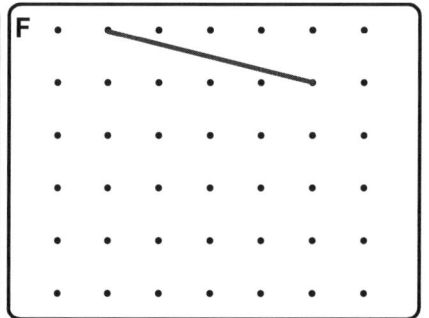

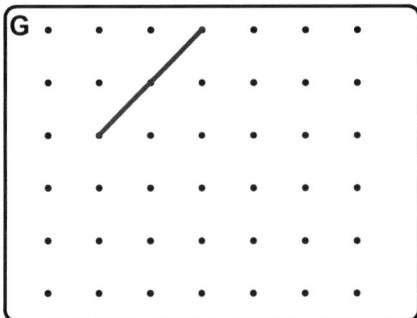

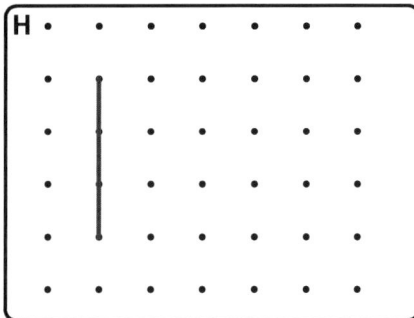

A

B

C

D

E

F

G

H

I

J

K

L

types of quadrilaterals: parallelograms

learn by heart

Quadrilateral: *4 sided shape*	Parallelogram : *Opposite sides are parallel*
Rectangle : *parallelogram with 4 right angles*	Square : *4 right angles & all sides equal*

Rectangles & Squares are special parallelograms

exercise 8b

1. Which of the shapes below are parallelograms? Circle 2 answers.

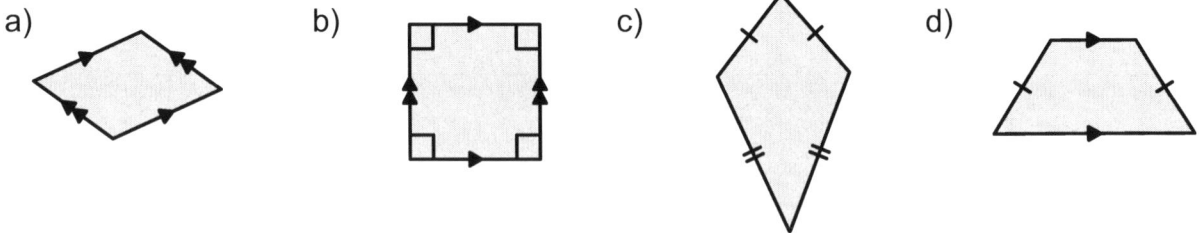

   a)   b)   c)   d)

2. Which of the shapes below are rectangles? Circle 2 answers.

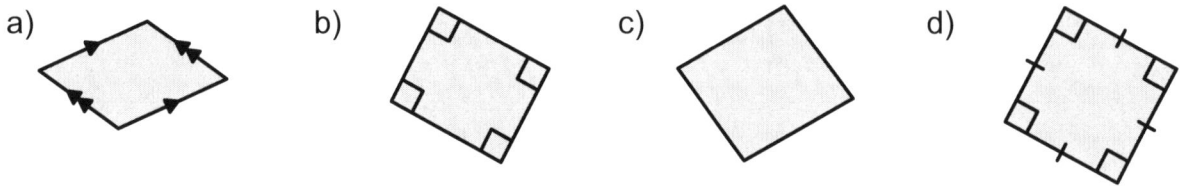

   a)   b)   c)   d)

3. Which of these shapes are squares?

   a)   b)   c)   d)

4. Copy the shapes and draw arrows on the parallel sides of these parallelograms:

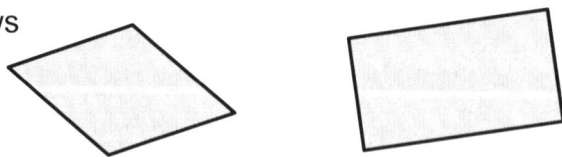

5. Which of these shapes are squares? Choose 2 answers.

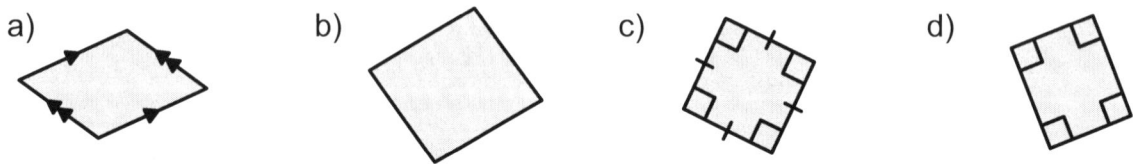

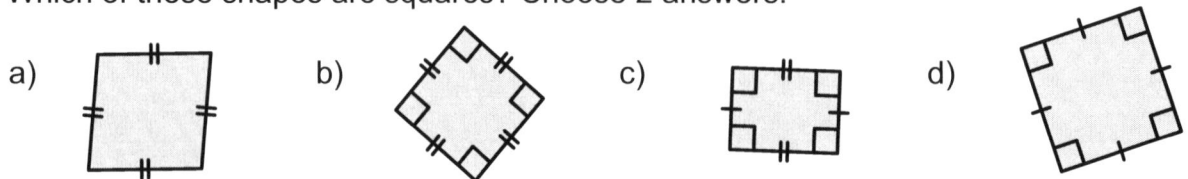

   a)   b)   c)   d)

6. Copy the diagrams and draw in extra lines to make 3 parallelograms:

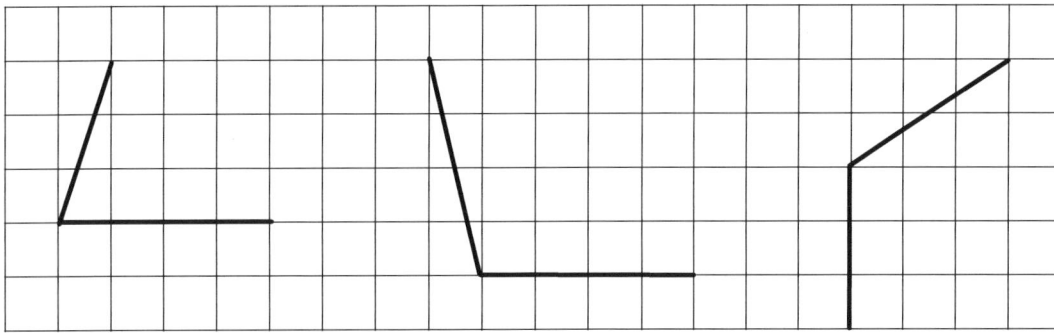

7. True or False?

a) A square has four equal sides.

b) The sides of a square are perpendicular to each other.

c) A square is a type of parallelogram.

d) A rectangle always has four equal sides.

e) The opposite sides of a rectangle are parallel.

f) A parallelogram can have four equal sides.

g) You can cut a parallelogram in half to make two triangles.

8. How many parallelograms are in the picture?

9. On square or dotty paper, copy and complete each diagram to make the shape indicated:

a) Square

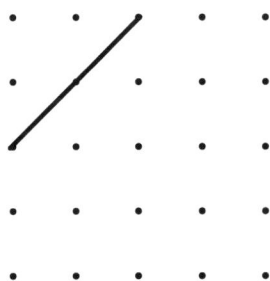

b) Rectangle

c) Parallelogram

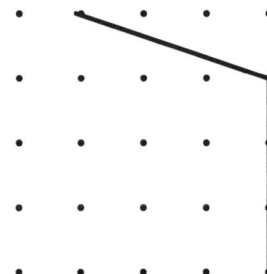

types of quadrilaterals 2

learn by heart

Rhombus	Trapezium	Kite
Four equal sides. Opposite sides parallel.	One pair of parallel sides.	Two pairs of adjacent sides equal.

Right-angled Trapezium	Isosceles Trapezium

exercise 8c

1. State whether each of these shapes is a rhombus, kite or trapezium:

a)

b) 60° 60°

c)

d)

e)

f)

g)

h)

i)

2. Which of these is a trapezium?

a)

b)

c)

d)

3. Sketch a parallelogram and a trapezium.
   Explain the difference between these two shapes.

Sort it Out!

Copy the table below and sort these shapes into the correct place:

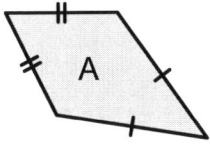

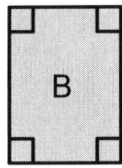

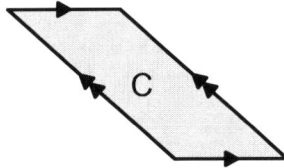

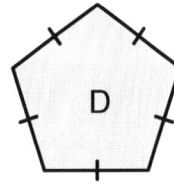

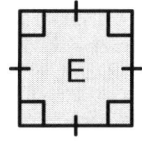

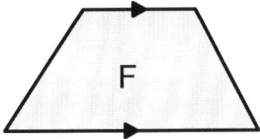

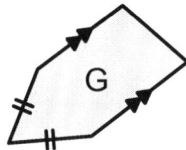

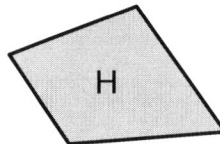

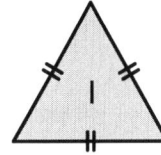

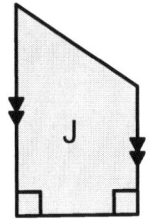

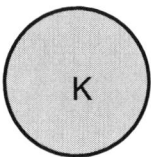

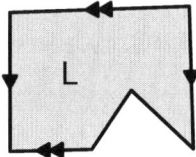

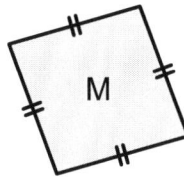

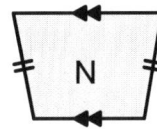

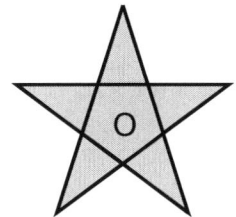

	Quadrilateral	Not a Quadrilateral
Has no parallel sides		
Has 1 pair of parallel sides	The shapes in this box are all _____	
Has 2 pairs of parallel sides	The shapes in this box are all _____	

Connect the Dots P

In each box, connect four dots to make the required shape

A kite	B rectangle	C rhombus
D trapezium	E square	F parallelogram
G square	H kite	I right angled trapezium
J rectangle	K rhombus	L parallelogram

measuring area

learn by heart

| Area *is* measured in square units | '1 square centimeter' is written $1cm^2$ 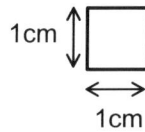 | '1 square metre', $(1m^2)$ equals $100cm \times 100cm = 10,000cm^2$ 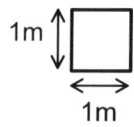 |

exercise 8d

1. Which of the following can be used to measure area? Circle all that apply.

   a) cm   b) mm^2 c) kg   d) kg^2 e) km^2 f) cm^3

2. Which of the following is largest?

   a) $1mm^2$ b) $1cm^2$ c) $1m^2$ d) $1km^2$

3. Which of the following is most likely the area of a school playground?

   a) $200mm^2$ b) $200cm^2$ c) $200m^2$ d) $200km^2$

4. Complete the units in each case:

   a) The area of the UK is approximately 242,000 _____.

   b) The area of the floor of a classroom is 70 _____.

   c) The area of a piece of A4 paper is approximately 600 _____.

   d) The distance from London to Sheffield is approximately 270 _____.

   e) The area of a finger nail is 80 _____.

5. Which of these is most likely the area of a football pitch?

   a) 1000m   b) $1000m^2$ c) $1000cm^2$ d) $1000km^2$

6. Which units would best measure the area of the front of a book?

7. How many square millimeters make a square cm?

   a) None   b) 1   c) 10   d) 100   e) 1000

8. How many square meters make a square kilometer?

   a) 100   b) 1,000   c) 10,000   d) 100,000   e) 1,000,000

9. a) Explain why the area of this shape is **not** 12 squares.

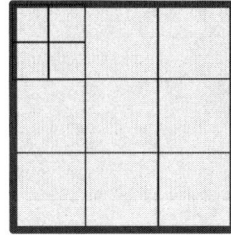

    b) What is the actual area of the shape?

10. Explain why the area of this shape is **not** 4 squares.

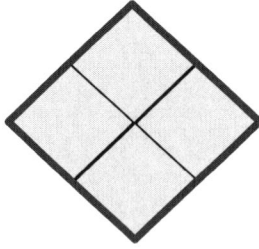

11. Do these two shapes have the same area? Explain your answer.

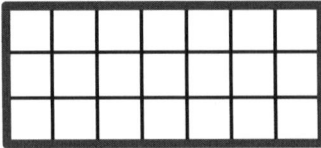

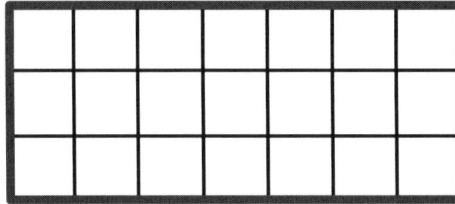

12. On squared paper, draw some rectangles with an area of 12 squares. How many different ones can you find?

13. Can you draw a triangle with a total of exactly 12 squares inside?

investigate perfect squares

14. A perfect square is a square made of whole squares.

    A perfect square can be made with 9 squares, like this:

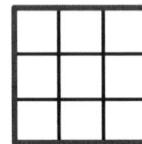

    On squared paper, try to draw a perfect square with an area of:

    a) 1   b) 3   c) 4   d) 5   e) 6   f) 8

    g) 9   h) 12   i) 15   j) 16   k) 25   l) 36

15. Can you predict which numbers will make perfect squares?
    Will 100 be a perfect square? How about 1000? How do you know?

⭐ **extra challenge**

learn by heart

| $1 cm^2 = 100 mm^2$ | $1 m^2 = 10,000 cm^2$ | $1 km^2 = 1,000,000 m^2$ |

When converting between area units, the conversion factor is (the length conversion factor)^2

examples

$3km^2 = $ _____ m^2?

$$3 \times 1000^2$$
$$= 3,000,000 m^2$$

$28,000 cm^2 = $ _____ m^2?

$$28,000 \div 100^2$$
$$= 2.8 m^2$$

km → m (length conversion factor = × 1000)
km^2→ m (1000^2 = × 1,000,000)

exercise 8e

1. Complete the following conversions:

   a) $5m^2 = $ _____ cm^2

   c) $0.9m^2 = $ _____ cm^2

   b) $1.8m^2 = $ _____ m^2

   d) $1.12m^2 = $ _____ cm^2

2. Complete the following conversions:

   a) $3km^2 = $ _____ m^2

   c) $0.5km^2 = $ _____ m^2

   b) $2.5km^2 = $ _____ m^2

   d) $0.01km^2 = $ _____ m^2

3. Match each area on the left with the same area on the right:

| A $1.8m^2$ |
| B $1,800mm^2$ |
| C $1,800,000m^2$ |
| D $108mm^2$ |
| E $10,800cm^2$ |

| F $18cm^2$ |
| G $1.08cm^2$ |
| H $1.08m^2$ |
| I $18,000cm^2$ |
| J $1.8km^2$ |

A	
B	
C	
D	
E	

4. Complete the following conversions:

   a) 2m^2 = _____ cm^2 b) 30,000cm^2 = _____ m^2

   c) 1km^2 = _____ m^2 d) 42,500cm^2 = _____ m^2

   e) 406m^2 = _____ cm^2 f) 6,500,000m^2 = _____ km^2

   g) 2,300cm^2 = _____ m^2 h) 4.5cm^2 = _____ mm^2

5. True or false?

   a) 1m^2 = 100cm^2 c) 1km^2 is longer than 1km

   b) 1m = 100cm   d) 1km^2 is larger than 1000m^2

6. In each pair, select the larger area:

   a) 1m^2 or 1cm^2 c) 4m^2 or 1000cm^2 e) 3m^2 or 300cm^2

   b) 1cm^2 or 90mm^2 d) 10cm^2 or 100mm^2 f) 0.1m^2 or 2000cm^2

7. Fill in the blanks:

   a) 99mm^2 + _____ = 1cm^2 d) 1m^2 + _____ cm^2 = 1.2m^2

   b) 9000cm^2 + _____ = 1m^2 e) 1,000,000m^2 + _____ = 1 km^2

   c) 3m^2 + 4,000cm^2 = _____ m^2 f) 2.6km^2 + _____ m^2 = 3km^2

8. Which of the following is largest?

   a) 500cm^2 b) 50m^2 c) 0.5km^2 d) 5mm^2

figure it out ⭐ extra challenge

Volume is measured in cubes.
Can you figure out how many cubic centimetres would fit inside a cubic metre?

A cubic metre (not to scale)

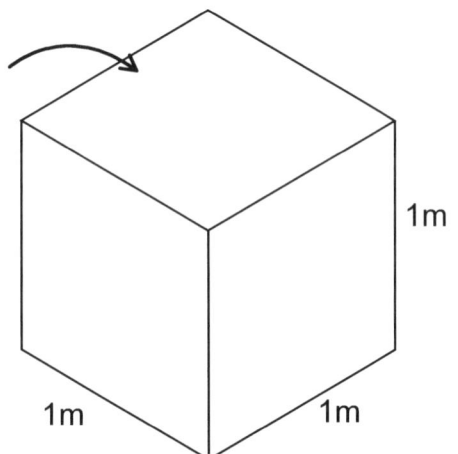

1m
1m
1m

A cubic centimetre

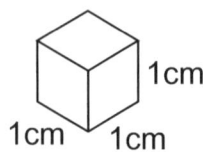

1cm
1cm
1cm

area of parallelograms (including squares & rectangles) 🖩

learn by heart

Area of Squares, Rectangles & Parallelograms: *base × perpendicular height*

examples

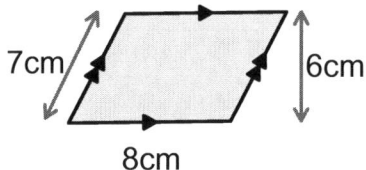

Calculate the area

= 8 × 6
= 48cm²

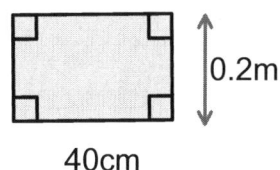

Calculate the area

= 0.2 × 0.4
= 0.08m²

exercise 8f

1. Work out the area of each shape. Pay careful attention to the units.

a)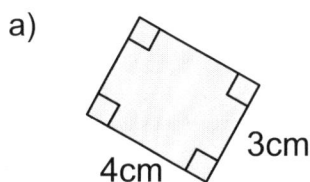

b)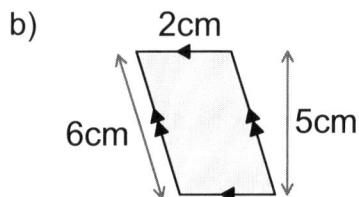

c)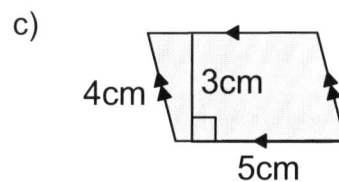

d)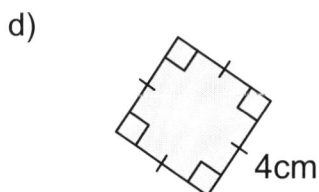

e)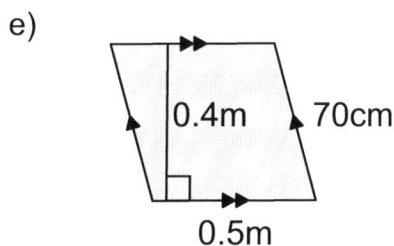

f)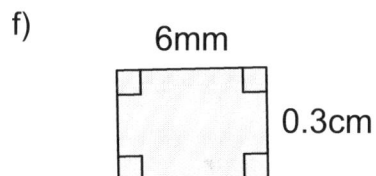

g)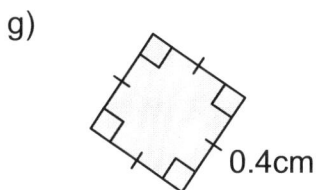

h)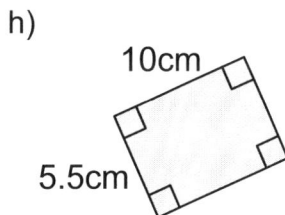

i)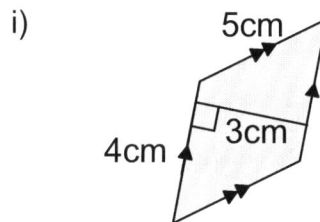

2. Given the area, work out the side length of each of these squares:

a)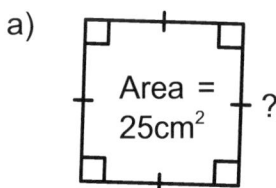

Area = 25cm² ?

b)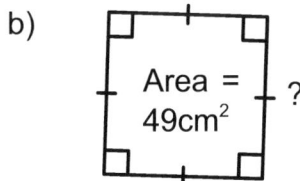

Area = 49cm² ?

c)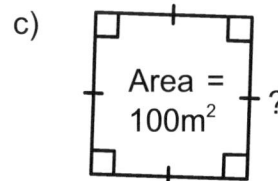

Area = 100m² ?

3. In these shapes, all lengths given are in centimetres.
Calculate the area, giving your answer as a decimal:

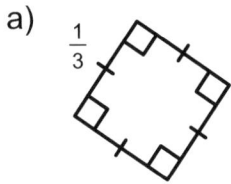

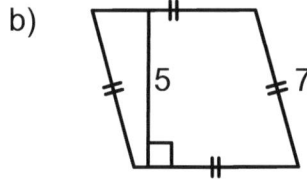

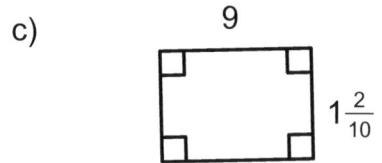

a) $\frac{1}{3}$

b) 5   7

c) 9 $1\frac{2}{10}$

4. Explain why we can't work out
the area of this shape:

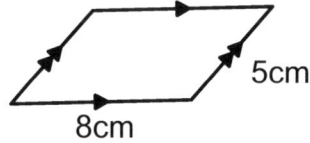

5cm

8cm

5. This rectangle and parallelogram have
the same area.

Can you work out the length marked ?

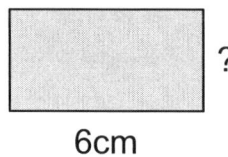

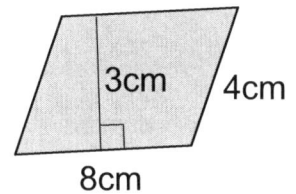

?   3cm   4cm

6cm   8cm

6. Which calculation works out the area of this parallelogram?

a) 5 × 10   b) 10 × 8   c) 7 × 8   d) 5 × 7

5   7

10   8

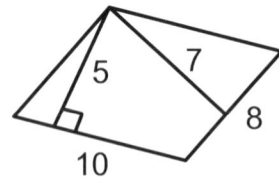

7. On square or dotty paper,
draw three different parallelograms with an area of 10cm^2

8. On square or dotty paper,
draw three squares with areas of 4cm^2 , 9cm^2 and 16cm^2

Draw it! P ⭐ extra challenge

Draw the following shapes:

A A square with an area of 25

B A rectangle with a perimeter of 18 and an area of 20

C A square where area = perimeter

D A rectangle where area = perimeter = 18

E Complete the parallelogram so that it has an area of 15

F A square where the area is half the perimeter

G A parallelogram with no right angles and an area of 40

H A parallelogram with no right angles that can split exactly into two right angled triangles

I A rectangle with a perimeter that is an odd number

J Draw two different rectangles each with a perimeter of 15.

K A square where area - perimeter = 12

L A rectangle where area + perimeter = 14

279

area of triangles

learn by heart

Area of a Triangle:
(*base* × *perpendicular height*) ÷ 2

example

Calculate the area

$= \frac{1}{2} \times 8 \times 7$

$= 28cm^2$

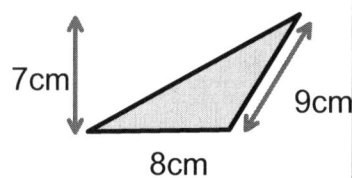

exercise 8g

1. In this triangle, the base is _____ long and the perpendicular height is _____ long.

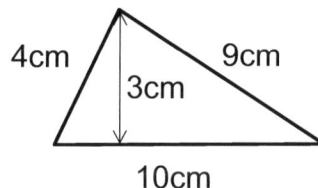

2. On each triangle the **base** is shown.
   Copy each diagram and draw on the perpendicular height.

a)

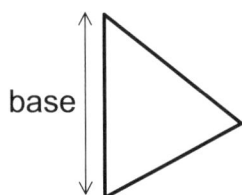

b)

base

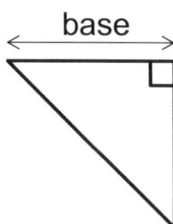

c)

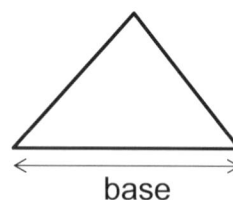

base

d)

base

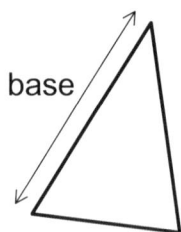

e)

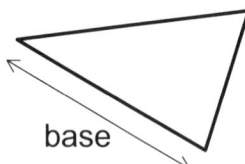

base

f)

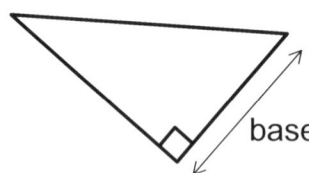

base

3. Which calculation works out the area of this triangle?

a) $\frac{10 \times 6}{2}$

c) $\frac{6 \times 8}{2}$

b) $\frac{6 + 8}{2}$

d) $\frac{10 \times 8}{2}$

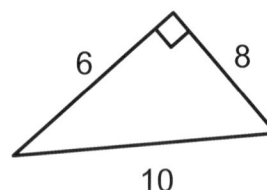

4. Which calculation can be used to work out the area of this triangle?

a) $\frac{15 \times 9}{2}$

b) $\frac{15 \times 12}{2}$

c) $\frac{9 \times 12}{2}$

d) $\frac{9 \times 12 \times 15}{2}$

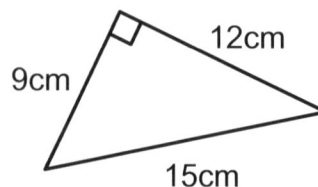

5. Calculate the area of each triangle. Lengths are all measured in cm.

a)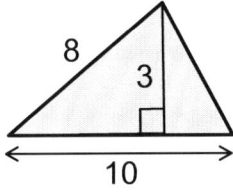

b)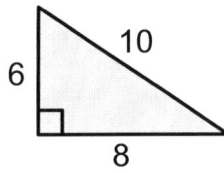

c)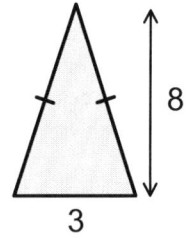

d)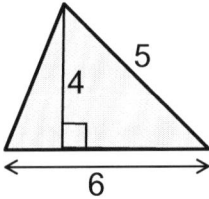

e)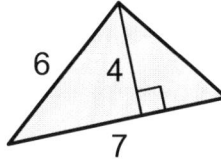

f)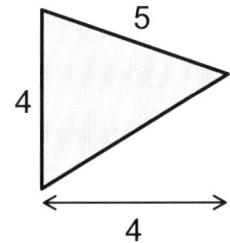

g)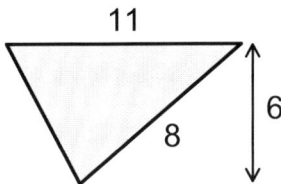

h)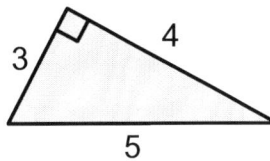

i)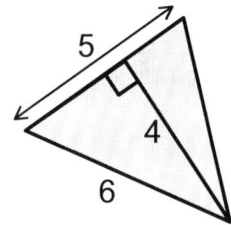

6. Draw two more triangles with the same area as the one given:

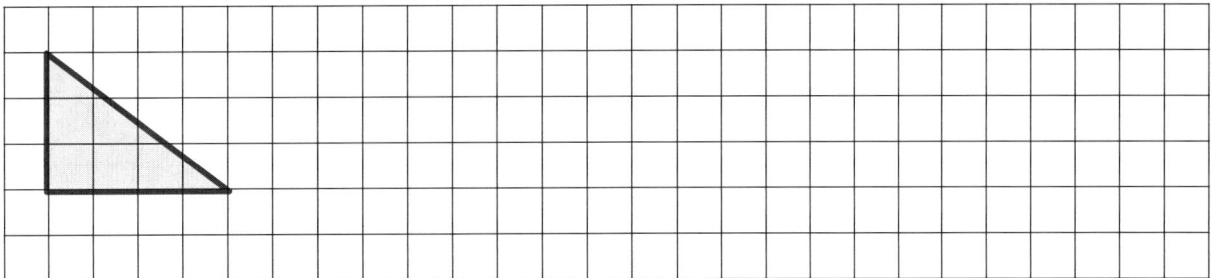

7. The area of the triangle is 3 times bigger than the area of the parallelogram. Work out x.

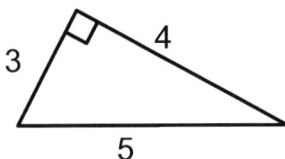

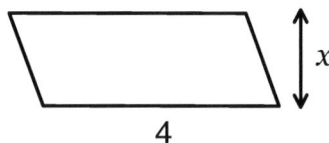

learn by heart

Area of a Trapezium: $\dfrac{a + b}{2} \times h$

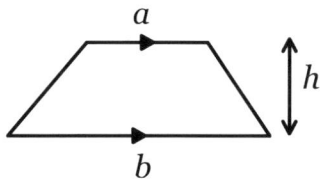

a and b are the parallel sides of a trapezium

example

Calculate the area:

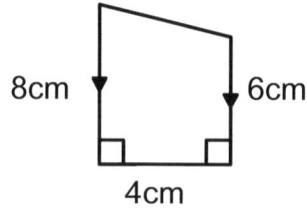

8cm   6cm

4cm

$$\text{Area} = \frac{8 + 6}{2} \times 4$$
$$= \frac{14}{2} \times 4$$
$$= 7 \times 4$$
$$= 28cm^2$$

exercise 8h

1.   Calculate the area of each trapezium:

a)

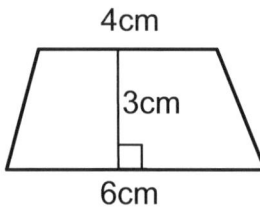

4cm

3cm

6cm

b)

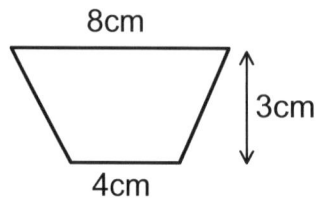

8cm

3cm

4cm

c)

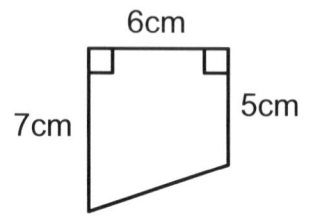

6cm

7cm   5cm

d)

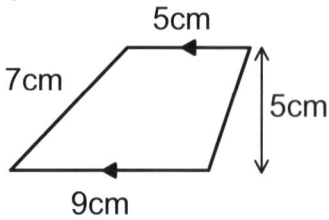

5cm

7cm

5cm

9cm

e)

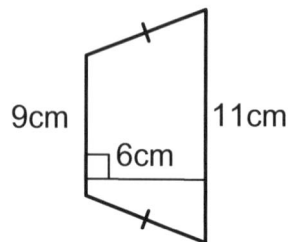

9cm   11cm

6cm

f)

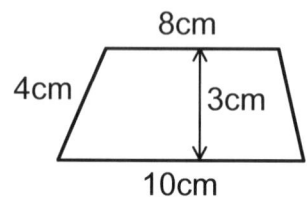

8cm

4cm   3cm

10cm

g)

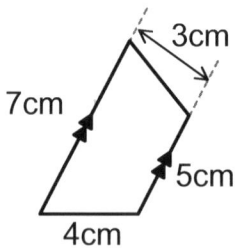

3cm

7cm

5cm

4cm

h)

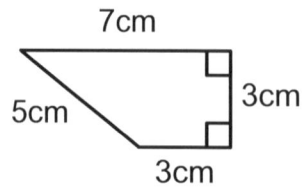

7cm

5cm   3cm

3cm

i)

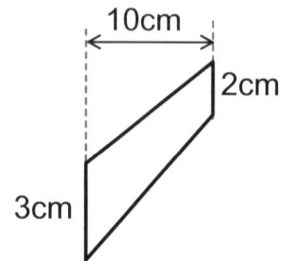

10cm

2cm

3cm

exercise 8i : mixed area practice

1. Calculate the area of each shape.

a)

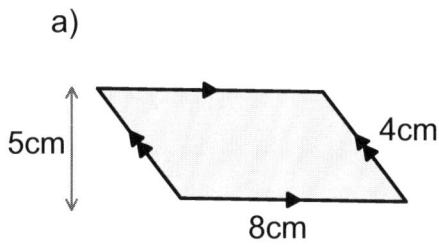
5cm
4cm
8cm

b)

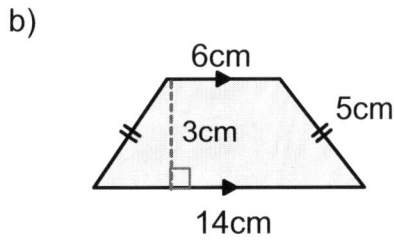
6cm
5cm
3cm
14cm

c)

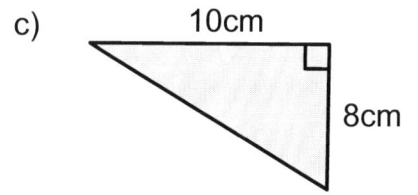
10cm
8cm

d)

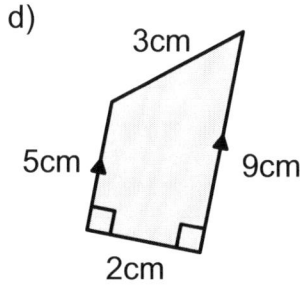
3cm
5cm
9cm
2cm

e)

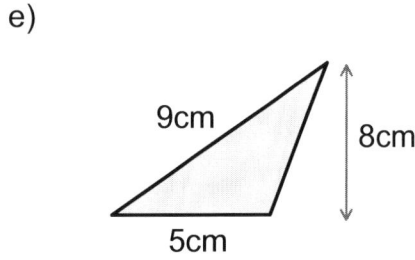
9cm
8cm
5cm

f)

units!

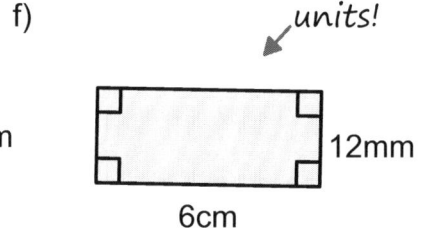
12mm
6cm

g)

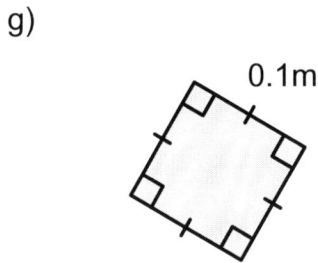
0.1m

h)

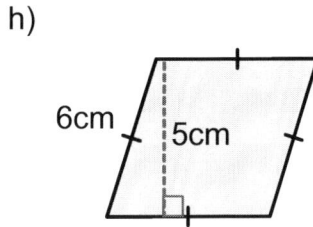
6cm
5cm

i)

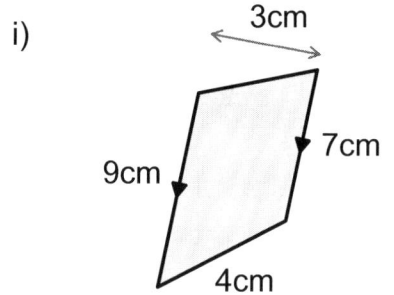
3cm
7cm
9cm
4cm

j)

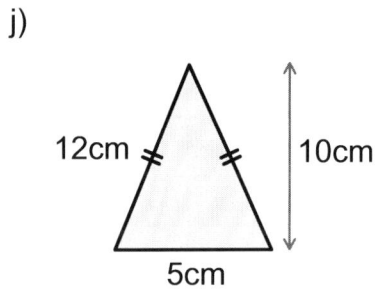
12cm
10cm
5cm

k)

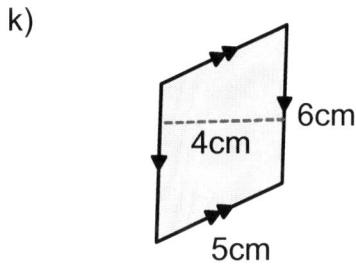
6cm
4cm
5cm

l)

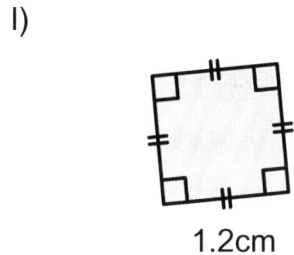
1.2cm

2. Draw a triangle, a trapezium and a parallelogram that all have
    the same area.

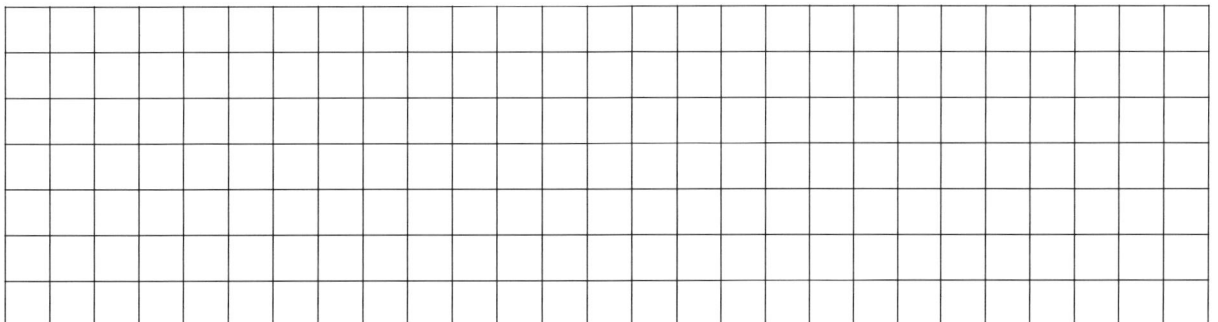

compound shapes

example

Calculate the area:

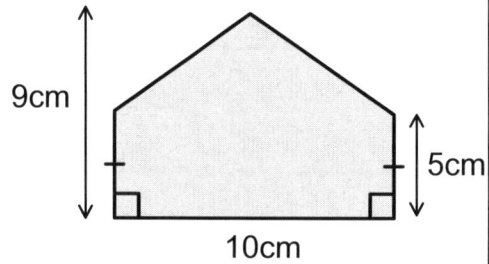

Area of Rectangle = 50cm²

Area of triangle = $\frac{4 \times 10}{2}$ = 20cm²

Total Area = 70cm²

exercise 8j

1. Calculate the area:

a)

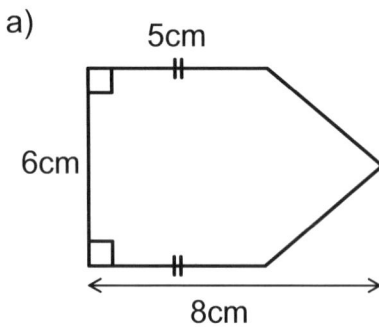

b)

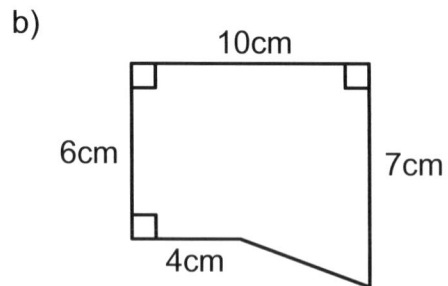

c)

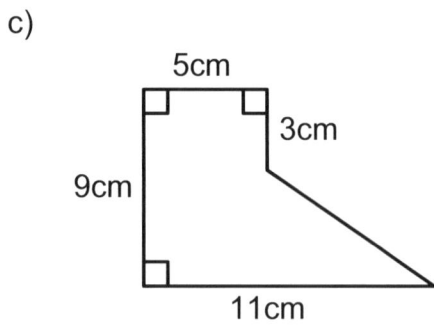

d)

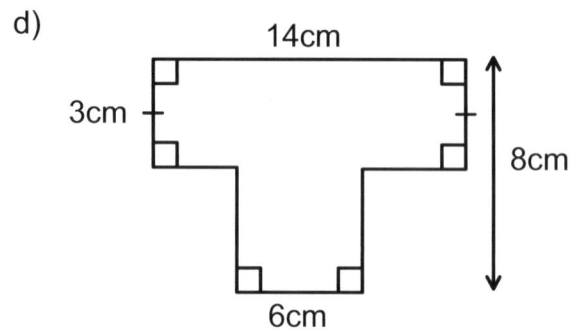

e)

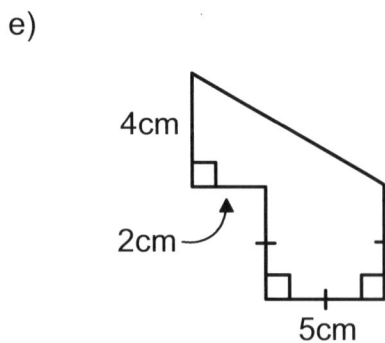

f)

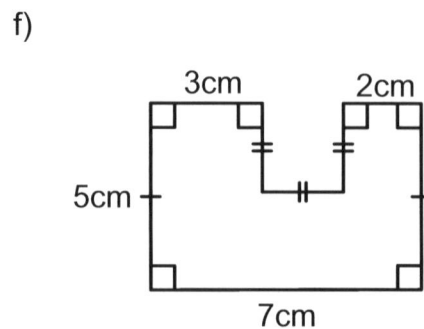

2. Calculate the area of these shapes. All the lengths are measured in cm.

a)

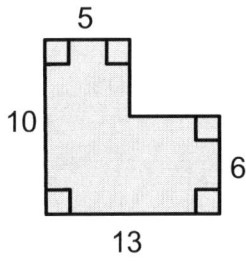

b)

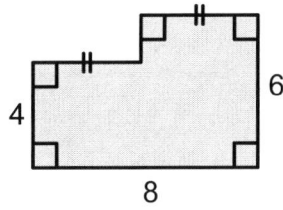

c)

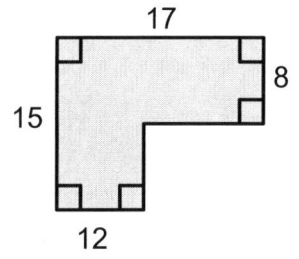

d)

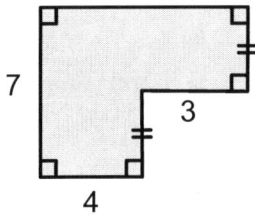

e)

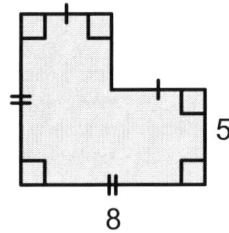

f)

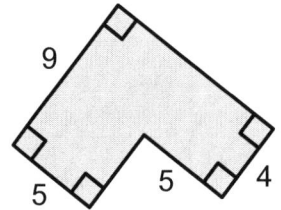

3. Calculate the missing dimensions. (All dimensions are in cm.) ⭐ extra challenge

a)

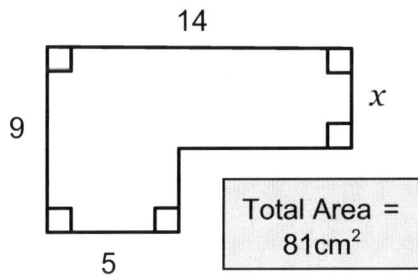

b)

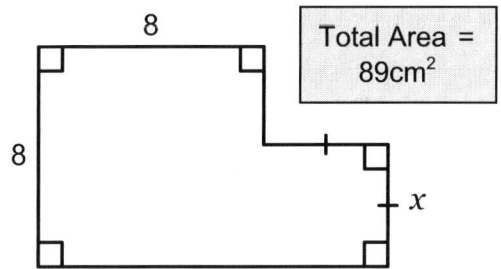

c)

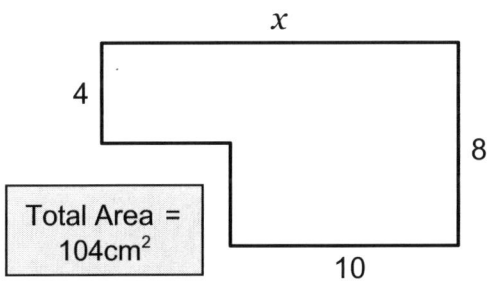

d)

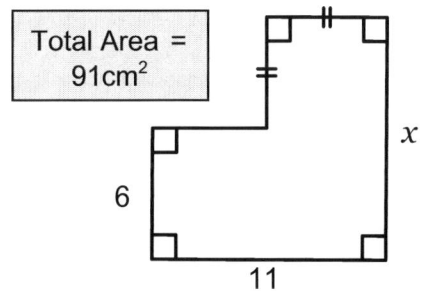

example

Calculate the area:

Area of Whole Rectangle = 90cm²
Area of Missing Trapezium =
$\frac{10 + 6}{2} \times 5 = 40cm²$
Total Area = 90 – 40 = 50cm²

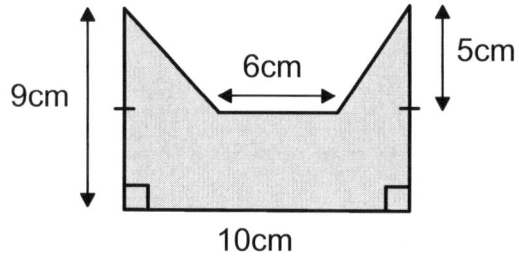

exercise 8k

1. Calculate the shaded area of each shape:

a)

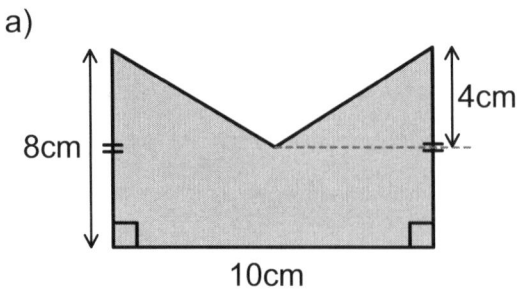

b)

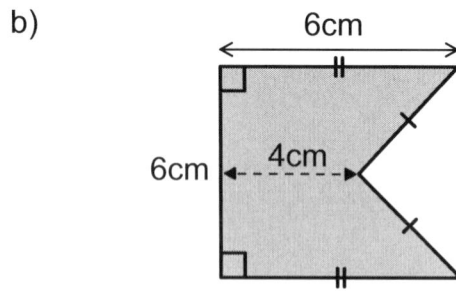

c)

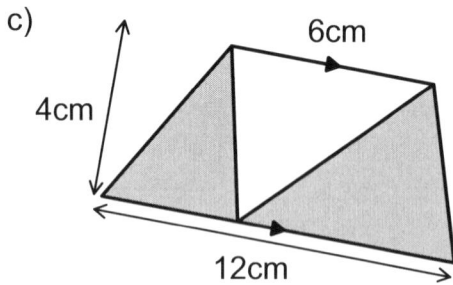

d)

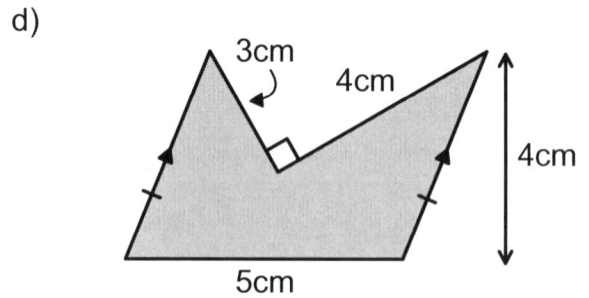

e)

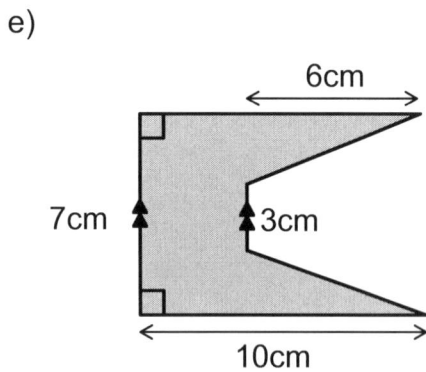

f)

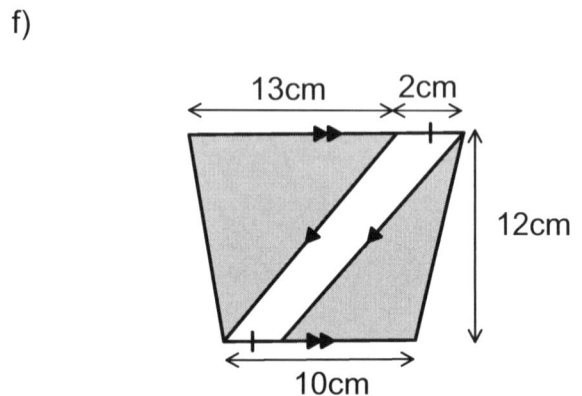

g)

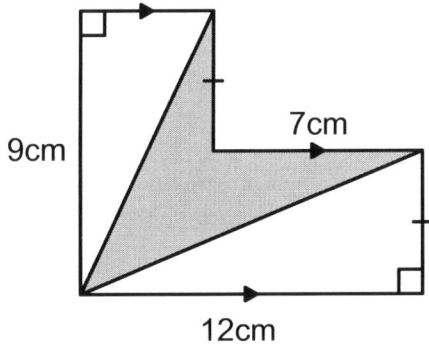

9cm

7cm

12cm

h)

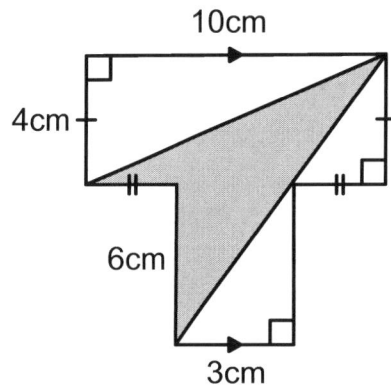

10cm

4cm

6cm

3cm

2. Each of these diagrams are squares.
   Calculate the shaded area in each diagram:

a)

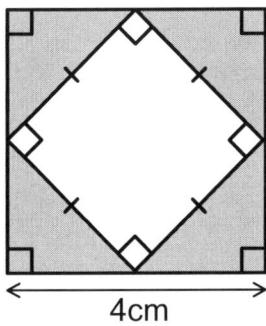

4cm

b)

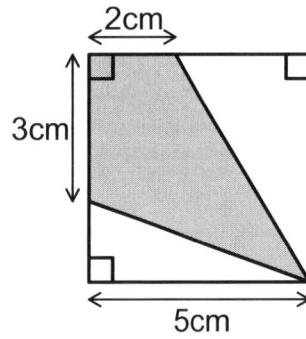

2cm

3cm

5cm

c)

4cm

10cm

d)

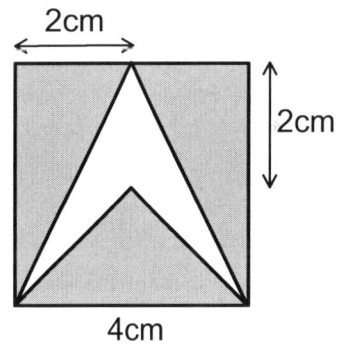

2cm

2cm

4cm

<u>challenge</u>

3. The line AB is a straight line.
   The area of the white triangle is 120cm².
   What is the area of the blue triangle?

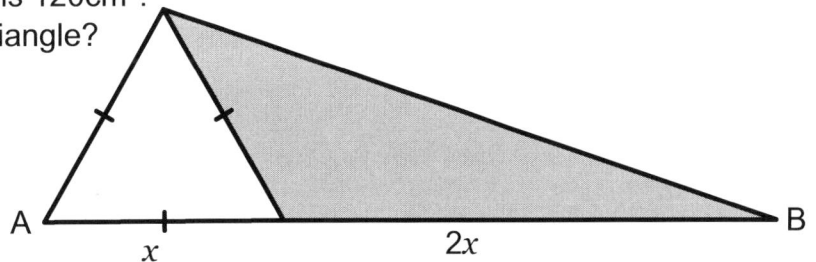

A   x   2x   B

area of circles 🖩

learn by heart

Area of a circle = πr^2

Recall that π (pi) is an irrational number that begins 3.141...

example

Work out the area of this circle. Give your answer to 3 s.f.

10cm

area = 5^2 × π = $78.5cm^2$

exercise 81

1. If the radius of a circle is 12cm, then the diameter is _____

2. If the diameter of a circle is 3cm, then the radius is _____.

3. Calculate the area of these shapes. Round your answer to 3 significant figures.

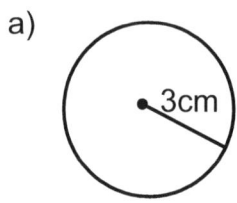

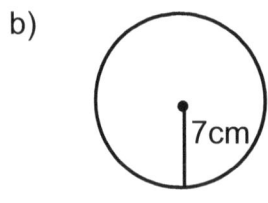

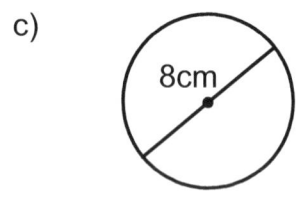

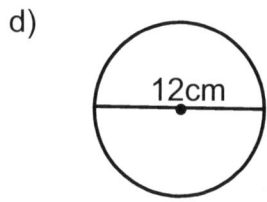

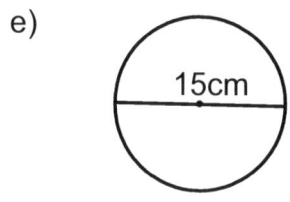

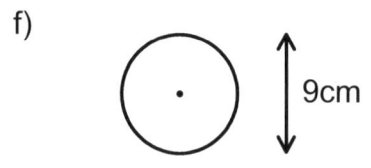

a)

3cm

b)

7cm

c)

8cm

d)

12cm

e)

15cm

f)

9cm

4. A circle is drawn inside a square. The side length of the square is 12cm. Work out the area of the circle to 3 s.f:

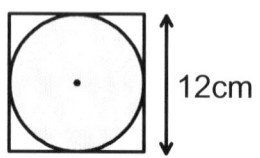

12cm

5. The diagram shows a circle inside a square. The circle has a radius of 3cm. What is the area of the square?

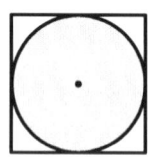

6. The diagram shows two identical circles inside a rectangle. Work out the area of 1 circle, correct to 1 d.p.

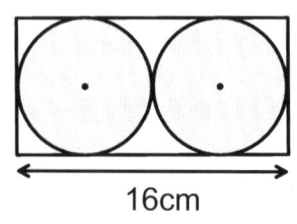

16cm

7. If the area of a circle is $1m^2$, then the area of this circle is also _____ cm^2

8. The diagram shows three identical circles inside a rectangle. The circles each have a radius of 2cm. Work out the area of the rectangle.

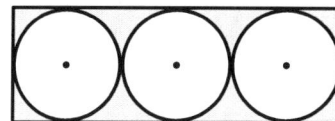

9. The diagram shows a circle inside a square. The area of the square is 64cm². Work out the area of:

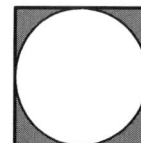

   a) the circle to 2 d.p.   b) the shaded region to 2 d.p.

10. The diagram shows four identical circles inside a square.

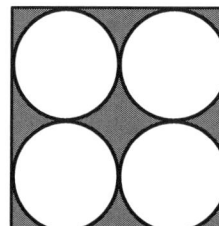

    a) If the square has an area of 36cm², what is the radius of each circle?

    b) Work out the area shaded blue to 3 s.f.

11. The diagram shows three identical circles inside a rectangle. Work out the area shaded blue to 1 decimal place..

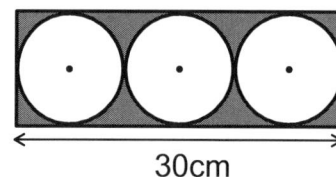

    30cm

12. The diagram shows two circles with the same centre point. The radius of the smaller circle is 3cm. Work out the area of the region shaded blue, to 2 d.p.

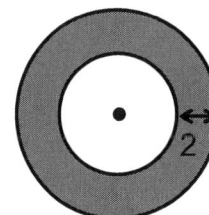

    2

13. The diagram shows two identical circles inside a larger circle. The radius of each small circle is 1cm. Work out the area shaded blue, to 3 s.f.

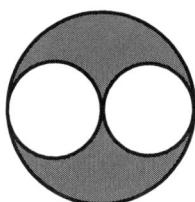

extension ⭐ extra challenge

14. The diagram shows a semi-circle. Work out its area to 3 s.f.

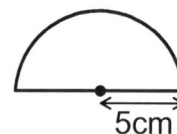

    5cm

15. The diagram shows a semi-circle. Work out its area to 3 s.f.

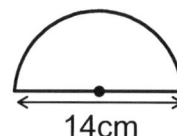

    14cm

exercise 8m

1. Calculate the area in square centimetres, rounding to 3 s.f where necessary:

a)

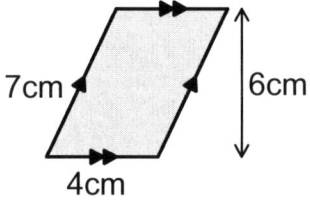

7cm   6cm   4cm

b)

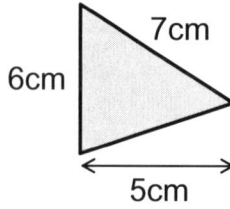

7cm   6cm   5cm

c)

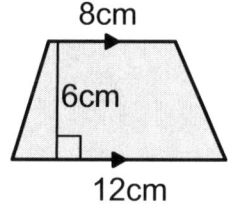

8cm   6cm   12cm

d)

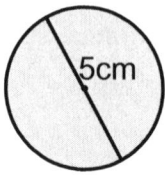

5cm

e)

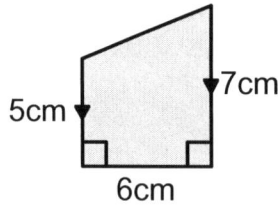

5cm   7cm   6cm

f)

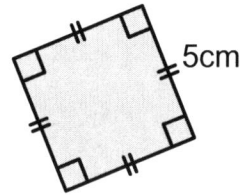

5cm

g)

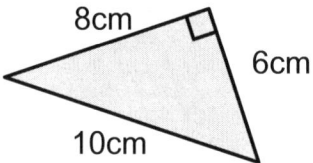

8cm   6cm   10cm

h)

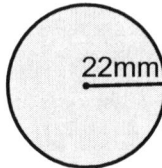

22mm

i)

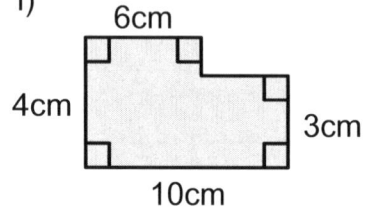

6cm   4cm   3cm   10cm

j)

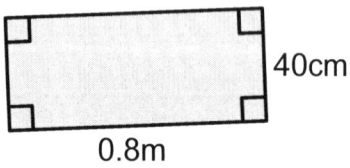

40cm   0.8m

k)

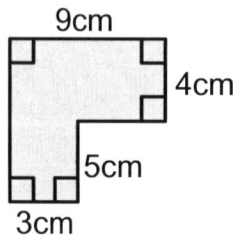

9cm   4cm   5cm   3cm

l)

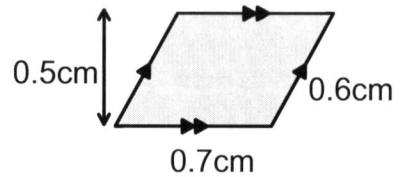

0.5cm   0.6cm   0.7cm

m)

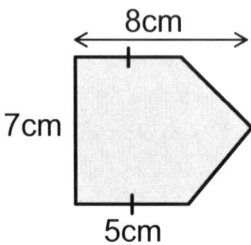

8cm   7cm   5cm

n)

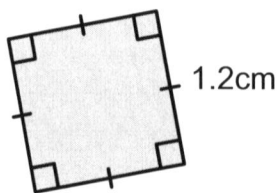

1.2cm

o)

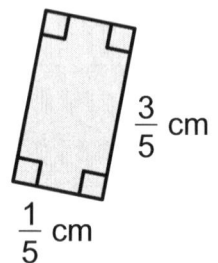

$\frac{3}{5}$ cm $\frac{1}{5}$ cm

290

more challenging ⭐ extra challenge

1. Given the area shown, can you work out the missing dimensions of these shapes, labelled with a ? Round your answer to 2 d.p. where necessary.

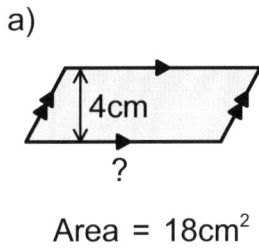

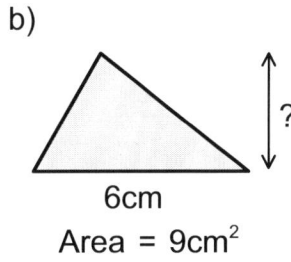

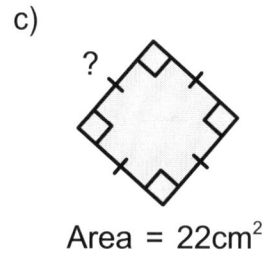

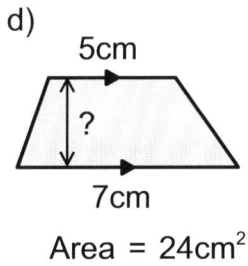

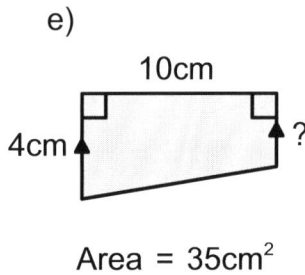

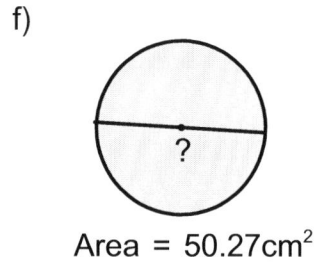

a)

4cm

?

Area = 18cm²

b)

6cm

?

Area = 9cm²

c)

?

Area = 22cm²

d)

5cm

?

7cm

Area = 24cm²

e)

10cm

4cm

?

Area = 35cm²

f)

?

Area = 50.27cm²

2. These shapes all have the same area.
Can you work out the missing dimensions?

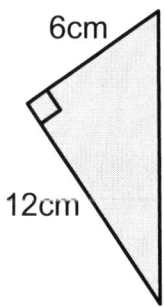

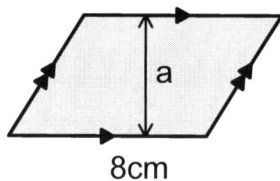

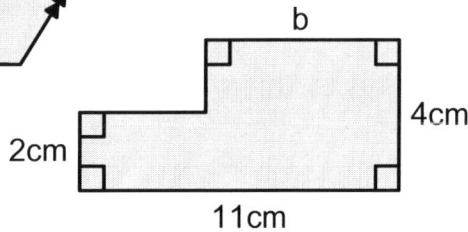

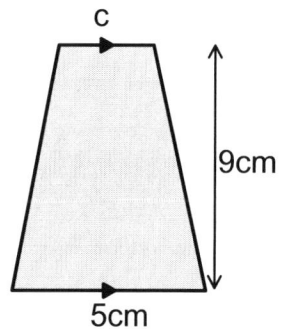

6cm

12cm

a

8cm

b

2cm

11cm

4cm

c

9cm

5cm

3. These shapes are drawn on a 1cm by 1cm grid.
By breaking them into triangles and rectangles, can you work out their areas?

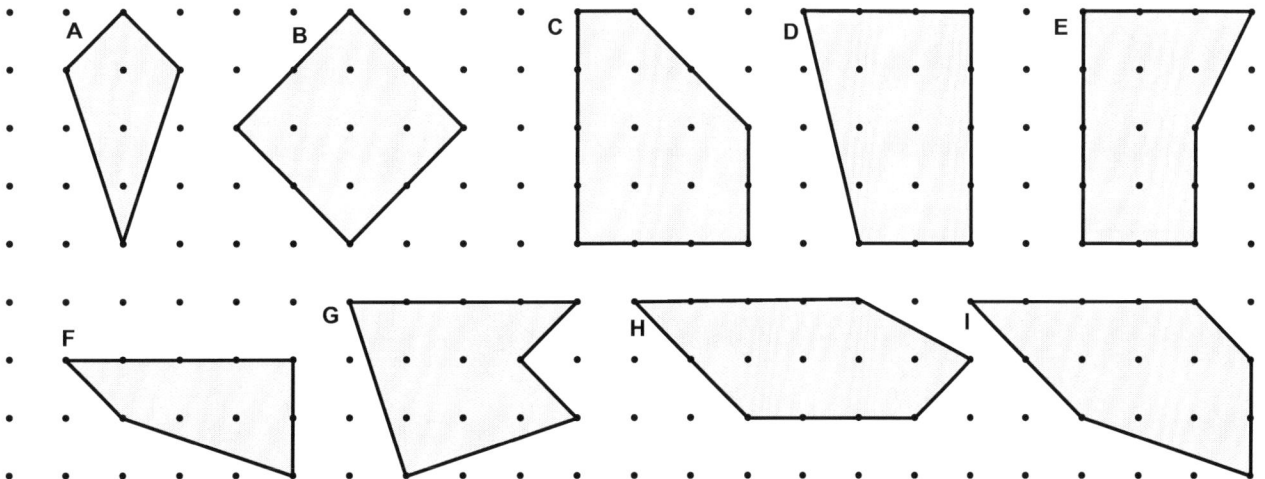

A B C D E

F G H I

Investigating Pythagoras: Tilted Squares ⭐ extra challenge P

In the 6th century BC, the ancient Greek mathematician Pythagoras discovered a curious fact about the area of squares drawn on the sides of triangles.

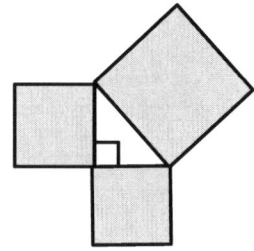

In this investigation, you are going to try and find the pattern that he discovered.

To begin, try finding the area of these tilted squares, by breaking them down into rectangles & triangles:

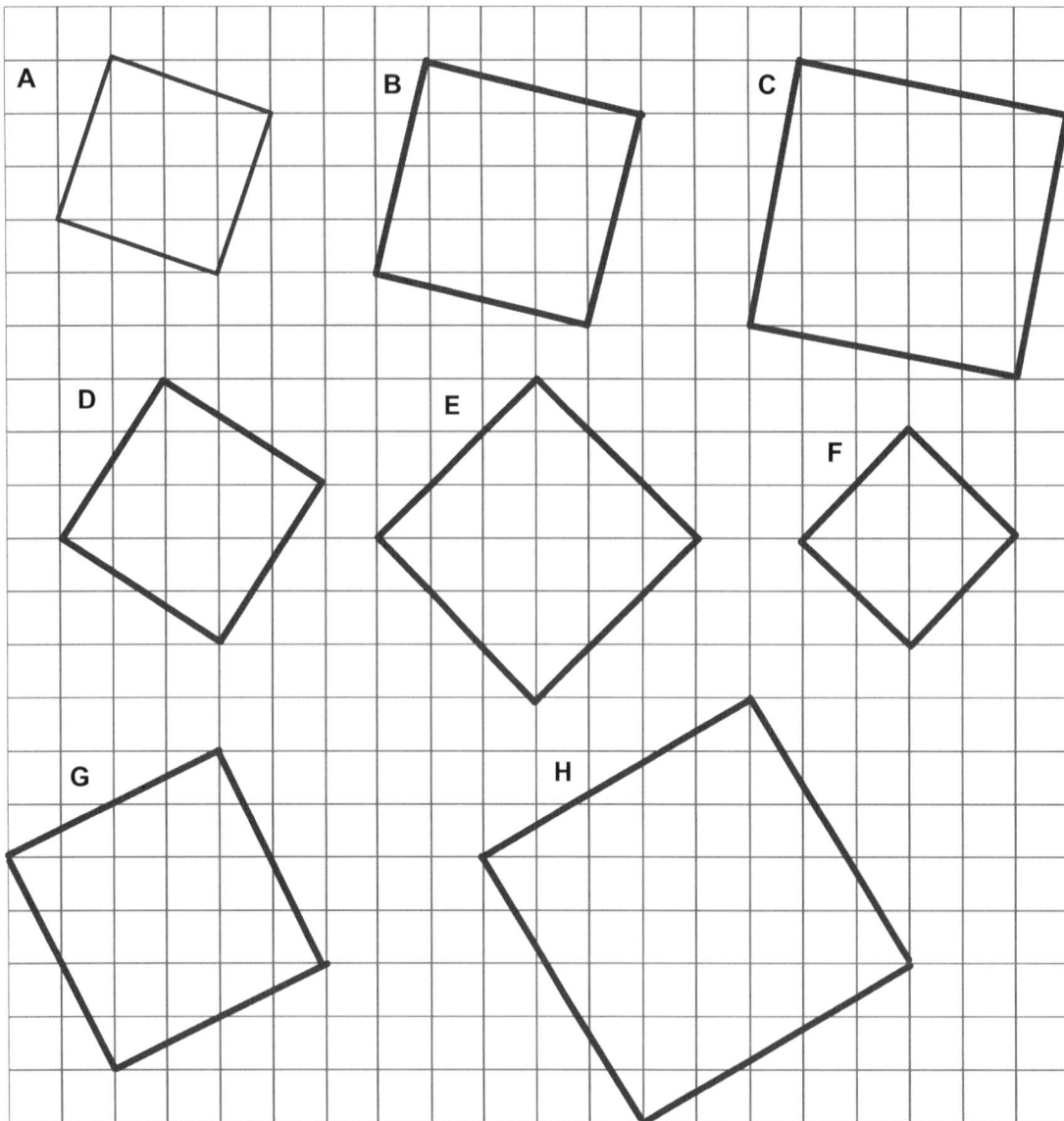

A B C

D E F

G H

Now try finding the area of these tilted squares drawn
on the sides of right angled triangles. What do you notice?

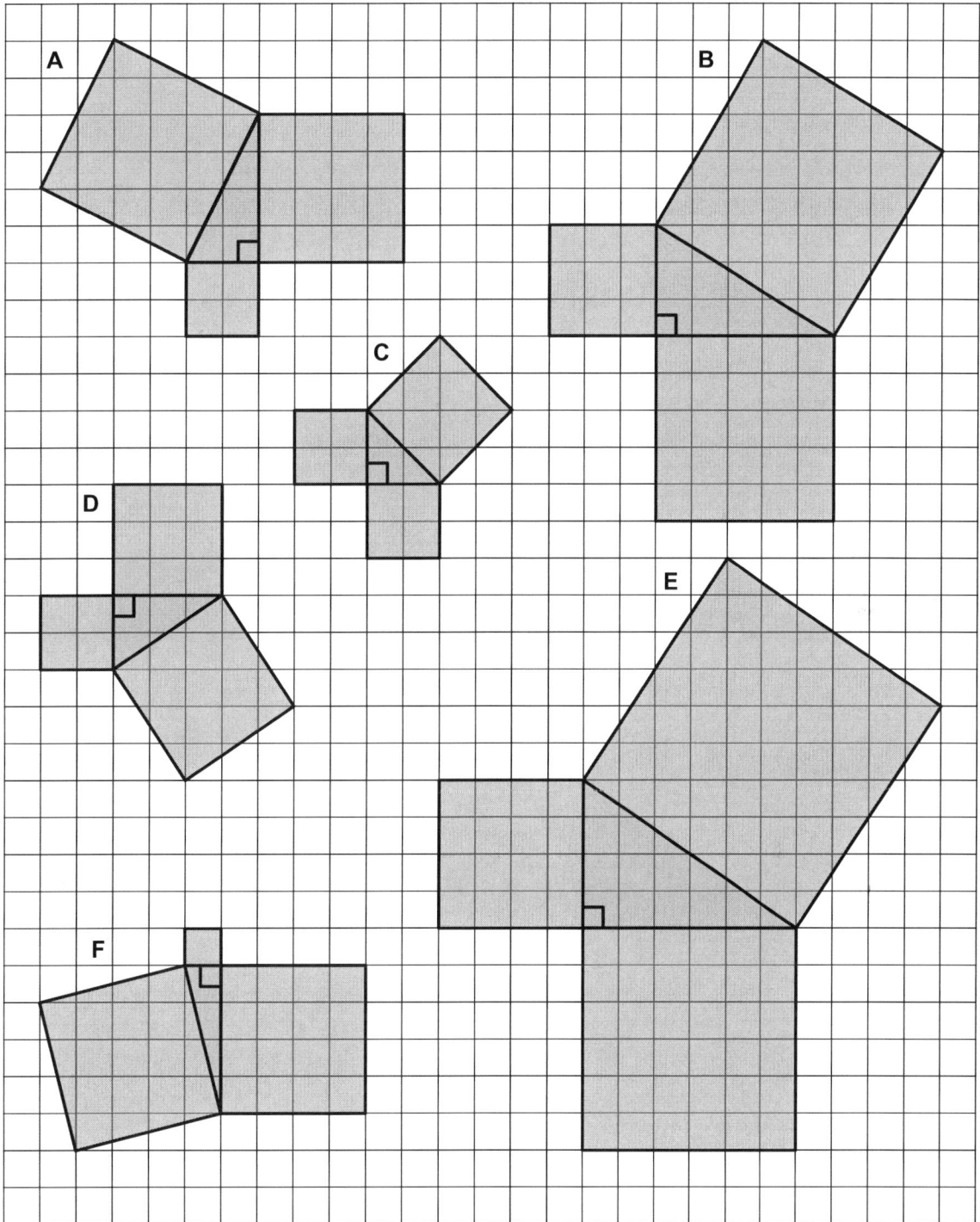

extra
challenge

P

pythagoras' theorem ▦

The hypotenuse is opposite the right angle

learn by heart

Hypotenuse: *the longest side in a triangle*

Pythagoras' Theorem: $a^2 + b^2 = c^2$

a^2

b^2

c^2

example

Calculate the length of the side marked x:

$x^2 = 20^2 - 8^2$
$x^2 = 336$
$x = \sqrt{336}$
$x = 18.33$ (2 $d.p.$)

8

20

x

recall

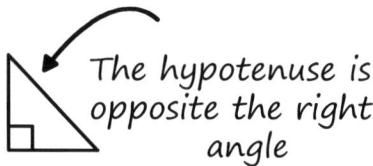

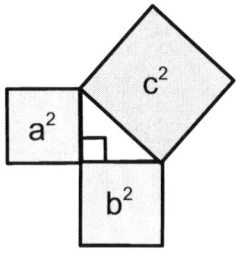

The square root of a non-square number is called a 'surd' - it is an irrational number that will continue forever with no repeating pattern.

exercise 8n

1. Find the length of the hypotenuse, correct to 1 decimal place.

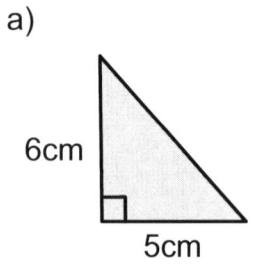

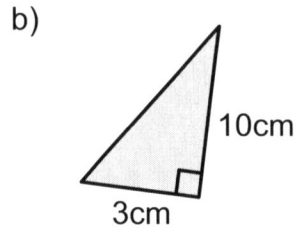

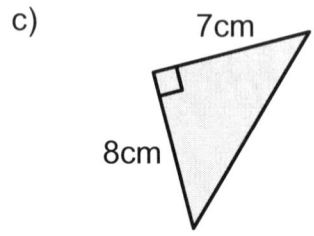

    a)

    6cm

    5cm

    b)

    10cm

    3cm

    c)

    7cm

    8cm

2. Find the length of the missing side, correct to 3 significant figures.

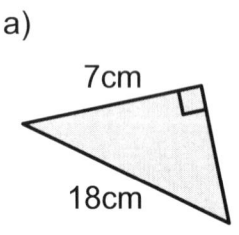

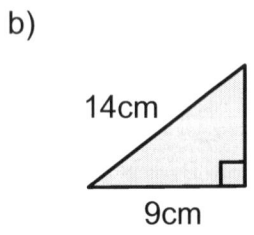

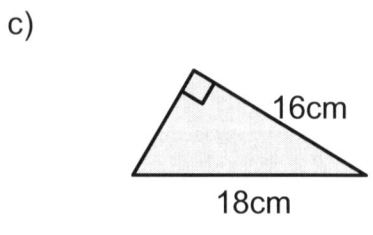

    a)

    7cm

    18cm

    b)

    14cm

    9cm

    c)

    16cm

    18cm

3. Work out the value of x for each diagram.
    Round your answers to 2 decimal places, where necessary.

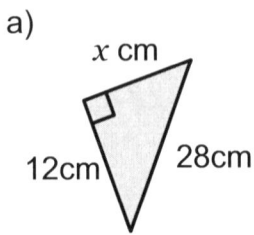

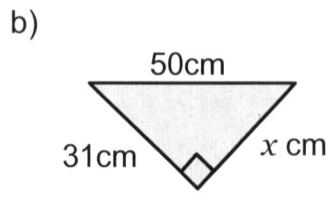

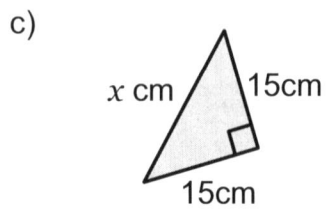

    a)

    x cm

    12cm

    28cm

    b)

    50cm

    31cm

    x cm

    c)

    x cm

    15cm

    15cm

d)

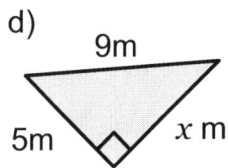

9m
5m *x* m

e)

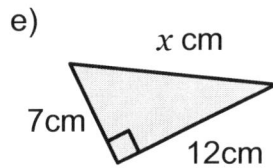

x cm
7cm 12cm

f)

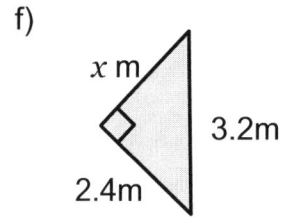

x m
3.2m
2.4m

4. Work out the missing sides of these triangles. The answers are all integers.

a)

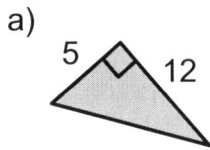

5 12

b)

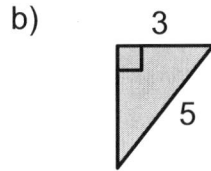

3
5

c)

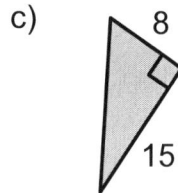

8
15

d)

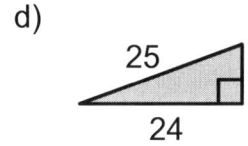

25
24

5. Work out the **perimeter** of each triangle.

a)

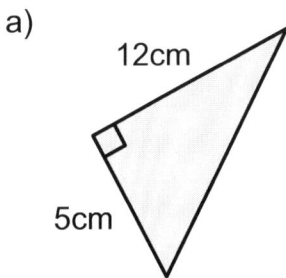

12cm
5cm

b)

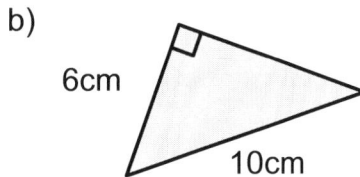

6cm
10cm

c)

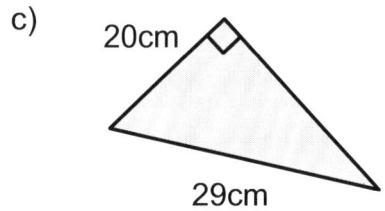

20cm
29cm

6. In each diagram, work out the length of the sides marked with letters.
    Where necessary, round your answers to 1 decimal place.

a)

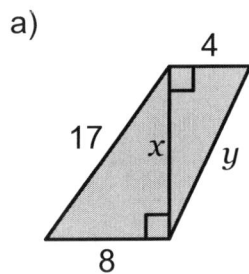

4
17 *x* *y*
8

b)

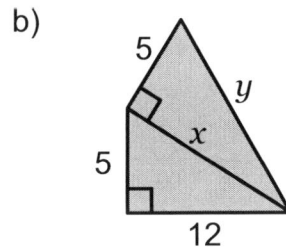

5 *y*
x
5
12

c)

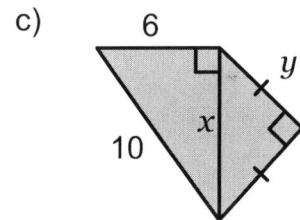

6 *y*
10 *x*

more challenging

7. Work out the area of each triangle. Hint: each triangle can be split into two right-angled
    triangles. Use Pythagoras to help find the lengths you need.

a)

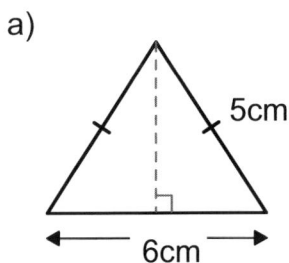

5cm
6cm

b)

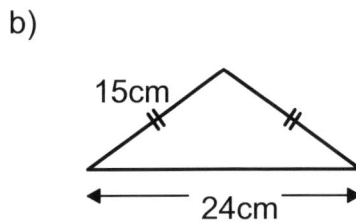

15cm
24cm

c)

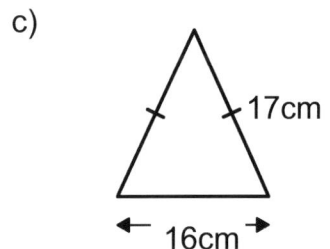

17cm
16cm

applying pythagoras' theorem 🔲 ⭐extra challenge

examples

Calculate the area to 1 d.p.:

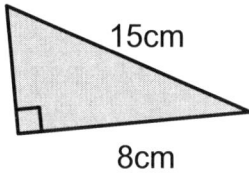

15cm
8cm

missing side^2 = $15^2 - 8^2$
missing side = 12.69 (2.d.p.)
area = $(8 \times 12.69) \div 2$ = $50.8cm^2$

Calculate the perimeter of this trapezium:

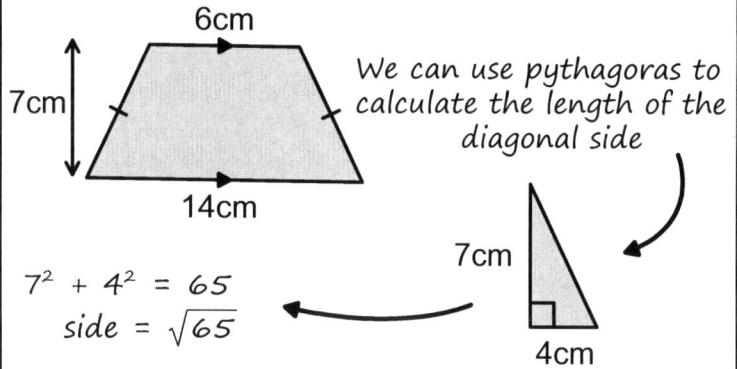

6cm
7cm
14cm

We can use pythagoras to calculate the length of the diagonal side

7cm
4cm

$7^2 + 4^2 = 65$
side = $\sqrt{65}$

Total Perimeter = $6 + 14 + 2 \times \sqrt{65}$ = 36.12cm

exercise 80

1.   Work out the area of these triangles,
     rounding your answer to 3 significant figures if necessary.

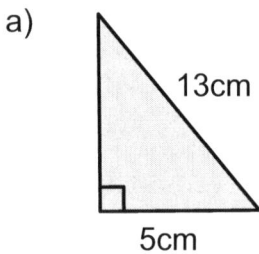

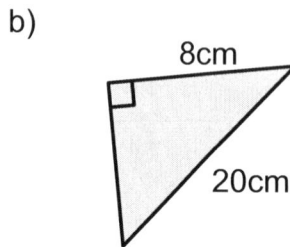

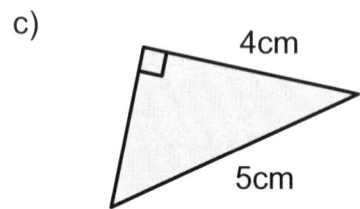

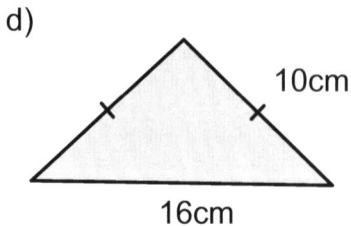

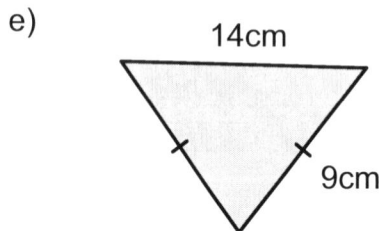

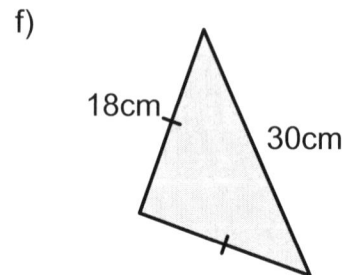

a)
13cm
5cm

b)
8cm
20cm

c)
4cm
5cm

d)
10cm
16cm

e)
14cm
9cm

f)
18cm
30cm

2.   Work out the perimeter of this trapezium,
     correct to 2 decimal places:

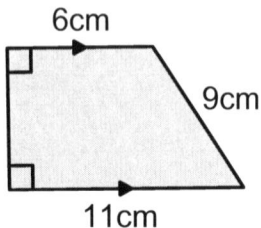

6cm
9cm
11cm

3.   Work out the length of the diagonal
     of this rectangle, correct to 2 d.p.

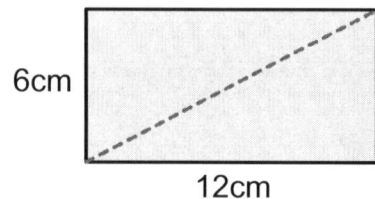

6cm
12cm

4. Mark walks 4km due east and then 3km due south. How far is he from where he started?

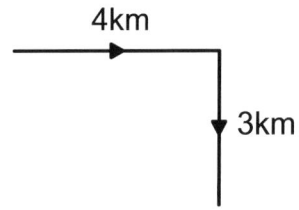

5. Find the perimeter of each of these shapes. Give your answers to 2 d.p.

a)

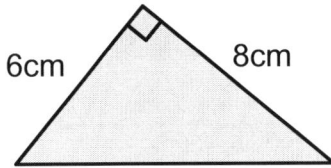

b)

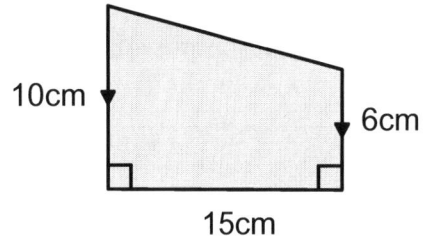

c)

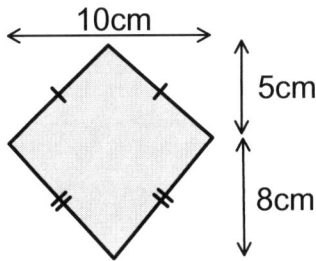

d)

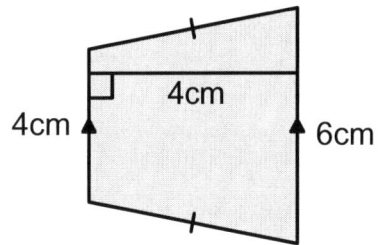

6. Work out the length of each diagonal line on this square grid.
Give your answers correct to 2 decimal places.

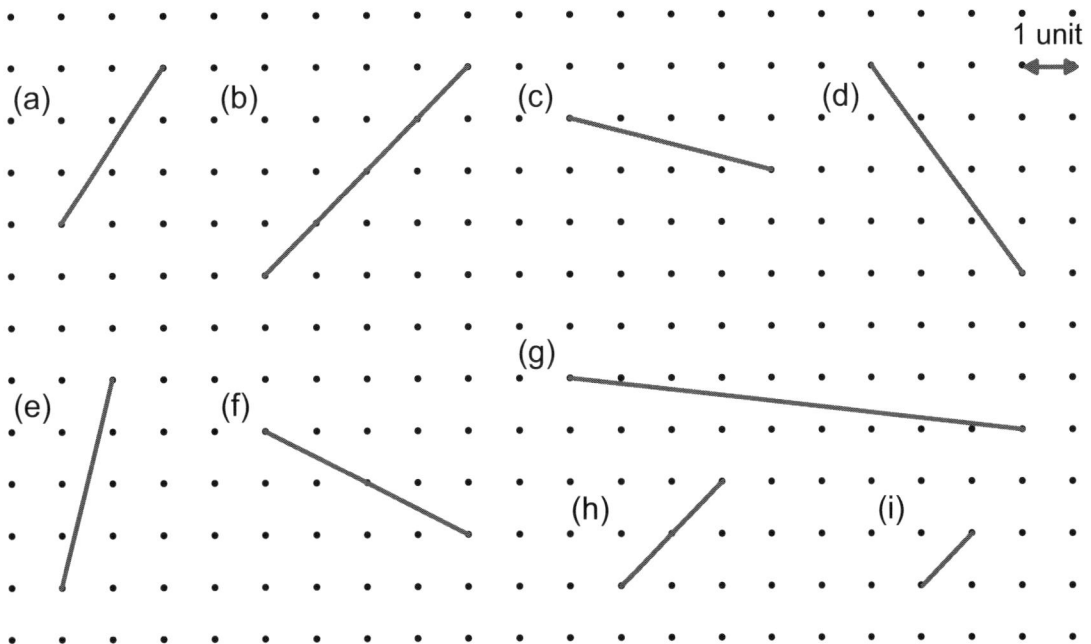

recall

Perimeter is the distance around the edge of a shape

The perimeter of a circle is its circumference.
The length of the circumference is given by C = πd

exercise 8p

1. Work out the area and perimeter of each shape.
    Round your answers to 1 d.p. if necessary:

A

Area = ...

Perimeter = ...

B

5cm

4cm

3cm

Area = ...

Perimeter = ...

C

5cm

8cm

10cm

17cm

Area = ...

Perimeter = ...

D

6cm

5cm

7cm

Area = ...

Perimeter = ...

E

10cm

3cm

4cm

3cm

Area = ...

Perimeter = ...

F

12cm

9cm

Area = ...

Perimeter = ...

G

3cm

Area = ...

Perimeter = ...

H

12cm

13cm

18cm

13cm

Area = ...

Perimeter = ...

I

8cm

9cm

5cm

Area = ...

Perimeter = ...

2. Given the area, work out the perimeter of each of these squares. Round to 2 d.p. 🖩

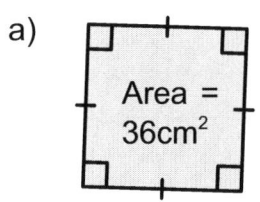

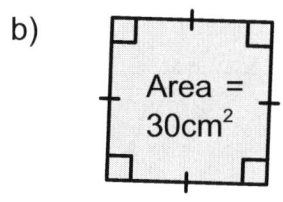

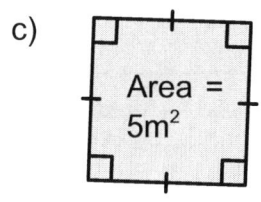

a)

Area =
36cm^2

b)

Area =
30cm^2

c)

Area =
5m^2

3. These diagrams are made from squares & rectangles.
In each diagram, work out the value of x. Round irrational answers to 1 d.p.

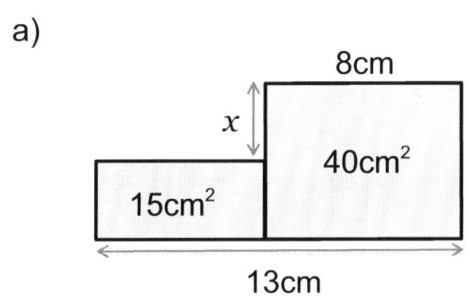

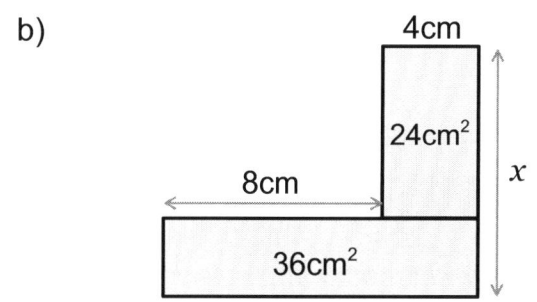

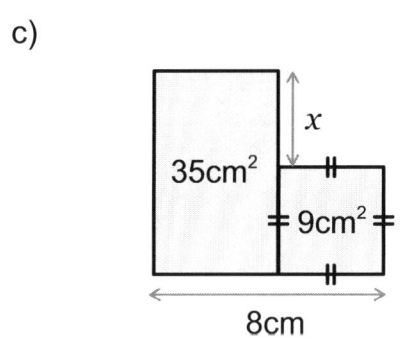

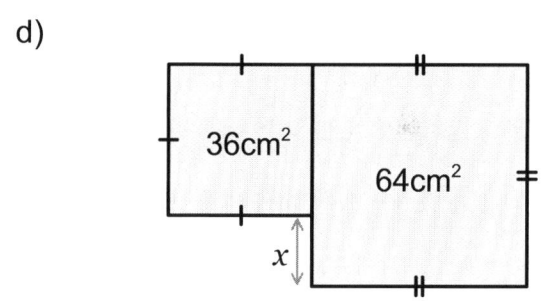

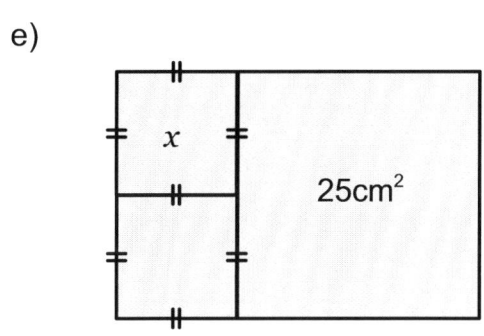

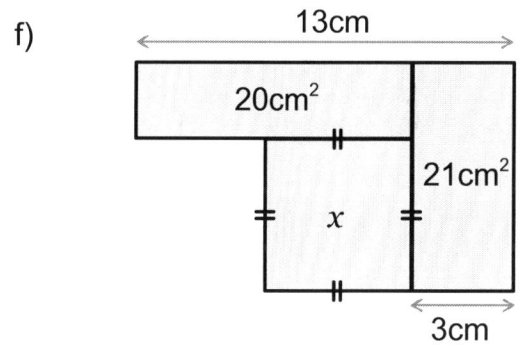

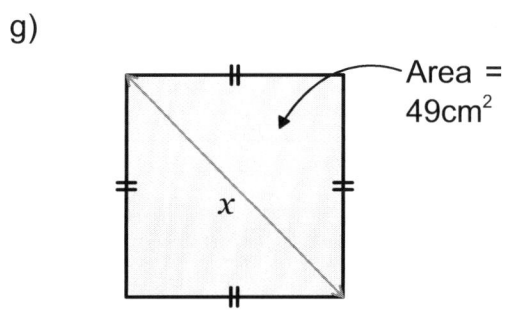

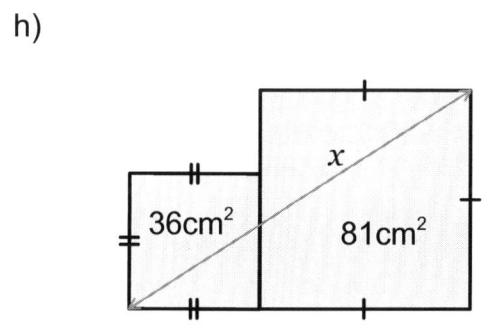

a)

8cm

x

40cm^2

15cm^2

13cm

b)

4cm

24cm^2

8cm

x

36cm^2

c)

x

35cm^2

9cm^2

8cm

d)

36cm^2

64cm^2

x

e)

x

25cm^2

f)

13cm

20cm^2

21cm^2

x

3cm

g)

Area =
49cm^2

x

h)

x

36cm^2

81cm^2

299

exercise 8q

1. The perimeter of each shape is given. Can you work out the area?

a)
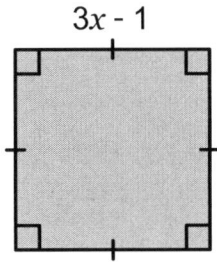
$3x - 1$

Perimeter = 32

b)
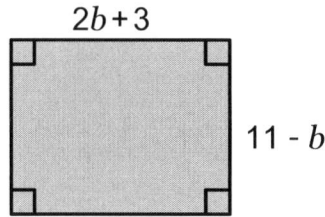
$2b + 3$

$11 - b$

Perimeter = 36

c)
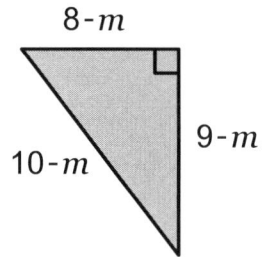
$8 - m$

$9 - m$

$10 - m$

Perimeter = 12

2. A gate consists of metal rods arranged as shown in the diagram. One of the rods is diagonal, the others are horizontal or vertical. Work out the total length of the metal rods altogether.

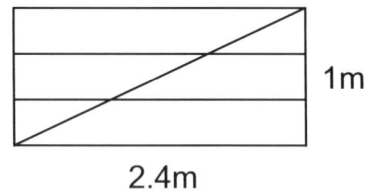
1m

2.4m

3. The area of the right-angled triangle is 30cm².

a) Work out the value of x.

b) Work out the perimeter of the triangle.

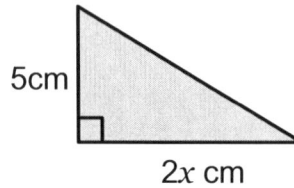
5cm

$2x$ cm

4. A shape is made by placing **8** regular hexagons together in a repeating pattern (regular means all sides are equal). Part of the pattern is shown in the diagram. Work out the total perimeter of the shape.

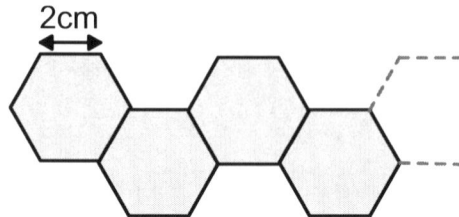
2cm

5. Two squares, each with an area of 36cm², are placed side-by-side to form a rectangle. Work out the perimeter of the rectangle.

6. The area of the parallelogram is four times the area of the triangle.

Work out the height of the parallelogram, h.

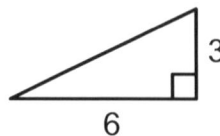
3

6

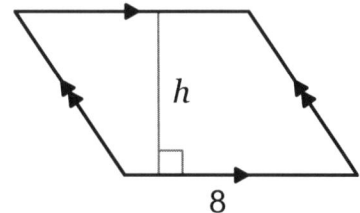
h

8

8. Eight rectangles are placed together as shown to form a larger rectangle with a height of 16cm.

   Work out the area of each small rectangle.

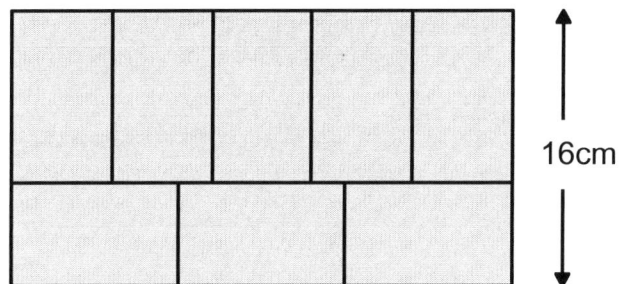

16cm

9. Laura needs to paint the lines for a hockey pitch. The layout of the pitch is shown on the right. This includes two semi-circles.

   Work out the total length of all of the lines on the hockey pitch.
   Round your answer to the nearest metre.

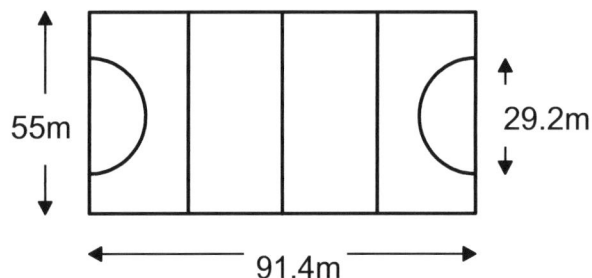

55m

29.2m

91.4m

10. The area of this isosceles triangle is 100cm². What is the length of its hypotenuse?

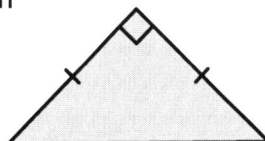

11. Two identical overlapping squares are shown in the diagram.
    The total overlapping area is 14cm².
    The total non-overlapping area is 70cm².
    Work out the width of each square.

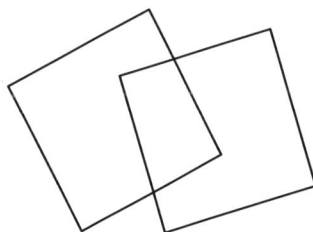

12. Each vertex of a square lies on the circumference of a circle. The square has an area of 36cm².

    a) Work out the diameter of the circle to 3 s.f.

    b) Work out the area of the circle to 3 s.f.

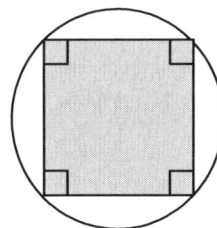

13. The diagram shows a trapezium.

    a) Work out the value of x.

    b) Work out the area of the trapezium.

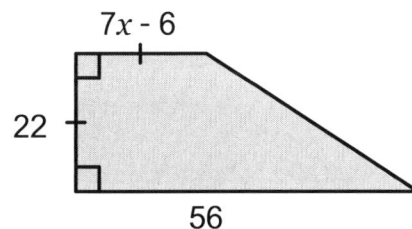

$7x - 6$

22

56

exercise 8r

1. Work out the missing side lengths, to 2 decimal places:

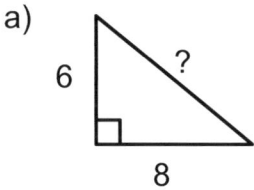

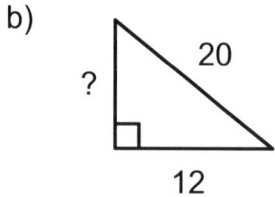

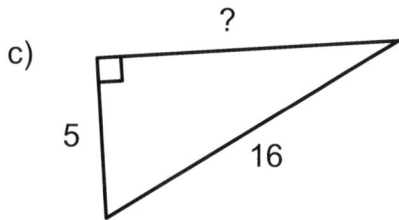

a)

6, ?, 8 (right-angled triangle)

b)

20, ?, 12 (right-angled triangle)

c)

?, 5, 16 (right-angled triangle)

2. Work out the area. All measurements are in cm. Round answers to 3 s.f. if necessary.

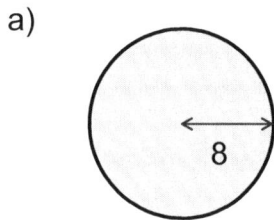

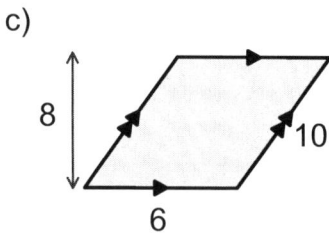

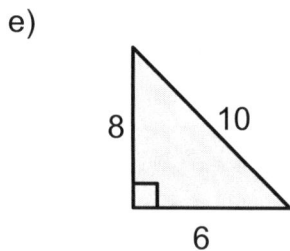

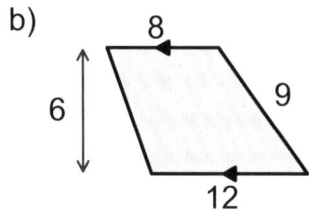

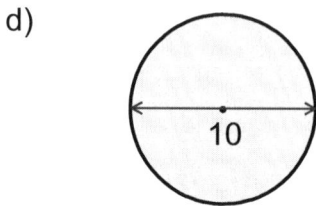

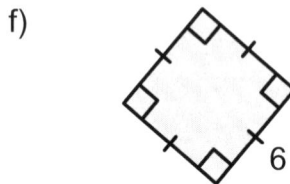

a)

8 (circle with radius 8)

b)

8, 6, 12, 9 (parallelogram)

c)

8, 10, 6 (parallelogram)

d)

10 (circle with diameter 10)

e)

8, 10, 6 (right-angled triangle)

f)

6 (square/rhombus)

3. Identify whether each shape is a parallelogram or trapezium:

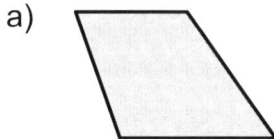

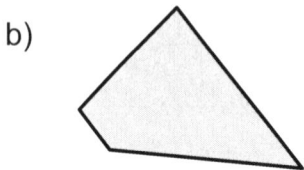

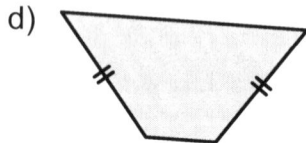

a)

b)

c)

d)

4. Complete the conversions:

a) $1m^2$ = _____ cm^2 c) $4,500cm^2$ = _____ m^2

b) $240cm^2$ = _____ mm^2 d) $300mm^2$ = _____ cm^2

5. Sketch a kite, a rhombus, a paralleogram and a trapezium and explain the differences between them.

6. Copy each diagram and add arrows for parallel lines and dashes for equal length lines to show that:

   a) This shape is an isosceles trapezium

   b) This shape is a rhombus

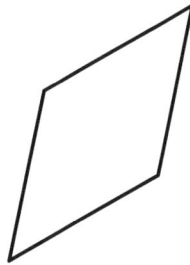

   c) This shape is a kite

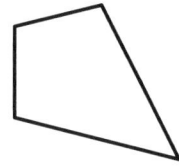

7. Which of these is most likely the area of a postage stamp?

   a) $4mm^2$ b) $6cm^2$ c) $2m^2$ d) $1km^2$

8. A shape with 4 equal sides is called a _____.

9. The area of a square is $100cm^2$. What is its perimeter?

10. The diagram shows 4 circles inside a square.

   a) Work out the area of one circle to 3 s.f.

   b) Work out the area shaded to 3 s.f.

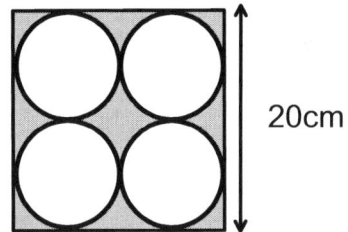

20cm

11. Copy and complete each shape:

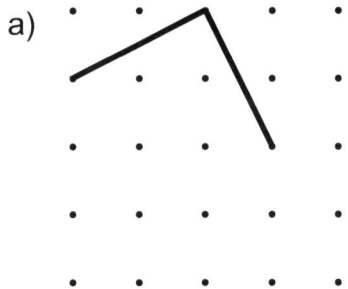

   a)   b)   c)

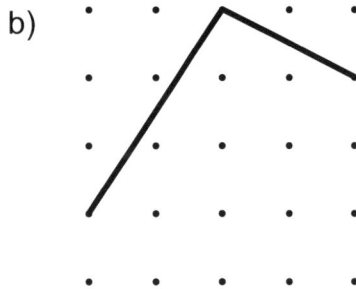

   Square   Parallelogram   Kite

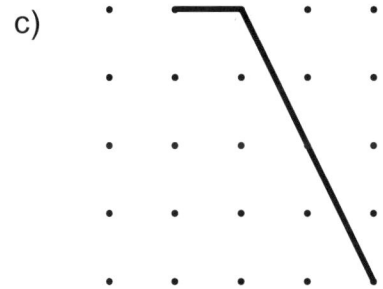

12. Work out the area of the triangle:

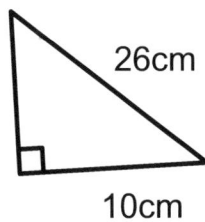

26cm

10cm

exercise 8s

1. Calculate the following:

   a) -12 × -8

   b) -12 + -8

   c) -12 - 8

   d) -12 - - 8

   e) $\frac{1}{3} \times \frac{1}{8}$

   f) $\frac{1}{3} \times 8$

   g) $1\frac{1}{3} \times 8$

   h) $\frac{1}{3} + \frac{1}{8}$

   i) $\frac{1}{3} \div \frac{1}{8}$

   j) $\frac{1}{3} \div 8$

   k) $3 \div \frac{1}{8}$

   l) 0.3×0.8

2. Write 0.084 in standard form.

3. Simplify $a^4 \times a^2 \times a$

4. Complete these statements:

   a) 6.1km = _____m

   b) 60cm = _____m

   c) 1.02km = _____m

   d) _____cm = 0.35m

   e) 150000m = _____km

   f) 1km = _____cm

5. Which of these cannot be evaluated? Circle 2 correct answers.

   a) $\sqrt{4.5}$ b) $\sqrt{-4}$ c) $\sqrt{0}$ d) $\frac{5}{0}$ e) $\frac{0}{5}$

6. How many minutes are there between 22.42 today and 01.12 tomorrow?

7. Write an expression for the perimeter of each shape:

   a)

   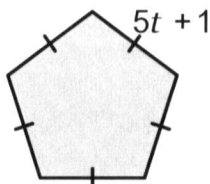
   $5t + 1$

   b)

   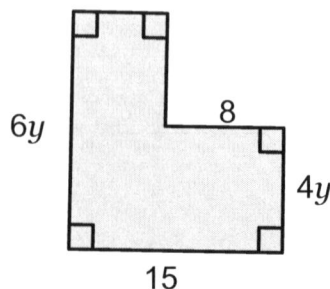
   $6y$ 8 $4y$ 15

8. Given that 4.7 × 8.2 = 38.54, calculate:

   a) 47 × 82

   b) 0.47 × 8.2

   c) 0.47 × 8200

9. Calculate:

   a) -24 + 8

   c) -3 × -15

   e) -14 + -18

   b) -17 - 9

   d) 8 - 25

   f) -12 + 26

10. Write as a power of 2:

   a) $(2^3)^5$

   b) $\frac{1}{2^3}$

   c) $(2^{-2})^{-3}$

   d) $\frac{2^4}{2}$

11. Work out the area of these triangles:

   a)
   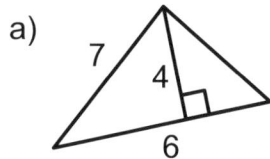

   c)
   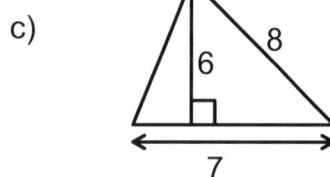

   b)
   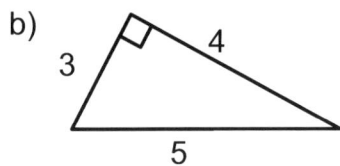

   d)
   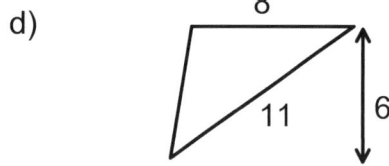

12. What is the reciprocal of:

   a) 6

   b) $\frac{1}{7}$

   c) a

   d) $\frac{1}{b}$

13. Calculate:

   a) $4 \div \frac{1}{10}$

   b) $\frac{3}{5} \div 7$

   c) $\frac{1}{10} \div 10$

   d) $7 \div \frac{1}{7}$

14. Simplify $2a - 6 - 5a - 4$

15. Write 4098 in standard form.

16. Write these numbers in order from smallest to largest: 0.81,   0.$\dot{8}$,   0.8$\dot{1}$, $\frac{8}{10}$

17. Use a calculator to write down the first six digits of $\sqrt[4]{2}$

18. **challenge!** Calculate $3 - \left(\frac{1}{4} + \frac{2}{3}\right) \times 2$ 🖩

cumulative review 2

exercise 8t

1. Work out:

   a) 0.04×1000　　　　b) $3 \div 0.1$　　　　c) 7×0.1

   d) $4020 \div 100$　　　　e) $14 \div 0.5$　　　　f) $0 \div 8$

2. Write in order, starting with the smallest:

   6.03　　　6.3　　　0.603　　　6.033

3. Work out:

   a) 3×-4　　　b) $2 + -3$　　　c) $-4 + -4$　　　d) $-8 \div -2$

   e) $-1 - -1$　　　f) -3×6　　　g) $(-4)^2$　　　h) $12 \div -2$

4. Work out, giving your answers in the simplest form:

   a) $\frac{1}{3} + \frac{1}{6}$　　　　b) $\frac{2}{5} \times \frac{3}{4}$　　　　c) $2 \div \frac{1}{6}$

   d) $1 - \frac{3}{7}$　　　　e) $\frac{1}{8}$ of 48　　　　f) $\frac{5}{6}$ of 24

5. Write $3\frac{2}{3}$ as an improper fraction.

6. Write $\frac{11}{4}$ as a mixed number.

7. Work out:

   a) 6^2　　　　b) 8^{-1}　　　　c) $\left(\frac{2}{3}\right)^3$

   d) $\left(\frac{1}{5}\right)^2$　　　　e) $\sqrt{4}$　　　　f) $\sqrt[3]{8}$

8. Work out:

   a) $(-3)^2$　　　b) $(-3)^3$　　　c) 3^{-2}　　　d) 3^{-3}

9. Work out the missing values:

   a) $6^{-3} \times 6 = 6^{\square}$　　　b) $6^{-2} \div 6^{\square} = 6^2$　　　c) $(4^3)^{-2} = 4^{\square}$

10. Work out:

   a) $6 + 3 \times 4$　　　　b) $\frac{8 + 6}{2}$　　　　c) $4 - 8 \div 2 + 7$

   d) $\frac{7}{2} - 2$　　　　e) $(6 + 3)^2$　　　　f) $3 \times 6 - 4 \times 5$

chapter 9: fractions, decimals & percentages

[Recommended Time : 9 - 13 hours]

Contents

comparing fractions

learn by heart

Unit Fractions have a numerator of 1, e.g. $\frac{1}{3}$ or $\frac{1}{100}$

$$\frac{1}{11} > \frac{1}{12}$$

For unit fractions, as the denominator gets bigger, the fraction gets smaller in size

If the denominators are the same, you can compare numerators, so $\frac{4}{10} > \frac{3}{10}$

To compare fractions with different denominators, first make a common denominator

examples

Which is bigger $\frac{1}{5}$ or $\frac{1}{12}$?

$\frac{1}{5}$ because it has a smaller denominator

Which is bigger $\frac{7}{5}$ or $1\frac{2}{5}$?

None – they are equal because $1\frac{2}{5} = \frac{7}{5}$

Which is bigger $\frac{4}{10}$ or $\frac{2}{3}$?

$\frac{4}{10} = \frac{12}{30}$ and $\frac{2}{3} = \frac{20}{30}$

so $\frac{2}{3}$ is bigger

Both fractions are changed to a denominator of 30 because 30 is the first number in the 3 and 10 times table

exercise 9a

1. Which is the largest fraction in each pair?

   a) $\frac{4}{7}$ or $\frac{5}{7}$
   b) $\frac{2}{9}$ or $\frac{1}{9}$
   c) $\frac{3}{6}$ or $\frac{1}{6}$
   d) $1\frac{2}{5}$ or $\frac{6}{5}$

2. Which of these is largest?
   $\frac{1}{3}$ $\frac{1}{4}$ $\frac{1}{5}$ $\frac{1}{6}$ $\frac{1}{7}$

3. Select all the numbers that are **more** than $\frac{5}{9}$:

   a) $\frac{1}{9}$
   b) $\frac{7}{9}$
   c) $\frac{9}{9}$
   d) 1
   e) $\frac{3}{9}$
   f) $1\frac{1}{9}$
   g) $\frac{1}{10}$

4. Which is **smaller**?

   a) $\frac{1}{3}$ or $\frac{1}{5}$
   d) $\frac{1}{10}$ or $\frac{1}{100}$
   g) $\frac{2}{3}$ or 1

   b) $\frac{1}{7}$ or $\frac{2}{7}$
   e) $\frac{3}{5}$ or $\frac{2}{5}$
   h) $\frac{5}{4}$ or 1

   c) $\frac{1}{3}$ or $\frac{1}{2}$
   f) $\frac{7}{5}$ or $\frac{3}{5}$
   i) $\frac{8}{3}$ or 1

5. Select all the numbers that are **bigger** than 1:

   a) $\frac{4}{7}$
   b) $\frac{7}{4}$
   c) $1\frac{2}{3}$
   d) $\frac{5}{5}$
   e) $\frac{12}{15}$
   f) $\frac{3}{4}$
   g) $\frac{11}{10}$

6. Write the biggest & smallest number in each row:

	Smallest	Biggest
a)		
b)		
c)		
d)		
e)		

a) A $\frac{1}{5}$ B $\frac{1}{3}$ C $\frac{1}{4}$ D $\frac{1}{2}$

b) A $\frac{2}{5}$ B $\frac{1}{5}$ C $\frac{3}{5}$ D $\frac{6}{5}$

c) A $\frac{3}{7}$ B $\frac{9}{7}$ C 1 D $\frac{1}{7}$

d) A $\frac{2}{3}$ B $1\frac{1}{3}$ C $\frac{1}{3}$ D $\frac{5}{3}$

e) A $2\frac{1}{6}$ B $2\frac{5}{6}$ C $\frac{10}{6}$ D $\frac{18}{6}$

7. True or False?

a) $\frac{1}{5}$ is less than $\frac{1}{4}$.

b) $\frac{1}{5}$ is less than $\frac{1}{6}$

c) $\frac{2}{3}$ is greater than $\frac{1}{3}$.

d) $\frac{3}{10}$ is smaller than $\frac{7}{10}$.

e) $\frac{10}{10}$ equals 1 whole.

f) $1\frac{3}{5} > 1\frac{2}{5}$

g) $\frac{12}{5}$ is smaller than 3

h) $\frac{1}{4} > \frac{1}{5}$

8. Complete these statements with the symbols >, < or =

a) $\frac{1}{2}$ ◯ $\frac{1}{4}$

b) $\frac{1}{3}$ ◯ $\frac{1}{5}$

c) $\frac{6}{6}$ ◯ 1

d) $\frac{2}{10}$ ◯ $\frac{7}{10}$

e) $\frac{3}{5}$ ◯ $\frac{2}{5}$

f) $\frac{1}{9}$ ◯ $\frac{1}{8}$

g) $\frac{3}{10}$ ◯ $\frac{6}{20}$

h) $\frac{9}{5}$ ◯ 1

i) $2\frac{1}{2}$ ◯ $\frac{5}{2}$

j) 3 ◯ $\frac{16}{5}$

9. Put these in order of size, from smallest to largest:

$\frac{4}{5}$ $\frac{1}{5}$ $1\frac{3}{5}$ $\frac{1}{10}$ $\frac{6}{5}$

10. Work out which fraction is largest in each pair:

a) $\frac{5}{8}$ or $\frac{3}{4}$

b) $\frac{3}{7}$ or $\frac{1}{3}$

c) $\frac{7}{9}$ or $\frac{5}{6}$

d) $\frac{1}{4}$ or $\frac{2}{9}$

e) $\frac{7}{10}$ or $\frac{2}{3}$

f) $\frac{7}{12}$ or $\frac{11}{20}$

11. Complete each statement using >, < or =

a) $\frac{1}{3}$ _____ $\frac{2}{5}$

b) $\frac{7}{8}$ _____ $\frac{3}{4}$

c) $\frac{3}{10}$ _____ $\frac{4}{5}$

12. True or false?

a) $\frac{3}{3} = 1$

c) $\frac{12}{15} = \frac{4}{5}$

e) $\frac{1}{9} > \frac{1}{10}$

b) $\frac{1}{5} > \frac{1}{4}$

d) $\frac{2}{5} > \frac{4}{10}$

f) $\frac{1}{5} > \frac{2}{3}$

13. Find **three** fractions in this list that are equivalent to $\frac{4}{6}$.

$\boxed{\frac{40}{60}}$ $\boxed{\frac{2}{5}}$ $\boxed{\frac{24}{26}}$ $\boxed{\frac{2}{3}}$ $\boxed{\frac{6}{8}}$ $\boxed{\frac{6}{4}}$ $\boxed{\frac{8}{12}}$ $\boxed{\frac{9}{15}}$

14. Which of these fractions are bigger than $\frac{8}{5}$?

$\boxed{\frac{11}{10}}$ $\boxed{\frac{15}{10}}$ $\boxed{\frac{18}{10}}$ $\boxed{\frac{24}{10}}$

15. Insert one of the symbols $\boxed{<}$ $\boxed{=}$ $\boxed{>}$ to make a true statement.

a) $\frac{4}{5}$ ◯ $\frac{1}{2}$

b) $\frac{3}{7}$ ◯ $\frac{1}{2}$

c) $\frac{5}{10}$ ◯ $\frac{1}{2}$

d) $\frac{9}{20}$ ◯ $\frac{1}{2}$

e) $\frac{6}{9}$ ◯ $\frac{1}{2}$

f) $\frac{7}{13}$ ◯ $\frac{1}{2}$

16. Which of these is largest?

$\boxed{\frac{3}{10}}$ $\boxed{\frac{2}{5}}$ $\boxed{\frac{7}{20}}$ $\boxed{\frac{9}{10}}$ $\boxed{\frac{8}{20}}$

17. Write each set of fractions in order, starting with the smallest.

a) $\frac{3}{7}$ $\frac{2}{7}$ $\frac{1}{2}$

b) $\frac{1}{2}$ $\frac{3}{11}$ $\frac{7}{11}$

18. **challenge!** Decide whether these statements are true or false: ☆ extra challenge

a) $\frac{24}{32} > \frac{4}{5}$

b) $\frac{50}{13} > \frac{25}{7}$

c) $\frac{8}{7} \geq 1\frac{1}{7}$

d) $8\frac{6}{9} = \frac{26}{3}$

e) $\frac{6}{14} = \frac{18}{35}$

f) $\frac{16}{17} \leq \frac{17}{18}$

converting fractions and decimals (recap)

recall

> If the denominator is 10,100,1000 etc → use place value, e.g. $\frac{3}{10} = 0.3$
>
> If the denominator is a factor of 10,100,1000 → use equivalent fractions e.g. $\frac{3}{5} = \frac{6}{10} = 0.6$
>
> Otherwise use short division → $\frac{1}{3} = 0.333...$

exercise 9b

1. Write these fractions as decimals:

   a) $\frac{3}{50}$ e) $\frac{6}{50}$ i) $\frac{1}{6}$ m) $\frac{3}{8}$

   b) $\frac{1}{5}$ f) $\frac{10}{25}$ j) $\frac{3}{25}$ n) $\frac{17}{1000}$

   c) $\frac{3}{20}$ g) $\frac{3}{5}$ k) $\frac{1}{9}$ o) $\frac{4}{25}$

   d) $2\frac{7}{1000}$ h) $6\frac{42}{1000}$ l) $\frac{9}{75}$ p) $\frac{15}{75}$

2. Write these decimals as fractions or mixed numbers:

   a) 0.9   b) 0.125   d) 0.03   e) 0.001

   g) 1.7   h) 3.81   j) 2.030   k) 0.071

3. Match pairs of equivalent fractions and decimals.
   Record your answers in a table.

A $\frac{3}{100}$	B $\frac{11}{50}$	C $\frac{3}{1000}$	D $\frac{14}{200}$		M 0.6	N 0.8	O 0.07	P 0.3
E $\frac{22}{50}$	F $\frac{3}{5}$	G $\frac{1}{5}$	H $\frac{3}{50}$		Q 0.2	R 0.202	S 0.03	T 0.22
I $\frac{10}{25}$	J $\frac{3}{10}$	K $\frac{4}{5}$	L $\frac{202}{1000}$		U 0.003	V 0.44	W 0.4	X 0.06

A	B	C	D	E	F	G	H	I	J	K	L

ordering fractions & decimals

examples

Which is bigger 0.7 or $\frac{9}{100}$?

$\frac{9}{100}$ = 0.09, **so 0.7 is bigger**

Which is bigger 0.35 or $\frac{4}{10}$?

$\frac{4}{10}$ = 0.4, **so $\frac{4}{10}$ is bigger**

exercise 9c

1. In each pair, decide which is bigger, or say if they are equal:

   a) 0.3 or $\frac{4}{10}$

   b) 0.07 or $\frac{3}{10}$

   c) 0.1 or $\frac{1}{100}$

   d) $\frac{3}{1000}$ or 0.05

   e) $\frac{2}{100}$ or 0.1

   f) $1\frac{3}{100}$ or 1.2

2. Fill in the gaps with >, < or =

   a) 0.4 _____ $\frac{32}{100}$

   b) $\frac{1}{10}$ _____ 0.15

   c) $\frac{12}{100}$ _____ 0.3

   d) 0.605 _____ $\frac{6}{10}$

   e) 0.08 _____ $\frac{8}{100}$

   f) $1\frac{3}{10}$ _____ 1.6

   g) $\frac{3}{5}$ _____ 0.4

   h) $\frac{6}{50}$ _____ 0.1

   i) $\frac{1}{25}$ _____ 0.02

3. Put these numbers in order, starting with the smallest:

   A 0.49   B $\frac{4}{100}$ C 0.05   D 4.9

4. Put these numbers in order, starting with the smallest:

   A $\frac{1}{4}$ B $\frac{4}{10}$ C 0.3   D $\frac{29}{100}$

5. Give an example of a decimal that is between $\frac{7}{10}$ and $\frac{8}{10}$

challenge

6. Fill in the boxes with digits to make this true:

$$\frac{1}{\square} < 0.3 < \frac{\square}{5} < 0.9$$

7. Decide whether each of these statements are true or false:

a) $0.3 > \frac{4}{10}$

b) $\frac{5}{10} = 0.5$

c) $\frac{6}{10} = 0.60$

d) $2.35 < 2\frac{4}{10}$

e) $0.301 \geq \frac{5}{100}$

f) $\frac{6}{100} < 0.51$

8. Which of these are more than $\frac{1}{3}$? Circle two answers.

a) 0.3   b) 0.34   c) 0.03   d) 0.3333   e) $\frac{34}{100}$

9. Which of these are less than 0.7? Circle two answers.

a) $\frac{65}{100}$ b) $\frac{7}{100}$ c) $\frac{7}{10}$ d) $\frac{6}{1}$ e) 0.70

10. Arrange the digits to make a true statement: ☐0 ☐1 ☐2 ☐3 ☐4

$$\frac{\Box}{\Box} < \Box . \Box\Box$$

- -

With Your Partner: 3 in a Line

Make a copy of the number line.
Take it in turns with your partner to choose a number from the list below.
Estimate where you think the number you have chosen goes on the number line and place a cross. Make sure your partner agrees the position!
The first person to get three numbers in a line, wins!

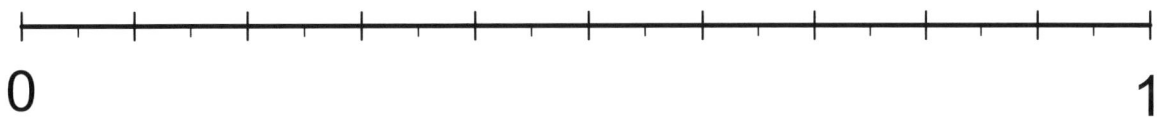

0   1

$\frac{2}{3}$	0.1	$\frac{3}{10}$	0.42	0.01	$\frac{1}{4}$	0.6	$\frac{3}{8}$	0.18
0.9	$0.\dot{2}$	$\frac{1}{5}$	$\frac{1}{6}$	$\frac{6}{5}$	0.203	$\frac{19}{100}$	$\frac{3}{100}$	$\frac{4}{5}$

313

exercise 9d: more challenging ★ extra challenge

1. Put these numbers in order of size, from smallest to largest:

   a)
A	B	C	D
$\frac{1}{5}$	$0.0\dot{1}$	0.12	$\frac{1}{8}$

   b)
A	B	C	D
$\frac{3}{100}$	-0.3	$\frac{1}{3}$	$-0.\dot{2}\dot{8}$

   c)
A	B	C	D
-9	$-9.\dot{1}$	-9.05	$-9\frac{3}{10}$

   d)
A	B	C	D
$-2.\dot{1}\dot{2}$	$-2\frac{12}{100}$	$-2\frac{1}{10}$	-2.2

   e)
A	B	C	D
$\frac{23}{100}$	0.023	$\frac{2}{11}$	$0.\dot{2}$

2. In each pair, decide which number is **larger**:

   a) $0.\dot{7}$ or $\frac{7}{10}$

   b) $0.\dot{2}\dot{3}$ or $\frac{23}{100}$

   c) $0.\dot{5}$ or $\frac{6}{10}$

   d) $0.\dot{7}\dot{0}$ or $\frac{7}{10}$

   e) $2.0\dot{5}$ or $2\frac{5}{10}$

   f) $0.09\dot{2}$ or $\frac{10}{100}$

   g) $0.\dot{0}1\dot{2}$ or $\frac{2}{100}$

   h) $0.\dot{8}$ or $\frac{89}{100}$

   i) $3.\dot{2}\dot{4}$ or $\frac{32}{10}$

3. Which of the following are between $\frac{3}{10}$ and $\frac{1}{3}$? Choose two answers.

   a) 0.33   b) $0.\dot{3}$ c) $\frac{34}{100}$ d) 0.30   e) $\frac{333}{1000}$

4. Write down all the decimals with 2 decimal places that are between 0.7 and $\frac{7}{9}$

5. Arrange the digits to make a true statement: | 0 | | 3 | | 5 | | 6 | | 7 | | 8 |

$$\frac{\square}{\square} < \square . \overset{\bullet}{\square} \leq \frac{\square}{\square}$$

terminating & recurring decimals to fractions

learn by heart

There are 3 types of decimal....

Terminating Decimals, e.g. $0.74 = \frac{74}{100}$

Recurring Decimals, e.g. 0.333.... we use an equation to write them as a fraction

Irrational Numbers: cannot be written as fractions

example

Convert $0.\overset{..}{8}\overset{.}{9}$ to a fraction.

$$\text{Let } x = 0.\overset{..}{8}\overset{.}{9}$$
$$100x = 89.\overset{..}{8}\overset{.}{9}$$
$$99x = 89$$
$$x = \frac{89}{99}$$

exercise 9e

1. Write each of these as a fraction:

   a) $0.\overset{.}{1}$

   b) $0.\overset{..}{3}\overset{.}{7}$

   c) $0.\overset{..}{5}\overset{.}{4}$

   d) $0.\overset{.}{2}3\overset{.}{1}$

   e) $0.6\overset{.}{5}$

   f) $0.2\overset{..}{5}\overset{.}{4}$

   g) $0.6\overset{..}{8}\overset{.}{1}$

   h) $0.43\overset{.}{8}$

   i) $0.9\overset{..}{0}\overset{.}{4}$

2. Write $3.\overset{.}{7}$ as a mixed number.

3. Prove that $0.\overset{..}{2}\overset{.}{8} = \frac{28}{99}$

4. Write $28.0\overset{..}{6}\overset{.}{5}$ as a mixed number.

5. Write as fractions or mixed numbers:

   a) 0.3

   b) 0.09

   c) 0.001

   d) 0.27

   e) 0.143

   f) 0.803

   g) 0.041

   h) 1.9

   i) 2.043

6. Which of these cannot be written as fractions? Choose 2 answers.

   a) π b) $\sqrt{12}$ c) 0.444...   d) 0.2121...   e) 0.6084

fractions and percentages

learn by heart

Percentage: *means out of 100*

examples

Convert $\frac{4}{50}$ to a percentage.	Convert $\frac{3}{75}$ to a percentage.	Convert 3.5% to a fraction.
$\frac{4}{50} = \frac{8}{100} = 8\%$	$\frac{3}{75} = \frac{1}{25} = \frac{4}{100} = 4\%$	$3.5\% = \frac{3.5}{100} = \frac{7}{200}$

exercise 9f

1. Convert these fractions to percentages:

   a) $\frac{3}{10}$ c) $\frac{7}{20}$ e) $\frac{18}{100}$ g) $1\frac{3}{5}$

   b) $\frac{1}{50}$ d) $\frac{8}{25}$ f) $\frac{6}{200}$ h) $\frac{3}{2}$

2. Convert these percentages to fractions (or integers), in their simplest form:

   a) 5%   c) 8.5%   e) 10%   g) 100%

   b) 60%   d) 1%   f) 4.1%   h) 200%

3. On a test Julie scored $\frac{14}{25}$. Andrew scored 85%. Who did better?

4. Write down the percentage of each shape that is shaded.

   a)
   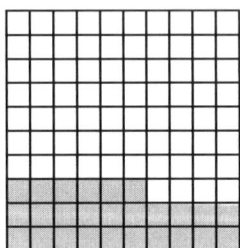

   c)
   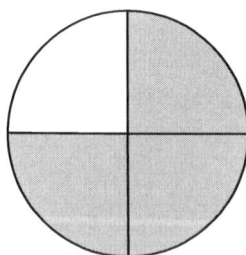

   e)
   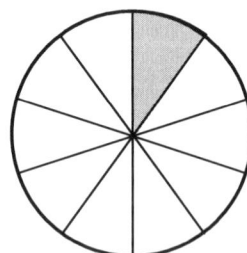

   b)
   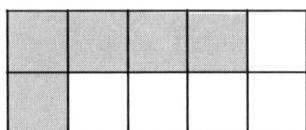

   d)
   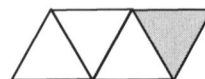

   f)

5. Put these in order of size, from smallest to largest:

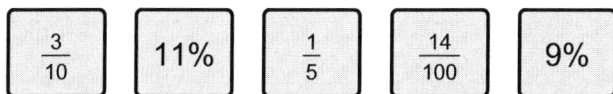

$\frac{3}{10}$ 11% $\frac{1}{5}$ $\frac{14}{100}$ 9%

6. Convert these fractions to percentages (no calculator)

a) $\frac{3}{30}$ c) $\frac{34}{200}$ e) $\frac{9}{300}$

b) $\frac{6}{75}$ d) $\frac{400}{1000}$ f) $\frac{9}{15}$

7. In which diagram is 50% shaded?

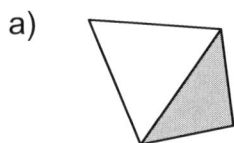

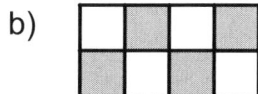

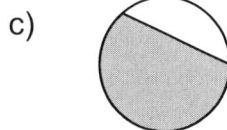

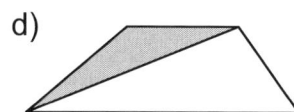

a)   b)   c)   d)

8. Put these in order of size, from smallest to largest:

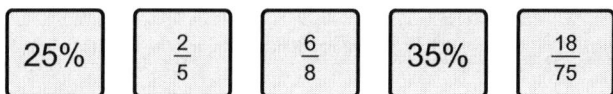

25% $\frac{2}{5}$ $\frac{6}{8}$ 35% $\frac{18}{75}$

9. Which of these equal 100%? Circle 2 correct answers.

a) $\frac{8}{8}$ b) $\frac{100}{1}$ c) $\frac{1}{100}$ d) $\frac{126}{126}$ e) $\frac{18}{3}$ f) $\frac{100}{0}$

10. Fill in each blank with >, < or =

a) $\frac{3}{5}$ _____ 60%   c) $\frac{8}{10}$ _____ 9%   e) $\frac{14}{70}$ _____ 20%

b) $\frac{2}{50}$ _____ 2%   d) $\frac{9}{25}$ _____ 40%   f) $\frac{6}{15}$ _____ 50%

11. Arrange the digits to make a true statement: 2   3   4   5   6

$$\frac{\Box}{\Box\Box} \; < \; \boxed{1}\,\boxed{7}\,\% \; < \; \frac{\Box}{\Box}$$

fractions, decimals and percentages 1

examples

Convert 0.452 to a percentage. $0.452 \times 100 = 45.2$ $0.452 = 45.2\%$	Convert 18.5% to a decimal. $\frac{18.5}{100} = 18.5 \div 100 = 0.185$	Convert 400% to a fraction or integer $400\% = \frac{400}{100} = 4$

exercise 9g

1. Write as a percentage:

    a) 0.21   c) 0.06   e) 2   g) 0.014

    b) 0.304   d) 1   f) 3.4   h) 0.0047

2. Write as a decimal:

    a) 18%   c) 100%   e) 18.5%   g) 0.8%

    b) 1.8%   d) 180%   f) 630%   h) 1.02%

3. Copy and complete the table of equivalent fractions, decimals and percentages.
    Give your fractions in their simplest form. Find your answers from the list below.

F	D	P
$\frac{1}{2}$		
$\frac{2}{10}$		
	0.9	
	0.09	
		2%
		25%
$\frac{3}{5}$		
$\frac{3}{20}$		
	0.4	
	0.8	
		8%
$\frac{3}{25}$		
		6.5%
$\frac{9}{20}$		
	2	

0.45   60%   0.2   0.12

90% $\frac{2}{25}$ $\frac{9}{100}$ 40%

0.15   45% $\frac{2}{5}$ 80%

0.065 $\frac{1}{4}$ $\frac{4}{5}$

200%   0.6 $\frac{13}{200}$ $\frac{1}{50}$

0.08   0.02   0.25

$\frac{9}{10}$ 12% $\frac{2}{1}$

9%   50%   20%

15%   0.5

4. Which of the following are the same as 2.8%? Circle two answers.

a) 0.28 b) 0.028 c) $\frac{28}{10}$ d) $\frac{7}{250}$ e) $\frac{28}{100}$

5. Convert 0.905 to a percentage.

6. Write 56% as a decimal.

7. Write $1\frac{3}{100}$ as a decimal.

8. Which of the following are equivalent to 200%? Circle two answers.

a) 2 b) 0.02 c) $\frac{6}{3}$ d) 200 e) $\frac{200}{100}$

9. Which is larger, 4.2% or 0.4?

10. Which is larger, 5.5% or $\frac{5}{10}$?

11. Put these in order of size, from smallest to largest:

a) $\frac{2}{5}$ b) 45% c) 0.04 d) $\frac{4}{50}$ e) $\frac{4}{20}$

12. Which of these are more than 100%?

a) 0.103 b) $\frac{3}{2}$ c) $\frac{1009}{1200}$ d) 1.6 e) $1.0\overset{..}{1}$

13. Which of the following are the same as 20%? Choose 3 answers.

a) $\frac{1}{5}$ b) 0.02 c) 0.2 d) $\frac{5}{25}$ e) $\frac{20}{200}$

14. Jane says "0.4 is equivalent to 4%." Explain why Jane is wrong.

15. Which is larger, 28% or $\frac{6}{20}$?

16. Which is larger, 85% or $\frac{21}{25}$?

17. Write each set of numbers in order of size, starting with the smallest.

a) $\frac{1}{2}$ 0.4 $\frac{23}{50}$ 35%

b) $\frac{3}{20}$ 12% $\frac{4}{25}$ 0.2

c) 0.1 0.08 $\frac{1}{5}$ 18%

d) 0.82 $\frac{19}{25}$ 87% 0.9

fractions, decimals and percentages 2 *(includes recurring decimals)*

examples

Convert $\frac{2}{3}$ to a percentage.

$\frac{2}{3} = 0.\dot{6} = 66.\dot{6}\%$

Convert $0.\dot{1}$ to a percentage.

$0.\dot{1} = 11.\dot{1}\%$

Convert $\frac{1}{8}$ to a percentage.

$\frac{1}{8} = 0.125 = 12.5\%$

exercise 9h

1. Write these as decimals:

   a) $\frac{1}{3}$ b) $\frac{1}{6}$ c) $\frac{5}{9}$ d) $\frac{2}{9}$

2. Write these as percentages:

   a) $\frac{1}{3}$ b) $\frac{1}{6}$ c) $\frac{5}{9}$ d) $\frac{2}{9}$

3. Katie scored $\frac{4}{9}$ on a test. Emily scored 48%. Who scored higher?

4. Fill in the blanks with >, < or =

   a) 25% _____ $\frac{3}{9}$ c) $\frac{1}{2}$ _____ $0.\dot{5}$

   b) $\frac{1}{6}$ _____ 0.7   d) $\frac{1}{3}$ _____ $0.\dot{3}$

5. Match each number on the left with its equivalent percentage on the right. Record your answers in a table.

A $\frac{2}{3}$	B $\frac{1}{9}$	C 0.4	D $0.\dot{3}$	M 3%	N 20%	O 45%	P 15%
E $\frac{3}{20}$	F $\frac{100}{100}$	G $\frac{9}{50}$	H 0.03	Q $33.\dot{3}\%$	R 5%	S $66.\dot{6}\%$	T 18%
I 0.45	J $\frac{6}{50}$	K 0.2	L $\frac{2}{40}$	U $11.\dot{1}\%$	V 100%	W 12%	X 40%

A	B	C	D	E	F	G	H	I	J	K	L

6. True or false?

   a) $\frac{1}{10}$ + 20% = 0.3

   b) $\frac{1}{4}$ + 0.25 = 50%

   c) $\frac{6}{10}$ - 60% = 0

   d) $\frac{4}{5}$ + 5% = 0.9

   e) 70% - 0.1 = $\frac{6}{10}$

   f) $\frac{2}{10}$ + 0.8 = 10%

   g) $\frac{3}{4}$ + 0.25 = 100%

   h) $\frac{1}{3}$ + 0.6 = 90%

   i) 0.9 - 9% = 0%

   j) $0.\dot{7} - \frac{7}{9}$ = 0%

7. Put these in order of size, starting with the smallest:

   a) $\frac{2}{3}$ b) 67%   c) 0.6   d) $\frac{33}{50}$ e) 66.7

8. Work out the percentage shaded:

   a)
   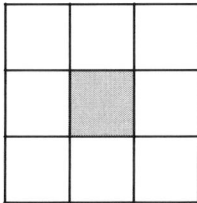

   c)
   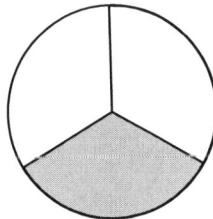

   e)
   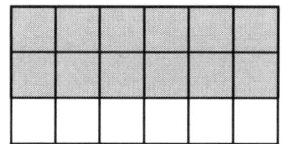

   b)
   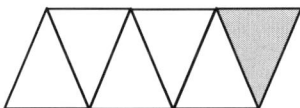

   d)
   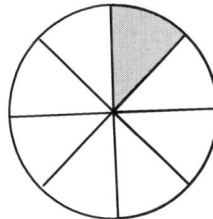

   f)
   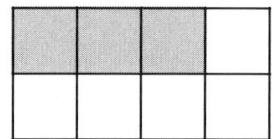

9. Which of these are more than 100%? Circle 2 answers:

   a) $\frac{9}{10}$ b) 1.01   c) $\frac{100}{101}$ d) 0.101   e) $\frac{101}{100}$

10. Write an integer in the gap to make this statement true: $\frac{4}{3} < $ _____ % $ < \frac{27}{20}$

Fractions, Decimals and Percentages - Odd One Out

In each box, cover up pairs that are **equivalent** to each other.
Find the number that is left over.

A

0.4	50%	13%
4%	$\frac{1}{4}$	40%
0.25	$\frac{13}{100}$	$\frac{1}{2}$

B

$\frac{3}{10}$	0.02	$\frac{1}{10}$
$\frac{3}{4}$	10%	0.2
2%	0.3	75%

C

$\frac{1}{5}$	0.15	$\frac{1}{2}$
0.25	15%	20%
0.5	5%	$\frac{5}{20}$

D

$\frac{3}{5}$	80%	$\frac{9}{10}$
70%	0.6	40%
$\frac{4}{5}$	0.9	$\frac{7}{10}$

E

5%	$\frac{1}{25}$	6%
0.06	0.4	$\frac{1}{20}$
$\frac{1}{50}$	2%	0.04

F

$\frac{13}{50}$	16%	0.13
20%	$\frac{3}{20}$	15%
$\frac{4}{25}$	0.2	0.26

G

25%	$\frac{12}{16}$	0.015
0.08	$\frac{2}{8}$	$\frac{1}{8}$
0.125	1.5%	75%

H

$\frac{1}{3}$	0.03	$\frac{3}{10}$
$\frac{3}{5}$	$0.\dot{3}$	$\frac{2}{9}$
$0.\dot{2}$	3%	60%

I

37.5%	$\frac{19}{50}$	0.88
$\frac{22}{25}$	$\frac{8}{9}$	0.38
$\frac{3}{8}$	19%	$88.\dot{8}\%$

J

120%	$\frac{9}{20}$	0.9
90%	18%	$\frac{6}{5}$
$1\frac{4}{5}$	0.45	1.8

K

105%	14%	$1\frac{1}{25}$
$\frac{7}{50}$	$1\frac{1}{20}$	$\frac{11}{10}$
1.4	1.1	$\frac{7}{5}$

L

$\frac{14}{9}$	1.3	$\frac{5}{3}$
$1.\dot{6}$	0.6	160%
$\frac{8}{5}$	$1.\dot{5}$	130%

percentage of an amount 1 🔢

learn by heart

$1\% = \dfrac{1}{100}$	$5\% = \dfrac{1}{20}$	$10\% = \dfrac{1}{10}$	$20\% = \dfrac{1}{5}$	$25\% = \dfrac{1}{4}$	$50\% = \dfrac{1}{2}$

To find 50%:	To find 10%:	To find 1%:	To find 20%:	To find 3%:
divide by 2	*divide by 10*	*divide by 100*	*× 10% by 2*	*× 1% by 3*

exercise 9i

1. Work out:

    a) 50% of 90

    b) 10% of 95

    c) 1% of 90

    d) 1% of 240

    e) 50% of 240

    f) 1% of 35

    g) 20% of 220

    h) 5% of 220

    i) 25% of 220

    j) 3% of 220

    k) 40% of 220

    l) 80% of 220

2. Copy and complete these percentage chains:

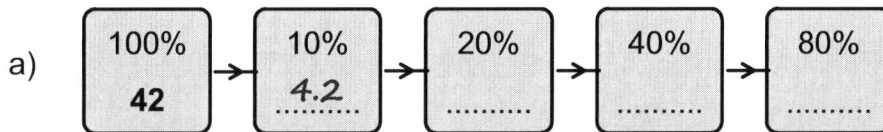

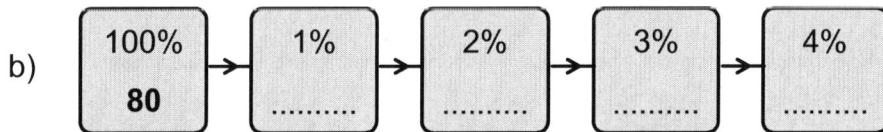

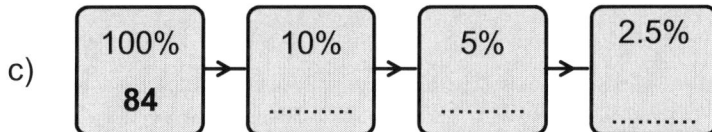

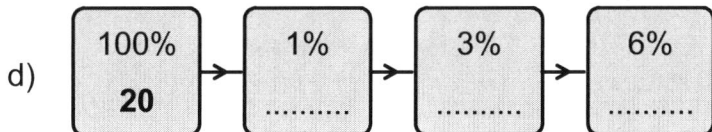

    a) | 100% **42** | → | 10% 4.2 | → | 20% .... | → | 40% .... | → | 80% .... |

    b) | 100% **80** | → | 1% .... | → | 2% .... | → | 3% .... | → | 4% .... |

    c) | 100% **84** | → | 10% .... | → | 5% .... | → | 2.5% .... |

    d) | 100% **20** | → | 1% .... | → | 3% .... | → | 6% .... |

3. Work out:

    a) 30% of 50

    b) 25% of 48

    c) 3% of 30

    d) 5% of 40

    e) 75% of 24

    f) 20% of 80

    g) 40% of 60

    h) 60% of 40

    i) 90% of 320

4. Use the cards (once each) to complete these statements.

    a) 50% of £9 = _____

    b) 1% of £45 = _____

    c) 10% of £450 = _____

    d) 50% of _____ = £35

    e) 10% of _____ = 7p

    f) 1% of _____ = 7p

    | 45p | £7 | £45 | 70p | £4.50 | £70 |

more challenging

5. Sue thinks of a number. 50% of Sue's number is 35.

    a) Work out 10% of Sue's number.

    b) Work out 1% of Sue's number.

6. Tyrell thinks of a number. 30% of Tyrell's number is 15.

    a) Work out 60% of Tyrell's number.

    b) Work out 3% of Tyrell's number.

Percentage of an Amount Puzzle

7. Use nine of the numbers on the left to make 3 true statements:

15%	20
3	18
50	30%
5.5	60
40%	20

☐ of ☐ = ☐

☐ of ☐ = ☐

☐ of ☐ = ☐

percentage of an amount 2

examples

Percentages of an amount can be added or subtracted to find more percentages.

Find 51% of 120

50% = 60
1% = 1.2   +
_____
51% = 61.2

Find 12% of 120

10% = 12
2% = 2.4   +
_____
12% = 14.4

Find 9% of 120

10% = 12
1% = 1.2   −
_____
9% = 10.8

exercise 9j

1. Copy and complete these percentage chains:

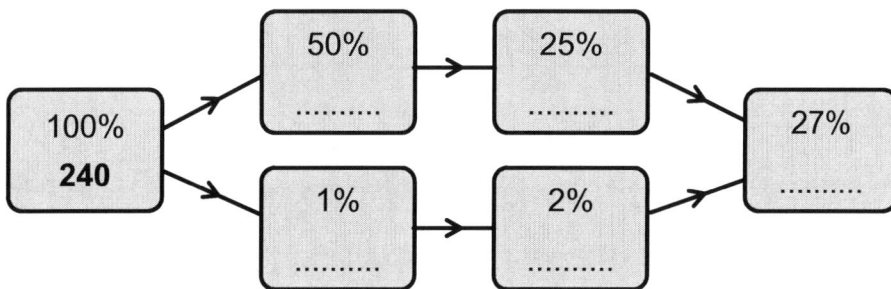

a)

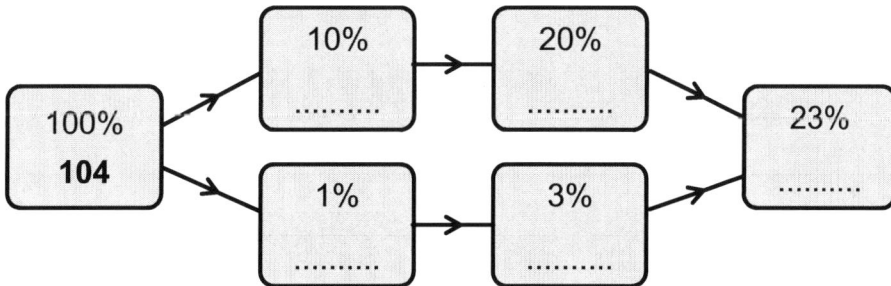

b)

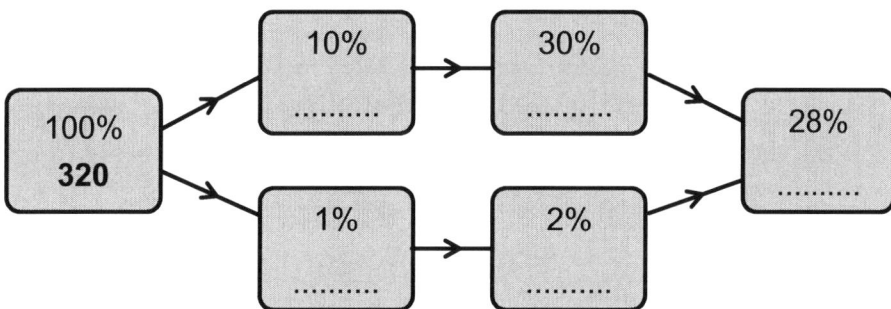

c)

2. Work out:

a) 11% of 140

b) 51% of 140

c) 60% of 140

d) 61% of 140

e) 49% of 140

f) 9% of 140

3. Copy and complete the table:

	Amount	1%	5%	10%	15%	32%
a)	30					
b)	400					
c)	128					

4. Use the cards (once each) to complete these statements.

a) 55% of £18 = _____

b) 31% of £30 = _____

c) 13% of £7 = _____

d) 19% of £48 = _____

e) 24% of £4 = _____

f) 74% of £1.50 = _____

96p	£1.11	£9.90	£9.12	91p	£9.30

5. Jasmine, Mark and Hailey each think of a number.

a) 10% of Jasmine's number is 28. Work out 15% of Jasmine's number.

b) 12% of Mark's number is 30. Work out 18% of Mark's number.

c) 14% of Hailey's number is 84. Work out 35% of Hailey's number.

6. Which of the following calculations works out 3% of 55?

a) (55 ÷ 3) × 100   b) (55 ÷ 100) × 3   c) 55 ÷ 300

matching activity

Match the percentages to a number on the right.
Record your answers in a table.

A 51% of 120	B 15% of 400	C 6% of 1050
D 11% of 72	E 60% of 110	F 20% of 41
G 25% of 34	H 23% of 35	I 35% of 160
J 64% of 12.5	K 61% of 120	L 5% of 1520

56	66
8	61.2
7.92	73.2
60	8.2
76	63
8.5	8.05

A	B	C	D	E	F
G	H	I	J	K	L

Percentage of an Amount Jumbled Answers

Copy and complete the table.
The answers are below, jumbled up.

100%	10%	1%	5%	15%	30%	86%
90						
25						
	8					
		6				
			12			
				6		
					9	

mixed up answers

3.75	13.5	1.25	4	0.9	4.5	30
36	206.4	24	0.4	1.5	72	9
7.5	516	2.4	77.4	4	12	600
12	25.8	60	40	240	4.5	30
0.8	180	21.5	34.4	0.25	80	68.8
24	2	0.3	27	3	2.5	90

percentage of an amount (calc) 🖩

learn by heart

Decimal Multiplier: *The decimal equivalent of a percentage*

examples

Calculate 42% of 60

= 0.42 × 60
= 25.2

Calculate 142.3% of 60

= 1.423 × 60
= 85.38

exercise 9k

1. Write the following as decimals:

   a) 40%   c) 0.4%   e) 100.3%   g) 350%

   b) 4%   d) 104%   f) 200%   h) 152.3%

2. Calculate:

   a) 5% of 74   c) 3% of 206   e) 3.5% of 25

   b) 9% of 81   d) 80% of 41   f) 28.1% of 108

3. Calculate 103.5% of 64

4. What is 20% of a billion?

5. Which is more, 15% of £200,000, or 25% of £120,000?

6. Which is more, $\frac{2}{5}$ of £50 or 18% of £70?

7. Which of the following will calculate 125% of 63?

   a) 1.25 × 63   b) 125 × 63   c) 0.125 × 63   d) 12.5 × 63

8. Calculate 236.5% of 94

9. If we multiply n by 0.8, it works out:

   a) 0.8% of n b) 8% of n c) 80% of n d) 800% of n

10. If we multiply n by 0.002, it works out:

    a) 0.002% of n b) 0.02% of n c) 0.2% of n d) 2% of n

Sarah's Homework 🖩

Below is Sarah's completed homework.
Mark her work. If she has made a mistake,
give her some feedback. At the end, give her a score.

Sarah's Score: / 12

1
Calculate
30% of 70

$10\% = 7$
$3 \times 7 = 21$

2
Calculate
3% of 300

$1\% = 3$
$3 \times 3 = 9$

3
Calculate
9% of 25

$10\% = 2.5$
$1\% = 0.25$
$9\% = 2.5 + 0.25$
$= 2.75$

4
Calculate
18% of 96

96×0.18
$= 17.28$

5
Calculate
1% of 183

$1\% = \frac{1}{100}$
$183 \div 100$
$= 1.83$

6
Calculate
75% of 24

$24 \times 7.5 =$
180

7
Calculate
90% of 18

$10\% = 1.8$
$9 \times 1.8 = 16.2$

8
Calculate
3.5% of
204

$3.5\% = 0.035$
204×0.035
$= 7.14$

9
Calculate
60% of 90

$90 \times 0.06 =$
$9 \times 0.6 =$
5.4

10
Calculate
4.5% of
2000

$2000 \times$
$0.045 = 90$

11
Calculate
6% of 120

$10\% = 12$
$5\% = 0.6$
$1\% = 0.12$
$6\% = 0.72$

12
Calculate
0.2% of 23

23×0.002
$= 0.046$

percentage increase & decrease (calc) 🖩 ⭐ extra challenge

examples

Increase 38 by 1.3%

$= 38 \times (100 + 1.3)\%$
$= 38 \times 101.3\%$
$= 38 \times 1.013$
$= 38.494$

Decrease 38 by 0.9%

$= 38 \times (100 - 0.9)\%$
$= 38 \times 99.1\%$
$= 38 \times 0.991$
$= 37.658$

exercise 91

1. Write each of these as a decimal:

   a) 45%   c) 1.8%   e) 108%   g) 207%

   b) 4.5%   d) 100%   f) 99.8%   h) 309.5%

2. Complete the following:

   a) Increase 90 by 6%   e) Increase 104 by 26%

   b) Increase 34 by 12%   f) Decrease 64 by 13%

   c) Decrease 18 by 52%   g) Decrease 104 by 5.5%

   d) Increase 4 by 3%   h) Decrease 12 by 100%

3. Which of the following will increase n by 3%?

   a) $n \times 1.3$ b) $n \times 0.03$ c) $n \times 1.03$

4. Which of the following will decrease a by 94%?

   a) $n \times 0.94$ b) $n \times 0.06$ c) $n \times 1.06$

5. For each multiplier below, state whether it will increase or decrease an amount and by what percentage. The first one is done for you.

   a) 0.4   *Decrease of 60%*   f) 1.03

   b) 0.8   g) 1.3

   c) 0.65   h) 2

   d) 0.05   i) 1.8

   e) 0.001   j) 1.08

Percentages: Who's Right? ⭐ extra challenge

Kim, George and Emma were trying to answer the questions below.
Each time, only one person was correct. Select the correct method for each question.

question		kim's method	george's method	emma's method
A	Calculate 80% of 15	15 × 0.8	15 × 0.2	15 × 1.8
B	Calculate 12% of 62	62 × 1.12	62 × 0.12	62 × 0.88
C	Calculate 5% of 35	35 × 0.05	35 × 0.95	35 × 0.5
D	Calculate 40% of 31	31 × 0.4	31 × 0.04	31 × 1.4
E	Calculate 150% of 72	72 × 0.5	72 × 1.5	72 × 1.05
F	Increase 16 by 20%	16 × 1.2	16 × 1.02	16 × 0.2
G	Increase 16 by 120%	16 × 1.2	16 × 2.2	16 × 2.02
H	Increase 50 by 3%	50 × 0.97	50 × 1.3	50 × 1.03
I	Increase 12 by 0.4%	12 × 1.4	12 × 1.04	12 × 1.004
J	Decrease 15 by 85%	15 × 0.85	15 × 0.15	15 × 1.85
K	Decrease 25 by 10%	25 × 0.9	25 × 0.09	25 × 0.1
L	Decrease 16 by 32%	16 × 0.68	16 × 0.32	16 × 1.32
M	Decrease 20 by 3%	20 × 0.7	20 × 0.3	20 × 0.97

decimal calculations review

examples

Given that 142 × 183 = 25,986 calculate 14.2 × 1.83 *14.2 is 10 times smaller* *1.83 is 100 times smaller* *The overall answer will be* *10 × 100 times smaller* = 25.986	Write 482 in standard form. = $4.82 × 10^2$	Calculate $\frac{42}{0.6}$ $\frac{42}{6}$ = 7 $\frac{42}{0.6}$ = 70 *smaller divisor = larger answer*

exercise 9m

1. Which of these cannot be calculated?

   a) $\frac{1.2}{0.4}$
   b) $\frac{1.2}{1.0}$
   c) $\frac{1.2}{0}$
   d) $\frac{0}{1.2}$

2. Calculate:

   a) 12 ÷ 0.5   c) 14 ÷ 0.01   e) 16 ÷ 0.4

   b) 18 ÷ 0.1   d) 2.8 ÷ 0.1   f) 12 ÷ 0.6

3. Calculate 426 ÷ 1000

4. Calculate 4.26 ÷ 0.01

5. Calculate $103 ÷ 10^2$

6. Given that 135 ÷ 15 = 9, calculate 1.35 ÷ 15

7. Calculate 21.24 ÷ 6

8. Which of the following will have the largest answer?

   a) $\frac{46}{10}$
   b) $\frac{46}{0.1}$
   c) $\frac{46}{1}$
   d) $\frac{46}{0.01}$

9. Calculate:

   a) 0.6 × 0.2   d) 1.2 × 0.3   g) 0.4^2

   b) 0.08 × 3   e) 1.8 ÷ 0.06   h) 0.1^2

   c) 1.9 ÷ 100   f) 0.4 × 0.8   i) 0.3 × 0.2 × 0.1

10. Which of the following is correctly written in standard form?

a) $4.2 \div 10^2$ b) 0.42×10^3 c) 4.2×10^{-3} d) 420×10^4

11. Given that $27 \times 14 = 378$, what is $378 \div 27$?

12. Given that $378 \div 9 = 42$, calculate:

a) $378 \div 0.9$ b) $37.8 \div 9$ c) $0.378 \div 9$

13. Given that $42 \times 108 = 4536$, calculate 4.2×1.08

14. Write 4.8×10^4 in ordinary form.

15. Write 2.7×10^{-2} in ordinary form.

16. Complete the calculation: $0.49 \times$ _____ $= 4,900$

17. Which of the following will make a number 100 times smaller? Circle 2 answers.

a) $\times 10^2$ b) $\times 10^{-2}$ c) $\times 0.1$ d) $\times 0.01$ e) $\times 0.001$

18. If each of these numbers is multiplied by 100, which will have integer answers?

a) 4.27   b) 0.843   c) 0.09   d) 5.687

19. Write in standard form:

a) 378   c) 4000   e) 6,850

b) 0.09   d) 22.9   f) 0.209

20. **Estimate** the answer to:

a) $2.999 \times 4,799$ b) $\dfrac{289 \times 6.99}{0.499}$

21. Match each calculation on the left with an equivalent calculation on the right:

A	170 × 0.1
B	170 ÷ 0.01
C	170 ÷ 1000
D	170 × 10

E	170 × 100
F	170 ÷ 0.1
G	170 ÷ 10
H	170 × 0.001

A	
B	
C	
D	

examples

Calculate $\frac{6}{5} + \frac{3}{4} \times \frac{2}{5}$

Remember to apply the order of operations $\longrightarrow$

$\frac{6}{5} + \left(\frac{3}{4} \times \frac{2}{5}\right) =$

$\frac{6}{5} + \frac{6}{20} =$

$\frac{24}{20} + \frac{6}{20} = \frac{30}{20} = 1\frac{10}{20} = 1\frac{1}{2}$

Calculate $\frac{12}{5} \times \frac{15}{4} \div \left(\frac{1}{3}\right)^2$

Remember cancelling fractions can make calculations easier $\longrightarrow$

$\frac{12}{5} \times \frac{15}{4} \div \frac{1}{9} =$

$\frac{3}{1} \times \frac{3}{1} \div \frac{1}{9} =$

$\frac{9}{1} \div \frac{1}{9} =$

$\frac{9}{1} \times \frac{9}{1} = 81$

exercise 9n

1. Calculate the following, giving your answers in their simplest form:

   a) $\frac{1}{4} \times \frac{3}{8}$

   b) $3 \times \frac{2}{7}$

   c) $\frac{1}{5} + \frac{2}{5}$

   d) $\frac{7}{10} - \frac{3}{10}$

   e) $\frac{2}{5} + \frac{1}{4}$

   f) $\frac{4}{5} - \frac{1}{7}$

   g) $\frac{1}{5} \times 7$

   h) $\frac{2}{5} \times 5$

   i) $\frac{4}{8} - \frac{7}{8}$

2. True or False: $\frac{3}{8} + \frac{4}{8} = \frac{7}{16}$

3. Calculate:

   a) $\left(\frac{1}{3}\right)^3$

   b) $\left(\frac{5}{7}\right)^2$

   c) $\left(-\frac{2}{3}\right)^3$

4. Use cross cancelling to multiply these fractions:

   a) $\frac{24}{10} \times \frac{5}{3}$

   b) $\frac{15}{36} \times \frac{12}{20}$

   c) $\frac{9}{14} \times \frac{70}{3}$

   d) $\frac{4}{5} \times 15$

   e) $24 \times \frac{2}{3}$

   f) $\frac{3}{10} \times \frac{15}{9} \times \frac{9}{2}$

5. Calculate $2\frac{1}{5} \times 7$

6. True or False:
   To multiply fractions we must first make a common denominator.

7. Write down the reciprocal of:

    a) $\frac{3}{10}$ b) 5   c) $\frac{1}{4}$ d) $3\frac{1}{2}$

8. Calculate the following:

    a) $7 \div \frac{1}{3}$ c) $\frac{2}{3} \div \frac{1}{4}$ e) $\frac{3}{5} \div \frac{1}{7}$

    b) $\frac{1}{4} \div 5$ d) $\frac{2}{9} \div 6$ f) $8 \div \frac{2}{3}$

9. What happens when you multiply a number by its reciprocal?

10. Calculate $1 - \frac{3}{5}$

11. Calculate $\left(\frac{2}{5} + \frac{1}{2}\right) \div 6$

12. Calculate $\frac{1}{2} + \frac{1}{3} \times \frac{2}{5}$

13. How many $\frac{1}{4}$'s make 3?

14. Calculate the following:

    a) $\frac{2}{3}$ of 36   c) $\frac{1}{100}$ of 94   e) $\frac{5}{4}$ of 32

    b) $\frac{1}{5}$ of 45   d) $\frac{1}{10}$ of 62   f) $\frac{2}{5}$ of -40

15. $\frac{3}{5}$ of a number is 15. What is the number?

19. Calculate the following, giving your answer as a fraction in its simplest form:

    a) $\frac{2}{3} \div 0.1$ c) $20\% \div \frac{1}{4}$ e) $\left(\frac{1}{4} + \frac{1}{5}\right) \div 3$

    b) $8 \div \left(1 - \frac{2}{3}\right)$ d) $\frac{2}{5} \div 0.5$ f) $0.1 + \frac{3}{10} \times 4$

22. Calculate $\frac{1}{3} - - \frac{1}{5}$

23. Calculate $\frac{1}{8} + -\frac{2}{8}$

24. Simplify $\frac{a}{7} + \frac{2a}{7}$

chapter review

exercise 9o

1. Fill in the table to show equivalent fractions (simplest form), decimals and percentages:

F	$\frac{1}{50}$		$\frac{3}{5}$	$\frac{1}{8}$				
D		0.2			0.1			
P						1%	8%	0.5%

2. Write as a decimal:

   a) $\frac{1}{8}$
   b) $\frac{23}{100}$
   c) $1\frac{3}{100}$

3. Work out:

   a) 4×0.6
   b) 0.3×9

   c) 0.4×0.2
   d) 0.04×3

   e) 50×0.3
   f) 0.3^2

4. Which of the following is equivalent to 5%? Circle two answers:

   a) 0.5
   b) $\frac{5}{100}$
   c) 0.05
   d) $\frac{0.5}{100}$
   e) $\frac{5}{1000}$

5. Which is larger, $\frac{2}{5}$ or $0.\dot{4}$?

6. Write the following as decimals:

   a) $\frac{1}{3}$
   b) $2\frac{7}{100}$
   c) $\frac{1}{9}$
   d) $\frac{3}{8}$

7. Which of these are equal to **4.3**? Choose all that apply.

   a) 10×0.43
   b) 43×0.1
   c) 0.43×0.1
   d) 430×0.01

8. Calculate:

   a) $12 \div 0.1$
   c) $0.3 \times 0.2 \times 0.1$
   e) $\frac{1}{3} \div \frac{1}{8}$

   b) $\frac{1}{5} \div 0.5$
   d) $\frac{1}{5} \div 5$
   f) $0.6 \div \frac{1}{5}$

9. Write 0.203 as a fraction.

10. To find 10% of a number, we can divide it by _____ and to find 1% of a number, we can divide it by _____.

11. Work these out, giving your answers in the simplest form.

   a) $\frac{3}{4} \times \frac{2}{5}$

   b) $\frac{1}{5} \times \frac{1}{6}$

   c) $\frac{2}{9} \times \frac{3}{4}$

   d) $\frac{1}{8} \times \frac{4}{7}$

   e) $\left(\frac{2}{3}\right)^2$

   f) $\frac{5}{12} \times \frac{3}{10}$

12. Work out: $\frac{1}{4} \times \frac{1}{4} \times \frac{1}{4}$ giving your answer in the simplest form.

13. Calculate:

   a) 20% of 300

   b) 5% of 40

   c) 1% of 900

   d) 3% of 900

   e) 15% of 20

   f) 30% of 220

14. Work out the missing fraction in each calculation:

   a) $\frac{2}{7} + \boxed{} = 1$

   b) $\frac{7}{2} \times \boxed{} = 1$

   c) $\frac{3}{5} \times \boxed{} = \frac{3}{15}$

15. Which of these are more than 0.4? Circle two answers.

   a) $\frac{4}{10}$

   b) $\frac{4}{100}$

   c) 0.40

   d) $\frac{3}{5}$

   e) $\frac{2}{3}$

16. Put these in order, from smallest to largest:

   a) 0.7

   b) $\frac{7}{100}$

   c) 0.707

   d) $\frac{71}{1000}$

17. Which of these calculations works out 23% of 50?

   a) 2.3×50 b) 0.23×50 c) $50 \div 0.23$ d) $0.23 \div 50$

18. Which of the following is equivalent to 0.5%?

   a) 0.5   b) $\frac{5}{100}$ c) 0.05   d) $\frac{0.5}{100}$ e) $\frac{5}{1000}$

19. Which is larger, $\frac{1}{7}$ or $0.1\dot{4}$?

20. Write each of these decimals as a fraction or mixed number:

   a) $0.\dot{2}\dot{3}$

   b) $0.\dot{7}$

   c) $0.\dot{5}0\dot{7}$

   d) $0.3\dot{5}$

   e) $0.2\dot{6}\dot{5}$

   f) $4.1\dot{0}\dot{6}$

Find the Greatest Integer

For each statement, work out the biggest whole number that could go in the empty box to make the statement true

A
$$\frac{\square}{45} < 1$$

B
$$\frac{\square}{100} < 24\%$$

C
$$0.8 > \frac{\square}{10}$$

D
$$\square\% < \frac{19}{100}$$

E
$$\square\% < 0.9$$

F
$$\frac{\square}{29} < 100\%$$

G
$$\frac{\square}{10} < 75\%$$

H
$$0.5 > \frac{\square}{100}$$

I
$$\square\% < \frac{3}{4}$$

J
$$0.7 > \frac{\square}{5}$$

K
$$\frac{1}{2} > \frac{\square}{12}$$

L
$$\frac{\square}{15} < 100\%$$

M
$$\frac{2}{5} > \square\%$$

N
$$\frac{\square}{10} < 50\%$$

O
$$\frac{\square}{16} < 25\%$$

P
$$\frac{\square}{15} < \frac{2}{3}$$

Q
$$\frac{\square}{3} < 0.5$$

R
$$\frac{\square}{4} < 101\%$$

S
$$\frac{\square}{8} \le 0.5$$

T
$$82\% > \frac{\square}{50}$$

U
$$\frac{\square}{20} \le \frac{3}{5}$$

V
$$2 > \square\%$$

W
$$\frac{\square}{10} < 0.1$$

X
$$\frac{1}{\square} > 20\%$$

cumulative review (chapters 1-9)

exercise 9p

1. True or false?

   a) $3^6 \div 3^6 = 0$ d) 23m = 0.23km   g) 0.7777 is a recurring decimal

   b) $a^5 \times a^3 = a^{15}$ e) $12^8 \div 12^5 = 1^3$ h) $0.23\dot{4} = 0.2344444...$

   c) $1^0 = 1$ f) $3 + 4 \times 5 = 23$ i) -4 + -3 = 7

2. Simplify:

   a) $2a + a$ c) $2a + 3 + 4a + 1$ e) $a^5 \times a^3 \times a^2$

   b) $2a \times a$ d) $3b - 4 - b - 5$ f) $3a \times 4b$

3. Which of these is the same as 8%? Circle 2 correct answers.

   a) $\dfrac{8}{10}$ b) $\dfrac{8}{100}$ c) 0.08   d) 0.8   e) 8.0

4. Calculate:

   a) -4 × -3   c) -4 - 3   e) -4 - - 3

   b) -4 + -3   d) -4 + 3   f) -4 × 3

5. Which two numbers are equal to their square roots?

6. Which of these numbers is the same whether you round it to 3 significant figures or 2 decimal places?

   a) 65.985   b) 4.209   c) 0.2856   d) 109.459

7. Which of the following is between 1.8 and 1.9?

   a) $\dfrac{12}{10}$ b) $\dfrac{15}{10}$ c) $\dfrac{174}{100}$ d) $\dfrac{183}{100}$

8. Evaluate the following, giving your answer as an integer or decimal:

   a) $\sqrt{64}$ c) $\sqrt[4]{16}$ e) $(-3)^2$ g) $\left(\dfrac{1}{3}\right)^2$

   b) $\sqrt[3]{27}$ d) $\sqrt[3]{-8}$ f) $(-3)^3$ h) $\left(\dfrac{1}{10}\right)^3$

9. Calculate:

   a) 4.98 + 0.745   b) 2.96 - 0.587   c) 238 ÷ 7

10. Which of these equal 1? Circle two answers.

    a) 5^0 b) a^1 c) 0^1 d) $(-1)^2$ e) $\sqrt{-1}$

11. Calculate:

    a) $\frac{3}{5} \times 2$ c) $6^6 \div 6^4$ e) 0.6×0.3

    b) $\left(\frac{1}{3}\right)^2$ d) -4 - 4 - 4   f) $1\frac{1}{10} \times 0.4$

12. Round:

    a) 4823 to 1 significant figure.   b) 0.04506 to 3 significant figures.

13. A height is measured as 14.8cm, correct to 1 decimal place.
    Write down the error interval for this measurement.

Percentage of an Amount Puzzle 2

Use all of the numbers on the left to make 4 true statements:

2	45
20%	20
10	30%
10	150
5%	50
200	10%

☐ of ☐ = ☐

☐ of ☐ = ☐

☐ of ☐ = ☐

☐ of ☐ = ☐

exercise 9q: additional cumulative review

1. True or False?

   a) $4 + 3 \times 2 = 14$

   b) $10 - 3 + 4 = 3$

   c) $20 \div 2 + 3 = 4$

   d) $6 - 2 \times 3 + 1 = 1$

2. Calculate:

   a) $5 - 2^2$

   b) $10 + 2 \times 4$

   c) $9 - (2 + 1)^2$

   d) $10 + 3 \times 4 - 6$

   e) $\frac{5 + 3 \times 10}{7}$

   f) $(2 - (3^2 - 10))$

3. What is the answer to $0.4 + 0.4 \times 0.2$?

   a) 0.48   b) 1.2   c) 1.6   d) 0.12   e) 0.16

4. Calculate:

   a) $\frac{1}{2} - \frac{1}{3} \times \frac{1}{4}$

   b) $1 - \left(\frac{2}{3}\right)^2$

5. Fill in the blanks:

   a) $8 + 2 \times \underline{\quad} = 16$

   b) $8 + 2 \times \underline{\quad} = 0$

   c) $\underline{\quad} \div 3 - 2 = 2$

   d) $(\underline{\quad} - 8) \div 2 = 11$

   e) $(\underline{\quad} + 1)^2 = 25$

   f) $8 + \underline{\quad} \times 3 - 5 = 33$

6. Calculate:

   a) $-8 \times -2 + 10$

   b) $-5 - 20 \div -4$

   c) $(-3)^2$

   d) $(-3)^3$

7. Solve:

   a) $7x = -21$

   b) $100 = 4x + 20$

   c) $\frac{x}{4} = 0.2$

   d) $x - 3 = -10$

8. The expression $\frac{5}{x}$ is undefined if $x = \underline{\qquad}$

exercise 9r

1. Without a calculator, work out $\sqrt[3]{12^6}$

2. The diagram shows two squares with integer side lengths. Work out the area of the shaded region.

3. How many square numbers are there between 1 and 5000?

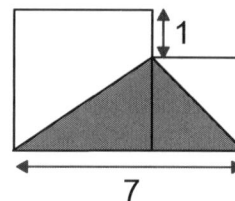

4. How many years is 1 billion minutes? Assume a year is 365 days and round your answer to the nearest integer.

5. 1000 tenths make _____

6. If $xy < 0$, which of these are possible?

   a) $xy = 0$ b) $x + y = 0$ c) $x > y$ d) $x + y < 0$

7. Which is longer, 1 million days, or 100 decades?

8. Work out the value of $0.\dot{3} + 0.0\dot{8}$

9. The perimeter of a square is 48cm. What is its area?

10. The diagram shows two circles inside a rectangle. Work out the area that is shaded. Give your answer to 3 s.f.

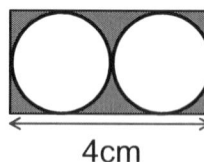

   4cm

11. If a is a positive number, which of these are true? Circle 2 answers.

   a) $a \div 0.1 = 10a$ b) $a \div 0.1 < a$ c) $a \div 0.1 = 2a$ d) $a \div 0.1 > a$

12. The diagram shows a triangle inside a square.
   The area of the square is 64cm^2.
   What is the area of the triangle?
   Give your answer to 2 decimal places.

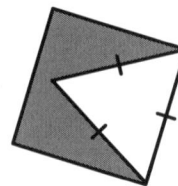

13. What is the value of $0.\dot{1} + 0.\dot{2} + 0.\dot{3}$

   a) $\frac{5}{9}$ b) $\frac{6}{9}$ c) $\frac{6}{10}$ d) $\frac{6}{11}$

14. Ajay has completed $\frac{4}{5}$ of his journey.

   He travels another 500m and the journey is now 85% complete.

   What is the total length of his journey? Give your answer in km.

Printed in Great Britain
by Amazon